CARRY ME
IN YOUR
HEART

PEARL BENISCH

CARRY ME IN YOUR HEART

The Life and Legacy of

⟡ Sarah Schenirer ⟡

Founder and Visionary of the
Bais Yaakov Movement

FELDHEIM PUBLISHERS
JERUSALEM   NEW YORK

Also by the author:
To Vanquish the Dragon
(Jerusalem: Feldheim Publishers, 1991)

ISBN 1-58330-576-9

First published 2003
Second, corrected edition published 2003

FELDHEIM PUBLISHERS
POB 35002 / Jerusalem, Israel

208 Airport Executive Park
Nanuet, NY 10954

www.feldheim.com

Printed in Israel

I wish to dedicate this book to…

Reb Yehudah Leib Orlean הי״ד
and his devoted staff of seminary teachers

❖

All Bais Yaakov teachers and Bnos leaders

❖

Bais Yaakov students and Bnos members —
our precious little Bais Yaakov children.

❖

To my dear special friends and co-workers.

To all of them whose marvelous, promising lives
were brutally cut off by the Nazi monsters
and their collaborators between 1939 and 1945.
No grave, no memorial, no trace was left of them—

ה׳ יקום דמם

MAY THIS BOOK BE A MONUMENT TO THEM.

תנצב״ה

Acknowledgments

הודו לה' כי טוב, כי לעולם חסדו.

FIRST AND FOREMOST, I WOULD like to express my deep gratitude to the Ribono shel Olam for granting me the time and opportunity to write this book. Throughout my writing, I overwhelmingly felt *siyata di-Shemaya*, Hashem's helping Hand, at every stage of my work. In His goodness, He kept on sending me important papers, letters, and photographs to document my story.

I am grateful to all of Hashem's emissaries, who so faithfully fulfilled His commands and did it with love and dedication.

My earnest thanks go to Mrs. Sarah Rafaeli, who for all these years so lovingly preserved the first Bais Yaakov report card, issued to her mother, Devorah Birnbaum, as well as Frau Schenirer's wedding gift to Devorah, so beautifully inscribed. I greatly appreciate Mrs. Rafaeli's meticulous copying of those precious mementos for me.

I am indebted to Mrs. Chavah Perkal, the daughter-in-law of Rabbi Moshe Reuven Perkal, for her interest in my work and for her tireless copying of all of Sarah Schenirer's most important letters to Hansi Ross; and also for the historic photographs, depicting Hansi's extensive work in establishing new Bais Yaakov schools per Sarah Schenirer's instructions. My heartfelt *yeshar koach* to you.

My sincere thanks to Rebbetzin Julia Mandel, née Wechsler, for her most valuable information about the life and achievements of her esteemed teacher, Chava Landsberg, the most dedicated and accomplished follower of Sarah Schenirer.

I am most indebted to Mrs. Pearl Altschuler for so painstakingly copying for me the most important documents and photographs of the Bais Yaakov movement from both before and after the war. I appreciate your preserving so lovingly those precious pieces of history.

My warmest thanks go to my Bais Yaakov friends for helping refresh my memory of many interesting events during our Bais Yaakov days. For their information and advice, I thank: Taubka Mushel-Jacobi, Renia Finkelstein-Rosen, Reizel Dym-Wohlhandler, Sara Blaugrund-Pfeffer, Yenta Verdiger-Ashkenazi, Rivka Leblowitz-Citron, Hilda Hollander-Naimon, and all the others who helped with a good word and encouragement.

I am foremost grateful to the esteemed Rabbi Noach Weinberg for his beautiful and most impressive Foreword to this book. It is the most powerful definition of Sarah Schenirer's personality and achievements. *Yeshar koach* for enhancing my story. May your wonderful work in Jewish education and outreach be crowned, *b'ezras Hashem*, with much success. Sincere thanks to Dr. Neil Golombek for his recommendation.

My warmest *yeshar koach* to Rebbetzin Chana Rotenberg for her beautiful and heartwarming Introduction to this book. It is a privilege for me to have her words in my book, as she, a favored student of Sarah Schenirer, gives a most valuable description of Bais Yaakov and Bnos. Thank you for sharing with me the deep feeling of pride of belonging to the great worldwide Bais Yaakov sisterhood.

My deep gratitude goes to Reb Yaakov Feldheim for his special interest in my book. His input of important information and data, and his valuable suggestions and comments, were greatly appreciated. His knowledge of the subject, his follow-up, and his continuous encouragement were remarkable. Thank you very, very much.

My sincere thanks go to my capable editor, Naftali Greenwood, and copy-editor, Deena Nataf, for their skillful work, as well as to Joyce Bennett for her assistance and support. Their understanding, unusual cooperation, and patience are greatly appreciated. In addition, I would like to acknowledge and thank Eden Chachamtzedek, for turning my handwritten pages into a professional, computerized manuscript. My gratitude goes to Bracha Steinberg for her lovely design of the book, beautifully suited to the subject, and to Michael Silverstein, for expressing the significance of my story through his artistically designed cover. A special thank you to the entire staff of Feldheim Publishers for turning my manuscript into a beautifully produced book.

I wish to express my gratitude to my husband Shymon for his share in the important chapter of my book dealing with the poverty in pre-war Poland. He contributed a valuable description of the tragic plight of the religious Jewish worker.

Last but not least, I wish to express my heartfelt thanks to my dear children and their spouses: Frieda and her husband Lenny Schwartz, Leib and his wife Rachel Reichman, and Mirrel and her husband Mordechai Eissenberg for their warm interest in my story, as well as for their valuable suggestions, sound advice, and productive criticism. May Hashem bless you for your constant help and support in every way. My warmest thanks to my dear grandchildren for being my sounding board, and for their valuable opinions, which represent the views of our younger generation. I highly regard your help and assistance, and above all, the *nachas* you are showering upon me. May Hashem bless you all.

Pearl (Reichman) Benisch
Bnei Brak/New York
Adar Alef 5763
February 2003

Introduction
by Rebbetzin Chana Rotenberg

LITTLE DID I KNOW WHAT I was in for when my dear friend Pearl Benisch honored me with the privilege of writing some words of introduction to her seminal account of the life of Sarah Schenirer, founder of the Bais Yaakov movement.

We, the Children of Israel, descendants of Avraham, Yitzchak, and Yaakov, we who are the recipients of the Torah, know that Hashem created the world and gave the Torah — His law — the precepts of conduct, to the Children of Israel. Our task is to do His will, and to be His emissaries, spreading His word to all of the nations of the world. Every generation's goal is to guard this legacy, to uphold it, to save it, and to transmit it to the next generation, until the end of days.

Throughout the ages, the Jews have been the *Am ha-Torah*, the Torah nation, marching forward, spreading the word of Hashem and teaching it to the world. Each generation produced its Torah leaders, who were at the helm. In earlier times, when the home was the center of Jewish life, girls and women remained modestly in the home, at their fathers' and husbands' sides, absorbing their teachings. Torah and observance of mitzvos were at the forefront. But then came Revolution and Enlightenment, with all their "isms," penetrating also into the Jewish homes.

But Hashem watches over His People. He put into the heart of Sarah Schenirer to gather the Jewish daughters, and to show them the treasures and beauty of adhering to the Torah and Jewish life in the face of the dangers lurking from the different "isms" confronting our nation.

Amidst the secular Revolution, Sarah Schenirer, too, created a Revolution — through the Bais Yaakov and Bnos movements. She was a pioneer in teaching the Daughters of Israel their role as partners in building the Eternal Nation.

In Bais Yaakov we learned what is important and what is not, what are the highest priorities in the life of a Jewish Daughter, and what's more — to be proud of these priorities, at all times and places, in all stages of life; how to live them, and how to give our lives for them if necessary. We learned that our highest ambition was to study Torah, live Torah, teach Torah, and implant Torah in future generations. Thus not only were we imbued with the Torah, we were also imbued with the idea of spreading it throughout all of *Klal Yisroel*. The Bais Yaakov movement elevated in our eyes and lives the status of Torah-learning to the highest degree, and singled out those toiling in it to be deserving of the highest prestige. These values were now placed on the highest pedestal.

Mrs. Benisch provides us with an original account of Sarah Schenirer's personality, and her achievements in those turbulent times. We are given a warm and descriptive glimpse of beautiful, heartwarming scenes of Jewish life and of Bais Yaakov and Bnos in pre-war Poland. We read descriptions of the different activities in which Mrs. Benisch took an active part. How much living *mussar* and *chesed* for us to emulate from the lives of those unassuming girls and women brought up in the spirit of Bais Yaakov, who gave their lives in all circumstances to ease the lot of their sisters and brothers regardless of their political affiliation or level of observance. *Ahavas Yisroel* to the highest degree.

Bais Yaakov gave them knowledge, but even more, it gave them role models to admire and to learn from. How much there was to learn from, admire about, and follow after people like the rabbis and teachers in the Bais Yaakov movement — Reb Yehudah Leib Orlean and Dr. Leo Deutschlander, for example, who with the approval and blessing of the Chofetz Chaim and the Gerrer Rebbe gave their all for *chinuch ha-banos*, for molding the Bais Yaakov girls into the model teachers and mothers of the Jewish nation. It was a quiet revolution, unheard of in terms of beauty and enthusiasm. It was a chapter of the renaissance of Torah in the life of *Am Yisroel*.

Then came the period of bestiality!

And who could not but stand in awe before all those Bais Yaakov and Bnos girls and women who with their quiet heroism and dedication stood up to the enemy and made the lives of those around them a little more bearable, sometimes saving them from torture or even death, while jeopardizing their own lives.

But look! On the horizon, the sun that we thought had set for good started to rise. And look! Those shattered bodies remained strong in spirit. Hashem had His plans. He guided the remnants of Bais Yaakov and Bnos, broken in body but resolute in spirit, to settle in the faraway corners of the globe. They brought with them the sparks of Torah and fanned them into flames.

Hashem gave these women new strength. He stood them up, and they built new lives even while still on the blood-soaked earth of post-war Europe. They searched for hidden children, they tried to save any *Yiddishe neshamos*, at the risk of their own lives. They married, they longed for their *"Mamme Tzion"* (Eretz Yisroel), and hoped to build their future there. But wherever they settled, they brought with them the love of Torah and of those who toiled in it. They built Jewish homes, each a *mikdash me'at*, a small *Beis ha-Mikdash*, an oasis of Torah, even in the farthest corners of the earth.

We are greatful to ha-Kadosh Baruch Hu for every individual whom He spared, among them my friend Pearl Benisch. Hashem granted her a wonderful memory, a thirst for knowledge, and a desire to emulate her great teacher. In His mercy He allowed this *ud mutzal me'eish*, this brand saved from the fire, to retain her prodigious, God-given memory in order to pass on this true history to all future generations.

I used to see Pearl passing our house on her way to Frau Schenirer, who lived next door to us on Kordeckiego street in Kraków. I remember her sitting in the classes of Reb Yehudah Leib Orlean and Frau Biegun, drinking thirstily from the fountain of knowlege, *yiras Shamayim*, and *ahavas Yisroel* which they and the other teachers passed onto us. Already then she displayed a great sense of responsibility for all those around her, which she has never lost. She has given the Jewish world an honest, pure account of Frau Schenirer's personality and a history of *Klal Yisroel* in pre-war Poland and beyond. *Carry Me in Your Heart* is a *leibidiker mussar sefer*, a living code of behavior.

No words written or spoken will justly describe the tremendous impact this book will make. It will be etched in the heart of whoever reads it, spurring them on to live a better, a holier life; to shake off the chains of materialism, to live a life of Torah values, and to bring about the coming of *Moshiach*, soon in our days.

Rebbetzin Chana (Zehnwirt) Rotenberg is a noted talmidah of Sarah Schenirer, and a teacher and staff member of the Bais Yaakov Teacher's Seminary in Brooklyn, New York.

Foreword
by Rabbi Noach Weinberg

RABBI YECHEZKEL (CHASKEL) SARNA, the rosh yeshivah of Yeshivas Chevron and a very great man, was addressing a gathering at the *bris* of Reb Moshe Chevroni's grandson — who was also a grandson of the Gerrer Rebbe. A large segment of Eretz Yisroel's Torah giants were there, among them the grandchildren of the following leaders of the previous generation: the Chofetz Chaim, the Slonimer Rebbe, the Vizhnitzer Rebbe, the Gerrer Rebbe, the Levush Mordechai, the Alter of Navardok, the Alter of Mir, and the Alter of Slobodka. Their grandchildren were all there at this *bris*.

Rav Yechezkel Sarna got up and said, "Everybody in this room thinks that it was his grandfather that did the most for *Am Yisroel* in the last one hundred years. The Chofetz Chaim, the Alter of Navardok, the Alter of Slobodka — the *talmidim* they had, the *yeshivos* they created. I'm here to tell you that it's none of them."

Rav Sarna was very confrontational, and the people present said, "Reb Chaskel, let's not have fights. Please sit down."

Reb Chaskel said, "I'll tell you more. The one who did the most for *Klal Yisroel* in the last one hundred years, never learned a *blatt gemara*."

"Outrageous!" everyone said. "Reb Chaskel, you're going too far."

He answered, "I'll tell you more. When I mention the name, you will all agree with me that it wasn't your grandfather, it wasn't one of these great rabbis, but yes, it was in fact this person who did the most for *Am Yisroel* in the last one hundred years."

Everybody started laughing. Can you imagine that the chassidim and the misnagdim would all agree on who did the most for *Am Yisroel* in the last century? Was it possible?

Reb Chaskel mentioned the name...and they all agreed with him.

The name was Sarah Schenirer. If it wasn't for that woman who never had a formal Jewish education, if it wasn't for that woman who got this idea of educating our girls, then *chas ve-chalilah* the face of *Am Yisroel* would look very different today indeed.

What did this woman have? She didn't learn a *blatt gemara* like the men do. She didn't even go to a Bais Yaakov. What did she have that gave her the merit to be the force that did the most for *Klal Yisroel* in the last one hundred years? Nobody told her to do what she did. She had a lot of detractors, people who wanted to excommunicate her.

The story is told that they came to the Chofetz Chaim to complain about this woman who was doing something new under the sun. "For three thousand five hundred years we didn't have any school for girls. And who is she anyway?" They asked him to take action. The Chofetz Chaim was very agitated. He ran into his room. They thought he was getting his coat, to go out to do battle. Instead, he came out with some zlotys, coins, and said, "Such a tremendous mitzvah and I shouldn't have a part in it? Here, give her this money."

Baruch Hashem, the Chofetz Chaim backed her, the Gerrer Rebbe backed her, the Belzer Rebbe gave her his blessing. But what made her do it?

There is a famous story of Rabbi Eliezer ben Hurkenos, who at the age of twenty-seven couldn't learn Torah, couldn't recite *Birkas ha-Mazon*, couldn't even say *kerias Shema*. He cried and cried until he reached Reb Yochanan ben Zakkai, who was able to finally teach him Torah. So much so, that he became Rabban shel Yisroel.

Why did Reb Eliezer ben Hurkenos merit to become the Rebbe of *Am Yisroel*? Because he was able to cry for Torah. You have to be willing to cry. Sarah Schenirer cried for the Jewish girls who were getting lost. In her autobiography she writes that she cried for those children. That's why she merited to become the Mother of Bais Yaakov, the Matriarch of future generations of *Klal Yisroel*.

Rabbi Noach Weinberg is the founder and Dean of Yeshivas Aish Hatorah.

Preface

I LAY DOWN MY PEN. My handwritten manuscript is finished. The story, however, is not. It goes on, living and growing, each generation adding page after page to the history of a great movement, that of Bais Yaakov.

Bais Yaakov revolutionized the Eastern European Jewish world by applying a novel idea, *chinuch ha-banos*, traditional education for Jewish girls — an idea so crucial at the time, and at all times, for the survival of authentic Jewish nationhood.

Bais Yaakov educators and, especially, Yaakov Feldheim, the publisher of my first book, *To Vanquish the Dragon*, repeatedly urged me to write a book about Sarah Schenirer, the founder of the Bais Yaakov movement. I repeatedly declined, considering myself inadequate to illuminate the unique personality of my great teacher and to assume the vast responsibility of such a project.

On one of my many visits to my publisher, Mrs. Marsi Tabak, the company's editor-in-chief at the time, asked me again about writing the book. Having become a friend of Marsi's by that time, I tried to soften my refusal by telling her a little story about Sarah Schenirer:

"Frau Schenirer never allowed us to hang her picture on the wall," I related. "'Don't hang it on the wall,' she used to say. 'Carry it in your heart.'"

This brought Marsi to her feet in excitement.

"Mrs. Benisch!" she exclaimed. "You have a book and you have a title: *Carry Me in Your Heart*. No more excuses," she added with finality. "Go ahead and write."

Thus, unable to disappoint my friend, I decided to write this story under the title she gave it. The result, I warned Marsi, would be not a biography but a book of reminiscences about my exceptional teacher and her great *talmidos,* who so excellently followed in her footsteps.

With that, I began to write. The ink in my pen flowed freely. So did the memories, flashing by in succession. I wrote about the great idea behind Sarah Schenirer's Bais Yaakov initiative and her vision of a worldwide movement. I recalled her struggles, unsuccessful at first, to realize the idea. I documented her powerful determination, her resolve to carry on against all odds and to bring her towering idea, that of Bais Yaakov, to fruition.

I recalled Frau Schenirer's wonderful lessons, her meaningful sayings, her sensible advice, and her inspirational discourses that influenced her students so profoundly — the everlasting impact we derived just from listening to her soul speaking, as we used to say.

How intently we pupils observed Frau Schenirer's behavior and her sublime attributes of mercy, love, and respect for every human being. Her willingness to help the needy and the distressed knew no limit. She gave and gave until her very last breath. And she is still giving....

No tribute to Sarah Schenirer, however, can be complete without mention of her great followers, the girls and women who emulated her ways in the most trying times ever known, who risked their lives, and who subjected themselves to torture, to help, sustain, and rescue others. Their story is also told here — before and during World War II and, especially, in the period shortly following the liberation. It was then that those *talmidos*, although hardly able to stand, bolstered others' morale, shared their time and their scanty resources with them, and helped them to reconstruct their lives.

Afterwards, finding the Bais Yaakov schools in Europe in ruins, those great students of Sarah Schenirer's followed her path of self-denial and established new Bais Yaakov schools in Europe, Israel, Australia, and the Americas. With hard work and determination, they surmounted all obstacles to build up Jewish communities in the post-war wilderness that was *Yiddishkeit* in the New World. With the enthusiasm and spirit that Bais Yaakov and its founder had invested in them, they turned the wastelands into blooming Jewish oases.

The memories in this volume sometimes overlap or leap from one era to the next. They do so because the story they tell, that of a unique, indestructible historical movement, defies rigid periodization.

Nevertheless, it all traces to one moment. As Dr. Judith Grunfeld often said, "Frau Schenirer threw a large stone into the waters of Jewish history, and that stone continues to ripple in ever-widening circles."

What a powerful throw that must have been. Indeed, its impact on Jewish history continues to grow, and so it will until the great day of Redemption.

Then Sarah Schenirer's dream of Bais Yaakov — "House of Jacob, let us walk in the light of Hashem"[1] — will be fulfilled in its entirety. At the End of Days, Frau Schenirer will look on as her Bais Yaakov — the House of Jacob — strides forward, followed by all mankind, in Hashem's glorious light.

---

1. *Yeshayahu* 2:5.

The Early Years

❧ *Chapter 1* ❧

It was 1883. Poland lay stricken, torn into three pieces by the greatest powers in Europe. Germany had grabbed the country's northern section, her pride — the two seaports of Gdansk and Gdynia, her gateways to the world, so crucial to her national and economic survival. Russia had savaged Poland's midriff — her capital, Warsaw, and the industrial city of Lodz. Austria had annexed the southern part of Poland, the area known as Galicia, with its lovely city of Kraków.

Kaiser Franz Josef, who ruled Austria at that time, was favorably disposed toward his Jewish minority. One may even say that the Jews of Galicia lived rather peacefully. They enjoyed freedom of trade and religion. Torah education flourished in Kraków. There were places of worship and study on every corner, as well as impressive synagogues such as the stately Alte Shul, the Kupper Shul, the Rema Shul, and a few others. In the Jewish quarter of Kazimierz, one could hear the sound of Torah day and night wherever one went. No wonder Kraków was nicknamed *Klayne Yerushalayim*, Little Jerusalem.

That year, a little girl was born to a prestigious, well-established Krakowian family — to Reb Bezalel and Reizel Schenirer, followers of the famous Belzer Rebbe. The Schenirers were a typical Chassidic family in Kraków — Reb Bezalel a towering Torah scholar; his wife an authentic *eishes chayil*; their sons learning Torah vigorously, following the Chassidic way of life; imbibing the warmth of the Shabbos atmosphere, the *zemiros*, the *divrei Torah*, and the warm, loving

3

family milieu. These were the surroundings in which little Surahleh grew up.

Kraków, like all cities in Poland, had no Jewish schools for girls. Jewish girls had to attend Polish public schools, sharing their classes with gentile girls. Schooling was compulsory until seventh or eighth grade; parents who were derelict in obeying the law were liable to heavy fines and, sometimes, imprisonment.

Surahleh Schenirer was a typical Krakowian girl — bright, intelligent, broad-minded, and graced with an unquenchable thirst for knowledge. She was eager to start school, eager to learn. She was interested in every subject taught. Thus, she became a top student in her class, excelling in all subjects — especially "religion hour," which the school provided once a week for Christian and Jewish children separately. She knew all the answers there, and it was no wonder: she spent the entire Shabbos studying *parashas ha-shavua* from her mother's *Tze'ena u-Re'ena* and delving into her beloved *seforim: Chok l'Yisroel* in Yiddish, *Beis Yehudah* with its Yiddish translation of Rashi, and others with which her father fondly supplied her.

Surahleh's teachers admired her for her interest in learning and her painstakingly prepared homework. Her classmates loved and respected her for her unflagging willingness to help. With her keen perception, she understood their needs even before being told. No wonder she was beloved by all. Only one thing kept her apart from her friends: they could not accept her deep commitment to Jewish values, her strong faith and *yiras Shamayim,* her love of the Creator and the world He created, and her admiration for everything she encountered in that world. They could not follow her ideas, although they adored her for her devotion and caring. They lovingly nicknamed her "Chassidka." It was a well-chosen sobriquet.

When she became aware of her father's business hardships, she offered to work to augment his income and help support the household. Talented in handicrafts, she became a seamstress without ever attending a dressmaking course. Soon, she became known as a capable maker of children's dresses. Satisfied mothers admired her sense of perfection and the minute details that she sewed into the little dresses that she made for their young darlings. She was very busy and worked hard, sometimes into the late hours of the night.

Seeing her daughter tired and often exhausted, Sarah's mother made her an offer: "Surahleh, you work so hard. You need a rest badly. Your friends are going to either Zavoja or Krynica for their summer vacation and to Zakopane in the winter. Go join them. I know how you love the beauty of nature, and there you'll be surrounded by the towering Tatra Mountains — and I also know how badly you need the vacation to replenish your strength."

"Thank you for your offer, dear Mother," answered Sarah, "but times are hard. God will give me the strength I need without our having to spend the money." After much arguing, however, Sarah succumbed to her mother's urgent plea. From then on, she interrupted her hard work for brief respites twice a year.

The girls were excited to hear that Sarah would join them for their vacation. They ran to her house and happily described the arrangements they had already made. "We're going to Zakopane this winter," Leah, the most enthusiastic of the group, cried out. "Surahleh, you're always the life of the party. You give us all so much joy and laughter. We love to go hiking with you," she added excitedly. "You always show us the beauty of nature, the Glory of God's creation."

"We've rented a room for the five of us," added Gittel, "so we can make our own food and not depend on the hotels in Zakopane, with their questionable *kashrus*."

What a pleasure it was to leave the muggy air of Kraków behind and travel to Zakopane, where they inhaled pure, crisp winter air and enjoyed the beautiful scenery. As Sarah's mother had noted, this charming winter resort was surrounded by the Tatras, the highest mountains in Carpathia.

The other girls slept late after the exhausting trip from

Kraków. Sarah, however, woke up early to heat the stove, put up a kettle of water for hot cocoa, buy fresh rolls, and make breakfast. The girls awakened to a warm room and a table set for an elaborate meal. "Oh, my!" they cried in appreciation.

"Surahleh, you shouldn't have gotten up so early. You're as tired as we are," Gittel said reproachfully. "Tomorrow," chimed in Leah with resolve, "I'll make sure to wake up early to make the preparations."

They spent the day pleasantly driving around in a beautiful horse-drawn carriage mounted on a large sled. The driver, dressed in a suit that bespoke prestige, led the vehicle up to the first stop on the mountain. From there the girls rented sleds to slide down the snowy slope. How pleasurable it was to feel the crisp mountain air and the sun's warm beams, protecting them from the cold wintry air. Up in the carriage, down on the sled — what a joy it was to spend the winter in Zakopane!

The next day, Sarah planned to hike up the mountain to see the sunrise. It was always a great experience to watch the sun fight the night, bringing light and warmth to the snowy mountaintops below. "What a great day it will be tomorrow, God willing. Girls, don't forget to bundle up and wear your spiked winter hiking shoes," Sarah cautioned.

"And of course, bring your walking sticks to help you conquer the heights," added Sheindele with excitement. With great joy they looked forward to the next day's experiences.

They had to get up before dawn to reach the summit in time for sunrise. Leah woke up even earlier to make her friends hot drinks. How disappointed she was to discover that Sarah had beaten her to it again! This happened for the rest of that vacation, and during all the vacations that followed. In Zakopane in the winter, in Zavoja or Krynica in the summer, nobody could beat Sarah to those chores.

The girls admired and respected Sarah's distinctive personality, her special love for people, her *middos* (character traits), and her way of seeing only the good in others. But there was no time for reflection that morning. They had to rush to get to the summit of the mountain on time. For hours they hiked in the deep snow, climbing higher and higher, until they finally reached their destination. But it was too late. The sun had climbed over the mountaintops. However, it was not too late to gaze down thousands of feet and enjoy a breathtaking view of the Morskie Oko, the Eye of the Sea, a round lake surrounded by the majestic mountains. It was a sight to behold.

Sarah couldn't get enough of the awe-inspiring spectacle; it could not satiate her soul. Her friends stared at and admired these wonders of nature that were spread out in front of their eyes. So did Sarah, except that her perspective was totally different. Her heart burst with awe for the Great Maker Who had created it all for one purpose only: for human beings to witness and enjoy Hashem's Glory. Sarah could not contain herself. She cried out in the words of King David:[2] "How mighty, Hashem, is Your Name in the whole world…. When I see the beautiful sky, the work of Your Hands, and the moon and the stars You created, I have to cry out, 'Who am I that You remember me?' You gave a spark of Your Glory and splendor to man, so he could appreciate the loving-kindness that You have bestowed upon mankind."

Then she turned to her friends. "Don't you see Hashem's greatness in this wonder of nature? Don't you feel what I feel? Aren't you as awed as I am?"

They laughed. "Look, our Chassidka's preaching her old-fashioned ideas to us. We love you, Surahleh, but please stop exhorting us with your pious thoughts and ways."

Four girls went down the mountain happy, their faces flushed, their spirits high. "What a wonderful hike it was," they repeated to each other. Sarah went down heartbroken. She stayed awake all night, thinking. Even my own friends don't follow my ideas, she admitted sadly. The noxious atmosphere that has enveloped the young Jews of Kraków has infected them, too.

---

2. *Tehillim* 8.

*   *   *

Sarah spent some summer vacations in Krynica, a renowned Polish health spa frequented by vacationers and, especially, people seeking relief from stomach problems and other maladies. People bathed in bubbly hot-spring water, to which healing properties were attributed. Drinking fountains also dispensed the naturally bubbly fluid, which people found refreshing and relaxing. Other fountains offered a less delicious mineral water that was believed to help stomach patients.

Observing the sparkling spring water as it burst forcefully from the earth and created a captivating geyser, Sarah described this experience in her personal diary: "I was fascinated by this natural phenomenon. Hashem created natural wonders and gave man a mind to search and explore these hidden treasures and to harness and use them for the benefit of mankind."

✤ Chapter 2 ✤

The young Sarah Schenirer was a typical broad-minded and inquisitive Krakowian girl. She was eager to learn, to know, to experience. As she wrote in her *Gesamelte Schriften* (Collected Writings), published in Yiddish:

> I used to work hard to supplement my family's income, often staying up until late at night. Then I started to work on myself, on my own education. *Chok l'Yisroel,* which my father so lovingly bought for me, became the source of my Jewish knowledge. There in Yiddish translation I followed every night the daily portion of *Chumash, Nevi'im,* Mishnah, and Gemara. I enjoyed it tremendously, as it enriched my understanding of the Jewish heritage and its beauty and depth of thought.
>
> But I also took a great interest in secular knowledge: education, history, world literature, etc. I especially admired the classical works of Polish and German writers. I loved reading them. From time to time, to quench my thirst for knowledge, I attended lectures and speeches on various subjects at the Polish folk universities. When I was in Vienna shopping for fabrics for my sewing trade, I enjoyed listening to reviews of classic German authors' works in the great auditorium of the Bayerishes Hoff. All these lectures were well-attended by Jewish youth, who listened to them enthusiastically since this was the only interesting knowledge available.
>
> I regretted going to those places, but unfortunately

9

there was no Jewish environment to meet these needs of Jewish youth. I was happy to have my Jewish education, with which I could censor what I heard. But what about the other girls? If only I could communicate the subjects they were so eager to know and, at the same time, inspire them with Torah wisdom and the beauty of the Jewish heritage. If only I could!...

In the winter of 1908, I went to Vienna to attend the great celebration of the sixtieth anniversary of Kaiser Franz Josef's coronation. It was a very impressive event, with all European dignitaries in attendance.

Great parades of military and home guard units marched through the streets of Vienna. Police troops protected the very distinguished entourage of the Kaiser and his esteemed guests, amidst music and song.

I thought about the immense glory and honor they give to this flesh-and-blood king, the enthusiasm and exaltation they shower upon the worldly ruler, who, like all human beings, will eventually turn into dust.

Why do our young people fail to understand and to give this honor and glory, this exaltation, to the Almighty, the King of kings? Instead, they pray to the Creator lethargically, as a burden, or just to please their parents.

If only I could explain to them how badly deceived they are. Instead of glorifying the Omnipotent Ruler, they render honor and pay tribute to the ruler of flesh and blood. Thus they substitute mere tinsel for true greatness and pure gold.

✤ *Chapter 3* ✤

The end of the nineteenth century found Europe in turmoil. All kinds of revolutionary ideas had been born and were spreading in the West. It did not take long for the strong winds of change to blow eastward — to Poland.

In the course of that century, the rising tide of assimilation in Germany, set in motion by the *Haskalah,* the so-called Jewish Enlightenment, lured young Jews and robbed them of their traditional values. They pronounced themselves equal to gentiles and free to mix with them, marry them, and become just like them. Unfortunately, these new ideas made inroads in the Polish cities.

The beautiful Reform temples that the *maskilim* built attracted a Jewish "intelligentsia" that was not worthy of the name — Jews who wanted to become Poles even if it sometimes ended up in conversion to Christianity, God forbid. None of it mattered as long as they had all the opportunities for advancement. Many Jews in the large cities fell victim to a gradual process of assimilation. In small towns, Jews still adhered to their tradition.

The great rabbis of Eastern Europe reacted to the onslaught of the *Haskalah* and launched a counteroffensive against it. They waged a continuous battle for many years.

The Torah giants of the time mounted a struggle against the influence of the *Haskalah,* the misnamed Jewish Enlightenment, each in his own way, each according to the conditions in his community. These warriors included Rabbi Yitzchok

Elchonon Spector, Rabbi of Kovno; the Ksav Sofer in Pressburg; Rabbi Shimon Sofer in Kraków; the Chiddushei ha-Rim, the Rebbe of Gur; Reb Yisroel Salanter in Vilna; and others.

Great *yeshivos* were founded in Poland and Lithuania. Reb Chaim of Volozhin founded the first yeshiva in the town of that name. Rabbi Yisroel Meir Hakohen (the Chofetz Chaim) established the yeshiva in Radin. Rabbi Yosef Yoizel Horowitz founded the *mussar* yeshiva in Navardok. Other *yeshivos* operating in Eastern Europe were those of Slobodka, Telz, and Mir. In Germany, the cradle of assimilation, Rabbi Samson Raphael Hirsch rose up to fight this dangerous affliction and cast his powerful influence not only across Germany but also in Poland and Russia. His world outlook and educational philosophy captivated young Jews and inspired them to follow the Jewish tradition. The Chassidic rebbes did their share, inspiring young Jewish men to embrace the Torah way of life and to study it with vigor and joy — thus sparing them from the claws of assimilation. The rabbi of Radomsk, the Tiferes Shlomo, founded thirty-eight great *yeshivos* in Poland. The Torah-true world had any number of institutions on which it could rely: the Kesser Torah *yeshivos*, Talmud Torahs, Yesodei ha-Torah, the Tomchei Temimim yeshiva founded by the Lubavitch movement, and others.

Nobody, however, thought about protecting an especially vulnerable part of the Jewish population — the girls — from the onslaught of the *Haskalah*.

*   *   *

Then a new storm roared in from the West: the idea of national liberation and self-determination for all. Jews found it alluring, of course, and later developed their own liberation doctrine, Zionism. The Zionist idea spread quickly, resulting in the establishment of all kinds of organizations with different ideological shadings. "We lovers of Zion wish to 'make *aliyah*' — to settle in Eretz Yisroel and build our homeland and our children's future there." Zionist organizations mushroomed under such slogans.

Who joined them first? Our Orthodox youth, of course. Who else had been nurtured at home with love of Zion? Who else yearned for *Eretz ha-Kedushah,* the land of sanctity? Our girls were among the first to be caught up with the Zionist idea, and they flocked to join the movement's various organizations.

Young Sarah loved Eretz Yisroel so deeply. It possessed her thoughts and dreams. She longed to be there — to behold its beauty, to feel its sanctity, to walk on the ground where our prophets and prophetesses lived and prophesied, to listen to the whisper of history, to hear every stone, every blade of grass telling us about the glorious past of this land, the splendor of the times of *Beis ha-Mikdash.* She could never speak of Eretz Yisroel dispassionately.

Years later, when I was in the Bnos youth movement, Frau Schenirer occasionally visited us for *shalosh se'udos,* the third Shabbos meal, or spent a special evening with us. Each visit was an experience that engraved itself in our minds and hearts forever. One such visit occurred on Tu bi-Shevat, the fifteenth day of the Hebrew month of Shevat, the new year of fruit trees. Following the custom, the girls had brought fruits from Eretz Yisroel to celebrate the occasion and to recite the appropriate blessings over the fruit of our land. The girls were singing when Frau Schenirer walked in, a smile on her face and a spark of joy in her eyes. Soon, she joined us in song with her usual vigor and enthusiasm.

She loved to hear the girls sing solo, especially when they sang her favorite songs. She turned to one of the younger girls: "*Nu,* Mirale [Schwartzmer], it's Tu bi-Shevat, we're eating the fruits of Eretz Yisroel. Sing your favorite song."

Mirale complied:

א מאנדל, א באקסער, א פייג
ברענגען אונדז א גרוס פון גאר ווייט
ברענגען אונץ א גרוס פון אונדזער לאנד

וואס מיר האבן עס באקומען

פון ג-טס האנד

אבער מיר האבן עס נישט יעצט

פרעמדע מענטשן האבן עס באזעצט

אין גיכן וועט קומען א צייט

ווען ג-ט מיט זיין חסד איז גרייט

באווייזן ווידער גרויסע וואנדער

מיט אן אויסגעשטרעקטע האנד

וועט ברענגען זיינע קינדער

צוריק אין היילייקן לאנד.

An almond, a carob, a fig
Bring us regards from our land
Which we received
From God's Hand.

But we don't have it anymore,
Strangers now occupy its shores.

But soon will come the time
When Hashem will restore
The Land to His children.
And they will return home
With joy once more.

Frau Schenirer joined in the last verse with passion and then turned to Bertha Horowitz. "Now please sing your favorite song, 'Yerushalayim, Mayn Mamme [Jerusalem, My Mother].'" Bertha complied as well, with deep emotion:

ירושלים, מיין מאמע

מיין גוף און מיין נשמה.

שוין צוויי טויזענט יאר

אין גלות גיזעסן

אבער פון דיר מאמע

קיין מאל ניט פארגעסן.

ירושלים מיין מאמע

מיין גוף און מיין נשמה.

Yerushalayim, my mother
My body and my soul,
Who has destroyed and disgraced you, Mother?
We are so far away, longing
And crying out our hearts to you
And Mother weeps
Praying for her children's return.

Then, we all sang together. It was Frau Schenirer's profound emotion that created that unforgettable mood of longing, pining, waiting, and hoping to be reunited with our beloved mother, Yerushalayim, soon.

*   *   *

One Friday night, a dear cousin of Sarah Schenirer's visited with her and suggested that she come along and enjoy a beautiful *oneg Shabbos* at the "Ruth" organization, to which she belonged. Unsurprisingly, Sarah gladly consented. She wanted to see how and what they were doing to promote *aliyah* — settlement of Eretz Yisroel. Maybe, she thought, I can be of help.

How disappointed she was when, instead of an *oneg Shabbos*, she found *chilul Shabbos* — desecration of the holy day — as the leaders unashamedly turned the lights in the hall on and off. Heartbroken, she turned to her cousin. "Please, let's leave. I cannot stay here a minute longer. How can this organization really love Zion, *Eretz ha-Kodesh* [the Holy Land], if everything they do destroys its *kedushah*?"

It had always pained Sarah to watch girls stray from the Jewish tradition. Now, however, it hurt her even more as she saw where these Zionist organizations were leading them. Oh! she thought. If only I could go out there and open their eyes to true love of Zion, love of the Ribono shel Olam, love of the Jewish tradition.

"But I am shy," she wrote in her diary. "Oh! If only I had the courage to run in the streets and scream, 'There is a Master Who created this world and leads it, Who with His loving-kindness nourishes us and bestows upon us all the goodness and beauty in this world!' If only I had the courage," she lamented.

Thus, even as a young girl Frau Schenirer had to battle against the influence of her own friends and cousins. She constantly struggled to combat their foreign concepts and to keep her inner self true to her lofty ideals.

Her diary, for instance, describes a happy event in her life that her friends wished to celebrate with her. They suggested that she and they go see a popular play at the theater.

She deflected their well-meant offer by recalling a *midrash* she had read on Shabbos: "When King David tried to get up at midnight and sing praises to Hashem, his *yetzer ha-ra*, evil inclination, taunted him: 'Are you out of your mind? All other kings sleep late into the day, and you want to rise at midnight?' King David replied cunningly, 'Very well, I'll spend my night at the theater.'

"'That makes more sense,' the *yetzer ha-ra* replied in satisfaction, and he left the scene.

"As soon as his despised foe left, King David arose and composed the *Tehillim*, the beautiful Psalms that we recite to this very day.

"How right he was," Sarah Schenirer continued. "Isn't our world likened to a theater, in which one actor wears a regal crown and another carries a beggar's cane? When the curtain descends after the earthly show, don't the king and the beggar go to the same grave?

"Isn't it better, instead of wasting time in this theater of life, to learn Torah and follow Hashem's commandments? We should remember that every day brings us closer to the moment of truth, when we will have to account for our deeds. Whether we wear a regal crown or carry a beggar's cane in this earthly theater, we all face the World of Truth when the curtain falls. We will have to account to the Eternal Judge for all our performances on this earthly stage."

* * *

On August 4, 1911, the 10th of Av, Sarah Schenirer wrote

the following entry in her diary:

> Just yesterday, on Tishah b'Av, I mourned the tragedy of the destruction of the *Beis ha-Mikdash*, the loss of the Holy of Holies, where God's *Shechinah* rested.
>
> Today, Friday, my personal happiness was destroyed. I lost my dear father, my teacher, my leader. I am left without his presence, his advice, his encouragement.
>
> I suffered two disasters, both a national and a personal tragedy, in one stroke. Who will comfort me? Who will comfort us? Then I remembered: a week ago [erev Rosh Chodesh Av, after her usual Yom Kippur Katan prayers at the Rema Shul] I went to pray at the grave of the saintly Rema. Interestingly, I realized for the first time that this great sage lived only thirty-three years, wrote thirty-three *seforim*, and passed away on Lag ba-Omer, the thirty-third day of the Omer. In his short lifetime, he attained such great heights.
>
> Suddenly I understood: Hashem gives man as much time as is needed to accomplish his purpose in life. My father too, in his short lifetime, achieved the goal for which he was destined.

She was comforted.

Cemetery next to the Rema Shul.

Her memory was correct. The Rema passed away on Lag ba-Omer. On his *yahrtzeit*, thousands of Jews from all over Poland would come to Kraków to visit the saintly grave of this holy man and to pray there.

One of the great rabbis who eulogized the Rema at his funeral said, among other things, that the saintly Rema had lived thirty-three years, published thirty-three *seforim*, and had thirty-three *ma'alos* (virtues). In admiration, the rabbi started to count them — but arrived at only thirty-two. There must be another one, he thought, racking his mind in distress. There must be another one.

"I know his thirty-third virtue," one of the mourners cried out. "On Purim night, when the Jews get together, eat and drink, sing and dance, and get drunk *Ad de-lo yada* in their merriment, they sometimes forget to daven *Ma'ariv*. At precisely that time the saintly Rema would leave his own Purim *se'udah* and knock on the doors of other Purim celebrants. As each door was opened, he would ask, 'May I have a little water to wash my hands? I have to daven *Ma'ariv*.'

"'Oh, my goodness!' the hosts would exclaim. And turning to their guests, they would say, 'Let's daven *Ma'ariv*. In all the excitement, we forgot to daven.'"

The Rema understood that amidst all the festivities people might forget to daven *Ma'ariv*, so he reminded them in a caring and inoffensive manner.

Sarah Schenirer herself passed away at the young age of fifty-two. Overcoming many difficulties, she brought to fruition her novel idea of educating Jewish girls in the spirit of Torah. By establishing the Bais Yaakov movement she saved not only the girls who enrolled in these schools but the entire Jewish generation of her time and all generations to come. In the eulogy at her funeral, the title *Gedol ha-Dor* was bestowed upon her. This was an unprecedented honor for a Jewish woman.

❧ *Chapter 4* ❧

It was early in 1911 when I bought myself a sewing machine," Sarah Schenirer wrote in her diary. "I purchased it with my hard-earned money. Now I had my own treasured possession! I took seriously to sewing. It's a tough profession, but one has to work," she philosophized. "We were placed in God's creation *le-ovdah u'le-shomrah*, to cultivate and protect it, both physically and spiritually. Idleness, laziness, is the mother of all evil. If man would only understand that he is here to contribute to the well-being of humanity, we would have a better world.

"I like to work," she continued. "It gives me time to think. Thoughts fly — thoughts of dreams, desires, and intentions, thoughts that make demands of me: muster your courage, go out into the world, speak to your sisters, the girls you love. Open their eyes and their minds. Show them what it means to be a Jewish daughter, a daughter of the King.

"Again, thoughts, thoughts. Don't delay, they urge me. Act, work, and perform. God will help you to accomplish your goal. Then come conflicting thoughts: You can't face an audience. True, you can speak one-on-one. But you're too shy to speak in public. You'll never do it!

"Never? Oh, God Almighty, I still hope to do it — maybe tomorrow, maybe some day, maybe soon."

*   *   *

Sarah Schenirer, whose heavy workload often forced her to toil until late at night, took a vacation twice a year at her mother's insistence. To carry the dual burdens of work and self-education, she had to relax and replenish her strength at regular intervals.

She vacationed at various spas and summer and winter resorts. As an ardent observer of God's nature, she was delighted to have those opportunities to observe and admire the beautiful country scenery. She was awed by the breathtaking views and considered it a *zechus*, a great privilege, to behold them.

She was also interested in meeting young girls in these places, or at weddings and other happy events that she frequently attended around Galicia. She discussed life with them and tried to interest them in her ideas. Some of the girls she spoke with were concerned with fashion, hairstyles, jewelry, and the like, to the exclusion of everything else.

"Other girls would come up to me," Sarah wrote in her diary, "and ask which organization I belonged to. These were intelligent, idealistic young people who strove to find meaning in life, who searched for an ideal. I tried to explain to them what the true ideal is. However, their minds were already made up. They had all joined various organizations that stood for the popular "isms" of our time, innocently believing that they could lead to the true goal in life.

"Oh!" the diary cried out. "If only I could establish an organization that would rebuff all those false ideas — an organization in which I could inspire young girls to embrace the Torah ideal and teach them how to love the Ribono shel Olam, to emulate His ways of loving-kindness, and to reach the true goal in life. Hashem," Sarah Schenirer implored the Almighty, "help me realize my dream!"

✳ ✳ ✳

It is Yom Kippur. Sarah Schenirer prays. She begs her merciful Father to forgive all her sins and those of *Klal Yisroel*. "Father in Heaven," she entreats, "even the sinners are all Your children. Help them return to You. Especially forgive those misguided, estranged daughters of Yours who do not know how to pray. Help me show them how to serve You in joy and bring them closer to You."

She continues to pray with love and devotion. She follows the *chazan* during the *Ma'ariv* service. She imbibes his powerful tones: *Chazak ve-ya'ameitz libecha ve-kavei el Hashem* — "strengthen and encourage your heart and have hope in Hashem." The words give her strength and encouragement. She resolves, "I will put aside my sewing and start planning and working actively to bring my ideals to realization at long last. *Kavei el Hashem* — with courage, I hope for *siyata di-Shemaya*, Hashem's help."

*　　　*　　　*

In 1914, the world was dragged into the Great War (World War I), disrupting Sarah Schenirer's plans and ideas. Panic gripped Poland. Young men were drafted. Women and children fled from Galicia to Vienna, where they felt more secure. Sarah Schenirer and her family were among them. It was a daunting experience. Masses of people descended on the city; housing was scarce. After much searching, the Schenirers found an apartment on the outskirts of the city. Sarah was heartbroken. Where would she find an Orthodox shul to attend on Shabbos? Her landlady put her at ease, "Don't worry, Sarah, there's a nice Orthodox synagogue within walking distance; you'll enjoy praying there." When she visited the shul on Shabbos, she was amazed to see that women did not carry their *siddurim* or *Chumashim* (as there was no *eiruv* in this, the Seventh District of Vienna). Everything had been prepared for them in advance.

After *Shacharis*, she heard Rabbi Moshe Flesch, rabbi of the congregation, speak about the *parashah* and current events. Rabbi Flesch was a student of Rabbi Salomon Breuer, and a passionate teacher of the writings of Rabbi Samson Raphael Hirsch. It was Shabbos Chanukah. Rabbi Flesch spoke with enthusiasm and warmth about Yehudis and how she had sacrificed her life to save her people.

Sarah, greatly excited, thought about the girls in Kraków. If only they could hear this message and share the inspiration she derived from Rabbi Flesch's oratorical skills. She resolved not to miss any of his Shabbos talks and, immediately after Shabbos, to take notes on what she had learned. The most memorable part of his Shabbos Chanukah message, she felt, was his elaboration on the sacrifice of Jewish women in all generations to save their people.

At this time she made her first acquaintance with the works of Rabbi Samson Raphael Hirsch. She was inspired by his idea of *Torah im derech eretz*, his courageous stance against the Reform movement, and his struggle against the *Haskalah*, which he waged with Torah-true values. How amazing it was, she thought, that in Germany, the citadel of assimilation, one man stood up and tackled a movement that had already become firmly entrenched by then. However, Rabbi Hirsch's remarkable influence spread far beyond Germany: his creative thinking and the unique style of his *seforim* captured the imaginations and minds of young people in many countries. Fascinated and intrigued by his novel approach toward Jewish tradition, they followed his ideas of Torah-true observance.

The Bais Yaakov Movement Is Born

⚜ *Chapter 5* ⚜

The Great War ended and young Sarah returned with her family to her beloved Kraków and the people for whom she cared so much. A distressing spectacle greeted her: organized youth who were following all those powerfully influential new "isms."

In order to spare the boys, our rabbis, the giants of the Torah, put up a great fight to repel the foreign currents that were flooding Poland. Nobody, however, cared about the Jewish girls. They believed that girls should be educated at home by their mothers. In agony, Sarah confronted our leaders' indifference to the tragic situation of the girls, who were left prey to these alien ideas.

Time and again she turned to the influential leaders of the Orthodox community and explained the need for traditional Jewish education for girls. She urged them to open their eyes and behold the disastrous plight of the Jewish daughters, the broken Jewish homes, and the tragic consequences this situation might, God forbid, bring upon the entire Orthodox way of life. With vigor and enthusiasm, she tried to inspire them with her vision of an educational system for girls that would mend the riven Jewish family.

It was all to no avail. Her entreaties and sincere reasoning fell on deaf ears. Nothing could convince the powers-that-be in the Jewish community that such a school was desperately needed. They denied the reality of the disintegrating Jewish family and, perforce, could not comprehend it. How it hurt Sarah to observe the beautiful tapestry of Jewish tradition, spun with love through ages by women of valor, suddenly torn and disgraced! The cold disinterest that our own people displayed toward her idea caused her untold anguish and disappointment, which she endured in silence.

How pitifully the situation compared with the warm concern for women's education that she had felt in Vienna. Here there was no Rabbi Flesch, let alone a Rabbi Hirsch, to breathe new life into the Jewish population. Thinking about Rabbi Flesch's lectures, Sarah felt with growing conviction that destiny had placed her in this world, at this particular time, to become the Yehudis of her generation — to save the Jewish girl, and with her the Jewish people at large, from destruction.

For young Sarah Schenirer, however, the going was tough. She met hostile opposition from left and right. Even her own friends ignored her ideas. Young people, hardened to the beauty of the Jewish heritage by the toxic atmosphere surrounding them, paid her no heed.

Mothers, however, shared their tragic stories with her. "My oldest daughter," one mother confided, "is a beautiful, charming, talented, smart girl. We all love her. She loves us too and respects us. But a terrible thing has happened," the mother continued, sobbing heavily. "She has joined the Communist party, which is outlawed in Poland, and has become a leading personality in it. She lectures in different towns and cities. But she won't speak in Kraków, so as not to hurt her parents. I fear for her life and safety because the government is hunting for Communist leaders to arrest them. My daughter doesn't care. She's fighting for her ideal — to bring justice to the world — and defends herself by saying, 'Wasn't it loving-kindness that you always taught us?'

"I have a younger daughter," she continued, wiping her tears. "I don't want her to follow her sister's lead."

Other mothers poured their hearts out to Frau Schenirer in the same way. One cried that her daughter was leaving home to join a nonreligious kibbutz in Palestine. Another lamented,

"Our daughters go to the movies after the Friday night Shabbos meal, which we eat early during the winter Friday nights. They just try to hide it from us."

Frau Schenirer listened to these heartbroken mothers' accounts of their daughters' irreligious and improper behavior. She armed herself with her notes from Rabbi Flesch's speeches and the writings of Rabbi Samson Raphael Hirsch. The collected writings of the latter became her inseparable companions, his translations of *Chumash* and *Tehillim* her favorite reading material. Realizing that she could not depend on the community leaders for any help, she resolved, "I shall break through my shyness once and for all and gird myself with courage to go out into the world and bring God's truth to the Jewish daughter."

On one occasion she mentioned to a few older students the passage in *Pirkei Avos* (Ethics of the Fathers),[3] *Be-makom she-ein anashim, hishtadel lihiyos ish* — "In a place where there are no men, try to be a man." "There are times, there are communities," she said, "where there are no men to care. Then you must stand up and be the 'man' who takes responsibility into his own hands," she added apologetically. Yes, she became a Torah giant who revolutionized the Jewish world with the novel idea of Torah education for girls.

Before she started to realize her plans, however, she consulted with her older brother in Czechoslovakia, with whom she was very close. She wrote him a letter explaining her plans. He discouraged her, saying, "Why do you need to get into fights with all those Leftist organizations?"

But when he saw her determination, he suggested that she visit Marienbad, where she could ask the Belzer Rebbe, Reb Yissachar Ber, for his advice.

"My happiness knew no limits when I received this answer," Frau Schenirer wrote later on. "Although I could hardly afford it, I immediately made arrangements to travel to

---

3. 2:5.

Marienbad and meet up with my brother there. He was a familiar figure in Belz, and we were given an audience with the Rebbe right away.

"My brother wrote the *kvitl*, the note to the Rebbe: 'My sister has decided to educate Jewish girls in the spirit of our tradition.' Fortunately, I was present in the room when the Rebbe pronounced the blessing, '*berachah ve-hatzlachah*.' [This meant that she had *carte blanche* to go ahead with her idea.] Those words, from the mouth of this great *tzaddik*, gave me courage and certainty that, with Hashem's help, I would succeed."

In contrast to other Torah personalities, the Rebbe showed that he understood the need for Torah education for girls.

With that, Frau Schenirer put her plans into action. She formed a group of Orthodox women, including the young Rebbetzin Halberstam, granddaughter of the Divrei Chaim, and introduced them to her idea of educating Jewish girls in the spirit of Torah.

"I want to return them to the traditional way of life," she explained,[4] "and to restore their pride in being daughters of the King, happy to fulfill His commandments with joy.

"The women showed great interest in my idea and undertook to help me arrange the first meeting with young girls. Now I will have an opportunity to speak to my beloved youth and give them an introduction to the true ideal, the Torah life.

"I was troubled. The older women were enthusiastic about my plans. But what will the youth say, the ones I want to reach?" She pushed away these disturbing thoughts. "I must go ahead with my plans, pray and hope, with Hashem's help, to succeed."

The first *oneg Shabbos* took place in the spacious, pleasant auditorium of the Kraków Orphanage. Due to the women's efforts, forty girls, mostly between the ages of sixteen and twenty, attended. Surprised and pleased with the nice beginning, she

---

4. *Gesamelte Schriften.*

delivered her first lecture with vigor and enthusiasm. She spoke on *Pirkei Avos*. "I discussed what the Sages said: *Va'asu siyag la-Torah* [Build a fence around the Torah],"[5] she tells us in her writings. "The girls listened with interest as I described the beautiful garden of exquisite flowers and blossoming fruit trees that Hashem planted for us, and how our Sages built fences around it to protect it from the onslaught of evil elements.

"However," she continued, "as I explained the 'fence' that our Sages built to protect the precious garden of the 613 Torah precepts from desecration — for example the 'fence' of *muktzeh* to protect the observance of Shabbos — I noticed sardonic expressions on the girls' faces, which told me, 'Is that what you brought us here for? To tell us about your old-fashioned ideas?'

"One by one they walked out shamelessly, never to return. I realized that my job would not be easy, but I did not give up. I resolved to try again."

Sarah Schenirer strongly believed in the power of youth. Young people, she felt, are intrinsically enthusiastic, energetic and active, striving for an ideal in life. They are loud and rebellious, but that is their privilege. They observe the establishment's faults and try to improve the world and create a better life.

Unfortunately, however, our youth got lost in the labyrinth of false ideas. They knew nothing of our people's history and were not inspired by the beauty of our heritage.

"I must try again to organize the youth," she wrote, "open their eyes, and show them the true ideal, the Torah ideal, which is worth all manner of effort and sacrifice."

She elected to start over with other young girls and chose a different and more stimulating method — an enthusiastic recitation of King David's glorious *Tehillim* and the poetic chapters of the great Jewish prophets. This time, girls flocked to hear her.

Believing in the inspiration of the written word, Frau

---

5. *Pirkei Avos* 1:1.

Schenirer immediately established a small library of Jewish books. She stocked it with the works of Rabbi Samson Raphael Hirsch, Marcus Lehmann's commentaries to *Pirkei Avos* and the Pesach Haggadah, as well as his original stories, issues of *Der Israelit* (a Jewish weekly published in Germany), and a few other books on Jewish thought. They were all she could find.

In terms of her ultimate goal, however, this second attempt also proved unsuccessful. The girls enjoyed an exciting lecture but flinched from taking responsibility for leading a meaningful Jewish life and committing themselves to fulfilling the precepts of the Torah.

Again, Frau Schenirer did not give up. Unsophisticated and blessed with the trait of unusual simplicity, this young woman had a far-reaching vision. She saw girls, not only in Kraków but throughout Poland, the rest of Europe, and beyond — attending schools in the Bais Yaakov network that she would establish, mastering the treasures of the Torah and Jewish history and heritage.

She envisaged girls growing in wisdom and understanding. She saw their characters being formed and their acquiring pure love of and devotion to their Father in Heaven. She saw a great and burgeoning Bais Yaakov movement spreading all over the world.

Rabbi Kahaneman, the Rosh Yeshiva of Ponivezh, had an apt expression for people like Sarah Schenirer. Once, at a fund-raising meeting for his yeshiva, he pointed at a large hill in Bnei Brak and explained to the audience, "One day there will be an impressive yeshiva campus on that hill."

"Rabbi, you're dreaming," people in the audience called out. "Yes, I am dreaming," Rabbi Kahaneman answered. "But I am not sleeping."

Such a person, too, was Sarah Schenirer. She dreamed...but instead of sleeping, she acted. She decided to start with girls who had not yet been contaminated by the surrounding anti-religious atmosphere.

Although she never relinquished her dream of inspiring and

working with youth, she now began with young children who still clung to their mothers' skirts, who sat on their father's laps on Shabbos nights, listening with excitement to the stories from the *parashah*.

I was one of those girls.

❧ Chapter 6 ❧

In my early childhood I could hardly wait for the long winter Shabbos nights, when Father, after the *se'udah*, seated himself in his favorite armchair, next to the tall green tile oven. How warm and cozy the dining room was! I climbed into my father's lap, eager to listen to this week's story.

I was fascinated by the beautiful tales my father spun for me about Avraham, our nation's forefather — his love for all human beings; his concern, along with his wife Sarah the matriarch, for hungry and thirsty wayfarers; their unusual hospitality; the loving-kindness that they extended to everyone. How exciting it all was. Avraham even prayed for the evildoers of Sedom — he begged Hashem to save them!

Some of the stories were agonizing, too. The tragedy of Yosef the *tzaddik* and how his brothers sold him into slavery made me cry. His brothers' jealousy, which caused this tragedy, made me so angry. His appointment as a viceroy in Pharaoh's house thrilled me. Then my heart broke when my father spoke about Yosef's brothers as they visited him in Egypt to buy food, and about Yosef's response: to hold Binyamin, their father's favorite son, hostage. How many tears I shed listening to the dramatic events that followed. What a joy it was to reach the denouement, as Yosef revealed himself to his brothers and so graciously forgave them.

Father retold the story the next year. This time, however, instead of crying, I asked him innocently, "*Tatte*, why didn't he learn his lesson from last year? Why did he go to look for his brothers again if he knew they'd sell him into slavery once more?"

Sarah Schenirer resolved to start with these innocent little girls like me. She would tell them about the great love that our Father, the Ribono shel Olam, has for His children, His concern for their well-being, the beauty of our heritage, Jewish history, and the truth of the Torah. She felt that if she started with young girls instead of adolescents, she would have a better chance of reaching them and bringing them to the path of Torah.

Chana Rivka Birenbaum was one of Sarah Schenirer's closest friends. Unfortunately, she was widowed early and was left with two young daughters. She later remarried, and her second husband, Rabbi Yisrael Moshe Schmidt, not having his own children, became a father to her two girls.

The two friends met and visited each other often. Chana Schmidt would bring her two young daughters, for whom Sarah Schenirer would fit dresses that she had made for them. During those visits, Sarah shared with Chana her ideas, her plans, and her dreams of establishing a girls' school that would teach Jewish history and illuminate the beauty of the Jewish heritage and the meaningful laws and traditions of our People.

One evening in early 1918, Sarah Schenirer visited her friend instead of the other way around. "I've decided to realize my dream today," she said in great excitement. "I will turn my workshop into a classroom and start the school," she declared with resolve, her voice rising with her usual vigor and her eyes sparkling with fire, as they always did when she was deeply moved.

Rabbi Schmidt heard the commotion and came into the kitchen to see what it was about. As a *mashgiach* in Yeshivas Chachmei Lublin (who traveled from Lublin to Kraków to spend Shabbos, *chagim*, and other occasions with his family), he appreciated the dire need for traditional education for Jewish girls. Hearing about Sarah Schenirer's decision to start the school, he was caught up in the excitement. Enthusiastically, he turned to Sarah with a spontaneous offer: "We have two young girls. Begin the school with them, and may Hashem bless your saintly endeavors."

*   *   *

That is how Hindy and Devoiraleh (Devorah) Birenbaum became the first students in the newly established Bais Yaakov school. Then came Mrs. G., who with tears in her eyes introduced her daughter Escia and pleaded, "My older daughter has gone astray. Please save at least my youngest child." Other mothers followed in the same fashion. Thus seven girls — Escia, Hanka, Sarah, Gittel, Bella, Hindy, and Devoiraleh — became the founding core of the Bais Yaakov movement.

Years later, at an event in Bnei Brak, I had the *zechus* to meet Rebbetzin Hinda (Hindy) Ehrenberg, one of the first girls in this class. At this exciting meeting, she spoke enthusiastically about being part of the Bais Yaakov beginnings. She introduced me to her three daughters: Sarah Frankel, Ahuvah Ehrlich, and Riva Abramowitz, all respected members of the community in Bnei Brak. As she wasn't feeling well at the time, she told them to fill me in with the details that she used to relate to them about her experiences at the newborn Bais Yaakov school.

"We loved that new private school," Rebbetzin Ehrenberg would tell her daughters. "We admired our teacher, who not only taught us something new, something exciting every day, but who also spoke to us with a warmth that only a mother can equal. She began with a simple question-and-answer session. 'What are you?' she would ask one of the girls in her motherly way.

"The girl already knew the answer: 'I am a Jewish girl.'

"'And what makes you a Jewish girl?' the teacher continued.

"'I believe in our *Beshefer* [Creator], Who created this world and gave us His holy Torah.'

"'Now, what is written in this Torah?'

"'It says that Hashem created the world and everything in it. He created man to enjoy all His creations and use them to serve the *Heiliger* [Holy] *Beshefer*.'"

The questions became more mature later on. The girls learned the purpose of Creation. They studied God's commandments and learned how to fulfill them. Increasingly, they understood that the Torah is God's unique truth.

Rebbetzin Ehrenberg remembers: "We could hardly wait for the next afternoon, when we would meet again, discover new treasures of Jewish wisdom, enjoy the exclusive company of Jewish friends, and listen to a loving, motherly Jewish teacher.

"One day, Frau Schenirer came into the room with a nicely wrapped package under her arm. '*Kinderlach*,' she said, her twinkling eyes adding to the suspense, 'I have a gift for each one of you. I hope you will like it.' We were excited, eager to see the surprise. She unwrapped the parcel and pulled out a snow-white, beautifully starched collar. She asked one of the girls to come over and put on the collar on her dress. Then she attached the collar with a specially sewn-on button. She did the same for each of us. We stood there in a half-circle smiling, happy with the beautiful gift she had so lovingly bestowed upon us.

"The happiest person in the room, however, was Frau Schenirer herself. 'This is the new Bais Yaakov uniform,' she pronounced. 'Be proud of it.'"

Thus the white collar became the first Bais Yaakov uniform. In many pictures taken before World War II, one can see Bais Yaakov girls proudly wearing their white starched collars. We will see these collars in many Bais Yaakov group pictures throughout the book — especially in the picture of Ita Goldknopf's Bnos group on page 70.

*   *   *

The seven girls "went to school" in that austere room, which Frau Schenirer, as she was called, cleaned personally. It had only a few furnishings: a table in the middle and some chairs around it. It lacked a teacher's desk, let alone a blackboard. However, the school grew rapidly. When the chairs did not suffice, the girls sat on the floor, writing on their laps. The Krakowian girls were soon joined by quite a few out-of-towners. One of them was Chavah Tauber of Bendin. She told me how things looked at the beginning, back there in Frau Schenirer's private apartment:

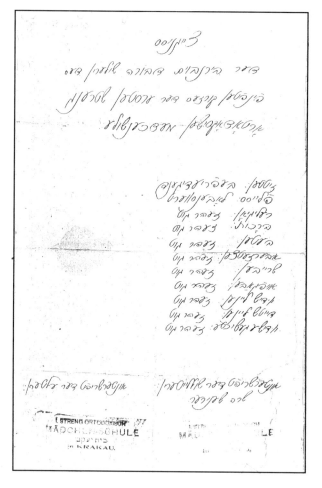

Devorah Birenbaum's report card.

"We were crowded in that room during the day, but we were happy, indescribably happy, as our revered teacher opened new worlds for us and gave us an opportunity, day and night, to observe the unique behavior and saintly ways of a great personality.

"We prepared our simple meals in her kitchen," Chavah continued, "and ate at the same table. Dinner was mostly buckwheat and a glass of milk. Plain, inadequate meals, you'd say; but if you looked at our spiritual food you would marvel at how rich, how gorgeous, how exciting it was. At night, we slept in the same room on the floor, and if we were lucky, we had a straw bed."

The sisters Hindy and Devoiraleh (Devorah) Birenbaum were the oldest girls in the first Bais Yaakov class and Devoiraleh was the first official graduate. Frau Schenirer gave the girls report cards for their mothers to sign and enjoy their daughters' accomplishments. They were neither printed nor even typed. Frau Schenirer had no typewriter either — not even an official school seal.

The report card was handwritten, as were Devoiraleh's great marks. Devoiraleh moved to Eretz Yisroel in 1934, brought her cherished *Report Kart* with her, and lovingly preserved it afterwards. She passed away a few years ago and bequeathed her precious treasure to her daughter, Sarah Rafaeli. It is my pleasure to reproduce this historical document on the facing page.

Mrs. Rafaeli also inherited the book that Frau Schenirer gave her mother as a wedding gift: *Rebecca: The Jewish Woman in Her Great Religious Profession,* by Avraham Levi. This book outlines the responsibilities of a Jewish woman as wife and mother. Frau Schenirer autographed it beautifully and signed it: "On the wedding day of my first Bais Yaakov student. Kraków, Adar 1930."

Devorah's older sister Hindy married before her, in 1925, making her the first of Frau Schenirer's students to marry. Her husband was Rabbi Yeshua Menachem Ehrenberg, a young but

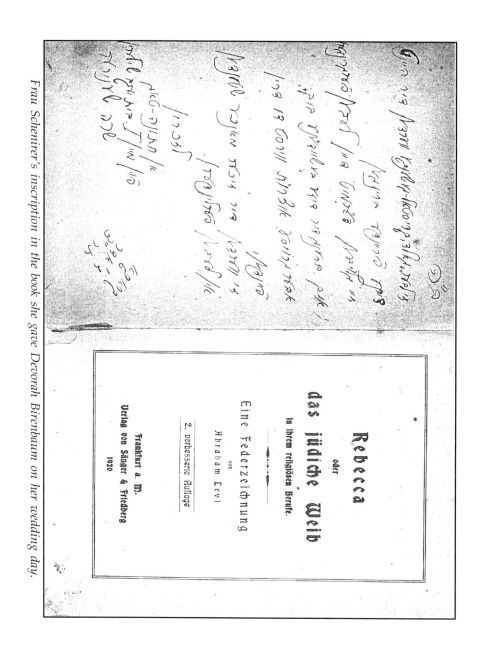

Frau Schenirer's inscription in the book she gave Devorah Birenbaum on her wedding day.

already renowned *talmid chacham*. After World War II, when they moved to Eretz Yisroel, he was given an important position as *Av Beis Din* in Tel Aviv.

After they married, the young couple lived in her parents' house, which Sarah Schenirer visited frequently. When Hindy's first baby girl was born, Sarah Schenirer of course came by to say *Mazel tov* and bless the newborn. She greeted the occasion with special excitement. "This is my first *einikel* [grandchild]!" she exclaimed enthusiastically — her face radiant, her eyes sparkling with joy.

Normally, only a biological grandmother can feel such happiness and *nachas* at the birth of her *einikel*. However, "Mother Schenirer" was able to do the same. I am sure that she continues to *shep nachas* upon the birth of each of her thousands upon thousands of *uhr-uhr einiklech,* in our generation and in every generation to come.

*   *   *

Unfortunately and tragically, Sarah Schenirer was denied her own biological children. However, she was granted the *zechus* to be a mother not to one, ten, or twenty children, but to scores, hundreds, thousands, generation after generation, of Jewish children. She was like Chavah, the first woman, a mother of *kol chai,* every living being. "Motherhood is a woman's calling," she would emphasize. "Hers is the greatest goal in life — to cleave and polish the most precious diamond, the soul of a child, and to develop his personality to perfection."

In the ancient world, there were generations of mothers who were not given this responsibility. Then, a great Jewish mother, our matriarch Sarah, was born. That Sarah showed future generations of mothers how to raise a child in holiness and purity. Even before the giving of the Torah on Mount Sinai, she demonstrated to the world a Jewish mother's responsibility to educate not only her own progeny but all Jewish children. As Rashi explains the verse, *Ko tomar l'Veis Yaakov,* "So shall you say to the House of Jacob":[6] speak first to the women, because it will be their responsibility to raise not only their own but all Jewish children in the ways of Torah.

"*Heinikah vanim Sarah*," the Torah says in *Parashas Vayera*.[7] Sarah nursed *children*. She had only one child, Rashi explains, but she nursed many children whose mothers brought them to her for nursing. She had so much to give and to offer, and was so willing to share it with others.

Throughout the generations, Jewish mothers have struggled and sacrificed to give their children a Jewish education. They sent boys at the tender age of thirteen to strange towns to learn Torah and to live the *essen teg* way — to eat each day in the home of a different kindly Jew, where they were fed by caring Jewish mothers who also felt responsible for other Jewish children's Torah education. At times, when a proper place was not found, the children had to suffer hunger and deprivation. Every such boy had a Jewish mother at home, worrying about where he would eat that day, where he would sleep that night. She feared for his health. If he fell ill, who would take care of him? The mother was always anxious about her youngster's well being.

Rabbi Meir Shapiro, of blessed memory, understood a mother's pain and concern, her sacrifice to raise her child in the Torah's ways. To ease the *talmid*'s suffering and the Jewish mother's worry and sacrifice, he founded Yeshivas Chachmei Lublin and equipped it with a modern dormitory and all conveniences.

Rabbi Shapiro admired Frau Schenirer and her efforts to introduce formal education for girls in the vocation of true Jewish motherhood. At his inaugural address when he became rabbi of the prominent *kehillah* of Piotrków, all eyes turned to him and all ears strained to hear this famous orator. They observed their new rabbi as he kissed the *paroches*, lifted his eyes, and

---

6. *Shemos* 19:3.
7. *Bereishis* 21:7.

uttered the first few words of his inaugural speech: "*Mazel tov, Mamme! Deyn Meyerke is givorn Ruv in Piotrków* — *Mazel tov,* Mother! Your Meyerke has become the rabbi of Piotrków." It is your struggle, your hard work and sacrifice, that made it happen.

Then he turned to the *ezras nashim* and continued: "You Jewish mothers, with great effort and self-denial, are bringing up your Meyerke or Shloimeleh or Duvidel, and with hard work are shaping his character, his personality. Who knows?" he cried out. "Who knows to what greatness you are bringing him up? He may also say *mazel tov* to you as he becomes a rabbi, a rosh yeshiva, or a great Torah scholar. Who knows? Maybe, just maybe, you are bringing up the *Moshiach,* the Redeemer of Israel. *Mazel tov* to all you Jewish mothers." Thus, with this moving introduction, Rabbi Meir Shapiro began his brilliant inaugural address.

*   *   *

Throughout Jewish history, we have seen Jewish women sacrifice their lives to save a child. People alive today witnessed many heroic acts of women in the rescue, or attempted rescue, of Jewish children from the claws of Hitler's torturers. One of these exemplary women was Tzila Orlean.

Tzila Neugröschl-Orlean (later Soroczkin) was one of Sarah Schenirer's early students and would herself soon become renowned as a teacher *par excellence,* first in Bais Yaakov schools and later at the Bais Yaakov Seminary in Kraków, where her well-thought-out lessons and wise advice made her the most beloved teacher there was. She also directed the first instructors' course for Bnos leaders, organized by Reb Gershon Friedenson. It was my good fortune to attend this course. Her lectures, delivered with profound thought and feeling, her discussions with us on all sorts of topics, and her instructions and practical advice are unforgettable. The model thus fashioned was then successfully replicated to create a promising institution for the education of Bnos leaders — which, unfortunately, was brutally

Chavas Schmuel, 1938; the first Bnos instructors' course.
Tzila Orlean, the leader, is in the second row, far right; the
author is in the top row, far right.

An early Fortbildungs Kurs, which Tzila Orlean attended as a
student. She is in the first row, second from left.

cut short by the tragedy of World War II.

During the war, Tzila Orlean taught *Tehillim* to small groups in the Kraków ghetto. In this setting, her teaching was not a lesson but a song — a song of faith and hope, a dream of speedy redemption. She painted a beautiful picture of Eretz Yisroel, of Lake Kinneret in its majesty and glory, exactly as if she had been there to witness it. When I had the *zechus* to be in Eretz Yisroel after World War II, I saw the lovely Lake Kinneret set amidst the magnificent tall mountains that surround it, with its beautiful waters that change from blue to various kaleidoscopic colors in the splendor of sunset. "How strange: I've already seen this picture," I thought. However, there was nothing strange about it. I *had* seen it: Tzila had painted it during her lessons in the ghetto, where we gathered secretly, endangering our lives because the Nazis forbade assembly under penalty of death. (Five people were considered an "assembly.")

Among camp inmates during the Holocaust, it was only Tzila Orlean, later Rebbetzin Soroczkin, whom the German authorities called not by number but by name, "Orlean." Yes, Rebbetzin Soroczkin made a name for herself, a *shem tov b'Yisroel*, to be remembered for ages.

She worked in the women's camp of Auschwitz as head nurse of the infirmary. This was God's doing; He sent her to Auschwitz as an "angel of mercy" to help ease His children's sufferings. She saved multitudes of lives at risk to her own. Moreover, even in Auschwitz, she continued to teach Bais Yaakov girls how to sacrifice their young lives to ease people's pain and suffering — and to save human lives. She formed a legion of girls who were ready at her command to endanger their lives to save others.

As mentioned, it was not uncommon for women to live lives of self-denial in order to provide a child with a true Jewish education. However, it was unprecedented in Jewish history for a woman to sacrifice her life, let alone to risk inhuman torture, to teach Torah to a Jewish child. But that is exactly what happened in Auschwitz, under the noses of doctors Mengele and

Königel (Kommandant of Block 10), may their names be obliterated.

A little boy, Jackie, had been transported to Auschwitz together with his family. They were led directly toward the gas chambers. Attracted by the unusual sights, the boy wandered off unnoticed to the women's camp, where one of the girls found him lost and confused. She hid him in her barracks, where she and the other girls shared their meager rations with him and concealed him during roll calls. He often visited Tzila at the infirmary, where he received an extra piece of bread or a bit of fresh water.

One day Tzila approached him with a suggestion: "You're already twelve years old; soon you will become a bar mitzvah. All you know about Jews is that they are tortured and degraded. It is time for you to learn about the beauty of the Jewish heritage. Come here every day, and I'll teach you to read Hebrew. You'll learn the *Chumash,* the most sacred book there is, the one we received at Mount Sinai. You'll learn about Hashem and the world He created, about our great Sages, about our holy nation which He chose to be the bearers of His Torah — the eternal truth."

Jackie was excited about Tzila's suggestion, and Tyly, her student and helper, went to work to acquire a *Chumash* from the girls who worked in the *Kanadakommando,* the detail that sorted the belongings of victims who had just been cremated. The girls were happy to do something for Tzila, who was always ready to help others. As hard as it was to search for the holy book, and as dangerous as it was to smuggle it into the camp, the girls were glad when they found it and brought it to Tyly for Tzila.

Tzila started to teach Jackie, who eagerly absorbed everything she told him. He was fascinated by her stories and excited to learn the beauty of our Torah. Now he proudly looked forward to becoming a bar mitzvah, a full-fledged Jew.

One evening as he sat in the infirmary listening to a story about our patriarchs, his face flushed with the excitement of learning about his heritage, the door suddenly opened and in walked Dr. Königel.

Königel was the most dreaded man in the camp. His block was always locked, separated from the rest of the camp. He was in charge of "scientific experiments" on girls, in which they were tortured to death.

When we arrived in Auschwitz, we encountered Pesa Sheroshewsky, a prominent Bais Yaakov teacher, walking past us with the other members of her labor detail. In the few moments that we had to talk as we passed each other, the most important message she gave us was a warning: "Avoid Block 10 at any price, even suicide." Now, the dangerous man who commanded the dreaded Block 10 had stepped into the infirmary.

Tzila instinctively hid the *Chumash*, but it was too late to hide the boy. Königel approached her and asked furiously: "What is this boy doing in the women's camp? And what are you doing with him?"

"Herr Obersharführer, let me explain," Tzila implored in a conciliatory tone.

It was no use. "Come with me, both of you," Königel commanded.

Everyone was seized with fright; only Tzila kept her composure and, with Königel and Jackie, walked toward Block 10 as the Nazi had directed.

"He opened the door," Tzila told me, "and I saw the inside of Block 10 for the first time: a large, well-lit room, furnished with all kinds of modern medical equipment. It looked like an ordinary laboratory."

"'Ha, Orlean,' he said venomously, closing the door after me and leaving Jackie outside. 'What were you doing with the boy?'"

"Let me explain, Herr Obersharführer," she replied calmly. "I was preparing him to become a bar mitzvah." She explained the meaning of this term and described what she had taught him.

"I had to tell him the truth," she told me later. "I assumed that I was doomed anyway."

The Nazi butcher stared at her in disbelief and had the boy brought in. "What were you doing with Orlean?" he demanded.

The child answered innocently, "Mrs. Orlean teaches me Bible. I learn about God and the world He created. She teaches me Jewish history and tells me stories about our patriarchs. I love it. And Mrs. Orlean is such a good-hearted lady; she always gives me something to eat when I come."

This beast of beasts, who performed "experiments" on Jewish girls — i.e., tortured them — was overwhelmed by the spectacle of this symmetrical display of innocence: that of the grown woman and that of the young boy. His heart of stone — moved at the sight of this great woman's pure love for a Jewish boy and the incredible sacrifice she had made to teach a strange child — gave forth a little spark of humanity. "He had tears in his eyes when he dismissed us," Tzila recalled.

He ordered her to return to the infirmary but assured her, "I will not harm the boy, but he has to be transferred to the men's camp. It is too dangerous for you and for him if he stays in the women's barracks."

Tzila was a unique teacher. Who else had the *mesirus nefesh* (self-sacrifice) to teach a child Jewish values in Auschwitz, under the threat of death and, worse, torture-experiments? She even taught the beast of beasts, Dr. Königel, how to see and appreciate greatness.

❧ *Chapter 7* ❧

It is October 1918. Finally, finally I am sitting in my own classroom with twenty-five children," Sarah Schenirer wrote in *Gesamelte Schriften.* "Their faces shone with joy as I taught them the meaning of a *berachah.* Only twenty-five children, but these are twenty-five Jewish souls who have been entrusted to me to be brought up in the true Jewish spirit. A little room with old chairs. It doesn't even have a blackboard," she continued, "but my heart is overwhelmed with joy. Here is the place where my dream, carried for so long in my heart, is being realized.

"I am happy that I'm not alone. Two people are at my side, helping me with this difficult beginning. I would like to record their names for posterity. One is the young Rebbetzin Halberstam, who works tirelessly to convince parents to send their children to my school. The second one is Mr. Mordechai Luxenberg, the father of one of my students, who works without rest, for hours, because he realizes the importance of the school. I feel uncomfortable knowing that he even forgoes his own Torah study for the benefit of the school. He realizes that the girls' education is so urgent at this time that he applies to it the Sages' interpretation on the verse, *Eis la'asos l'Hashem heifeiru Torasecha*:[8] 'It is time to act for Hashem; set aside your Torah.'"

Soon the workshop had become so crowded that Sarah Schenirer had to rent a small flat at 1 Katarzina Street, at

---

8. *Tehillim* 119:126.

which she proudly posted a sign on the front door: BAIS YAAKOV SCHOOL FOR JEWISH GIRLS.

The girls learned, ate, and slept in the new quarters. They cooked their simple meals there, and then cleaned up to use the same rooms for study. At night, the rooms became a dormitory, the out-of-town girls sleeping on beds and on the floors. Despite the primitive conditions, the girls were jubilant. They learned something new every day, with vigor and enthusiasm. Jewish tradition became their life. Jewish heritage and history opened a new world for them, and excitedly they imbibed everything that was offered to them. They were very intelligent, broad-minded, sophisticated, and inquisitive. Frau Schenirer encouraged them to ask questions; only thus, she knew, would they obtain the right answers and avoid confusion.

Enrollment grew unexpectedly fast and quickly outstripped Frau Schenirer's ability to do all the teaching herself.

Fortunately, by now her students had already grown in Torah wisdom. They thrilled to the revelation of the Torah's treasures, devoured the teachings of our great rabbis, followed the Torah ways of our giants and, above all, absorbed Frau Schenirer's great enthusiasm in observing the mitzvos. When they "graduated," it was then time for these fourteen- and fifteen-year-old girls to go out into the world to spread their newly gained Torah knowledge and its joys to other Jewish children.

Frau Schenirer went from city to city and from town to town to organize Bais Yaakov schools. On her first trip, she took along Gittel Teitelbaum, dressed in a long skirt with a mature hairstyle to make her look older, to be the first teacher in one of those towns. The whole community attended the gathering, and Frau Schenirer introduced Gittel to the women. Gittel stood up, her dark eyes sparkling as usual when she got excited, and addressed the audience. She told them about Bais Yaakov and the revival of Jewish tradition in girls' education. Her warmth and enthusiasm captured the mothers' hearts. Then Frau Schenirer turned to them. "Would you like this young woman to teach your children?" she asked. A resounding ovation was the answer.

Thus Gittel became a teacher at the first Bais Yaakov school outside of Kraków. The other girls — Hanka Grossfeld, Ida Bauminger, Escia Goldstoff, and the rest — followed the lead and staffed the newly established schools. Later, they became the driving force behind the establishment of Bais Yaakov schools in cities, towns, and hamlets, bringing their newly acquired knowledge and its spirit to many Torah-starved Jewish children.

Frau Schenirer had an exhortation that she regu-

A group of Bais Yaakov teachers in the Fortbildungs summer camp. Seated, left to right: Hanka (Grossfeld) Biegun, Ida Bauminger, Gittel (Teitelbaum) Pass; standing: Frymcia Zuckerbrodt, Esther Teitelbaum.

larly delivered to her teachers-to-be and the rest of us: "A Jewish daughter has to have two pockets," she began, smiling as she pointed to her own. "In one pocket, she should carry the motto, *Kol kevudah bas Melech penimah* — 'The glory of the King's daughter [a Jewish girl] is inside.'[9] She should stay in her tent modestly and quietly, not calling attention to herself. But in the other pocket, she should carry the principle, *Eis la'asos l'Hashem* — 'There is a time to act for Hashem.' There is a time when she must go out to spread God's truth to the world. *Penimah*, inside her, always rests the glory of being the King's daughter. But she should remember that, as a princess, she is a leader, not a follower. She sets the style and leads the way. Let others follow.

"Girls," she continued, giving her teachers-in-training her

---

9. Ibid., 45:14.

most encouraging smile, "be aware that you are going out into a hostile world. They will want to change *you*. Have the strength to repel the pressures. Remain what you are, proud Jewish daughters with God's Glory *inside* you. Never forget. Remind yourself again and again. You are not a commoner. Each of you is a favored daughter of the King of kings. You have to lead the true path, and if you do, others will follow you! *Bais Yaakov, lechu ve-nelcha be'ohr Hashem*[10] — 'House of Jacob, let us walk in the light of Hashem, and they will follow you in His radiance!'"

---

10. *Yeshayahu* 2:5.

✣ *Chapter 8* ✣

The idea of women's liberation made large inroads in Poland in the early 1920s. Polish women awakened to the Enlightenment that had been proclaimed in the West and rebelled. No longer did they wish to be "little women" whom men placed on a pedestal, adorned with jewelry, and worshiped for their beauty and charm. No longer would they be objects whom mothers sent to finishing schools so they would learn a little history, literature, piano, etiquette, and of course French.

The women were tired of all that. They wanted to join the world of men, to be their equals, to be liberated — free to have an opportunity to study the sciences, law, and medicine, to join men in the professions and in politics, and above all to learn. Women struggled for opportunities to gain knowledge, to pry open the doors of study centers and universities. Thus, "popular" universities sprang up in every city, and nowhere more than in Kraków, where bright, intelligent girls thirsted to absorb all the knowledge they could. Soon the *volks universities*, as they were called, became crowded.

What sort of girl led the throng? The Jewish girl, of course. Who else had such a tremendous yearning for knowledge? Sarah Schenirer herself — as she wrote in her diary — went to listen to those well-known scientists and educators. She also wanted to learn, to know. How disappointed she was, however, when once she heard a great educator speak about evolution. His speech was riddled with atheistic ideas. Is that what they teach our girls? she asked herself. The experience honed her determination to cry out to those Jewish girls and tell them, "Yes, you have a thirst for knowledge. So come and see; there is a wealth of Jewish thought and ideas for you to learn and enjoy. All decent thoughts and great ideas, even in world literature, stem from Torah and Talmudic knowledge."

But what of the idea of women's liberation, newly arrived in Poland? "Girls, open your eyes," she said in response. "The Jewish woman was liberated at the dawn of history. Thousands of years ago, our matriarch, Sarah, was a liberated woman. God Himself liberated her, giving her equality in greatness with her husband, Avraham. How? Come, girls, and learn:

"Hashem promised Avraham that his wife Sarai would bear him a son who would become the forefather of a great nation. Avraham, knowing that Sarai at her age could not bear children anymore, made Hashem a humble offer: let my son Yishmael be the one. 'Out of the question!' Hashem answered. 'A father of this great nation must be born not only of a great father but also of a great mother.'

"To underscore Sarah's greatness, Hashem said to Avraham, 'Do not call her Sarai anymore; add the letter *hei* to her name, as I did to yours, and from now on call her Sarah.'

"You see, girls," Frau Schenirer used to say, citing the newly published book, *Der Torah Kval*, by Rabbi Zushe Fried-man, "Hashem did not want Sarah to be merely a jewel in Avraham's crown. He gave her a diadem of her own, crowning her as a special individual in her own right. 'Just as you, Avraham, are an *av hamon goyim*, the father of a multitude of nations, so she will be an *eim hamon goyim*, the mother of a multitude of nations.'

"God made Sarah a liberated woman so that she, together with Avraham, could bear and raise a child who would become the father of this great Jewish nation. Sarah proved that she was a liberated woman by sending Yishmael away, realizing what a bad influence he was on Yitzchak. She was free to do what she considered right in order to save the *kedushah*, the purity, of Yitzchak, the forefather of the Jewish nation. She did not care what the world would say. She did not even care how it would affect her work in bringing people under the wing of the Almighty. There is only one truth, she knew, and she fought for it.

"Avraham was distressed by the idea of expelling his own son. But Hashem told him, 'Do not be upset about the boy and about your maidservant. Everything that Sarah tells you, heed her words.'[11] Rashi explains: 'Because she is greater in prophecy than Avraham'; she knows that in the future Hashem will call Yitzchak the seed of this nation, and she is right to protect him from Yishmael."

Frau Schenirer leaned over us as she delivered this message. Then, smiling, she would say, "*Nu*, girls, what do you think? Wasn't our matriarch Sarah a free, liberated woman?

"And so was our matriarch Rivka," she continued, "by taking responsibility for telling Yaakov to obtain the blessing that his father was about to give Esav. She was dictated by a true prophecy: that it was Yaakov who would carry on the future of the nation."

Before Pesach, when she taught us the Haggadah, she would stress, "You know, girls, the Jewish midwives in Egypt were *free* to act against Pharaoh's decree and his orders that they kill every boy upon birth. They were free, unafraid of Pharaoh. They did everything possible to save the Jewish male infants. And God blessed these midwives and made *batim*, 'estates,' for them: an estate of priesthood for Miriam, an estate of kingship for Yocheved.

"And again, according to Rabbi Zushe Friedman, Hashem made them to *be* estates, *foundations*, examples for future women, who would be free to sacrifice their lives to save Jewish children. Thus, throughout Jewish history, we see that Jewish women have been free and unafraid to do Hashem's will, even if this sometimes means sacrificing their lives to save the Jewish People."

---

11. *Bereishis* 21:12.

Yes, even in our times, in the concentration camps, enslaved by the Nazis, tortured and degraded, enclosed behind barbed wire and electric fences, the Jewish woman was free. Under the noses of Göth and Mengele, the Jewish woman was independent and fearless — free to do what was right, to ease human pain, to save lives even at the risk of losing her own life in the process.

The Seminary and
Its Founders

✤ Chapter 9 ✤

The Kenessiah Gedolah (Great Assembly) of Agudath Israel, held in Vienna in 1923, was the first Orthodox body officially to acknowledge the importance of Bais Yaakov, the institution created to educate Jewish girls in traditional Torah values. Moreover, they assumed some responsibility for its existence.

Dr. Schmuel (Leo) Deutschlander, at the time chairman of Keren ha-Torah, the branch of Agudath Israel that raised funds to support *yeshivos*, took a special interest in the Bais Yaakov movement. He first met Sarah Schenirer in 1924, at the Agudath Israel convention in Kraków. This simple woman of motherly bearing made a tremendous impression on him as she spoke fervently about her novel idea of equipping Jewish girls with authentic traditional education. Her anguish came through as she expressed disappointment over the neglect of Jewish education for girls at a time when it was so crucial for the survival of Orthodox Judaism.

Dr. Schmuel (Leo) Deutschlander

The new school that she had founded, Bais Yaakov, reacquainted girls with their glorious Jewish past. It taught them how to love Hashem, Who created this beautiful world and lovingly gave it to mankind to use and enjoy. It instilled profound gratitude to the *Heiliger Beshefer* (Holy Creator) for His limitless beneficence. It inspired girls with desire to serve Hashem devotedly and to observe His commandments with joy.

Most of all, Dr. Deutschlander was impressed by Sarah Schenirer's personality and character traits: her faith, her burning desire to reach out to Jewish girls, and her hope of realizing her dream.

Driven by the sparkle in Frau Schenirer's animated eyes, Dr. Deutschlander, a sensitive, talented, and dedicated Orthodox educator, quickly shared her enthusiasm. He resolved at once to pledge all his abilities to the fulfillment of her sweeping vision of a great worldwide Bais Yaakov movement. Those abilities, moreover, were formidable: scholarship, educational brilliance, and the special skills needed to design and organize a school system worthy of the name.

His boundless devotion and tireless work on behalf of Bais Yaakov made him a pillar of the movement. The Jewish People is indebted to him for his tremendous contribution to the rapid fulfillment of Frau Schenirer's great idea of *chinuch ha-banos,* Torah education for girls. It is, however, important to note that before Dr. Deutschlander came into the picture, the humble Bais Yaakov Seminary, led by Sarah Schenirer alone, had already produced twenty-two teachers for twenty-two Bais Yaakov schools, with 4,490 students. The next year, with Dr. Deutschlander's help organizing the "Fortbildungs Kurs" in the summer of 1925 (see below), there were forty-nine participants. The Bais Yaakov network then grew to forty-nine schools and 6,585 students. See the graph on page 99, which shows the growth of Bais Yaakov from 1923 until 1933, published in the *Bais Yaakov Journal* in 1933.

*   *   *

Before anything else, Dr. Deutschlander tackled Frau Schenirer's immediate need for experienced teachers to staff her new seminary. To meet the need, he created the Fortbildungs Kurs, an intensive two-month summer course for teachers. Inaugurated in 1925 with forty-nine participants, it aimed to broaden and enrich the participants' own education. Above all, however, Dr. Deutschlander wished to equip the young Bais Yaakov educators with skills and techniques in writing systematic lesson plans. With his educational system, as well as his organizational and professional brilliance, Dr. Deutschlander turned this Bais Yaakov school into an official high school and teachers' seminary recognized by the Polish educational authority.

To attain the goals of his course, he recruited the most renowned Orthodox educators, such as Dr. E. Janos Ehrentrau, *dayan* in Baden, near Vienna; Miss Rosalie Mannes of Zurich; and Miss Judith Rosenbaum (later, Dr. Judith Grunfeld) of Frankfurt. It would be their duty to teach the girls Torah wisdom and Jewish history, explore the ideas of the Jewish Sages, and instill true Jewish values and ideals. Dr. Deutschlander himself delivered lectures on *Navi* and *Tehillim* with depth of thought and poetic flair. A scholar and an exceptional teacher, he made a tremendous impression on the girls, who listened to him enthusiastically and regarded him with great admiration and respect.

Many of the forty-nine girls who attended the first Fortbildungs Kurs later became teachers at the Bais Yaakov Seminary and mainstays of the Bais Yaakov school system.

✳   ✳   ✳

Promoting Jewish education for girls was Judith Rosenbaum's goal in life. Nothing motivated her as powerfully as the wish to broaden the young minds and horizons of Jewish girls. She thirsted to share her enthusiasm for Jewish education and reveal the treasures of Jewish thought and wisdom. Judith received her teaching diploma from the prestigious Frankfurt Teachers' Seminary at the end of the 1924/25 school year and had made plans to enroll at the University of Frankfurt in 1925/26 to begin working on a doctorate in education.

She wanted to spend her vacation teaching and initially expected to do this at the Hirsch School in Frankfurt. After an unpleasant experience while substituting there, however, she became disappointed in the administration's cool, insensitive approach to education and decided to seek a different employer. Her first thought was to go to Eretz Yisroel, where she hoped to find fertile soil in which her warm, sensitive manner of teaching would be appreciated. There she expected to attain true satisfaction from her efforts.

"I went to Moreinu Yaakov Rosenheim, president of the Agudath Israel World Organization and a friend of the family," she recalled years later, "and asked him to recommend a suitable school in Eretz Yisroel where I could accomplish something worthwhile for Jewish youth. Moreinu Rosenheim replied, 'I know of a perfect place for you. Go to Poland and look up Frau Sarah Schenirer, an unusual woman who has the revolutionary idea of educating religiously neglected Jewish girls in the spirit of Torah.'

"'Frau Schenirer,' Moreinu Rosenheim continued, 'established a school called Bais Yaakov where she educates girls in Jewish knowledge and values. The school is rapidly expanding and new schools are being founded in surrounding cities and towns. To staff them, she had to turn her young students into teachers.

"'That's the place for you,' he emphasized. 'A place that needs you.'"

Judith vacillated. She perceived Poland as a backward country relative to her native Germany. To help her make up her mind, Moreinu Rosenheim contacted Dr. Deutschlander who, with his own skills of persuasion, convinced this young, very talented pedagogue, trained in Central Europe, to come to Robov to help Sarah Schenirer in her tremendous undertaking. This was no small feat on Dr. Deutschlander's part, since the village of Robov was considered primitive even in Polish terms. Nevertheless, this sophisticated young lady left the comfort of Frankfurt to help Frau Schenirer realize her dream.

One of the first Fortbildungs summer courses. "Fraulein Doktor" Rosenbaum is in the second row, wearing a polka-dot dress. Behind her with the black tie is Bella Gross. To Bella's right, in white, is Escia Teitelbaum. Standing at the far right is Ida Bauminger.

Years later, when she recalled her experiences during her first few days in Robov, she spoke with excitement about the girls who attended the course. "They were lively, intelligent, broad-minded girls with an unusual thirst for knowledge. They were eager to listen, to know, and to discuss the topics we studied. They were full of questions, hanging onto me for answers.

"I had to prepare my lessons until late at night to be able to satisfy their inquisitive minds. After a few days of hard work, I felt exhausted. The job was too difficult. I was ready to quit.

"I approached Frau Schenirer and tendered my resignation: 'To my deepest regret, I cannot continue working. I am not experienced enough, and the preparation required to do my job properly is beyond my ability. I just cannot continue.'

"Frau Schenirer responded simply, as usual. 'Stay another two days.' I stayed not two days but five years. I realized that history was being made in this primitive Carpathian village and I wanted to be part of it.

"It was hard work," she continued, "but it was a pleasure to teach these intelligent, open-minded girls. They loved literature and admired the world's classics."

She withdrew from a chest a miniature leather-bound copy of Goethe's *Faust*. "This is a gift from my favorite and most beloved student," she explained, eyes moist with nostalgia. "This girl was a rebellious student and lover of *Faust* and other secular literature. Eventually, however, she became both a lover of Torah and a pillar of the Bais Yaakov movement and seminary."

At the time, the girls were still inspired by Western literature and were influenced by its loud proclamation of humanitarian ideas.

This sophisticated young woman, raised in Western culture, applied her personality and persuasive powers to dispel the girls' admiration of the "great" Western civilization. "Girls," she would say, "the world's great writings are full of nonsense. If you find a meaningful thought and a decent moral concept in world literature, you should know that it was stolen from the rich treasure-house of Jewish knowledge."

She dismissed the tendency of Polish youth at the time to admire in wide-eyed fashion the humanitarian ideas of the West. As she did so, she exposed the true nature of the Polish nobility and showed the youth timeless and reliable Jewish precepts.

Unfortunately, we not only saw but also experienced the West's inherently bestial behavior toward humanity.[12]

Miss Rosenbaum's interest in, love for, and devotion to Bais Yaakov were remarkable. Her deep faith and *yiras Shamayim*, combined with her modern education, immediately commanded the admiration of her forty-nine students, all of whom were eager to learn, to know, and to absorb her teachings and her unusual enthusiasm for the Torah truth. Teacher and students quickly came to love and understand each other. The girls lov-

---

12. For the details of this bestiality, see *To Vanquish the Dragon*, by this author (Jerusalem: Feldheim Publishers, 1991).

ingly called her "Fraulein Doktor."

Frau Schenirer also loved the young teacher, and the two personalities quickly developed a unique mutual respect and admiration. Frau Schenirer was fond of Judith's talents, her professional teaching methods, and the way she produced a co-ordinated, systematic curriculum at the seminar. She also admired Miss Rosenbaum's profound Jewish knowledge, her *middos,* and her devotion to the Bais Yaakov girls.

As deeply as Judith Rosenbaum respected Frau Schenirer's character, she was similarly awed by her saintly soul. "When I listened to Frau Schenirer speaking," she recalled much later, "I heard her *neshamah* (soul) talking to me." She especially admired Frau Schenirer's exceptional *middos* and altruism. Above all, however, she cherished Frau Schenirer's Bais Yaakov idea. Together they forged a unique union of German precision and professionalism and Chassidic enthusiasm and joy.

Frau Schenirer's staff at the early Bais Yaakov seminary came mostly from Central European countries (Germany, Switzerland, Austria), where different communities practiced different customs and lifestyles. They sometimes looked strange to the Krakowian girls at the seminary, with their Chassidic upbringing. Still, all the students held their teachers in uncommon esteem and loved and admired them deeply.

The students at the seminary were diverse: from different countries, different communities, and different backgrounds. They came from Germany, Austria, Czechoslovakia, Lithuania, Congress Poland, and Galicia. However different their characteristics and values were, they were all outstanding. For example, those from Lithuania excelled in their knowledge of the Hebrew language and the commentaries, and those from Germany were superb in fathoming difficult paragraphs in the sophisticated German that Rabbi Samson Raphael Hirsch used in his writings.

Frau Schenirer admired the girls' diverse qualities and, demonstrating her humility, expressed her appreciation for their help in certain areas — even in the classroom. She loved her girls and respected their differences. She did not wish to transform the seminary into a melting pot. She installed behavioral rules and enforced them strictly, but she respected the students' distinctive characteristics and lifestyles. She also instilled in her students mutual love and respect for every individual, and for her distinction and uniqueness.

Frau Schenirer was aware of the influence that the non-Jewish culture of our countries of residence has had on us. No matter how we resist the *galus* environment, Frau Schenirer insisted that the local culture leaves indelible impressions. In response to this, she quoted a warning dictum from the Gemara: "Eat the contents, discard the skin." God created a variety of fruits with different tastes, she explained — some juicy, some sweet, some tart, others exotic. Hashem gave them all to man for his enjoyment. Man is invited to taste them and ingest their nutritious meat but must be careful to discard the covering. Some fruits have a bitter rind, others a thick and unhealthy peel, yet others a hard shell. Discard the skin and enjoy the wonderful fruit. Respect each girl, admire her positive traits, and discard the foreign influence of her native country.

*   *   *

Frau Schenirer, in her thoughtful approach to relations among the girls, succeeded in creating an unusual atmosphere of love, respect, and harmony everywhere the girls went — at the seminary, the Bais Yaakov schools, and the Bnos organizations. The worldwide love and unity among the Bais Yaakov sorority was remarkable. It was the first thing a stranger coming in contact with Bais Yaakov noticed. During the war, traveling from one city to another, a Bais Yaakov girl never had to worry about where to stay. Wherever she had to go, she found a family — a Bais Yaakov girl who opened her doors and heart wide to receive her dear sister and help her in any way possible.

✿ *Chapter 10* ✿

The Bais Yaakov Seminary held its second summer intensive course in Jordanów, another small mountain village but more developed than Robov. The girls had better accommodations with beautiful surroundings and views. They learned under the open sky with zest and enthusiasm. Thus, they spent another summer in Jordanów and then moved on for three summers in Rabka, a resort town in the Carpathian Mountains. These were most meaningful summers for the Bais Yaakov Seminary students and for the young teachers who joined them.

Tzila Orlean, standing at left, lecturing at Rabka. In the background, surrounded by mountains, is the beautiful scenery of the Polish village.

They had the most wonderful teachers, a capable and devoted staff who delivered their lectures with profundity and ebullience. The girls listened with excitement to the Torah teachings and joyously absorbed everything offered them. The teachers not only taught the girls but also lived with them in the beautiful surroundings, and together they experienced those very special summer months.

Whenever Frau Schenirer discussed these summer courses, where teachers and teachers-to-be underwent further training, she mentioned her satisfaction upon observing her teaching staff, whose lectures created an atmosphere of Torah and *yiras Shamayim*.

It pleased and excited Frau Schenirer to recall the many joyous events and outings that the girls enjoyed during those intensive courses. Frau Schenirer was happy to join them, especially for outings of the sort that she had loved as a young girl. On every such occasion she had something interesting to point out, something whose existence and purpose in Creation she could explain. She philosophized about its benefit for man's growth and development.

Frau Schenirer enjoyed hiking with the girls up the mountains, especially the towering Tatras. There, too, she expressed her thoughts: "Girls, you know it is easy to go downhill. Climbing up and ascending the heights is harder. Every obstacle you overcome brings you closer to your goal. You just have to carry the proper climbing equipment and take the right steps to avoid falling."

They always tried to reach the summit in time to see the sunrise, to observe the sun struggle to conquer the darkness and bring light to the world. Again, as in Zakopane, Sarah Schenirer was overwhelmed by the breathtaking view. "How mighty, Hashem, is Your Name in the whole world,"[13] she cried out. The girls sang together with her in awe and passion, *Ha-Shamayim mesaprim kevodo ve-gam ha'aretz mala chasdo*

---

13. *Tehillim* 8:2.

— "The Heavens proclaim His Glory and the whole world is full of His loving-kindness." Gazing down at the magnificent view, they felt the whole universe joining them in an outpouring of love and admiration for the Creator.

How different it was for Sarah Schenirer to share this wonderful event with her Bais Yaakov girls than it had been on a similar occasion, when as a young girl she had climbed with her friends to the mountaintop in Zakopane. As she and her friends had admired the breathtaking spectacle of the Morskie Oko lake, thousands of feet below, surrounded by towering, mighty mountains, her friends had commented on the beautiful view. However, when she expressed her awe for the Creator and the wonderful world He had created, they laughed and called out, not for the first time, "There goes our 'Chassidka,' preaching her ideas to us."

How delighted Frau Schenirer was now, rejoicing in this great experience with her own Bais Yaakov girls, who like her were inspired and awed by the Omnipotent Creator of the infinite universe. On other outings, Frau Schenirer would remark: "Girls, look at this immense cosmos and observe. Every creature serves Hashem, playing its role exactly as its destiny dictates. Together, they create the beautiful, harmonious universe in accordance with Hashem's will.

"If only we could serve Hashem as they do, fulfilling the purpose for which we were created, albeit by our own choice. We would reach the highest *madreigah* [level] of all: servants of God. We would earn the title that the Almighty bestowed upon His most beloved son, Moshe — *eved ne'eman,* His loyal servant."

*　　*　　*

Frau Schenirer loved to discuss those fruitful and delightful occasions in the Fortbildungs Kurs. Years later, she would share her thoughts and feelings with students or staff. She loved recalling those wonderful summer weeks, living with her girls in the bosom of nature, educating and inspiring them with the true Torah ideal, imbuing them with the great responsibility of teaching the young children entrusted to them to love the Ribono shel Olam and His children, and instilling in the young teachers the deep satisfaction of forming the souls of young Jewish children and polishing them to perfection.

She especially enjoyed reminiscing about the parting evening of the summer course, when, after the students passed their final examinations, she spoke to them with concern:

"Now, I realize that you know very well how to learn and how to teach. My concern is that you should succeed in raising each of your charges to be a *mentsch*, a loving and caring human being imbued with Jewish ideals — a personality who, by her behavior, will bring *kiddush Hashem* to *Am Yisroel* and to Bais Yaakov."

The girls spent the whole day preparing for the parting event. They were excited in anticipation of a meaningful experience.

Their expectations were on the mark. At the start of the evening, the girls lit a bonfire and arranged benches around it. The lush lawn where the event took place had been silent witness to the hours of intense study, interesting discussions, and friendly warmth among all the participants. Lively young feet danced there cheerfully with the devoted teachers, and young voices sang Torah verses set to joyous melodies.

The flame gathered intensity, spreading light and warmth. The speakers inspired their listeners with heartwarming encouragement. They expressed confidence that the students would successfully use their acquired knowledge and experience to educate their pupils in the true Bais Yaakov spirit.

Then came the students' speeches. Movingly they expressed gratitude to their beloved Frau Schenirer and their faithful, caring teachers, with whom they lived together in the bosom of nature. Passionately they recounted the wonderful time they had during those meaningful and exciting weeks of living in such close proximity to their unique mentor and teachers. They were eager to emulate the fascinating, extraordinary behavior and *middos* that they had encountered.

Frau Schenirer sat and observed her beloved daughters, the future educators of the young generation. She studied their exalted faces, their eyes sparkling in the light of the flames, and noticed a tear rolling down the cheek of one girl, then another, and then another.

"Those were tears of sadness, brought on by the need to part with such a wonderful spiritual life," she wrote. "But on many other faces I saw the happiness of being able during these few weeks to acquire a bountiful spiritual treasure.

"I read their thoughts," she remarked. "They proclaimed, 'Let us continue to raise our banner of Torah higher and higher, so that we may inspire our estranged sisters to return to their roots and share with us the supreme joy of a Torah life.' I sent a silent prayer to Hashem, and a hearty blessing to my dear children to succeed in their saintly aspirations."

Here is a picture of a group of girls attending the Fortbildungs Kurs in Rabka. In the center is Ita Goldknopf, one

Judith Rosenbaum, in the chair, lecturing at Rabka. Gittel Teitelbaum is right in front of Dr. Rosenbaum.

of those special students, the pioneers of the Bais Yaakov movement.

Below is another interesting picture of Ita. Here she is a leader of her Bnos youth group in Warsaw. Not much older than the members of her group, she is their big sister, their beloved Bnos leader who later became their advisor, their devoted and caring friend, and their mentor in life.

Ita Goldknopf, in the center, surrounded by her Bnos group. Notice the white collars mentioned earlier.

Ita had her three mentors sign her autograph book at the conclusion of the 1930 Fortbildungs Kurs in Rabka. The first two inscriptions, written by Chava Landsberg and Judith Rosenbaum, express short, sincere advice for the future, written with love. But the third one, written by Sarah Schenirer (reproduced on the facing page) makes you stop and marvel at the personality of this great woman. Amid her hectic schedule of responsibility for the Bais Yaakov movement, her founding of new schools, and her personal interest in every human being, this remarkable woman — who used to lament about Lady Time limiting her activities — found the time to fill a whole page of her favorite pupil's autograph book with blessings, expectations, and hopes. She even drew a *sefer Torah* to remind Ita to learn and heed all of its concepts and commandments.

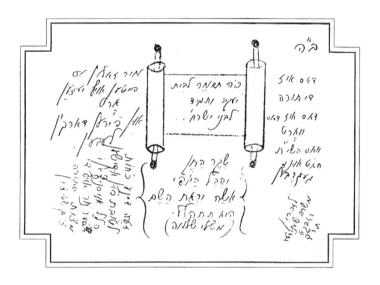

Sarah Schenirer's inscription in Ita's autograph book.

*　　　*　　　*

Frau Schenirer's favorite student did not let her down. The young "Itka," influenced by her revered teacher's love of Eretz Yisroel, attended a Bnos *Hachsharah* (an *aliyah* preparation facility for girls) in Warsaw. Luckily, she received an immigration certificate to Eretz Yisroel as a member of the Gur-Aryeh group. She left the home of her prestigious family of Gerrer Chassidim, and went to Eretz Yisroel to realize her dream of settling in the land of holiness and fulfilling the true love of Zion. She took in stride the numerous hardships she encountered there. She happily helped the group's leader, Miss Devorah Gur-Aryeh, to establish and run the home for the single girls in the group, all of whom had "made *aliyah*." She also taught the girls Jewish subjects in order to imbue them with the faith and courage to overcome the difficulties of living in

Eretz Yisroel. They all married distinguished members and leaders of communities in the Holy Land.

Later on, when Ita became engaged to the son of Rabbi Gershtenkorn, the founder and leader of Bnei Brak, the rabbi told his community, "I have brought a beacon to the city, a beam of light that will add sparkle to your lives." So she became. Apart from helping her father-in-law with his many activities on behalf of his community's spiritual well-being, she herself was a beacon of strength, offering encouragement and help to every individual in need. Her love of and attentiveness to anyone in distress, and her willingness to help, were remarkable. As a one-woman *chessed* organization, she often turned to her father-in-law for helping solving the personal problems of those who came to her. Even when her father-in-law complained of his inability to handle all her requests, she never stopped imploring him to help those troubled citizens.

Ita Gershtenkorn also gave classes in her home for girls and women, creating an atmosphere of learning and spirituality in what had become her beloved city. She was the one to whom the people of Bnei Brak turned for advice and help. With attentiveness, love, concern, charm, and grace, she helped them tackle the vicissitudes of life.

A true *talmidah* (disciple) of Sarah Schenirer, Ita Gershtenkorn used her abilities to help build an Orthodox city in *Eretz ha-Kodesh*.

*   *   *

On the facing page, we have a picture of two great friends attending the summer seminary who later became the pillars of the Bais Yaakov Seminary. On the right is Tzila Orlean, and on the left is Hanka Grossfeld, later Mrs. Biegun, the wife of Reb Yosef Biegun, known as the "little Chofetz Chaim" due to his great *lamdus* and exceptional *middos*. Hanka subsequently became the most outstanding teacher at the Bais Yaakov Seminary, renowned for delivering her lessons, especially in *Chumash*, with deep understanding of the text and the com-

Reb Yosef Biegun

Hanka Grossfeld and Tzila Orlean.
Kraków, 1935.

mentaries. Her creative mind presented the students with a world of deep thought and original insight into the Sages' exegesis.

Parts of Hanka's lecture on *Parashas Re'eh*,[14] which made such a great impression on me, have slipped from my memory. However, the essence of the elaborate discourse touched me unforgettably.

"You see, girls," she taught, "Hashem showed you so profoundly, so clearly, the absolute truth, the *tov,* and He also showed you the opposite, the evil, the falsehood, the *ra.* He told you explicitly, 'Choose the true goodness, the life, and not the opposite.' Make sure," she stressed, "to know the difference in your mind, in your heart. Know it so clearly, so surely, that you will remember the ultimate truth no matter how convincingly the false prophets present the lie.

14. *Devarim* 11–16.

"God has given these false prophets every opportunity and every tool to entice you with falsehood. Beware! They will come to you in a variety of forms and shapes, dressed in different clothing, speaking varied languages.

"They will show you many great discoveries of practical conveniences, and will try to impress upon you faithless ideas with convincing facts, or they may introduce a false approach to life by citing new developments. Don't believe them. As the Torah says,[15] if a prophet comes and shows you signs and miracles to convince you to follow his unholy, idolatrous ways, don't believe him! God sent him to test you, to see if you have faith in Him, if you love Him with all your heart and all your might."

How timely her words still are! And how often they helped us to withstand the pressure of the deceitful ideas that constantly surround and attack us with powerful words and ostensible facts to lead us astray.

---

15. Ibid., 13:2–4.

✣ *Chapter 11* ✣

The Bais Yaakov Seminary at 10 Stanislawa Street was built of more than iron beams and bricks. It was built with the hard work and enormous dedication of two great Bais Yaakov patrons, the aforementioned Drs. Schmuel Deutschlander and Judith Rosenbaum.

When Dr. Deutschlander came to help Sarah Schenirer in her undertaking, she was already conducting her Bais Yaakov classes for children, as well as classes for older girls — whom she taught and prepared to become teachers. This was already the beginning of the Bais Yaakov Teachers' Seminary.

At the first Fortbildungs Kurs in 1925, which was organized by Dr. Deutschlander, there were already forty-nine Bais Yaakov Seminary students attending; a few of them were already teachers. With Dr. Deutschlander's professional help, this evolved into the official Bais Yaakov Teachers' Seminary.

Dr. Deutschlander, seeing the pitiful living conditions at the school — which was at that time located in a top-floor apartment of a tenement house, where all the teaching was conducted — decided to make a total effort to create a home for this remarkable, fast-growing movement. As the chairman of Keren ha-Torah, he had fundraising connections and experience. Wasting no time, he began to comb the great cities of Europe and America. At every stop, aided by the local Agudah, he established a committee to raise funds for what had become his most urgent project and applied his charm, wisdom, and eloquence to introduce the idea of Bais Yaakov schools to large audiences.

He told them about the teachers' seminary in Kraków, which turned out enthusiastic teachers and sent them all over Poland to spread traditional Torah education among Jewish girls. Describing the dire need to build a home for this institution, he issued a passionate plea that usually got a warm response from important donors. In Vienna, he raised large sums by conducting public sales of bricks for the seminary building in Kraków. Below is a reproduction of the original "brick" (or "building stone," as they called it in German), distributed and sold to the public in Austria and Germany, dated April 1927.

The "brick" sold to raise funds for the Kraków seminary building.

In New York, Dr. Deutschlander found a great supporter for Bais Yaakov in the renowned personality of Rabbi Dr. Leo Jung, head of Keren ha-Torah in the United States. Dr. Jung became a great admirer of Sarah Schenirer and her life's work, the Bais Yaakov movement. Undertaking to help the Bais Yaakov school system in every possible way, he wholeheartedly devoted time, effort, and influence to fundraising for the construction of the Bais Yaakov Seminary.

Dr. Jung attended the groundbreaking ceremony of the seminary building in Kraków, held on September 13, 1927. A year later, he wrote the following in a fundraising report published by Dr. Deutschlander:

> Last summer in Kraków, I saw the type of Jewish girl that these schools turn out. It is a type utterly unheard of before, filled with missionary zeal to spread Judaism among Jewish girls.... These young women will inscribe their names in golden letters in the annals of contemporary Israel. [Our Sages say that] the House of Jacob [Bais Yaakov] is Jewish womanhood.... I can imagine no claim more irresistible, inspiring, and promising than that of Bais Yaakov.

Dr. Deutschlander spent vacations from his hard work of fundraising in Kraków, where he found his rest and relaxation in his beloved seminary. He used the time to lecture and speak to Bais Yaakov and the Bnos youth movement on his favorite subject, *Tehillim*. The girls impatiently awaited his annual two-month visits to the seminary. They loved his classes, which he delivered with depth of thought and poetic flair. Thirstily they imbibed every thought-provoking idea he offered; delightedly they listened to every word he said.

The greatest joy, however, was his — the *nachas* that he got from his Bais Yaakov girls — until to the dismay of both sides, he had to leave again for another arduous round of fundraising.

*   *   *

Fortunately, Dr. Deutschlander not only provided Sarah Schenirer with a prestigious colleague in the person of Dr. Judith Rosenbaum, but he himself also obtained a capable fundraising assistant.

"Fraulein Doktor" spent her free time and vacations traveling all over Europe, visiting large cities and speaking to women's organizations. She inspired them with the idea of Bais Yaakov schools for girls. She told them about the teachers' seminary that had already come into being and had begun to place graduates in Bais Yaakov schools in cities and towns all over Poland. She convinced the women of the need to give the seminary a home. Of course, such an important project required funding, i.e., donations. Usually she obtained very handsome sums.

This fundraising was an exhausting and difficult undertaking. For Fraulein Doktor, however, nothing was too hard where the benefit of Bais Yaakov was concerned. She made great efforts to secure appointments with wealthy manufacturers, whom she solicited for large donations. She once told me what these experiences were like:

"Once, no matter how hard I tried, I could not get an appointment with a certain wealthy and generous donor. I did not give up; I went to see him anyway," she continued with a confident smile.

"The receptionist asked me if I had an appointment, of course. I said that I didn't, but that I must see the chairman of the company. 'Please let me in,' I said. 'It's very important.'"

The receptionist was impressed with this beautiful young lady, who carried herself with such aplomb. When she asked the chairman if he would receive her, he told her to get the visitor's

Judith Rosenbaum, "the Shnorer," on a fundraising trip in Amsterdam.

business card. When she asked the visitor for a card, Judith wrote her name as "Dr. Judith Shnorer," and handed the receptionist the card. Soon she was admitted to the chairman's office. He, too, was moved by her regal bearing and her composure.

"Dr. Shnorer, you have a very unusual name. I've never heard it before," he said in an interested tone of voice.

"I am surprised. Have you never heard this expression?" she asked. "Not in your home, not even in your parents' home?"

"Yes, I did," he chuckled. "A *shnorer* — that's what we used to call poor people who knocked on the door for charity."

"So you *have* heard of it!" Judith spoke up. "I'm the biggest *shnorer* in Europe. I'm knocking on your door and appealing to your Jewish heart for a generous donation. I am *shnoring* for a very unusual cause, in which you will surely be as interested as I am."

With that, she enthusiastically introduced to him the novel idea of religious girls' education and described at length the Bais Yaakov movement and the need to build a home for the teachers' seminary. She came away with an unexpectedly generous donation, and had turned the chairman into a great supporter of the Bais Yaakov movement.

In the meantime, the committees organized by Keren ha-Torah all over Europe and the United States were hard at work. By dint of their efforts, construction of the semi-

Construction of the seminary building, 1928.

nary building was proceeding rapidly by 1928 (see photograph). The ground floor and first floor were ready two years later, and 120 students moved in as the construction work continued.

Agudath Israel in Kraków became heavily involved in all aspects of the Bais Yaakov schools. The men's committee — Reb Uscher Spira, Senator Moshe Deutcher, Reb M.S. Frankel, Reb Moshe Heitner, and Senator I. Bauminger — devotedly promoted the schools in the cities and towns of Poland, and were especially active in the construction of the seminary building.

Years later, Dr. Judith Rosenbaum Grunfeld told me, "During part of the construction, we were already teaching on the ground and first floors of the building and were exposed to the dust and the noise of the construction work above. Every morning I saw Mr. Spira come to the site and check on materials and workers. Once I said to him, 'Tell me, you're busy in real estate and housing construction; how do you have time to come here

Fortbereitungs Kurs. Sitting in the first row of teachers, 3rd, 4th, and 5th from left are Gittel Teitelbaum, Escia Teitelbaum, and Ida Bauminger. Standing behind Ida Bauminger is Zelda Zehnwirt, later an important leader of Bnos in America. This was a preparatory course which girls from Kraków who did not live in the dormitory were required to attend before being admitted to the seminary.

The seminary building at 10 Stanislawa Street, Kraków. The students are discussing a wonderful lecture they just heard.

to check on things every morning?"

"'Dear Fraulein Doktor,' he answered, 'when I leave this world, I will not be able to take any of the houses I built with me. The only building I will take with me is 10 Stanislawa Street.'"

That is exactly what he did. He carried that six-story building on his tortured shoulders through the gas chambers and the crematoria, to the Throne of Glory and the Kingdom of True Reward.

A group of seminary girls on the roof of the seminary building.

✿ Chapter 12 ✿

The first significant help Dr. Deutschlander gave Sarah Schenirer, as we know, was in recruiting dedicated young co-workers for the fledgling Bais Yaakov Seminary.

He persuaded the youthful Miss Betty Rothschild, later Mrs. Betty Wreschner,[16] to come from Switzerland to help Frau Schenirer realize the Bais Yaakov dream. Miss Rothschild's students admired her for teaching the difficult subject of *dinim*, the *Kitzur Shulchan Aruch*, with enthusiasm and joy. With her happy disposition and ever-willing smile, she imparted joy of life and excitement to the girls.

Chavah Landsberg of Breslau, Germany, was a lecturer (docent) at the University of Breslau. Dr. Deutschlander persuaded her to leave her lovely, warm, comfortable home for the relatively primitive conditions at the Bais Yaakov Seminary in Kraków. He inspired her with the possibility of helping Sarah Schenirer in her tremendous effort to train girls to teach in Bais Yaakov schools all over Poland and Hungary.

Chavah Landsberg was a born teacher whose entire life revolved around girls' education. Unsurprisingly, she accepted Dr. Deutschlander's offer without hesitation and, with her usual enthusiasm, she eagerly joined Frau Schenirer in her lofty work in 1927. Miss Landsberg found her métier at the seminary, devoting her every fiber to this remarkable undertaking. She presented no salary demands and asked no ques-

---

16. For more information about her, see Chapter 54.

tions about the hours. Meeting Sarah Schenirer, she felt so inspired by her personality that she was ready to give everything she had to realize Frau Schenirer's Bais Yaakov dream, which now became her own.

Chavah Landsberg had much to give — a tremendous store of values. She kept on giving; to the seminary, the Bnos, and Basya (a Bnos branch for elementary school girls). She was always ready for anything needed at any time. She was a bright, intelligent young woman with a vast knowledge of Jewish subjects and sources. She had a remarkable mastery of Tanach and the great Jewish Sages who interpreted it. Besides being a Hebrew teacher *par excellence,* she was a most capable purveyor of secular knowledge. Under her tutelage, even those subjects became tools in furthering the true Jewish education of Bais Yaakov girls. The girls, admiring her erudition and knowledge, eagerly listened to her inspiring lessons.

Miss Landsberg did not have a permanent visa to stay in Poland, and in 1929 — to her pupils' great regret — the Polish authorities forced her to leave. Until then, she was continually hunted by the Polish police as an illegal alien, until she was forced to give up and relinquish the work that she cherished, the girls whom she loved, and above all, her priceless mentor — Sarah Schenirer.

Miss Landsberg was not only a great teacher, but working together with Frau Schenirer, she became her profound admirer. Under Frau Schenirer's intense and noble influence, she emulated her courageous ways of putting her vision of a great Bais Yaakov movement into action. Therefore, Miss Landsberg was glad to take Dr. Deutschlander's suggestion to come to Vienna and help him to establish a Bais Yaakov seminary there. She taught there several years, educating girls to become teachers, who in turn headed Bais Yaakov schools in various towns in Romania, Czechoslovakia, and Hungary.

In the late 1920s, the Chief Rabbi of Verbau, Shmuel Reich, had awakened to the Bais Yaakov movement and urged local Agudah organizations to follow the world Agudah movement in supporting and establishing Bais Yaakov schools in their localities. The local organizations responded favorably, and at their behest the Bais Yaakov Seminary in Vienna sent students to cities and towns all over Czechoslovakia, Hungary, and Romania, to open and direct Bais Yaakov schools.

Chavah Landsberg visited these schools and helped the teachers meet whatever needs they had. Ayalah Rottenberg, a Bais Yaakov student in her hometown of Sighet, Romania, remembers one such visit.[17] Miss Landsberg brought one of her students, Chaya Haas (later Rafaelowitz), to be their new teacher. Miss Landsberg was in constant contact with the teachers, always ready with encouragement, advice, and teaching materials — just like her mentor, Sarah Schenirer.

By the early 1930s, there were more than twenty Bais Yaakov schools in Czechoslovakia, established by the Bais Yaakov Seminary in Vienna and aided by local branches of Agudath Israel. Additionally, the Austrian Bais Yaakov movement organized evening groups and Shabbos lectures for women and girls.

The picture on the facing page shows one of the many summer groups for girls organized by Dr. Deutschlander and led by Chavah Landsberg. Chavah Landsberg is surrounded by her students. During these summer courses, Miss Landsberg devoted the richness of her mind and the warmth of her loving heart to the training of these eager, receptive Jewish souls, turning them into Bais Yaakov teachers for the ever-increasing demand to open new schools.

In 1936, the Austrian-Czech border became difficult to cross due to strained relations between the countries. Travel permits were taxed heavily, making it difficult and, at times, impossible for girls from Slovakia and that part of Europe to travel to the seminary in Vienna. Therefore, Dr. Deutschlander decided to

---

17. Ayalah Rottenberg's book, *Echoes of Yesteryear* (Jerusalem: Feldheim Publishers, 2003), highlights her experiences as a Bais Yaakov student in both Sighet and Eretz Yisroel.

send Miss Landsberg to Pressburg (Bratislava) to establish a Bais Yaakov seminary that girls from Czechoslovakia and the vicinity could attend. With her usual vigor and enthusiasm, she rushed to Pressburg to perform her mission. Thus she founded the first Bais Yaakov Seminary in Czechoslovakia, with a prestigious staff of capable educators from the Vienna seminary. She also had the good fortune to obtain contributions from some renowned luminaries, among them Rav Shlomo Zalman Unsdorfer, who lectured every Shabbos on *Pirkei Avos*. The school soon became known as a distinguished educational institution.

The beginning, however, was difficult. Miss Landsberg started the school in two small rooms on Kaputziner Street. Like her mentor, Sarah Schenirer, she met with opposition not only from the assimilated Jewish population but also from the Orthodox community, which had never heard of educating Jewish girls in *limudei kodesh*. Girls were taught how to pray from the *siddur*; anything else was out of the question. But Chavah Landsberg defended her position courageously. Like her be-

Chavah Landsberg, fourth from left in first row, surrounded by her students.

loved teacher and advisor, she educated and enlightened the religious population in the necessity of Jewish education for girls.
With her eloquence and intelligent arguments, she convinced
them that girls' religious instruction had great merit.

Miss Landsberg vigorously carried on with her plans and installed the systematic seminary curriculum. Her professional
yet warm and enthusiastic approach to teaching won parents
over at once. At the school, besides vast Jewish knowledge, the
girls acquired excellent secular instruction. Parents continued
to enroll their daughters — those in Pressburg, those from distant towns, and even some from villages — in this exceptional
school. Above all, they admired this remarkable teacher, who
cared for their children as only a mother can, and who imbued
them with good *middos* and the rules of proper behavior.

It is no wonder that, alongside the girls' love and adoration,
Miss Landsberg earned the parents' respect and admiration as
well. They appreciated her warm, yet very effective, approach
to girls' education. In no time, she became the most popular
woman in town apart from the local rebbetzin. Pressburg families considered it a privilege to have her as a Shabbos or *Yom
Tov* guest, and waited in a lengthy line for the honor of receiving her in their homes.

Her noble personality and flawless character, combined
with exceptional Jewish and secular scholarship, made a lasting
impression on her pupils. She forged them into truly devoted
Bais Yaakov teachers, who spread Torah truth among Jewish
girls in cities and towns all over Slovakia, Romania, and Hungary.

Chavah Landsberg educated her students in proper ladylike
behavior and applied her teachings in this matter strictly. Notwithstanding her great humility, she required her girls to run
to greet her and take her briefcase from her when she entered
the school.

A student of hers from Jerusalem, now a noted teacher at
the Bais Yaakov Seminary in Brooklyn, described an incident
during her school days that made a great impact on her. A girl

brought Miss Landsberg her coat, placed it on her desk, and left. The teacher called her back: "Don't you know that you must help your teacher put on her coat?" she asked, surprised. The girl, embarrassed, did as she was told. The incident taught the girl a lesson for life: how to respect teachers and, similarly, parents, *talmidei chachamim*, the elderly, and others.

"It taught me, too," the student from Jerusalem said, completing her account of the episode. "To this day I remember to teach the girls that rule of proper behavior, even if the outside world does not accept it." Even today, Chavah Landsberg's students emulate her method of teaching with enthusiasm, devotion, and joy, just as she had learned it from Sarah Schenirer.

Chavah Landsberg's work in Pressburg was very successful. Her students were happy and eager to learn, and hungrily absorbed every word she taught them.

Miss Landsberg was not only a teacher and a principal; she was also a tutor. She spent her evenings voluntarily teaching girls who, due to various problems, could not attend the morning sessions. She also taught evening groups such as Bnos and Basya on both weekdays and Shabbos. Additionally, she lectured to women twice during the week and once on Shabbos. Although in frail health, she typically worked fourteen-hour days at the very least.

Unfortunately, Miss Landsberg's stay in Pressburg did not last more than two years. Lacking a permanent visa, she was again sought by the police. This time she was forcibly deported to her hometown, Breslau. Students, parents, and the whole community were heartbroken.

The Pressburg Jewish community geared up for her upcoming expulsion from Germany. Knowing of her fervent desire to settle in Eretz Yisroel, Agudah activists toiled to equip her with an *"aliyah* certificate" — a licit immigration permit from the British Mandatory authorities. Considering her fragile health, they wished to spare her the alternative — the dangerous route of "Aliyah Beit," clandestine immigration.

Even during those trying, tense times while waiting for her

aliyah certificate, Miss Landsberg corresponded regularly with her two most capable students, Netti Michaelis and Julia Mandel (*née* Wechsler), who had taken over the teaching and principal's duties at the seminary. Her letters contained assistance, advice, encouragement, and plans for curricula and events at the school she loved so dearly. Her worthy followers sustained her work with great devotion and self-sacrifice until 1942, when they were brutally stopped by the Nazis.

As for Chavah Landsberg, in 1939, Moshe Weiss, the president of the Pressburg seminary, acquired a certificate for her after arduous efforts. After arriving in Eretz Yisroel before the war, she was immediately recruited by Rabbi Hillel Lieberman to teach in his Bais Yaakov Seminary in Jerusalem. There, she quickly earned the reputation as a most capable and beloved teacher. As she lectured to her students, sometimes for hours at a time, she elevated them to spiritual heights. Her lectures and behavior made an everlasting impression on them. They drank from her inexhaustible well of Jewish scholarship, always thirsting for more. She taught them how to teach their pupils *middos* — respect for parents, honor for *talmidei chachamim*, and reverence for teachers. She stressed the importance of the special Bais Yaakov code of behavior and made her students proud to distance themselves from popular slang and mannerisms. She inspired them to take pride in being Bais Yaakov girls and to behave as such.

Chavah Landsberg's whole life was Bais Yaakov — teaching, inspiring, giving without limit of her time, knowledge, love, enthusiasm, joy of teaching, everything she possessed. When the Bais Yaakov Seminary in Jerusalem decided to drop English from the curriculum, she spent her afternoons teaching English to small groups of girls in her home — without pay, of course — because she considered this subject important for future Bais Yaakov teachers.

She gave until she forfeited her health, her youth, her personal life (she never married), and, in the end, her young life. She was sick for years, yet she kept on working, never complaining, until the sickness took its toll on her and she passed away at the young age of forty-six. She pursued her life's calling to shape the minds, souls, and characters of Jewish girls, just as Sarah Schenirer had taught her.

"My great mentor's parting words to me," she recalled to her students, "were, 'May you merit to get lots of joy and *nachas* from *your* Bais Yaakov girls, as I do from my own.' My dear girls, this great blessing has come true through you. I pray that your educational work will be the cornerstone of the building Hashem is readying for us, the *Beis ha-Mikdash*. Even if you encounter difficult times in your life, God forbid, know that I will be there with you."

It is no wonder that one of her students, Brachah Diskin, eulogized her in the following way: "If they had asked Sarah Schenirer, 'How should the epitome of a perfect Bais Yaakov teacher look?' she would have answered, 'Just like Chavah Landsberg.'"

Chavah Landsberg is second from the right, over the sign.

The Vanguard: Bais Yaakov's First Builders

❧ *Chapter 13* ☙

In Kraków in 1923, shortly after the first Kenessiah Gedolah, Agudath Israel helped Frau Schenirer acquire premises for the new school, and later even a whole floor, at 30 Augustianska Street. It also assumed financial responsibility for the existing Bais Yaakov schools and for the establishment of new schools.

This lifted a burden from Sarah Schenirer's shoulders, and she continued to work hard toward the fulfillment of her second dream — the development of a rich literature of Jewish thought for young girls. Fortunately, she found a capable publisher in the person of Reb Gershon Friedenson, who enthusiastically accepted the assignment and went straight to work on publishing two monthly journals: one for children called *Kindergarten* and another for youth under the title of *Bais Yaakov Journal*.

The beginning was exceedingly difficult, but Reb Gershon, realizing the great need for periodicals to further the education of Jewish girls, disregarded any hardships he encountered. His exceptional dedication and unflagging efforts to

Reb Gershon Friedenson, publisher of Kindergarten and the Bais Yaakov Journal, organizer of Bnos, and founder of Chavas Schmuel.

produce quality literature for Bais Yaakov knew no limits. Enthusiastically he attempted to persuade the community and its leaders to share his sense of the need. His arguments fell on deaf ears, but he did not give up. Starting over again and again, he finally published the debut issue of the *Bais Yaakov Journal* in 1923. The cover page of this first edition is reproduced here.

The cover page of the first edition of the Bais Yaakov Journal.

However humble this endeavor was, Frau Schenirer was overjoyed to see it fulfilled. Having worked closely with Reb Gershon, she knew how much sacrifice and hard labor had been invested in it. It took a chain of struggles to create the first few issues. Reb Gershon and his devoted staff went to great efforts to find Orthodox Jewish writers — there were not too many — who would train young talents to explore their literary abilities.

However, the *Bais Yaakov Journal* quickly became an Orthodox publication of high literary stature. Articles on Jewish thought and education were written by Sarah Schenirer, Reb Yehudah Leib Orlean (author of *Dos Yiddishe Leben*, Jewish life), Reb Nuteh Berliner, Rabbi Avraham Mordechai Rogovy, Reb Alexander Zushe Friedman, Reb Binyamin Mintz, Dr. Heshel Klepfisch, and other great writers. Reb Schmuel Schachnowitz regularly contributed interesting stories, and Israel Emiot, Reb Eliezer Schindler, and Reb Alter Schnur provided poems and great essays. So did many other towering authors.

When the hundredth issue of the *Journal* came out ten years later, in 1933, Frau Schenirer acknowledged its tremendous contribution to the development of the Bais Yaakov movement. She also expressed her appreciation and gratitude to Reb Gershon Friedenson for his indefatigable efforts in producing the *Journal* and *Kindergarten,* two badly needed founts of literature for Orthodox youth.

Frau Schenirer promoted the *Journal* and convinced her pupils to do the same in the communities where they lived or taught. Still, she continued to bewail the lack of understanding of this important project in the Bais Yaakov world. Mothers often complained to her about a shortage of Jewish books. She would reply, "Have they already read what is available — the *Bais Yaakov Journal*?!"

In Kraków, a story circulated about Frau Schenirer's having once spoken to an audience of Bais Yaakov mothers in a small town. She told them about a teacher who would give their daughters individualized tutoring on a host of interesting subjects. The women grew excited: "Who is that teacher? She's just what my daughter needs. But she must be very expensive!"

"No," Frau Schenirer replied, "she's not expensive at all. Her name is the *Bais Yaakov Journal* and she costs only one zloty. One zloty to teach your daughter everything I just mentioned. Isn't that a bargain, ladies?" she concluded with a smile.

Not only did Frau Schenirer advertise the written word, she strongly encouraged us, her students, to write our own monthly bulletin, which we often did for our regular Rosh Chodesh evening celebrations. Sometimes, she would even come to listen to our recitations.

At the first Chanukah celebration after World War II, at Kibbutz Chofetz Chaim in Zeilsheim, Germany,[18] we, Frau Schenirer's surviving students, published a beautiful newspaper — handwritten, of course. Rabbi Dr. Sacks, a chaplain from America who had been posted to the DP camps, was present at that evening. He was so impressed with the newspaper that he asked for a copy.

Below is a poem I published in this paper, rendered from the Yiddish in free translation.

מיין װארט

נישט אין שטילער נאכט

ביים לבנה שיין

האט מיין װארט ערװאכט

מיט צאַרטלעך גיפיל

גירופן צום זיין

קיין ליריש גיזאנג

גיװעזן מיין שפראך

נישט קיין דיכטער קלאנג

װאס פריי זיך צערלאכט

נאר ס'איז א װארט װאס

דער גרויל פון קריג

אין טויט שרעק האט זי גיבוירן

א װאָרט װאס האס שרין אין דער װיג

נקמה צוגישװאוירן

א װאָרט װאס האט די מאמע לייד

גיבאדן אינים בלוט

18. A "kibbutz" is any type of collective. Kibbutziim were organized in post-war Europe within the DP camps.

מיט פײַער אײַזענע קײט
אויסגעהאַמערט גוט

אַ וואָרט וואָס שטורעמט
אַ וואָרט וואָס בליצט
אויף יעדן וועלטן עק
וואָס האָט אויף
מענטשהײַט'ס שטערן אויסגעקריצט
אַן אייביק חרפה פלעק

אַ וואָרט, וואָס איבער אַלע וועלטן
ווי אַ גיווײסינס ביס וועט פֿליִען
די אום-פֿאַרשעמטע וועלט פֿאַרשטעלטן
נישט לאָזן מער זי רוען

אַ וואָרט פֿון האָפֿענונג און פֿון מוט
צו מײַנע טײַערע ברידער
אַ וואָרט וואָס פֿאָדערט
אַ וואָרט וואָס מאָנט
דעם קאַמף אױפֿנעמין ווידער

אַ וואָרט וואָס פֿאָדערט מיט זײַן קראַפֿט
מעשׂים פֿאַר פֿאָלק און בורא
אַ וואָרט וואָס בױט, אַוואָרט וואָס שאַפֿט
אַ צוקומפֿט על פי תורה.

אַז אונדזער וואָרט זאָל ווידער קלינגען
מיט האַרציק זיניקע רייד
אַ נײעם שיר חנוכת בית זינגען
מיט אַ פֿול מויל פֿרייד.

My Word

Not in silent night
By moon shining bright
Did my word alight.

Not a joyous tune
Lovely lyric verse
Did my word disperse.

But it was a word
Which in a cruel war

Agony had borne
A word that yet in cradle
Revenge had sworn.

A word that mother pain
Had bathed in blood
And dried with a burning chain
Hurled cruelly by a brute.

A word that, in desperation
Around the world did fly
Alarming the nations
For help bitterly cried
In vain.

A word that
On humanity's face
Burned a seal of shame
That will never erase
The curse upon her name.

A word of hope and courage
To my forlorn brethren:
Pick up the fight;
The obstacles weather.
Stand up and strive
To start a new life.

So once again our word
Will with happy laughter ring,
Thankful to our Lord
Will with joy, a new
Shir chanukas ha-bayis sing.

*   *   *

By 1925, the Bais Yaakov system had grown to forty-nine
schools, and there were 6,585[19] — yes, six thousand, five hundred and eighty-five — students, but no textbooks. Teaching

19. See the graph on the facing page, which was originally printed in the
Bais Yaakov Journal by Eliezer Schindler in 1933. It was part of a lengthy
article about the growth of the Bais Yaakov movement from 1923 to 1933.

was done from notes that teachers had taken from Frau Schenirer's lessons, plus new material that Frau Schenirer prepared for them.

דער אויפשטייג פון דער בית-יעקב-באוועגונג אין פולין
The Growth of the Bais Yaakov Movement in Poland
1923 – 1933

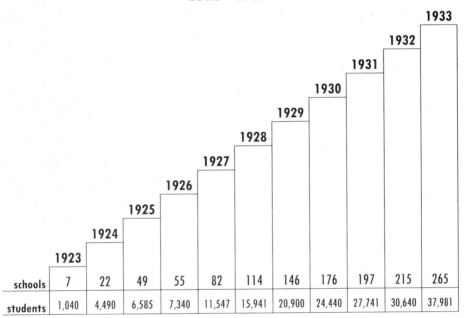

	1923	1924	1925	1926	1927	1928	1929	1930	1931	1932	1933
schools	7	22	49	55	82	114	146	176	197	215	265
students	1,040	4,490	6,585	7,340	11,547	15,941	20,900	24,440	27,741	30,640	37,981

There were no photocopy machines, of course, so Frau Schenirer produced four or five copies of her material using carbon paper. Her students helped to copy and distribute her lectures to the schools. It sounds amazing today, but even then it was considered a miracle. What is more, it was essential. Frau Schenirer was not only the originator of a great idea — the Bais Yaakov movement — and the creator of a new and lasting way to educate Jewish girls, but she was also an exceptional writer.

Today, writers descend to the level of their readers. They mimic their language, their style, and their tastes. Their aim is to satisfy the masses and turn out bestsellers. Good writers, in contrast, try to enhance their readers' lives: enrich their minds, broaden their horizons, impress them with beautiful literary style, and teach them refined language.

Even in an era of good writers, Frau Schenirer's style was superior. Professional literati could hardly approach it, let alone mimic it. Her spoken and written lectures, her letters, and her words of encouragement or advice were couched in an exceptional style. Her diaries, collected writings, prose, and poetry were unique. *They were Sarah Schenirer.* They expressed her personality and sang a continuous song of her noble soul. One finds this style only in the sayings of our great Sages and *meshorerim* (lyric masters). She embodied the style of **hu hayah omer** — "he *was* what he *said*"; Sarah Schenirer, too, was what she said — and wrote.

*   *   *

Frau Schenirer rhymed spontaneously when she spoke to children or her girls. An example follows:

איך ווייס אליין

אז איך בין קליין

און קען נישט אלע מצוות טיען

איך וועל מיך באמיען

נישט צו פארגעסן

מאכן א ברכה פאר יעדן עסן

I know
I am still a little girl
And am not asked
All of Hashem's demands to meet.
But I will try not to forget
To recite a blessing
Before I eat.

She wrote and directed her own plays, which, as she said, she created to sanctify Hashem's Name. She portrayed our patriarchs and matriarchs and retold their sacrifices for the Almighty. She loved poetry and wrote it for various occasions.

Once I heard Yenta Ashkenazi (*née* **Werdiger**) — a friend of mine, a pupil of Frau Schenirer, and a capable Bais Yaakov teacher — reciting one of her verses. It is presented below in free translation from the Yiddish:

חוען איך בין אמאל געבליבן
איין דער פרעמד אין איין קלייד,
אוְן א גאנצע ואך געטראגן
האב איך עס אויף דער לינקער זייט

געטראגן צו מענטשנס געלעכטער
נאך מער פון צו פריינד די שלעכטע
וויל בעהאלטן האב איך אויף שבת
מיר די זייט די רעכטע

Once when I was in
A strange city stuck
For quite a while to stay,
I had nothing to wear,
Save the dress I wore that day.

Disregarding people's stares,
I wore it all week
On the wrong side.
So to be able proudly
To don it on Shabbos
On the gorgeous right.

Sarah Schenirer not only wrote this poem, but also, in her simplicity, meant it; and, I am sure, would have done exactly as it said.

*   *   *

Several years later, in 1927, by which time the *Bais Yaakov Journal* had become a publishing house and had branched into book publishing, the first textbook for Bais Yaakov schools appeared. It was written by Reb Eliezer Schindler, a talented *litterateur* and a sensitive poet who turned out beautiful songs for children and youth. Additional textbooks followed, by Reb

Nuteh Berliner, Reb Alexander Zushe Friedman, Reb Yehudah Leib Orlean, and additional dedicated Orthodox writers. For Orthodox Jewish literature, 1927 was a year of great efflorescence in status and quality. For Frau Schenirer, the publication of the first Bais Yaakov textbook was a reason for boundless joy. She now had the tools to do her job.

Still, she was not satisfied. The publishing enterprise brought Jewish values to the Bais Yaakov system only. "We cannot rest on our laurels, happy with what we are doing in our Bais Yaakov schools," she explained. "We have to bring Torah education to the masses of Jewish youth who are not aware of their rich Jewish heritage."

She strongly believed in the power of the written word. "We have to go out into the wide world," she said, as well as wrote in the *Journal,* her concern evident in every word, "and circulate from city to city, from door to door, to spread the word of Torah. Only by advertising our publications can we reach larger audiences."

The staff of the Bais Yaakov Journal at work. Left to right: Benjamin Mintz, Leib Horowitz, A.G. Friedenson, Dovid Zvi Silberstein, Nuteh Berliner, Moshe Friedenson.

✤ *Chapter 14* ✤

It was shortly after the Second World War. My friend Rivka Pincusewitz came from Belgium to visit me in the United States. She wanted to reunite with classmates and friends from her seminary days and to meet the people who had established Bais Yaakov in America, the system that was growing in numbers of schools and students in New York and other localities. She wanted to spend some time with Rebbetzins Vichna Kaplan, Chavah Pincus, Basya Bender, Rivka Springer, Chana Rottenberg, and several others who, under the leadership of Rebbetzin Kaplan, had made the miracle of the Bais Yaakov movement come alive in America. This was the place where, as the Jewish saying went, "even the stones are *treif*." Here, in the religious desert of America, they had established an oasis of Orthodox education and, through it, true Jewish life.

Rivka fulfilled her heart's desire to spend several weeks in her friends' pleasurable company. We met to reminisce about the past and to share our God-blessed achievements after the war. We wanted to know the difficulties and struggles of Rebbetzin Kaplan, this great disciple of Sarah Schenirer's, who undertook to emulate her teacher and establish the Bais Yaakov movement in this religious wasteland, and who carried it to unimaginable heights in numbers and education endeavors.

At one of her meetings with friends, Rivka found out that Eliezer Schindler, the pillar of Bais Yaakov literature, had survived and was living in the United States. With his articles in

Reb Eliezer Schindler, writer for the Bais Yaakov Journal and composer of the Bais Yaakov anthem.

every edition of the *Bais Yaakov Journal,* he had inspired young readers with his thought-provoking ideas and, especially, his beautiful and heartfelt poetry and songs. We sang them constantly in the streets, in school, at home, and wherever we went. Of course, we were eager to meet the great writer again.

Rivka immediately looked up Schindler's address; he was living in a farming community in New Jersey. She promptly obtained his permission to visit, and asked me to accompany her.

It was a very moving experience. He was delighted to meet us, his readers — for we, like him, were people who had come from a lost world.

The subdued lighting in his home recreated the atmosphere of the long-forgotten world that he still inhabited. We conversed and reminisced about his work, his songs, and his devotion to and love for Bais Yaakov.

Then he sang his favorite songs as his wife accompanied him on the piano. The songs and the music carried us, too, into that lost world. Afterwards, he told us a story so moving that his voice occasionally broke, and we wept unabashedly.

"Once, while visiting Poland, I was in a store in Lodz," he began. "When I looked out the window, I saw children coming from school. All the children were singing the anthems of their organizations except for ours, who had no anthem to sing. It broke my heart. I sat down, took out a brown paper bag, and started to write the lyrics and the music. That's how Bais Yaakov got its first anthem."

Here is the anthem in the original Yiddish, as it is still sung:

מיר זענין ווי פייגאלעך פרייע
מיר זענען ווי בלימאלעך אין פעלד
מיר זענין חברות גיטראייע
מיר קינדער פון יעקב'ס גיצעלט.

מיר לערנען און שפילן צוזאמען
מיר לעבן צופרידן ביינאנט
קיין שנאה ביי אונדז נישט פארהאנען
די תורה, זי איז אונדזער באנד.

מיר זענען גיטריי אונדזער בורא
מיר היטן זיין הייליק גיבאט
מיר שווערן צו היטן די תורה
צו דינען דעם הייליקן ג-ט.

We are like free little birds,
Like flowers we spread a lovely scent
Of devoted love to each other,
We children of Yaakov's tent.

We sing and study together,
In friendship and joy we unite.
Hate has no place among us;
The Torah, she is our light.

We are loyal to our Creator,
Fulfilling every word of His Law;
We swear to uphold the Torah,
To serve God in joy and in awe.

"Now our children had an anthem to sing, and they sang it in school, jumping up and down on the steps, in the streets, on the way home, always with joy."

"You loved our little Bais Yaakov girls so much," I told him, sharing his overwhelming sense of loss. "You published your beautiful songs in *Kindergarten* for them. You brought so much joy and happiness to their young lives. Why did you decide to isolate yourself on this lonely farm in New Jersey, of all places? Why don't you continue to write your interesting articles? Don't you know that young people are thirsting for your moving poetry and songs?"

"I cannot do it anymore," he answered, his face creased with pain and profound sorrow. "My Bais Yaakov children are gone. I have nobody to write for. I cannot accept today's youth. I cannot make peace with the new world."

How bitter, how sad.

❧ Chapter 15 ❧

Taubka Jacobi, née Mushel, often visited Sarah Schenirer, her revered and beloved teacher. On one such visit, she invited Frau Schenirer to a play, *Yaakov and Esav,* that the girls would perform upon the *siyum* (completion of study) of *Sefer Bereishis* at her Bais Yaakov school in Bendin, Poland. Without hesitation and despite her busy schedule, Frau Schenirer traveled to Bendin to see the girls perform.

"She loved the play and laughed heartily at the funny scenes," Taubka recalled years later. "Frau Schenirer enjoyed the small things in life, and we were happy to provide her with them whenever we could.

"I remember when I was still in seminary, we made a little party once on Purim and gave the teachers token gifts," she continued. "We gave Frau Schenirer a nice autograph book that she happily accepted. 'The girls will write their original creative thoughts in it,' she remarked. She always encouraged them to think on their own and be creative.

"We gave Dr. Judith Rosenbaum a doll that held a rose in one hand and a whip in the other," Taubka chuckled at the very recollection. "Frau Schenirer liked the funny gift and the thought behind it. Fraulein Doktor, as we lovingly called her, used to hold a wonderfully aromatic rose in one hand. She impressed us with her beauty, her knowledge, her charm. She showered her love upon us. In her other hand, however, she clutched a whip — her readiness to rebuke us when we misbehaved. We all loved the joke and got a hearty laugh out of it."

Frau Schenirer appreciated a wisecrack. She would often tell a joke and then laugh together with the listeners. She also shared a funny story with the girls:

"There was a little girl in Bais Yaakov. She came from a non-committed home and her parents knew little about Jewish laws and customs. She had enrolled in Bais Yaakov because her friends were very happy there and she wanted to share their joy. Her mother, accepting this, kept track of the girl's behavior and noted the enthusiastic stories that her daughter brought home. One day, the girl came home and told her mother that each night before going to bed, she must place *negel vasser*, 'nail water' — a mug of water in a small bowl, with which she would wash her hands and recite *Modeh Ani* in the morning — near her bed. Her mother agreed to do this. What is more, to keep her daughter happy, she continued to fulfill this request, supplying her with *negel vasser* each evening.

"One day she approached Frau Schenirer in a state of severe annoyance. 'My daughter's teacher told the girls to have nail water placed near their beds every evening, which I am doing. But it has become ridiculous. All my mugs are rusty from the nails I've been putting in the water!'"

Frau Schenirer explained the misunderstanding. "We call it 'nail water' because the girls are required to wash only their fingertips, their nails." Problem solved! But Frau Schenirer's charming rendition of the story made us giggle anew each time.

❧ Chapter 16 ❧

In the early 1920s, Sarah Schenirer struck a deep and lasting friendship with Miss Hansi Ross of Frankfurt — all as a result of a missed train.

Frau Schenirer was rushing to the railroad station in Kraków, where she was supposed to catch a train to southern Germany for an important meeting. In her haste, she boarded the wrong train, which was waiting at the platform she usually used. Thus, instead of reaching her destination, she detrained in Frankfurt. What a misfortune! She missed her meeting.

"It must be *bashert* [willed by God]," she consoled herself. "Since I was brought here, Hashem must have had a reason for it." But now she needed lodging for the night. After making inquiries at the station, she was directed to the Ross family, who ran a small kosher hotel in the neighborhood where the Orthodox Jews lived.

She went there at once, eager to have a kosher meal and get some rest after her frustrating experience. She knocked on the door and was greeted by a lovely young woman, who ushered her into the establishment with a most disarming smile.

"I am Hansi Ross," she introduced herself, "the owners' daughter." The visitor introduced herself in turn.

Hansi's face lit up. "Do I really have the *zechus*, the merit, to meet the famous Sarah Schenirer?" she exclaimed enthusiastically. "The founder of the Bais Yaakov schools for Jewish girls that I've heard so much about?"

They took an immediate liking to each other. Like magnets,

they were drawn to each other spiritually. As they talked into the evening, Frau Schenirer discovered that her host, Miss Ross, was none other than the granddaughter of Rabbi Samson Raphael Hirsch.

What a happy turn of events, or let us say *hashgachah pratis* (personal Divine Providence) it was: Hashem had placed her aboard the wrong train and taken her to Frankfurt to meet Hansi, the renowned Rabbi Hirsch's great-granddaughter.

Hansi took after her great-grandfather. She had inherited his great mind, his familiarity with the deep well of Jewish knowledge, his enthusiasm for *Yiddishkeit,* his burning desire to bring faith in Hashem and the truth of His Torah to the masses.

With all those qualities, Hansi felt an urge to teach, to inspire girls to take pride in being Jewish daughters, to share with them her love of the beautiful Jewish heritage, to teach them the Torah, the Prophets, and the Writings. She wished to transmit the profound Jewish knowledge that she had acquired from her parents, from her distinguished uncle, Rabbi Breuer, and foremost, from her diligent study of the important works of her famous great-grandfather, Rabbi Hirsch.

In her quest for perfection in the performance of God's commandments, Hansi studied Jewish laws and ways intensively, with special emphasis on the rules of *tzeniyus* (modesty).

Frau Schenirer and Hansi got to know each other in the course of their intensive conversations. Hansi admired Sarah Schenirer's great concept in founding the Bais Yaakov system, and her unusual love of and concern for Jewish girls. She was taken by Frau Schenirer's remarkable enthusiasm and the pleasure with which she carried out her commitment to restore those spiritually starving girls' faith in Hashem and joy in fulfilling His commandments.

Frau Schenirer, in turn, adored this young girl and her deep desire to give, to share everything she had with others. Instantly, a lasting friendship developed between them. They shared the same idea: to establish new Bais Yaakov schools where more and more Jewish girls could learn about their heritage.

As a result of this encounter, and of subsequent correspondence between the two, a lasting partnership developed. Frau Schenirer encouraged Hansi to establish new schools and advised her about where to locate them. Their common interest required them to help each other and, for this reason, they continued to correspond frequently and extensively.

Thus Hansi, guided by Sarah Schenirer, would establish a Bais Yaakov school somewhere in Germany, recruit capable teachers from the Hirsch Seminary, and, when satisfied with the quality of the teaching, move on to found another school elsewhere.

They needed each other's help in acquiring teaching materials, which were very scarce at the time. Frau Schenirer offered Hansi books on Jewish values and modesty, written in Hebrew with a Yiddish translation, and suggested that she provide the girls in her newly established schools with the *Bais Yaakov Journal* and *Kindergarten* as reading material.

Frau Schenirer asked Hansi to send her copies of *Der Israelit,* which was published in Frankfurt. She loved this journal and, in one of her letters, said that she would appreciate it if Hansi could obtain all of the 1926 issues (see below). In her 1926 correspondence, she repeatedly asked for a list of all the works of Rabbi Samson Raphael Hirsch, Dr. Nathan Birnbaum, and Marcus Lehmann, as well as all novels suitable for an Orthodox library. [She urged every Bais Yaakov school to start a library of its own.]

The next page shows one of Frau Schenirer's letters to Miss Ross, dated in April 1926, in the original Yiddish. She frequently asked forgiveness for not replying promptly to letters written to her. Below is a translation of the most interesting paragraphs:

bs"D, Kraków, Sunday, *Parashas Shemini*, 1926

My beloved spiritual sister!

I now realize how, thank God, one heart knows and feels another. I just meant to write to you, and here I've received

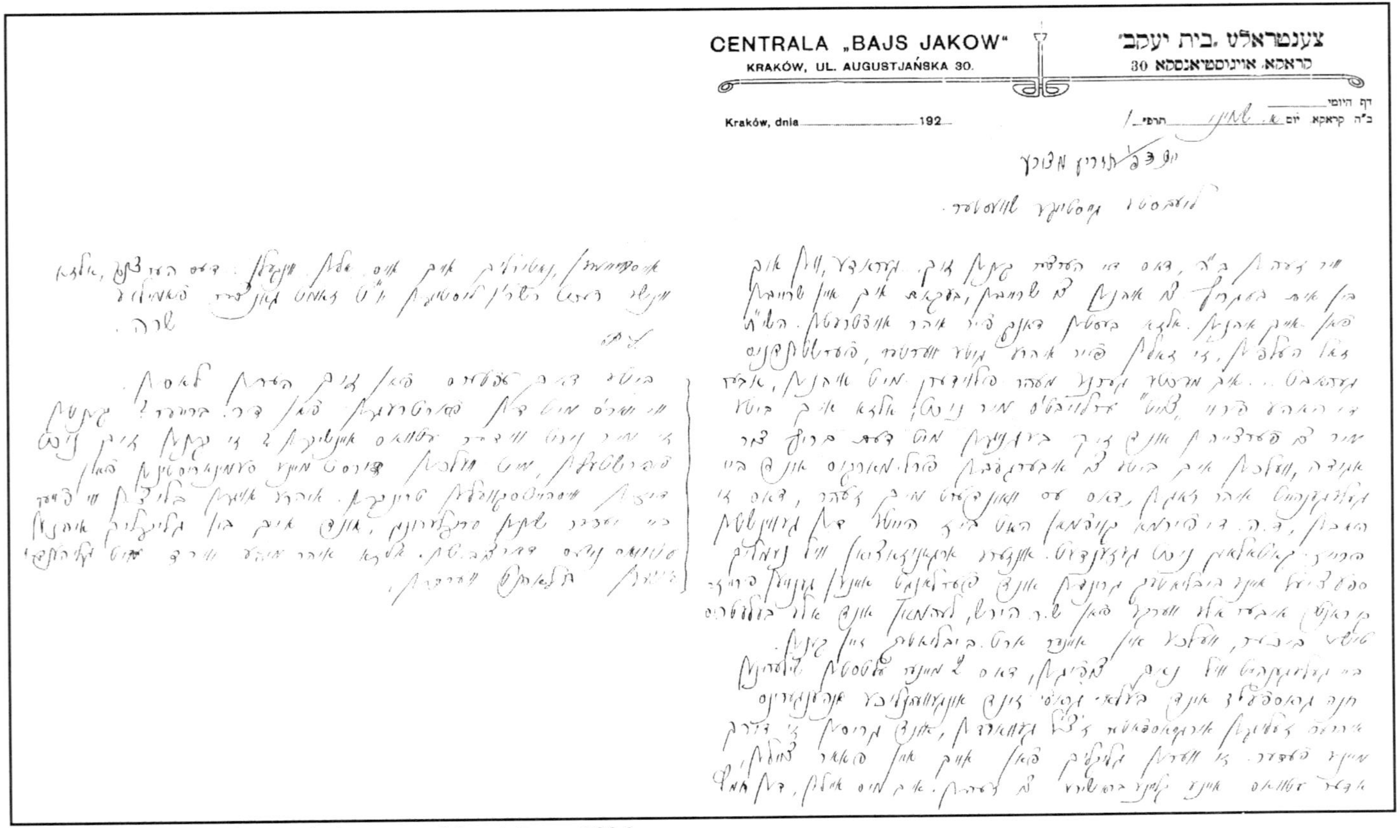
CENTRALA „BAJS JAKOW"
KRAKÓW, UL. AUGUSTJAŃSKA 30.
צענטראלע „בית יעקב"
קראקא, אויגוסטיאנסקא 30
Kraków, dnia 192

One of Frau Schenirer's letters to Hansi Ross, 1926.

a letter from you. Thank you for letting me know about your public appearance (a successful one, I'm sure). Let's hope that, with Hashem's help, your precious words will be highly appreciated and will inspire your audience.

I would love to write you more, but unfortunately, "Lady Time" does not allow me that pleasure. Please forgive me and read the [enclosed] letter about our work that I wrote to the Agudah, which I ask you to deliver. You will find the details there.

I wish to mention that my two favorite oldest students, Hanka Grossfeld and Bella Gross, have become great admirers of your late great-grandfather. They send their regards through my pen and would be happy to receive a few words from you or a little brochure of his.

Please write to me about Dr. Breuer's lecture. You cannot imagine how thirsty my seminar girls are to drink from the spring of knowledge that you send me from time to time. Their eyes sparkle with fire whenever they hear a new beautiful thought. I wanted to let you know how greatly we appreciate your efforts and how enthusiastically your written words are received.

Wishing you a *chag kasher ve-sameach* [a happy and kosher Pesach] and best regards to your family.

Sarah

As early as 1926, we read Sarah Schenirer's letters of praise to Hansi for her great work in organizing schools, forming Bnos groups, and teaching and lecturing to women. Hansi even found the time to work with the Frankfurt Agudah for ORT-Trade youth groups that were preparing for *aliyah*.

In a letter she wrote in April 1927, Frau Schenirer expressed her disappointment that Miss Ross had to leave the summer Fortbildungs Kurs a night before the course was to end. Thus, she missed the meaningful parting evening with Dr. Judith Rosenbaum. She writes:

At the time, we saw and felt how spiritual bonds are much, much stronger than physical, even biological, ones. I wrote to Reb Yaakov Rosenheim, describing the evening in detail. If you are interested, you can read it and send it back to me for filing with my important papers.

I would greatly appreciate it if you could send me the six weekly copies of *Der Israelit* from the middle of Elul to Rosh Chodesh Cheshvan. I can't get *Der Israelit* in Kraków. I would also like to know how much it would cost to obtain a complete set of *Der Israelit* for 1926. I need it badly.

Did you get in touch with Miss Rosenbaum about our plans? Did you work on them with her? You should know that she is an unusual treasure for the Bais Yaakov movement. Take advantage of it, for the benefit of our Jewish girls.

I'm preparing for a trip to establish a rather large number of new schools this week. As I hear, you are constantly founding new schools. I admire your superhuman effort in this direction and, *baruch Hashem*, your unusual success. I was also very happy to hear about Rosi Langer's achievements in our work. Is she accepting more girls in her class?

May Hashem give me the *zechus* of seeing the fruits of your great accomplishments for our Jewish daughters.

I have to conclude this letter; it is late at night and I still have to pack for the trip.

I wish all our friends and co-workers a happy and healthy summer.

> With warmest regards,
> Sarah Schenirer

In another letter on the eve of Yom Kippur of the same year, she wrote:

At the beginning of the new year, I don't wish to be guilty of not answering your letter. But, you must know that I have little time to tell you about the summer course. We'll have to leave it for next time. I just want to wish you a good *chasimah tovah* [a good inscription in the Book of Life].

You may wonder why I've added the word "good" to the expression *chasimah tovah*. Isn't *"tovah"* good in itself? The renowned Sanzer Rav, the Divrei Chaim, *zt"l*, was asked the same question and replied, "True, everything Hashem does for us is surely good. But we ask Him to let us feel that the 'good inscription' is good for us."

So, I wish you and your family a GOOD *chasimah tovah*.

> Next year in Jerusalem,
> Sarah Schenirer

During the days between Rosh Hashanah and Yom Kippur 1930, she wrote:

Again a year has sunk into eternity, and I did not repent. I still don't fulfill my correspondence responsibilities.

In a letter dated Rosh Chodesh Nissan [April] 1931, Frau Schenirer wrote to Hansi Ross among others:

It makes me so very happy to know the vast devotion with which you are working toward our ideal. May Hashem help your great effort to bring truly good results.

May the flame of love and fear of God grow in the hearts of your students, day by day, until it becomes an erupting volcano that will overcome both the inner and outer obstacles with its tremendous power.

Wishing you much success in your work.

Have a happy and kosher Pesach.

> Sarah Schenirer

Warmest regards to all your Bais Yaakov children. Please read them my letters that appeared in *Kindergarten*. I'd appreciate it if they'd write to me sometime.

> Sarah Landau[20] Schenirer

---

20. In the last few years of her life, Frau Schenirer was married to Rabbi Yitzchok Landau, a grandson of the Tiferes Shlomo, the Rebbe of Radomsk.

Frau Schenirer's extensive correspondence with Hansi informs us about Miss Ross' plans to make *aliyah*. Her love and longing for Eretz Yisroel prompted her not only to prepare young people for *aliyah* but also to settle there herself. When Frau Schenirer learned about her decision, she also urged her to establish additional Bais Yaakov schools in Europe on her way to the Holy Land, in accordance with her instructions.

Thus, Sarah Schenirer instructed Hansi Ross to establish a school in Bartfeld, Czechoslovakia. There she faced opposition from the local rabbi, who claimed that there was no need for it. "No other youth organization exists in our town," he asserted. In one of her letters, Frau Schenirer advised Miss Ross, "If the rabbi feels that way, don't force the issue. His brother lives in Frisztak, Poland, where the local rabbi also did not allow us to establish a Bais Yaakov. The Agudah leaders there wrote to the Chofetz Chaim and asked him about it. 'No question,' the saintly Chofetz Chaim answered. 'It is not only permissible but also urgent to establish a Bais Yaakov school there.'" His responsum, printed in Issue 106 of the *Bais Yaakov Journal* (see facing page), included the following remark by Sarah Schenirer:

> I myself participated in founding the school in this city [Frisztak]. Unfortunately, seventy girls had already joined various nonreligious organizations before the decision to do this was made.

The following is the translation of the Chofetz Chaim's letter concerning the Bais Yaakov schools:

> *bs"D*, 23 Shevat 5693 [February 19, 1933]

To the esteemed champions, lovers, and appreciators of Torah, those concerned [*chareidim*] about the Word of God:

When I heard that God-fearing and concerned people had volunteered to establish Bais Yaakov schools in the cities, for the purpose of teaching Torah and piety, moral virtues, and practical and religious studies for Jewish girls, I

מכתב מבעל „החפץ חיים" זצ"ל ע"ד בתי ספר „בית יעקב"

ב"ה, יום כ"ג חורש שבט תרצ"ג

אל כבוד האלופים הנכבדים חובבי ומוקירי תורה החרדים לדבר ד'
כאשר שמעתי שהתנדבו אנשים יראים וחרדים לדבר ד' ליסד
בערים בי"ס „בית יעקב" ללמוד בו תורה ויראת שמים. מדות ודרך ארץ
או תורה לילדות אחב"י. אמרתי לפעלם הטוב יישר ד' חילם ומעשה
ידיהם יכונן כי ענין גדול ונחוץ הוא ב'מינו אלה אשר זרם הכפירה ר"ל
שורר בכל תקפו והחפשים מכל המינים אורבים וצודים לנפשות אחב"י,
וכל מי שנגעה יראה ד' בלבבו המצוה ליתן את בתו ללמוד בבי"ס זה,
וכל החששים והפקפוקים מאיסור ללמד את בתו תורה אין שום בית
מיחוש לזה בימינו אלה, ואין כאן המקום לבאר באריכות. כי לא כדורות
הראשונים דורותינו. אשר בדורות הקודמים הי' לכל בית ישראל מסורת
אבות ואמהות לילך בדרך התורה והדת ולקרות בס' צאינה וראינה
בכל ש"ק מש"כ בעוה"ר בדורותינו אלה, וע"כ בכל עוז רוחנו ונפשנו
עלינו להשתדל להרבות בתי ספר כאלו, ולהציל כל מה שיש בידנו
ואפשרותנו להציל.

הכותב למען התורה והדת

ישראל מאיר הכהן מראדין
כעהמח"ס חפץ חיים ומשנה ברורה

pronounced their enterprise worthy and prayed that God
would strengthen them and bring their actions to fruition.
Theirs is a great and needed endeavor in these times, as the
tide of heresy is rising vigorously and all manner of miscre-
ants are lurking and hunting for Jewish souls. Anyone who
is concerned about *yiras Hashem* [fear of God] should consider it a mitzvah to enroll his daughter in such a school.
Those who fear or have doubts about the prohibition
against teaching their daughters Torah need not concern

themselves with it in our times. Although this is not the place to explain the matter at length, times have changed. In earlier times, it was the tradition in every Jewish home to follow the path of Torah and the faith and to read *Tze'ena u-Re'ena* every Shabbos. Due to our many transgressions, this is no longer the case. Therefore, every effort should be made to establish as many schools of this type as possible and to rescue as many Jewish girls as can be rescued.

> On behalf of Torah and the faith,
> Yisroel Meir Hakohen of Radin
> Author of *Chofetz Chaim* and
> *Mishnah Berurah*

*   *   *

Miss Ross established schools in Romania, Czechoslovakia, and elsewhere. Captivating young girls with her charm, wisdom, and enthusiasm, she inspired them to lead the Torah way of life joyfully, as Frau Schenirer had taught her.

Hansi Ross established and staffed so many schools that she also spent the year 1933 in Europe, still *en route* to Eretz Yisroel. On the facing page we reproduce a postcard that Frau Schenirer mailed to Miss Ross in Kaschou (Koszyce), Slovakia. In the picture on page 120, dated Lag ba-Omer [May 24] 1932, Miss Ross is surrounded by all the girls who attended the new Bais Yaakov school that she founded in that town. It seems to have several classes, as evidenced by the different ages of the girls and the rather large number of teachers who inspired them with the great idea of Bais Yaakov and imbued them with enthusiasm for and love of the Jewish heritage. The picture shows about 150 girls with Miss Ross in the center. We can only imagine how much effort Miss Ross put forth to recruit the wonderful staff that helped her organize and direct a school as large as this. And Frau Schenirer's extensive correspondence with Hansi shows us an additional aspect: the great assistance that the local Agudah gave Miss Ross in all her undertakings.

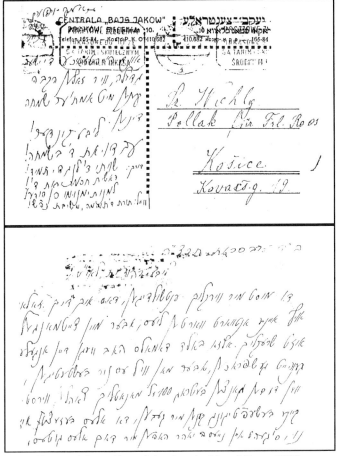

Postcard from Frau Schenirer to Hansi Ross, 1932.

In another letter from Sarah Schenirer to Hansi in Kaschou, we see that Miss Ross was evidently organizing a large Shabbaton, and she asked her mentor to join them. Unfortunately, Frau Schenirer had to turn down the invitation: "I cannot leave because of my responsibilities to the seminary and the Bais Yaakov schools. Founding and staffing new schools requires lots of attention, as you know," she wrote, "and it is even more difficult especially now that the borders between the two countries have been tightened.

"I would love to join you, my dear children, at this very im-

Bais Yaakov of Kaschou, Slovakia, founded by Hansi Ross; Lag ba-Omer, 1932. Miss Ross is in the center of the second row.

portant event. But even if I cannot be there physically, you should know that I am with you in my soul and my heart. Often, when I work at night, my thoughts go to you.

"I think of you all, my Bais Yaakov daughters, and I care for each of you individually. I pray that you should understand that only when *Toras Hashem temimah*, only when we fulfill the Torah completely, is it *meshivas nafesh* — only then does it give us joy, happiness, and peace.[21]

"Yes, my dear children, you should be *shleimusdik*, perfecting whatever you do every day of your life — be it at work, at shul, or in the street, when you keep Shabbos, say your prayers, or dress modestly. Even when you do *chessed* and work on your Jewish virtues, remember to do it with joy and enthusiasm. Always strive for Torah-true *shleimus,* perfection.

"Our Torah is not bankrupt. It does not pay 10 percent, 50 percent, or even 99 percent on its 'dollar.' It offers and expects 100 percent. Only when you imbibe the Torah as something

---

21. See *Tehillim* 19:8.

that is *temimah*, complete, can you expect it to be *meshivas nafesh*, to grant true peace.

"The trouble with our youth is that they don't take pride in doing a perfect job, regardless of the profession. They give 40 percent, 50 percent, whatever, just enough to achieve monetary satisfaction.

"We must teach our Bais Yaakov and Bnos girls," Frau Schenirer stressed, "to strive to attain *shleimus*, perfection, in Torah, for this will assure them everlasting joy and happiness in life."

"Be young," she wrote, repeating Mordechai's message to Esther in the Megillah, as she often did. "Don't be indifferent. Act with vigor and enthusiasm, take risks and make sacrifices, to help your people and, if needed, to save their lives.

"Do you know what youth means?" she asked rhetorically. "Youth," she answered forcefully, "is happiness, optimism, *joie de vivre,* hope, belief in ideals, belief in yourself, and the enthusiasm to live and strive for it.

"To be phlegmatic, cold, and indifferent is to be anti-youth. We have to work and strive, not only for our sake, but to bring every Jewish girl under the wings of the true faith. You should know that falling into ecstasy is easy, but to keep it up for months, years, for all your life, *always* to do what is expected of you with enthusiasm, is difficult. However, this is our calling. Go ahead! Work! And with God's help, you will be able to bring the greatest and holiest ideal, that of Torah-true life, to all Jewish girls."

How prophetic Frau Schenirer's words were. Today, the whole world screams for peace. The UN preaches it. Every demonstration, every rally expresses the desire for peace in a crescendo. The message of peace, peace for all nations, for all the world's children, is shouted in every corner of the world. Peace, peace, peace…yet the outcome of it all is wars and the murder and torture of innocent people. If they could only understand that true *shalom* is achieved only by *shleimus*. Striving for Torah-true perfection is the only assurance of world peace. As

Hillel says in *Pirkei Avos*:[22] *Ohev shalom ve-rodef shalom* — be a lover of *shalom,* peace, and strive for it with *shalom,* perfection. Love human beings and lead them to Torah. Only this will assure true peace.

*   *   *

Since Hansi Ross followed Sarah Schenirer's instructions and established Bais Yaakov schools in Europe on her way to Eretz Yisroel, it took her a few years to reach the land of her dreams. However, she had not come there to rest. With her usual vigor she looked for a place where there was a need to establish a Bais Yaakov school.

She ended up in Tiberias, a city at that time completely devoid of *Yiddishkeit,* and an economic and cultural wasteland. She had to fight to obtain even the most primitive conditions. She was discouraged from starting up her enterprise, and ridiculed from all sides, from the Left and the Right, just as her mentor, Sarah Schenirer, had warned her she would be. "Surmount all the obstacles," she had said. "Hashem will help you to attain your ideal, just as He has always helped me."

Instead of giving up, Miss Ross established a beautiful Bais Yaakov school in Tiberias. In short order, children attended it enthusiastically and their parents were pleased with their achievements. The children admired their great teacher, who taught them proper values with depth and feeling. They appreciated the milk that she obtained from the authorities, after a fight — hot milk in the winter and cold milk in the summer. They loved the other nourishment she provided them: motherly compassion and understanding. She repressed her own needs. Sometimes she went to sleep without supper, her pantry bare until she received her meager, belated salary. But the satisfaction and joy in her accomplishment were sufficient rewards for her.

Hansi Ross' next stop, after activating Bais Yaakov schools

---

22. 1:12.

in Tiberias and Tzefas, was Petach Tikvah, a new community where she had been called to start a Bais Yaakov school. The school was a great success and after seeing it properly functioning, she went to Jerusalem.

Hansi Ross Perkal

There, she married Rabbi Moshe Reuven Perkal and established a family. She became a mother to her husband's children (he was a widower), and gave them a loving home, saturated with sanctity, wisdom, and spirituality. Even then, she did not abandon her life's calling. She became a teacher in the Bais Yaakov school that Rabbi Hillel Lieberman had established.

All her life, she was a teacher, mentor, leader, and advisor. In everything she did, she followed the instructions of her spiritual mentor, Sarah Schenirer. She was proud to mention, at every occasion, Frau Schenirer's strong influence on her. Often she remarked, "Frau Schenirer's unusual enthusiasm and joy in doing God's will guided me in my life's endeavors."

No wonder that whenever Rabbi Perkal, a chassid, was asked, "How come a *yeketeh* — a woman brought up in Frankfurt, Germany — matches a chassid so beautifully?" he would answer, "In her innermost being, she is a great chassid."

Emulating Her Maker

ఌ Chapter 17 ఌ

Girls, do you remember? Frau Schenirer often reminded us of our favorite verse in King David's *Tehillim*:[23] "[The only thing I seek is] to live in the house of the Lord all the days of my life." "You know this beautiful Psalm by heart. We recite it twice a day each year, from Rosh Chodesh Elul until Hoshana Rabba. We pray with King David and repeat what he so sincerely asks of Hashem. His greatest longing, his deepest desire, is to dwell in God's House all the days of his life.

"King David spoke his mind. He sang what he felt in the deepest recesses of his heart. His words were the epitome of truth. How could he wish to dwell in God's House all the days of his life?" Frau Schenirer wondered. "He had to take care of his kingly duties, to take heed of and solve the problems of the country and of the Jewish People. He had to deal with other kingdoms, meet with his ministers, and make crucial decisions according to Hashem's will. As we know, all of this is time-consuming. How could he pray to dwell in God's House all the days of his life?"

Frau Schenirer answered her own rhetorical question with emphasis. "Girls, King David taught us a very important lesson in this Psalm: the whole universe is a House of God. Wherever we go, whatever place we occupy, we can make it a dwelling for Hashem. Whatever we do, every day and every minute of our lives, we dwell in Hashem's House if we do everything with His

---

23. 27:4.

A group of Krakowian girls at Bnos summer camp. Holding the ball is Escia Teitelbaum, laying on the grass is Rozia Dym, standing on the right is Balka Grossfeld, and third from right is Rozia Weiss.

will in mind.

"My dear children, know and remember that in everything we do, say, and feel, in dealing with people or in practicing our professions with honesty and truth according to God's commandments, we dwell in Hashem's House all of our lives. Thus did King David dwell in Hashem's House, in everything he did, every day of his life."

On one occasion, a girl asked, "Is everything you just mentioned *the same* as sitting and learning Torah all day in yeshiva or davening in shul, singing Hashem's praises all the time?"

"*Kinderlach*," Frau Schenirer replied, addressing her response to the entire class, "King David did not enumerate the duties he performed every day; he just prayed that everything he did all day, and all the days of his life, would be considered 'sitting in Hashem's House.'"

Then she returned to the questioner. "I understand your question and the questions of others who did not ask. You should know that all of your responsibilities as a Jewish daughter and a Jewish mother, even the most mundane ones, are *equally* considered dwelling in Hashem's House if you fulfill them with God's will in mind.

"Women's prayers, even if said not in shul but anywhere — at home, any time they can spare from family duties and demands — are as precious to Hashem as prayers uttered in shul. Their home is Hashem's House. The lullaby that a mother sings to her baby is her most moving prayer, her holiest dreams and expectations — a prayer of love and hope, of faith and gratitude, a powerful song of praise and glory to Hashem's Name. Yes, girls, it *is* the same, if not more.

"We read *Parashas Beha'alosecha* in shul this past week, in which Hashem says to Aharon, 'When you light up the lamps....'[24]

"When Aharon saw all the tribal chieftains and the tribespeople themselves making offerings for the construction of the Sanctuary, he was crestfallen. He and his tribe had been excluded from the dedication of the Sanctuary.

"Then Hashem said to him, 'You will *light* and *guard* the lamps.' Thus, Rashi explains, your life's calling is greater than theirs. You will light the lamp that will illuminate all of Jewry and you will guard it, lest it ever be extinguished. You will be the nation's teacher, as Moshe said to the tribe of Levi:[25] 'They will teach Your laws to Yaakov, and Your Torah to Yisrael.' The other tribal chieftains will build sanctuaries, shuls, and yeshivos, which might be destroyed, God forbid, and they will have to rebuild them again and again. But your light will last forever, illuminating Jewish life.

"Jewish women often feel bad and ask, as the daughters of Tzelofchad did, 'Why should we be excluded?' Why shouldn't we build sanctuaries, learn in *yeshivos*, and pray three times a day in shul? The world of men is active and bright; why should ours be different?"

---

24. *Bemidbar* 8:2.
25. *Devarim* 33:10.

Frau Schenirer answered with joy and love. "Hashem told the Jewish women, 'Your calling is greater than theirs. You will kindle the Shabbos light, which will burn from Shabbos to Shabbos, illuminating your home with sanctity and peace. You will be the mother, the teacher, who spreads the light of Torah to your children, your family, and everyone around you. Even during sleepless nights when you sing your baby a lullaby, when in fatigue you rock the baby, you are sitting in Hashem's House. Your calling is *greater*."

Frau Schenirer paused for a moment to let the idea sink in and become part of our being, the philosophy of our lives. And it did.

*   *   *

A lullaby of a Jewish mother's hopes and dreams, sung to her child, follows in the original Yiddish and free translation.

שלאפזשע מיר מיין יינגאלע מיין קליינער
די אייגאלעך די שוואַרצינקע מאַך צו
אַ יינגאלע וואָס האָט שוין אַלע ציינדאלעך
לאָזט גאָנצע נעכט די מאַמע נישט צו רו.

אַ יינגאלע וואָס וואָקסט אַ תלמיד חכם

וואָס וועט מיט מזל באָלד אין חדר גיין
און לערנען וועט ער חומש און גמרא
זאָל וויינין ווען די מאַמע וויגט אים איין.

אַ יינגאלע וואָס וואָקסט אַ תלמיד חכם
אַ גיניטער סוחר אויך צו גלייך
אַ יינגאלע אַ שיינער חתן בחור
זאָל ליגן אזוי נאַס ווי אין אַ טייך.

אַ יינגאלע אַ גרויסער תלמיד חכם
דערוויייל ביזטו אין וויגאלע ביי מיר
ס'וועט קאָסטען אסך מי און מאַמעס טרערן
ביז וואָנען וועט אַ מענטש אַרויס פון דיר.

Sleep, oh sleep, my dear, my little boy.
Your sweet black eyes close tight.
A boy who has all his little teeth,
Does not let his mother sleep all night.

A boy, a growing Torah scholar,
Soon with God's help *cheder* will attend,
Where he'll learn *Chumash* and Gemara
Should cry and cry all night without end?

A boy, a great Torah scholar
Also a smart businessman-to-be,
My little chassid, a handsome young man,
Should lie in his crib wet as in the sea?

A boy, a clever young man-to-be,
You still lie in the cradle close to me.
It will take mother's tears and prayers too
Till she sees a *mentsch* become of you.

❧ *Chapter 18* ❧

Frau Schenirer had another motto: Limnos yameinu kein hoda — "Teach us to count our days rightly, so we will know."[26] It stared at us from every wall in every Bais Yaakov building. It was constantly on her lips.

At various occasions, she mentioned it with different interpretations. "*Ha-yom katzar ve-ha-melachah merubah.*[27] How short the day is," she would complain, "and how much there is to do. Time is the most precious gift Hashem granted us. He gave everyone the same amount, twenty-four hours a day, and each person uses it as he pleases. Children, use it wisely. Count your days, count your hours. *Know* that every minute, every second, *counts*. The here-and-now is only one moment; it comes, and then it is gone. You have to seize the next moment, the next chance, the next opportunity, and to use it more properly. You cannot retain it. You cannot save it. Once it is used, you can only store it away in a treasure chest so one day you can recount it. Learn, and know, how to count your days."

*   *   *

I dislike digital watches; they only tell you the time. I like my face watch, on which I can see the large minute hand in motion. I can watch the time *moving* from minute to minute, urging me to follow it, slowly but surely, with the same "watchful"

---

26. *Tehillim* 90:12.
27. *Pirkei Avos* 2:15.

determination, filling the minute properly and devotedly, then moving satisfactorily to the next one. If only we could do the same!

Frau Schenirer did it, and did it all the time. When she wrote lesson plans for distribution to her young teachers or penned letters of advice and encouragement to them, it was always late at night — 2:00 or 3:00 A.M. She did not have time to answer all important correspondence. She tried, but her students made her surrender. "Frau Schenirer," they pleaded, "you must rest a few hours to be able to carry on with your busy schedule tomorrow."

"Oh, Lady Time," she lamented, "I have so much more to do, and you're holding me back."

Even though Frau Schenirer put every minute, every second to use, she never had time for all of her activities. She always strove to impress upon her girls the importance of every second.

Once she visited a Bais Yaakov school in Rzeszów, a large Jewish town in Galicia. One of the little girls who attended the school was Rivka Bendelman, who subsequently became my sister-in-law (now Reichman). Reminiscing with me some sixty years later, she described Frau Schenirer's visit, a very important and exciting event.

"I was a little girl at the time, only ten or eleven years old. I don't remember much about that afternoon, but I still recall the little story she told us. It impressed me so much that not only do I still remember it but I try to live by its message even to this day.

"'*Kinderlach*,' Frau Schenirer said before she left, 'I am now taking the train back to Kraków. It is scheduled to leave at five-thirty. I am sorry to leave you, my dear children, but I must rush not to be late. If I'm just *one minute* late, my train will be gone and I will not be able to catch it anymore. *Kinderlach*, can you imagine that I'll miss my ride if I'm only *one minute* late? That may show you, my dear children, how precious, how important, every minute is.'"

Thus, in her simple, direct way and style, she successfully impressed even her youngest students with the great value of time.

My father, another great inspiration in my life, taught me another thought about time. When I was about fifteen years old, I was supposed to deliver the first speech I had ever made in my life, to an audience of five hundred Bnos girls. It was on the weekly Torah portion.

Understandably, I had butterflies in my stomach and repeatedly asked my father, before I left that Friday night, if the speech I had prepared was appropriate. He encouraged me, as always, stressing that there is nothing wrong with being individual and creative.

"But my daughter, it's getting late. You have to be on time. When you come late, it is considered *geneivas zeman,* theft of time. You are stealing others' time; you are transgressing the commandment of *Lo signov,* Do not steal.

"You are stealing the most precious commodity man possesses: time. Be careful, my child."

I remain careful to this day. I can be late in any matter of concern to me alone, but I am always punctual, or several minutes early, when I have to speak to an audience.

My father's powerful lesson remains with me today. I dread the thought of wasting people's time. My revered father's warning — "Do not steal man's greatest treasure, time" — still resonates in my ears.

✣ *Chapter 19* ✣

Pride was Frau Schenirer's worst enemy. She always warned us not to fall under its influence. "Stay as far as you can from this evil trait," she counseled.

Frau Schenirer posted her best students — young, intelligent, bright girls — to difficult positions in small towns, which were even more demanding than large cities. Both there and in specific neighborhoods of larger cities, they became community leaders as well as teachers. These pioneers faced a hostile secular environment that opposed any new religious development which might challenge the secularists' supremacy in the community. Worse still, the secular feared Bais Yaakov as an obstacle to their efforts to sway youth away from religion. Bais Yaakov was also opposed from the Right, as a revolutionary movement in girls' education.

Although the young teachers found it very difficult to struggle against these clashing oppositions, both the Left and the Right ultimately learned to respect them. They brought honor to the Bais Yaakov movement, and Frau Schenirer was overjoyed at their success. But as pride was her most despised enemy, Frau Schenirer, upon hearing about the honors with which the community would shower her teachers, became worried that her students would fall victim to this terrible trait, God forbid.

I once heard Frau Schenirer speaking to the teachers. A new semester was about to begin; after long vacations in Kraków, the girls were ready to return to their teaching positions in their respective cities and towns.

"My dear children," she addressed her young teachers, "I am very proud of your achievements of last year. *Baruch Hashem*, it was a successful year for Bais Yaakov. I know how much intensity, love, and devotion you invested in your work. You deserve the respect and honor of your community. But girls, you must remember that all your talents, your wisdom, your intelligence — everything you possess — are gifts from Hashem to help you fulfill your purpose in life. The profession you have chosen — educating children to become God-fearing Jews who walk proudly in the path of Torah — is the most rewarding profession there can be.

"Look how great and satisfying this vocation is, girls," she continued enthusiastically, her eyes sparkling. "One smile from a child gives you more joy than any other job you can think of. However," she cautioned her young teachers, "you must know that all the glory and honor belong solely to the Almighty, Who equipped you with everything you need to carry out your mission. Therefore, all your achievements in life should focus only on bringing glory and honor to Hashem and sanctifying His Name.

"Let me tell you a story," she continued, flashing her lovely smile. "There was once a *maggid* [preacher], a well-known scholar and a very interesting lecturer, a man whom everyone loved and admired. He was once invited to a city to give an important sermon on Shabbos day. The community was excited about the chance to hear this renowned orator.

"Our *maggid* spent Friday night at an inn with a few people who had accompanied him. He spent the whole night talking to himself: '*Shalom aleichem*, Rebbe; we're so grateful that you accepted our invitation. Esteemed Rabbi, we cannot wait to hear you. The neighboring communities envy us for being privileged to host you this Shabbos.

"'The synagogue is packed but silent in anticipation of the great speaker. You can hear a pin drop.

"'Rebbe, your speech was dynamic. We were inspired by

your presentation. Your every word penetrated our souls.

"'We wish we had you here more often. Such a great scholar and speaker, but so humble. What an exceptional man. His words are like pearls, sparkling with wisdom, flashing with humor. Did you hear him? He was fabulous!'

"On and on it went: a repetitive litany of praise.

"One of the *maggid*'s followers, sleeping next door, couldn't figure it out. 'Why should our rebbe, the very embodiment of humility, drench himself in such a torrent of praise?' he asked, perplexed. He could hardly wait for morning to come, so he could speak to his revered rebbe. Finally, he got the chance and mustered his courage. 'My esteemed Rebbe, I was puzzled last night to hear the Rebbe heaping so many praises upon himself. I could not understand what it meant.'

"'Listen, my friend,' the Rebbe answered. 'When a person speaks in public, gives a sermon or lecture, and with God's help succeeds, he is liable to be inundated with personal compliments from all sides. When that happens, that person will be severely vulnerable to attack by the most despised inclination: pride. Pride waits for the moment when it can defeat you. Due to its sweet ammunition of pleasantry and deceptive satisfaction, its advances are very difficult to withstand.

"'To defeat this crafty enemy, we must prepare ourselves thoroughly. Here is how I do it: I pay myself every compliment that I could possibly hear, again and again, until the very sound of them makes me bored if not nauseated. It's no wonder that after a speech, all the praise directed to me sounds so cheap, even ugly, that it cannot attract me. This is the weapon I use to fight the cunning and mighty power of pride.'"

Having finished the story, Frau Schenirer addressed the teachers directly: "Now you've heard that there is a way to shield yourselves from this despised inclination, which can make you arrogant, God forbid. Beware of it! As teachers, you must have the humility to listen and pay attention to every child, to share her concerns, and to help her with her problems. Remember, the soul of a child is a precious jewel that has been entrusted to you to cleave and polish. God gave you the potential, but you can realize it only by treating even the youngest child with love and respect. Use the advice of this great, humble orator and fight pride with the weapon he suggested. May God bless you and help you to succeed in all your endeavors, so you will render honor to Whom it belongs, to our Father in Heaven and, for that matter, to the Bais Yaakov movement."

ad the house hotel · 2 rosslyn hill · hampstead · london · nw3 1ph
t 020 7431 8000 **f** 020 7433 1775
w www.thehousehotel.co.uk

Othello – Thurs :

the house hotel

♦♦♦♦♦ AA accommodation

❧ *Chapter 20* ❧

Frau Schenirer had innumerable responsibilities apart from her schools. Everyone in distress, in need, or ill, found their way to her. Her door and her heart were always open to troubled souls. She was willing to help in any way possible. She was especially concerned about referring the ill to the right sort of medical care and helping patients who needed complicated operations to travel to the finest surgeons in Vienna.

For all this she needed money. She personally knocked on doors and visited stores to raise funds. Whenever an emergency occurred, she told her students to close their books and go out to collect for the cause.

"One year on Purim," Taubka Mushel Jacobi recalled, "Frau Schenirer divided us seminary girls into pairs to collect *tzedakah* on different streets in the city.

"It was my privilege to join Frau Schenirer herself for the collection that day. When we returned in the evening, a queue of poor people was waiting for her. Patiently she distributed the alms and her blessings to every person in need."

*　　*　　*

A sick boy had to be sent to Vienna for a serious operation, and it took Frau Schenirer weeks to collect the requisite funds to cover the cost. "Do you recall," my friend Renia Finkelstein asked me, "how Frau Schenirer entered our class aglow with joy one evening? 'Girls,' she announced, beaming, 'I was finally able to send the boy off to Vienna, thank God! Now, let us all

139

pray for his speedy recovery.'"

Fundraising for the ill and the needy was not Frau Schenirer's only act of loving-kindness, however.

An orphan girl from a town in Galicia desperately wanted to enroll in the seminary. Once her aunt from Kraków visited her and, hearing of her niece's desire to go to Kraków to study, took her home with her. But instead of enrolling her in the seminary, the aunt put her to manual labor. The girl was devastated. Rivka Horowitz and other girls who discovered the problem called the case to Frau Schenirer's attention. In no time, Frau Schenirer brought the girl into her own home, met all of her needs, and, of course, sent her to the seminary. This girl eventually became one of Sarah Schenirer's most devoted and capable teachers.

*   *   *

Renia Finkelstein's mother founded an organization that she called, "For the Needy Who Are Ashamed to Beg." She was successful in her work. When she collected money for her organization, she visited only friends, relatives, and wealthy people who could afford to be generous.

Mrs. Finkelstein was also a close friend of Frau Schenirer; the two sometimes set out to collect charity together. Frau Schenirer approached storekeepers. If they knew her, they would hand over a five-zloty bill. Otherwise, she would get only one zloty or half a zloty. But she would not turn down even a quarter.

Mrs. Finkelstein begged Frau Schenirer not to visit places that gave her *groschen* only. "You are demeaning yourself," she said.

Frau Schenirer answered with a smile: "My dear, by knocking on a door where I get only 25 *grush*, I earn merit for three people: the one who gives it, the one who receives it, and the one who collects it. How can I deprive them of giving charity, even if only in a small way?"

Due to the post-World War I baby boom, the schools were

overcrowded and classes were given in two shifts. I was placed in the afternoon shift; it made me almost the only youngster in the neighborhood who had her mornings free. This is how I had the privilege of assisting Frau Schenirer from time to time.

I lived on the corner of Dietlowska and Kordeckiego Streets; Frau Schenirer also lived on Kordeckiego. Whenever she came from home, or came from the seminary on Stanislawa Street, she passed my house. One day, I stepped out of my doorway to do an errand and saw her coming. She beat me to the greeting, as usual. "Good morning, Peraleh," she said with her big smile. "I'm happy to see you. I need someone to collect money with me."

"Of course, Frau Schenirer, I'm so glad to have an opportunity to help," I answered without hesitation, despite the errand I was about to perform. How could I refuse Frau Schenirer? The errand would have to wait.

So we went together, the great Sarah Schenirer and little Peraleh, to collect money for *tzedakah*. What a lucky opportunity, I thought in excitement. Frau Schenirer strode energetically as usual and I trotted shyly behind her. First she visited the stores on the Dietlowska. Everybody knew her there, and she was greeted with respect. Five zloty, two zloty, one zloty, one zloty, one zloty — the bills fluttered into a special charity bag she took along. However, what she left with the donors was more precious: a genuine smile and a heartfelt blessing.

As I stepped out of my house another day, there was Frau Schenirer again with her friendliest greeting: "Peraleh, how happy I am to see you! Come with me to collect *tzedakah*." Again I obeyed. This time Frau Schenirer led me to some large apartment buildings. She knocked on strangers' doors, presented her request, and explained the importance of the matter: a young boy had to be rushed to the hospital for the removal of a malignant growth. Some people responded generously; others gave trifling donations. I was ashamed to see how disgracefully the "little" donors treated the great Frau Schenirer.

However, Frau Schenirer was not offended. She gave everyone the same "thank you," the same smile, and the same warm blessing. I was overwhelmed by her humility, and by her willingness to accept the smallest donations from all kinds of people with a smile and with respect. I admired her unusual determination to achieve her goal regardless of the circumstances and the situation. I was proud to collect *tzedakah* with Frau Schenirer. Furthermore, as we walked, I had an opportunity to talk with her and listen to her wise advice.

However, I was still a shy little girl who was ashamed to go door-to-door asking for charity. No matter how often I went, I could not overcome my shyness. I admit with great regret that once, when I saw Frau Schenirer approaching, I stayed indoors until she was far away in order to evade that day's charity mission. Briefly I was pleased with my behavior, but that night I was beset by severe pangs of guilt. I repented for what I had done and resolved not to do it again. "What would Frau Schenirer say about it?" I wondered. I never told anyone what I had done, but even now, so many years later, I remember this little incident and deeply regret the lost opportunity to have done one more mitzvah together with Frau Sarah Schenirer.

❧ *Chapter 21* ❧

It is after World War II. Frau Schenirer's students are scattered all over the world. Wherever they landed, they found themselves in strange countries with strange languages and unfamiliar surroundings. However, against all odds, they courageously started all over. They established families and built homes for their children, for the future. In everything they did, they were driven by an unusually strong desire to continue the chain of the family tradition.

Despite the hardships, they did not think only about themselves. They cared for others and concerned themselves with the needs of their neighbors and their community. They were always ready to help the ill and share their limited resources with the poor. If they did not have enough funds for the needy, they went out to collect charity, following the path of their great teacher.

*   *   *

Before the High Holidays in 1986, I was in Israel as usual and discovered that my precious friend, Tyly Yogel Rinder, the White Angel of Auschwitz, was terminally ill. I went to the hospital to visit her, stopped at the nurses' station, and asked for her room number. "Are you asking about Tyly, our very special patient? She is in the room across the hall," the duty nurse answered, leading me to her room. "Everyone here admires her."

"Tyly is more than a special patient; she's an extraordinary human being," I enlightened the duty nurse. "In Auschwitz they called her *der weiser Engel,* the White Angel, and she fully deserved it."

The nurse led me to her bed. I did not recognize my dear friend. If I was shocked, I tried not to show it. But she recognized me at once. Straining, she raised her head and greeted me with her lovely smile. "It's so good to see you again," she said, beaming. She asked me about my family and — concerned about everybody — about our friends in New York.

Tyly's husband was there, and then her daughter came in. "How are you, Mommy?" she asked. "I feel better today, my child," she tried to assure her. "Did you get all the donations? It's Thursday; you've got to distribute the money tonight. It is already late, the poor people have to buy food for Shabbos."

"Yes, Mother. And I have the list of names and addresses. Just tell me how much to give to each one." Tyly gave her daughter all the information she needed.

Wishing to share in this mitzvah, I added a donation of my own. Tyly thanked me and explained, "Unfortunately, I cannot do the collecting now, so my devoted donors bring their weekly contributions when they visit me," she said appreciatively.

I could not help but marvel: here is a terminally ill woman, still in her prime, fifty-some years old, in excruciating pain — collecting money and distributing alms to the needy from her hospital bed.

Her sister Tzipora told me, "Whenever I visit her in the hospital, she doesn't even answer when I ask her how she's feeling. 'There are more important things to do here,' she says. 'Look at the woman in the next bed. She cannot sit up to eat. Please help her.'

"'Very well,' I answer. After I help the woman, I turn back to Tyly. 'But I must talk to the nurses, to make sure they are giving you the painkillers the doctor has prescribed,' I say.

"'Oh please, Tzipora,' Tyly stops me, 'don't disturb any of them now; they work so hard and now they're having their lunch. It can wait. But' — she remembers to tell me — 'did you manage to take care of distributing the clothes I collected?

They're all in very good condition.'"

"You see," Tyly explained to her sister, "I put away three beautiful dresses in my bedroom." She described them and told Tzipora where to look for them. "They are for Sarahleh, the bride. And the other clothes...please write down that the gray dress is for Mrs. Gold, the junior outfit will be just right for Racheli...." So Tyly continued, listing each item of clothing and who should receive it. Her own comfort mattered the least.

"I come after work to take care of you and you even don't tell me how you feel," Tzipora said, very upset. But nothing helped.

"Tzipora, don't forget to bake a cake for the nurses," Tyly reminded her sister. "They love your home-made cake."

A terminally ill woman who acts thus can only be an angel or a true *talmidah* of Sarah Schenirer.

Several days later, on the eve of Yom Kippur, our precious Tyly left this world — a world in which her every day, every hour, was filled with acts of charity and loving-kindness. In the most tragic times and circumstances, she endangered her life to help others and save their lives. Now, on the Day of Atonement, our White Angel ascended to Heaven and, before the Heavenly Court, we hope she pleads for the atonement of her beloved people.

"For ages they have endured unbearable pain and distress for Your Holy Name, Hashem. Now they are experiencing bitter times of uncertainty. Master of the Universe," we can imagine her imploring the Almighty with her usual determination and love, "oh, Father in Heaven, have compassion on *Bnei Yisroel*, for they are Your children. Have pity on them, as a father pities his children. Declare that they have suffered enough and speed the full, Ultimate Redemption of the Jewish People."

❦ *Chapter 22* ❦

Ita Goldfinger was a Bais Yaakov girl from Chrzanów, a town not far from Kraków. She was studious, correct, sincere and, above all, always ready to help others.

Frau Schenirer often visited the Bais Yaakov school in Chrzanów. The children loved each visit and looked forward to the next one. They admired her simplicity, humility, and love for and interest in every girl. An invisible magnet drew both young children and older students to her. It was her pure soul that spoke to and inspired them.

Whenever she visited, the women of the Chrzanów community gave her a grand reception in a beautifully decorated auditorium. They set all kinds of colorful fruits and other delicacies on tables covered with white tablecloths. Frau Schenirer gazed at the table in admiration but, in her humility, did not even realize that it had been set for her. As the girls encircled her, waiting for her to sit down and taste the wonderful food they had prepared, she was oblivious to it all. All she wanted was to see how her children were doing.

She pointed to one of the girls. "What's your name?" she asked.

"Chana," answered the girl.

"Come to the table, Chanaleh, and tell me what blessing you make on this fruit or on the cookies."

Chana answered correctly. Frau Schenirer's face lit up with satisfaction. She praised the girl and encouraged her to continue in her achievements.

"Did you girls learn what blessing to make first when you want to taste everything on the table? Who knows?" she asked with her most encouraging smile.

One girl raised her hand. "What is your name?" Frau Schenirer asked.

"Gittel," the girl answered.

"Now tell me, Gitteleh, what would you eat first and what next? What would be your first blessing?"

"I learned," answered Gitteleh, "that you first say the blessing over *mezonos,* foods made from grains, because they are more important than fruit."

Frau Schenirer, her face radiating pure joy, called the girl closer. She hugged her and kissed her forehead. "I'm very proud of you, Gitteleh. Continue to learn so diligently and you'll become a fine Bais Yaakov teacher."

Then she turned to one of the older girls and asked, "What did you learn today?"

"We learned about *tzedakah* today," the girl answered proudly.

"How nice." Frau Schenirer was pleased. "Tell me, girls, what kinds of *tzedakah* did you do this week?" Hands were raised eagerly.

"I made an extra sandwich for a girl whom I noticed coming to school without lunch," said one girl.

"We formed a group that collects pieces of challah and distributes them to the needy for Shabbos," a second girl answered.

"Another group collects prepared meals from families and delivers them to Jewish patients in hospitals that don't provide kosher food," a third girl declared. So the answers went on.

Frau Schenirer, impressed with her young pupils' charitable deeds, spoke to them with enthusiasm. "Girls, I'm very proud of your charitable activities. I see you understand the importance of *tzedakah. Tayere kinderlach*, dear children," she continued with motherly love, "I want you to know and to remember that the greatest virtue of the Jews is *rachmanus* —

compassion, love, concern: the ability to notice other people's needs and help to the best of your ability under any circumstances." Thus Frau Schenirer inspired her students to feel the greatness of this virtue.

*   *   *

Ita Goldfinger took her words to heart and, while still very young, tried to emulate Frau Schenirer. She knew who was in need and always found a way to help. I first met her in the United States in 1949 when, as a young woman, she regularly gathered donations to supply poor people with food for Shabbos. This was only one of her many responsibilities that required fundraising. For years she raised funds for Komemiyut, a new moshav (cooperative farming village) in Israel led by the late Rabbi Binyamin Mendelson, which was struggling to sustain its schools and other important institutions. She collected for additional causes, which seemed to vary each time I encountered her.

She visited me one Sunday in the early sixties in the midst of the most severe blizzard I can remember. "Ita," I asked in amazement, "how did you make it in this terrible weather? The snow is knee-deep, there are patches of ice on the road underneath, and the wind cuts into your face mercilessly. Who would venture into the street today? I know you're probably collecting for a very important cause, but in this blizzard?"

"Okay, okay," she interrupted. "You're right, my dear. I need the money badly for a very urgent case that cannot wait. But I did not come to you for a donation today. I want you to come with me to collect the funds I need."

"Are you out of your mind, Ita?" I replied. "I can't take the car out in this weather; nobody can. Do you want us to walk in the snow from house to house, from street to street, from avenue to avenue, to collect donations? It's insane!"

"You're right again. Nobody can take his car out today. The schools and *yeshivos* are closed. People can't go shopping. Everyone's home today. It's an excellent time to approach people."

"I can't walk in this deep snow. I'll double my donation. Just don't make me go with you! Please," I begged.

But Ita was determined. "Let me tell you a story," she began.

I was always eager to hear a good story. "Go ahead; I'm listening," I said encouragingly.

"I had a dream," she continued. "I was in Heaven and I met wonderful women there — valorous, righteous women who ascended to Heaven after their worthy lives on earth. There they thrilled in the glory and splendor of the Heavenly Court; they basked in the delight of being in the proximity of their Creator.

"Then I noticed a well-groomed lady in a stylish outfit. Her eyes sparkled beautifully. Why did they sparkle so? I asked. 'Because she always saw only good in people,' I was told. Her lips were incandescent, shining with rainbow colors. 'Yes,' I was told, 'that's because she spoke beautifully to audiences, extolling Hashem's Name.' She wore diamond-studded gold earrings because her ears were always attentive to others' troubles. She wore a lovely hat because her mind was always busy preparing lectures and speeches to glorify God's Name. Her hands were adorned with gorgeous rings because she gave charity with an open hand. She earned her stylish outfit by clothing the needy.

"But," I asked, "why is this great woman walking around without shoes?

"'Oh, yes,' came the answer. 'She is barefoot because she never collected donations by foot.'

"Now," Ita concluded, "do you want to walk barefoot in Heaven?"

"God forbid," I answered, touched by her story. "Ita, you got me. But make me a promise: if I go with you now, I'll wear nice shoes in Heaven."

She laughed, but I meant it. And then I recited a verse that Frau Schenirer often uttered: *B'veis Elokim nehalech be-ragesh*, "Let us walk to God's House with feeling."[28]

"Ita, do you remember how Frau Schenirer used to inter-

---

28. *Tehillim* 55:15.

pret that verse? Apart from the original translation, which she loved, she appended to it the word *tamid,* always, and added her own interpretation, based on the letters of the word *be-ragesh,* "with feeling": the *beis* stands for *barad,* hail. The *reish* stands for *ruach,* windstorm. The *gimel* stands for *geshem,* rain. And the *shin* stands for *sheleg,* snow. The point Frau Schenirer tried to impress upon us was this: whenever you visit the House of God to do any mitzvah for Him, do it in any weather: in rain, in ice, in snow, even in a blizzard like today's. And do it with feeling, with joy. Ita, we're going to do the mitzvah of collecting *tzedakah* as Frau Schenirer taught us: *in any weather.*"

I put on my knee-high boots and we went out to conquer the weather. In fact, the blizzard did not feel so terrible; it merely added color to our cheeks. The deep snow was not so bad; when one of us fell, the other picked her up. It was a great adventure. What is more, Ita was right: we found everyone at home that afternoon and collected $250, a fortune at that time. We came home exhausted but fulfilled.

"Ita," I said in admiration, "you acted like a true *talmidah* of Sarah Schenirer's today. Not only that, you also made me follow in her extraordinary ways of doing *tzedakah. Yasher koach,* may you always continue to perform acts of charity and loving-kindness in good health and with joy."

✤ Chapter 23 ✤

The recollection of one of Frau Schenirer's favorite verses, "Let us walk to God's House with feeling," reminds me of other interesting occasions when she quoted and interpreted it.

Foremost, she said it when it came time to go to shul with the girls on Shabbos and the weather was inclement. The girls, thinking it unwise to venture into the street in a winter blizzard or a heavy summer rainstorm, tried to convince Frau Schenirer to stay indoors lest she or another girl catch cold. But Frau Schenirer's determination was unswayable. Her only answer was her favorite verse, accompanied by her profound emotional interpretation of the word *be-ragesh,* "with feeling," each Hebrew letter representing a different kind of inclement weather.

"You see, girls," she explained, "King David urged us to walk to the House of God with passion — *B'veis Elokim nehalech be-ragesh* — in any kind of weather." Her purpose was to impress upon the girls the importance of praying inside a synagogue, with a *minyan,* all the time, in whatever weather. This marked a departure from the practiced custom; in Poland, young ladies did not pray in the synagogue until they were married. Again, Frau Schenirer came up with a verse for this situation, along with her own interpretation. It was *Tehillim* 122:1 — *Samachti b'omrim **li** Beis Hashem neilech,* "I rejoiced when the groom said to me, '*Harei aht mekudeshes **li**'*; I am now a married woman." Frau Schenirer interpreted, "I rejoice, because now as a married woman I will be able to pray in

151

Hashem's House with a *minyan*."

Frau Schenirer was not finished. She wanted to add a thought to the power of prayer.

"Girls, when you vacation with family or friends, or when you're in a summer camp, do you ever go into the field in the early morning? To see the wide open spaces, to observe the universe waking up after the long, dark night, singing a praise to the Almighty with faith and hope for a bright, happy day? Do you ever consider praying together with nature, joining her in her great *Hallelu-yah* to her Maker? Try it and breathe free, be overtaken by the vast space of the universe. You feel that the field, the meadow, the hills, and the river are one great House of Hashem. You hear the birds singing. You see the flowers prostrating themselves, scenting the garden. You listen to the spring whispering, the leaves swishing, the tall trees rustling. Each is praying in its own way, in its own language, to the Creator of the World. You become part of this tremendous outpour-

A Krakowian Basya group at the Bnos camp. Standing, at the far right, is their devoted Bais Yaakov teacher, Escia Teitelbaum. Neither she, nor any of these lovely girls so full of promise, survived World War II.

ing of love and gratitude to the Almighty. You feel closer to Hashem."

Now Frau Schenirer broached her innovation. Over the opposition of the married women — "We're crowded enough in shul as it is; there's no room for girls," etc. — she insisted that her students pray in shul with a *minyan*. "Never mind if a girl says, 'I can pray at home with more devotion,'" Frau Schenirer explained. "If you pray with a *minyan*, you can hear the reading of the Torah. That's even more important for women than praying. Furthermore, if you pray with a congregation, the merit of each worshiper is included in the united communal prayer. You become part of this great, meritorious service to Hashem, which our Father in Heaven loves and desires most: Jewish unity, unity among His children."

Thus, it became the custom at the seminary for the girls to accompany Sarah Schenirer to the Rema Synagogue for *Minchah* every erev Rosh Chodesh to recite the Yom Kippur Katan service with a *minyan*. Once she was there, Frau Schenirer prayed with such concentration and fervor, that she put not only her girls, but all the women present, in a Yom Kippur mood. When she repeated after the cantor, "Take us back,

The Rema Shul, Kraków.

O Lord, to Yourself, and let us come back...,"[29] her entire personality turned the prayer into an urgent plea: O Father in Heaven, have mercy on Your children, forgive their sins and help them to repent, to return to You.

After the emotional service, Frau Schenirer escorted her girls to the adjacent cemetery. There they visited the holy graves of the great rabbis of Kraków — the Rema, the Bach, the Megaleh Amukos, Rabbi Shimon Sofer, and other *tzaddikim* — reciting *Tehillim*, entreating them to plead before the Almighty on our behalf. Those days were very special events in the lives of the seminary girls — days of indelible impressions that would guide them for the rest of their lives.

---

29. *Eichah* 5:22.

Days of Awe

✣ Chapter 24 ✣

In my frequent travels between America and Israel, I make sure to spend the High Holidays in Jerusalem, the city of sanctity. There I remember what Frau Schenirer so lovingly instilled in us: that one should always try to pray with a *minyan* in shul, so that one may gain the merit of the congregation and have one's prayers answered as part of this great assembly.

My dear teacher, I thought as I arrived for the High Holidays in 1974, Hashem granted me the great privilege of being able to pray on Rosh Hashanah in His holy city, Yerushalayim, the city of peace and unity. Now, I felt a heavy responsibility to find a proper shul with a proper *minyan*. I went into the old Jewish neighborhoods of Jerusalem and searched for an old, old synagogue, where pious *tzaddikim* and great chassidim prayed in the authentic Chassidic tradition, with the sublime devotion and fervor that typify that movement.

I found such a shul in the Meah She'arim neighborhood: the Breslover *Beis Midrash*. I was graciously offered a seat among the esteemed women of the congregation, who told me that another section of the women's gallery had recently been built on the opposite side for newly observant young women, newcomers to *Chassidus*, who came to pray there. I wanted to join them. The older women discouraged and cautioned me: "It's very crowded there and they bring babies who cry. You won't get to pray in peace."

I joined the young women anyway. The overcrowding was exactly as advertised; there was not even standing room, let alone a place to sit. Women stood in the stairwell, sat on the steps, filled every spot large enough for their feet. I had also been told the truth about the crying babies, whose mothers attempted to calm them.

"Don't you have babysitters?" I asked one of them.

"No, but that's not the only reason we bring the children with us," she explained. "We want our babies to experience the praying in shul, to breathe the atmosphere of the holy place."

Dear God, I prayed. Listen to the crying of those little babies. May their innocent tears intermingle with those of the Jews who shed them while praying to You with feeling and devotion. May all those tears rise together through the always-open Gate of Tears and approach the Heavenly Court to plead with You to forgive Your people.

Then the service came to a recess before the blowing of the shofar. I looked down into the men's section to contemplate the great assembly and engrave it into my mind forever. A very pretty young woman with beautiful blue eyes stood next to me and seemed to gaze into the men's section as I did. But I was mistaken: she neither looked nor listened; with tremendous concentration, she was talking to her Father in Heaven in plain Hebrew, as a child would speak to her father.

"Oh God, forgive me," she pleaded with Hashem, "for all those years that I did not know You and did not pray to You. Oh dear Father, forgive me," she continued with a broken heart. "Almighty God, I thank You for the light You showed me. I bless You for the richness of our heritage that You exposed to me. How can I ever thank You enough for Your loving-kindness?" she cried to Hashem, tears streaming down her cheeks.

I turned away. Inadvertently I had overheard an intelligent young woman crying from the depths of her soul for having been bitterly misled in her youth. I heard a throbbing heart extolling the Almighty for His loving-kindness in showing her the right way. I was overwhelmed to have the privilege to encounter a woman with an extraordinary Jewish heart that pulsated with such love for the Master of the Universe.

The recess was over. The assemblage fell into silence — a ponderous silence in anticipation of a great event to follow. Then the *ba'al tokeya* (shofar-blower) began the blessings with such passion, such ecstasy, that the worshipers trembled in exalted awe of Hashem.

"Blessed are You, O Lord our God...for sanctifying us with the commandment of hearing the sound of the shofar."

The men stood in silence; the infants stopped crying. Only the silent sobbing of the mothers, of the women, could be heard.

The *ba'al tokeya* moved on to the second blessing. "Blessed are You, O Lord our God...Who has kept us alive" — through all those tragic years — "and proudly erect, and Who has brought us here today to this experience [of hearing the holy sound of the shofar]."

Where others might have given only lip service to this blessing, this *ba'al tokeya* delivered an outpouring of a broken Jewish heart and a pure Jewish soul, expressing his congregation's love and devotion to the Almighty. The sublime passion and sanctity of his blessings were such that I was confused for a moment: was it the heavenly voice of angels praising the Almighty, or was I listening to the saintly voice of a great human being who soared over the choir of the angels directly to the King's own Throne?

As I observed the young women at prayer, with such devotion, enthusiasm, fresh passion, and abundance of love for the Creator, I felt I could not stand next to them. I had an observation: it seemed to me that we "*frum*-from-birth" people were like "old hands" with our Father in Heaven. We already knew what the "Groom" wanted of us and we tried to satisfy His wishes and follow His commandments. He knew that we loved and believed in Him, because everything we did reflected these truths. Trusting in His love, we knew that everything He did was for our own well-being. We tried to be good, devoted brides. The young people I was witnessing, in contrast, were on a honeymoon with the Master of the Universe. Everything they did was new and exciting to them. Their every experience made them more familiar with their Groom. They studied His commandments and tried to satisfy His wishes with a love and enthusiasm that would never grow stale.

By now, the crowded women's gallery was soaked in tears and throbbed with devotion, love, and an extraordinary yearning for proximity to Hashem. Surely, I thought, the Heavenly Gates will open wide to receive their prayers and forward them directly to our Father, our King, Who will forgive our sins and, in His pity and mercy, judge us favorably.

At that moment, I recalled how Frau Schenirer had urged us to pray in shul with a *minyan*. In a congregation, she said, every worshiper's merit is included in the united communal prayer. Each individual becomes part of the great merit that the congregation earns by its devoted service of God. Thus, I prayed and hoped that my humble supplications would intermingle with the congregation's overwhelming worship and, together with their saintly prayers, would sneak through the open Gate and reach the Throne of the Heavenly Judge, to be answered according to the immense merit of this congregation.

I thanked the Master of the Universe for directing me to this extraordinary house of worship and for the tremendous inspiration I had gained on that unforgettable Rosh Hashanah. Since then, I have spared no effort every Rosh Hashanah to pray in that shul, together with those special worshipers, who to my good fortune have also become my friends.

❧ *Chapter 25* ❧

It is Rosh Chodesh Elul in Kraków; the High Holidays are approaching.

During the month of Elul, when Frau Schenirer was in town Wednesday nights, she gave the Bnos girls the weekly lecture on *"Yahadus,"* a combination of Jewish thought and halachah. *"Kinderlach,* my dear children, did you hear the shofar blowing in shul this morning?" she would begin. "This is the voice of the King of the Universe, the voice of our Father in Heaven, calling His children to come back, to return to Him. It is the voice of the *teruah,* the cry of alarm, reminding mankind of the Day of Judgment, when the future of the whole world and each creature is decided.

"All of creation stands in awe of the Almighty Judge. Every being, from man to the smallest creature, trembles in fear of the verdict. Even the fish," she emphasized, her face taking on a fear-inspiring expression, "shiver in fear of Hashem's judgment. How much more should we human beings dread the Day of Judgment! The shattering sound of the *teruah* awakens the Jewish children to repent and return to their Father, Who is so eagerly waiting to receive them.

"Yes, Hashem," she said passionately, "Your children wake up from their sleep and rush to shul before dawn, so that they may say their *selichos* [prayers of penitence] early. It is said[30] that the most propitious time for Divine favor is the very early

---

30. *Tehillim* 88.

hours of the morning. That's why Your children rush to say their penitential prayers early, very early. They pray, they cry out with broken hearts, they repent and beg their Father in Heaven to forgive their sins and help them to return to Him in love.

"Girls," she continued, now turning personally to us, "every year before the High Holidays, I implore you to remember, on those days of awe and Hashem's good will, to beseech Your Father to let you come back to Him in joy and love. Then all your prayers for mundane material needs will be satisfied anyway.

"Girls, do you remember the parable I told you last year?" she asked. We all nodded. "Still, I'd like one of you to retell that beautiful fable."

One of the most articulate girls stood up and faced the class. "Once there was a mighty king," she started, "who had a very bright and talented only son. The king taught him everything he could absorb. He was preparing his son to govern his country's greatest province and to be a benevolent, caring ruler there. The young man grew in the knowledge and wisdom that befit a promising future ruler. Unfortunately, though, he also grew in arrogance. Overconfident, he began to disobey and rebel against his father, the mighty king.

"The devoted father tried everything he could think of to persuade his beloved son to change his ways. He warned him of the unfortunate consequences of his behavior for his future. Nothing helped. The stubborn young man continued to misbehave until his father, with great regret, gave his only son some money and exiled him to a place the youngster had never seen.

"Now this young man found himself in a strange and unfamiliar land. After he used up the money, with no means of support, and after much searching, he finally found a job as a shepherd.

"He had to take care of the herd all by himself and provide it with pasture and water to drink. He followed his charges around and gave every young sheep his devoted and concerned care. In the summer, he had to do this in scorching heat; in the winter, he shivered from cold.

"The older shepherds had a hut which sheltered them from the elements, but our young man could not afford a hut. Sometimes he thought, in regret, that he could have been a prince who took care of people in pleasant and honorable surroundings. 'Instead,' he said to himself, 'I'm a poor shepherd who takes care of sheep and can't even afford a hut to shelter me from the burning summer sun and the freezing winter cold.'

"One day there came a report that the king would soon visit the area and that everyone was invited to pay homage to him. The king even promised to grant the visitors' wishes. In his desperation, our young man joined the visitors to greet the king on the day of his graciousness and good will.

"'What is your wish, young man?' the king asked as he approached him.

"'Your Majesty, I am a poor shepherd who hasn't even a hut to shade himself from the sun and the cold. Gracious king, if in your goodness you would grant me my wish for a hut, I would be forever grateful,' he concluded, prostrating himself.

"'Your wish is granted,' said the king, brokenhearted as he recognized his son. 'How sad, my son,' he thought. 'You could have asked me for permission to return to my kingdom and reclaim your glory and honor. Instead, you asked for a hut. How piteous! How disappointing!'"

The parable finished, Frau Schenirer stood up. "Thank you for telling the tale so beautifully, with all its details. Now," she turned to us, "I know you remember, but my dear children, I'd like you to recall the moral of the story, and when you are standing before the King, your Father in Heaven, on the great Day of Atonement, to remember what to pray for. You will beg your Father in Heaven to show you the most important, the most essential grace: to forgive your sins and the sins of all Jews and to redeem His suffering children at long last. To restore their bygone glory and honor. And to let them rebuild their Holy Temple, where Hashem's Presence will dwell again, this time forever.

"Dear girls! This should be your primary wish. Once it is granted, as we hope it will be, it will satisfy all our worldly needs. In the meantime, Hashem will fulfill all your mundane wishes until the great day of complete Redemption arrives, speedily, in our days."

✤ *Chapter 26* ✤

It is an old Jewish custom in Elul, when the Jews arise early in the morning to say *selichos*, that the *shamash* (sexton) arises long before dawn, circulates through the Jewish quarter, knocks on windows and shutters of Jewish homes, and rouses his congregants to rush to shul before daybreak to beg Hashem for atonement of their sins by reciting the prayers of penitence.

יידאלעך, יידאלעך
טייערע כשר׳ע יידאלעך
שטייטס אויף, שטייטס אויף
צו עבודת הבורא.
עס ווערן די שטערן
שוין שווער צו גיפינען.
שטיי אויף יידאלע
און נעם דיין פידאלע
צו שחרית גיזאנגגען.

"*Yidalech, Yidalech,*
Dear faithful Jews,
Arise from your slumber
And like a lion strong,
Run to shul to worship
Your God," he intones
In a melodious sing-song.
"The stars are fast disappearing,
Heaven's darkness is clearing.
Rush, rush, *Yidaleh*

And take your '*fiddaleh*.'
Strike its fine string,
And a praise to the
Almighty sing.
Run, *Yidaleh*,
To exalt Hashem's Glory.
Hurry, hurry."

The Jews in Kraków lived in tenements that were four or five stories tall. Therefore, the *shamash* could not knock on all the Jewish windows or shutters. To rouse the Jews for *selichos*,

קומו לעבודת הבורא...

The "Selichos klapper",
Bia'le, Poland, 1926

he could only sing loudly, clearly, and passionately. This he did.

For years I never heard the *shamash* singing; I had been fast asleep in those early hours. Once, however, I resolved to hear him. I set my alarm clock for 4:00 A.M. I answered its call, rushed to the bedroom window, and pressed my face to the pane.

I saw the street below, illuminated by tall gas lamps that cast a soft, pleasant — if dim — light. The street was quiet; there was not a living soul in sight. I waited and waited.

Then I saw him: a little old man with a long gray beard, carrying a big lantern to light his way in the poorly lit streets. I opened up the window. A cold breeze blew into the room, causing me to shiver. But the old man walked along steadily, his moving, melodious voice touching every fiber of the Jewish heart:

יידאלעך טייערע כשר'ע יידאלעך

שטייטס אויף, שטייטס אויף
צו עבודת הבורא.

Yidelach, tayere, kushere Yidelach,
Shtayts oyf, shtayts oyf, tzu avoydas ha-Boyre….

I will never forget his fervent voice, pleading, urging his fellow Jews to get up to serve, to worship their Maker.

❧ Chapter 27 ❧

Frau Schenirer's lessons before and during the High Holidays were laden with thought-provoking ideas and calls for deep soul-searching. Especially in the days between Rosh Hashanah and Yom Kippur, she repeatedly reminded us of our responsibilities to each other and our duty to love all Jews without limit and to see only the good in them. Since every Jew has some good traits, if we look only at them we will surely love all fellow Jews, and all the more our friends, classmates, and neighbors.

How attentive and watchful Frau Schenirer was in monitoring her pupils' treatment of one another. It made her very upset to hear one girl insult another. "How can a Bais Yaakov girl do that?" she would ask. "My girls love their friends; how can they hurt them?"

Then came a powerful lesson in soul-searching. "It's easy to blame someone else. It's as old as the world. The very first man, Adam, did it. When Hashem asked him why he had eaten the forbidden fruit, he answered, 'The woman You gave me made me eat it.' When the Almighty asked Chavah why she did it, she said the snake made her do it. Hashem did not accept their excuses. God created man and then took a rib from him to create woman separately, as an individual human being. He taught us that every individual is responsible for his actions and should not blame anyone else for his wrongdoings.

"We should search ourselves for the reasons for our actions," Frau Schenirer stressed. "Then we will repent and our

Father, in His loving-kindness, will forgive our sins as He forgave the sin of Adam and Chavah. But," she cautioned us, "if we insult someone or hurt him in any way, we must first ask him to forgive us before we ask the Almighty for atonement.

"Girls," she said, gazing at us intently, "this is the time to search and to ask for forgiveness from anyone whom we harmed, even in the slightest way."

Indeed, Frau Schenirer asked quite a few of her young teachers for forgiveness. "I am sorry I could not answer your letter," she told one of them. "We were very busy this month, establishing new Bais Yaakov schools out of town. I know it's an important matter, and I will try, God willing, to answer you personally while you're here during the Holidays. Please forgive me." She asked another young teacher's forgiveness in a slightly different way: "I regret not answering your important letter, but I was up this week until the early hours of the morning and had no time to answer. The infamous 'Lady Time' is keeping me from doing everything I want to do. Please forgive me; I will try to answer all your questions soon," she promised.

One Wednesday night, Frau Schenirer came to Bnos in her usual fashion to deliver her weekly *Yahadus* lesson. It was during the Ten Days of Repentance, between Rosh Hashanah and Yom Kippur. "A *gemar chasimah tovah,* girls, you should have a good inscription into the Book of Life," she greeted us with a smile, her face sparkling with joy and enthusiasm. We knew what a grueling day she had had, yet she looked as fresh and spirited as if this lesson was her first task today. Her appearance alone was a great inspiration to us.

"Girls, do you remember what we talked about before Rosh Hashanah? We discussed soul-searching, right? And we learned about the difficult task of asking forgiveness from people we might have hurt. Do you remember?" she repeated her question.

A resounding, "Yes, we remember," came the chorus in reply.

"Was it difficult?" she asked one of the girls.

"Yes, it was very, very hard," the girl admitted, "but we tried to follow your suggestions and prayed for Hashem's help."

"I am very proud of you, my dear children," Frau Schenirer said with a note of satisfaction. "Now, before Yom Kippur, we must undertake an even more difficult assignment. As Reizel admitted, it is so hard to ask forgiveness, to bend your pride, to lower yourself and beg for mercy. Now think, my girls, how much more difficult it is to wholeheartedly *forgive*.

"She insulted me in front of others, you remember. She made fun of me or she hurt me so badly that I still feel the pain. Worse still, she unethically took away my job, which I used to supplement my parents' income. How can I forgive her for besmirching my good name? By doing that, she cost me my job and may have deprived me of a chance for a *shidduch*! How can I forgive her, my teacher, when I still feel the excruciating pain of rejection and neglect that she caused me? How can I forgive? How can I forget?

"Yet, my dear *kinderlach*, we come to the Almighty Judge on the Day of Atonement and beg of Him to *selach lanu*, forgive us, for all the sins we committed against Him. *Selach lanu* for all our transgressions, our misdeeds, our omissions. We recite a long list of our sins and beg and implore our Father in Heaven to forgive us, absolve us, and allow us to atone. To forgive and forget. To turn over a new leaf and grant us good life.

"And the congregation cries out Hashem's promise three times, loud and strong: *Va-yomer Hashem, salachti kidevarecha*, 'And Hashem said, "I forgive you, according to your word"';[31] To wit: He will say 'I forgive you' after you say 'I forgive you' to others. You see, girls, we must find the courage and strength to say 'I forgive you' to others wholeheartedly. We must forgive and forget what others did to us, to turn over a new leaf, to begin a new relationship with those who hurt us. Then we can ask the Almighty to forgive us, to wipe the slate clean for the coming year, and to inscribe us for a life of close-

---

31. *Bemidbar* 14:20.

ness to our Father in Heaven. Then we may cry out Hashem's promise three times, loud and strong: 'And Hashem states, "I forgive you, as you have asked"; I will forgive you according to your having said, "I will forgive!"'

"Girls, it is not easy. It is dauntingly difficult. It requires all the strength we can muster. But we Jews are capable of attaining the towering virtue of 'to forgive and forget.'

"Before this Yom Kippur, try to achieve this greatness, a greatness befitting the daughters of the King."

❧ *Chapter 28* ☙

One year, before the Great Day of Atonement, Frau Schenirer turned to us: "My dear children, Yom Kippur is approaching, the holiest day of the year. We must prepare for the solemnity of the Yom Kippur prayers — especially Kol Nidrei, which ushers us into the great Day of Atonement just before evening.

"We walk to shul immersed in earnest thoughts of repentance, filled with deep awe for the Creator, our Father in Heaven, and confident that our ultimate Judge will judge us in mercy and loving-kindness.

"We walk through the silent streets of the town, engulfed in an atmosphere of sanctity and awe. Dressed in white, we feel like angels who neither eat nor drink but just praise and exalt the Almighty all day.

"As we enter the shul, we are overtaken by the frightfully awesome atmosphere that permeates the place. The multitude of candles and large *yahrtzeit* lamps envelop the shul in soft light, reminding our adversarial angels of the soft penetrating light of Torah that our dear children spread throughout the world with their pure, devoted learning.

"At the very beginning of the service, Hashem gives us His answer with His magnificent light: *Or zaru'a la-tzaddik u'le-yishrei lev simchah* — 'Light is sown for the righteous, radiance for the upright,'[32] God promises. The splendid eternal light will envelop the righteous and bring radiance to the pure of heart.

---

32. *Tehillim* 97.

The congregation repeats this verse several times with deep emotion, believing and trusting in the Almighty to keep His promise.

"Then, girls," Frau Schenirer continued, "the cantor chants the moving prayer, *Al da'as ha-Makom, ve-al da'as ha-kahal* three times, to make sure that, with the consent of the High Court and the earthly council, we are allowed to pray with transgressors. The congregation remains silent, digesting the idea that we should not ignore the sinners of Israel and exclude them from our prayers. If they come and wish to pray with us, we should give them the opportunity to repent. Hashem will let them atone for their sins, because the repentance of sinners sanctifies Him."

Here she presented one of her favorite examples, that of the four species. "On Sukkos, we are commanded to make a very important blessing over the four species: the *esrog*, the *lulav*, the *hadas*, and the *aravah*. "The commandment is not fully performed unless you combine all four species into one unit. Only then, by clutching the four as one entity, do you fulfill the commandment.

"Children," she stressed repeatedly, "this is an allegory of our people. The Jewish nation is one, in which all kinds of Jews are combined into one great entity, *Bnei Yisroel*. There are four species in our midst, too.

"The *esrog* [citron] is an unusual citrus fruit. With its beautiful form, scent and taste, it is likened to the great *tzaddikim*, who with the grandeur of their visage, their continual Torah study, the kindnesses they perform, and their scent of holiness, leave an important impression in this world. For ages, even in the most difficult times, Jews have sacrificed their possessions and made strenuous efforts to acquire a perfect, unblemished specimen of this fruit, in order to fulfill this great mitzvah with special joy.

"The *lulav* [palm frond], the tallest and most impressive of the species, the king of fruit trees, has no scent. However, its regal bearing reminds us of the heavy, sweet, and tasty fruit that it carries proudly. The *lulav* symbolizes the Jew who is proud of being Jewish. He, and his children — his fruits—learn Torah and savor the sweetness and delectability of the holy fruit. They bring pride to the Jewish People and glory to Hashem's Name.

"Then comes the *hadas* [myrtle], the lovely branch of fine tiny leaves that spreads a beautiful aroma but has no flavor. The *hadas* represents Jews who do not know how to learn Torah but spread a heavenly scent with their good deeds and fine character traits.

"Now we come to the *aravah* [willow branch], which has neither flavor nor scent. It has no body or will of its own; it just sways to and fro. This represents Jews who have neither Torah nor good deeds. Having no strong will of their own, they lurch from one direction to the other. Nevertheless, they are still rooted in the solid, life-giving soil of *Yiddishkeit*. Knowledgeable or ignorant, they grow near the waters of the Torah.

"We must combine the four kinds of Jews into one entity, one great Jewish nation. Only then, when we are united, will our prayers to Hashem be complete and will Hashem's blessings be showered upon us."

✒ *Chapter 29* ✒

Stay Still and Look. I remember the very interesting article under this title in *Der Israelit,* which was published weekly in Frankfurt. Frau Schenirer suggested that our leaders read it with their groups on Shabbos, so we could discuss it at the next weekly *Yahadus* lesson.

The author beautifully and skillfully expressed the idea of the importance of a moment of silence — no activity; just looking, seeing, and admiring the greatness of Hashem.

"Dear children," Frau Schenirer stressed when we discussed it in class, "you should know that this is the first and most important lesson Moshe Rabbeinu taught us: the lesson of gratitude. At the moment when our people escaped from Pharaoh, they stood in desperation between the churning sea ahead and the pursuing Egyptian army behind. They were afraid, and Moshe said, 'Do not fear. Just watch and see how Hashem fights for your well-being with love and care. When you realize this, you will be overwhelmed and full of thanksgiving to your Maker, ready to repay Him in whatever coin He requests.'

"Moshe said to his people, 'Stand by, and witness the deliverance which the Lord will perform for you today....'[33] Stand watchful and you will see Hashem's salvation of *Klal Yisroel*, the deliverance of His children. In your private lives, too, stop for a moment, look around, and observe properly what's been happening to you. You will see *hashgachah pratis*, God's per-

---

33. *Shemos* 14:13.

sonal Providence watching over you, and you will be overwhelmed with gratitude for His beneficence.

"So it is in everyday life, in everything we do," Frau Schenirer enlightened us. "Just pay attention to what other people do for you and your convenience. Be aware that someone bakes your bread and sews your clothes. Someone waters the gardens surrounding you and cleans the street on which you walk. Whatever you use was made by someone for you. Realize that you could not exist if you had to do everything yourself. When you appreciate what other people are doing for you, you will be filled with gratitude for them. You will feel like showing your appreciation by giving them a big 'thank you.'

"Girls," Frau Schenirer stressed, "every time someone does for you something personally, say 'thank you' to him. Even if he's paid for doing it, you still owe him a 'thank you.' Two words. It costs you nothing to say them, and you'll see how much it means to the recipient. What encouragement and joy it will bring to his work. Your appreciation will help him to do his job with more interest and satisfaction."

Thinking about this lesson in gratitude, I wonder how many people thank tired, hardworking waiters who try to please you at your late-night event. Believe me, those two words would do them a world of good, as they would for others who try to make your life comfortable.

I once heard Reb Yehudah Leib Orlean speak on the subject of gratitude. More than half a century after he uttered these remarks, the memory of the example he mentioned remains vivid whenever I speak about gratitude:

> Do you ever realize that you ought to be thankful to people who walk the streets? Imagine that you're walking on a deserted street at night. No one is in sight. You are frightened. How appreciative would you be now if people were in the streets?
>
> It's late at night, and you are going to *selichos* before Rosh Hashanah. It's dark. It's midnight, 1:00 A.M., 2:00

A.M. You're not afraid; people are walking to shul in all directions, like you. Did you ever think of thanking all those people just for being there at night? Yes, the passersby make you feel secure. You are relaxed. It's true even during the day. Think how you would feel if the streets were deserted. You would be scared. You would panic. Now, realize how grateful you should be to all those people out there, who let you walk fearless and calm.

What a wonderful lesson to remember.

*   *   *

I would like to end this chapter with the following lovely story: Once my daughter-in-law traveled by bus with her six-year-old daughter, Goldie, from Tel Aviv to Bnei Brak, so she could spend Shabbos with her grandparents. As they were getting off the bus, Goldie said, "*Todah rabbah*" (Thank you very much) and "*Shabbat shalom*" to the driver. A young woman who was also getting off at this stop asked the little girl, "Why did you thank the driver? Isn't it his job to drive the bus?" Goldie, without thinking it over at great length, answered simply, "I had to say 'Thank you' to the driver because he brought me safely to my grandmother's house."

Little Goldie taught this young woman and all the other passengers a great lesson in gratitude, which she had learned from her mother — who had learned it from her grandmother, a student of Frau Sarah Schenirer's. Thus Frau Schenirer transmitted her thoughts and lessons to her pupils, who will inspire all future generations.

✣ Chapter 30 ✣

At another class on the High Holidays, Frau Schenirer took up the theme in *Shemos* 14:14: *Hashem yilachem lachem ve-atem tacharishun* — "The Lord will do battle for you, but you shall remain silent!" "Girls," she said, "there is another very important thought in that verse.

"In the first, perilous steps of our nationhood, before Hashem instructed us to act — 'Go forward!'[34] — He commanded us to 'remain silent.' He taught us a great truth in life: stay still, just concentrate and reflect. *Then* act, go forward. There is a moment for silence, a time for reflection, an important, significant time, before you act.

"Yes, *kinderlach*," she continued, flashing a smile laden with significance, "there is a time for *action*. 'Teach us to count our days rightly.'[35] Perform your Jewish duties every hour, every minute of the day.

"But you should know that there are other moments, weighty, active moments, of *silence* in a day. They are times of *cheshbon ha-nefesh,* of inner reckoning, when you take out your treasure chest; count your days, hours, and minutes; and reflect on your actions and resolve to do better the next day.

"Girls," she said, "when you go to sleep at night after a tiring day, you relax. It's quiet. You are alone with yourself and the truth. Try then to catch a few minutes of your time and do

---

34. Ibid., verse 15.
35. *Tehillim* 90:12.

your *cheshbon ha-nefesh*."

What an impression her soft-spoken but forceful words had on us. I felt the urgency of her plea as she repeated, "Remember, if it's a few minutes, a quarter of an hour, an hour, or whatever you spend on it, do your daily reckoning. Think about your day and how you filled it. Make it a habit, and you will see how much happier your next day will be."

She continued her inspirational lecture with another thought-provoking idea:

"Hashem gave us a whole week to act, to do our mundane work, and then He granted us a day of rest, Shabbos, on which to do our spiritual work; to learn, to teach, to spend time educating the children, to sing and pray, to worship Hashem and seriously recount our weekly activities. But He also gave us special days of reflection, of *cheshbon ha-nefesh*.

"Such a day is Rosh Hashanah. The Day of Judgment brims with moments when we are commanded to stay still and do nothing. We may not even learn or pray. We must only stand in awe, listening to and understanding the compelling sound of the shofar, urging us to return to our Father in Heaven. Those are precious moments of reflection, of reckoning, of thanksgiving, and of resolve.

"He also gave us the great day of Yom Kippur, when we do absolutely nothing. We don't eat, we don't drink, we don't even wear shoes. We just pray, begging and imploring our Maker to forgive us. We just *listen* to the voice of the *chazan*, representing us before the Almighty Judge, pleading and vouching for us. Most of all, we *listen* to the whispering of our own hearts, broken and sincere. Twenty-five hours of nothing but reflection, of *cheshbon ha-nefesh*."

May Hashem help us to count our days rightly, *limnos yameinu, kein hoda* — so that we will know.

Chessed and Its Far-Reaching Effects

✥ *Chapter 31* ✥

Frau Schenirer taught the girls to enunciate and understand their prayers. Once she tested them in translating the High Holiday prayers into Yiddish. Satisfied with the outcome, she asked, "Girls, who knows some of them by heart?"

Chavah Tauber, one of the students whom Frau Schenirer highly admired — an intelligent girl known for her extraordinary memory — raised her hand. Acknowledged, she stood up and recited the entire Rosh Hashanah service by heart. Frau Schenirer was proud of her beloved pupil, but disapproved of her overconfidence and reproached her strongly for it. However, her rebuke was soft, as usual, and this time it came with a bit of slang: "Chavahleh, don't be a *knakker* [a cute Yiddish word that denotes a "big shot"]; recite your prayers from the *Machzor* like everybody else."

Chavah admired and respected Frau Schenirer profoundly, as only the most devoted student could. People used to call her Frau Schenirer's *chassidah*, her "disciple." She loved her teacher and always tried to emulate her. She took a special interest in the downtrodden. People about whom others did not care, people who were neglected, people who did not get the attention, respect, or appreciation that they deserved — these were *her* "disciples." If a capable and knowledgeable teacher was eclipsed by a newcomer who was more attractive, more charming, and more admired by the girls, she took the underdog's side — showed her more love, took more interest in her, and inveighed upon the students to appreciate her vast knowledge and capabilities and give her more attention. Chavah treated her classmates the same way, always boosting the morale of any girl who felt left out. She behaved the same way in Auschwitz, always showering others with encouragement and hope.[36]

*   *   *

We have already noted that Frau Schenirer loved to listen to her girls singing solo. Chavah, besides her other talents, had a beautiful voice. Frau Schenirer liked to seat Chavah next to her and ask her to sing her favorite songs, which were usually Biblical verses set to music. Chavah knew what her teacher liked best and rendered them with their lovely melodies and the fullness of their meaning and emotions. Once she sang *Tehillim* 94:18, a verse they both adored: *Im amarti matah ragli chasdecha Hashem yis'adeini,* "When I think my foot has collapsed, Your kindness, O Lord, supports me." Frau Schenirer beamed with pleasure at the sound of it.

"When you see that you're giving way," she explained, "be aware that Hashem, in His loving-kindness, will support you." Indeed, Chavah knew this song very well and sang it through all her life — to herself and to others. In the most trying times in Auschwitz, when she felt herself giving way, the words of the song she had sung to her revered teacher reverberated in her ears loud and clear. "Don't despair; Hashem will support you soon, very soon. Just hang on a little longer and don't lose hope."

During these most trying years, she sang the verse to her campmates. "Don't give up!" she kept encouraging the walking skeletons. "You think you've reached your nadir, that you can-

---

36. Chavah was also the first one to notice Soviet troops approaching the camp, dressed in white camouflage uniforms to avoid being spotted on snow-covered ground. "Girls, get up," she said. "The liberation is coming. We will be freed today." Then she cried out in strong, clear tones, "This is the day that the Lord has made — let us exult and rejoice in it" [*Tehillim* 118:24].

not fall any deeper, that you have come to the end of your endurance. Don't despair, don't lose hope. Hashem, in His mercy, will support you. Hold on a little longer, and with His help you'll soon see the light at the end of the tunnel."

All her life Chavah gave people advice in coping with their problems, her wisdom and faith encouraging them in times of distress. After the war, I met her again in Jerusalem and visited her at her home on Bar Giora Street.

I visited Chavah whenever I was in Jerusalem. I loved every visit — her company, her wit, her keen remarks, her interesting stories, and her reminiscences of the bygone times at Bais Yaakov. She usually had company when I came; sometimes someone was even waiting his turn. People from all walks of life approached her for advice. Many asked for help in solving their woes; others sought answers in their confusion about faith or other life problems. Still others expected her to provide wise answers that would liberate them and clear their minds of doubts.

Somehow, she had advice and encouragement for everyone. Wherever possible, she also offered practical assistance. I have seen people enter her home in distress and exit relaxed and relieved. I do not know how she did it, but it reminded me of our teacher, Sarah Schenirer, who helped people in need and distress with that "special touch."

I recall a story told by Reb Binyamin Süssman (the father of my friend Sarah), who was very devoted to Bais Yaakov and close to Frau Schenirer. "It was shortly before Passover," he began. "Frau Schenirer came running to my house late in the evening. She did not have time to sit down; she just laid some money on the table and asked me to do her a big favor.

"'There's an important man in our community who's had a financial failure and needs help desperately. Please slip the money into his coat pocket when he stands up for *Shemoneh Esrei*, so he will not know who put it there. I know you'll have to disturb your own prayers to do it, but Hashem will surely forgive you, considering the great deed you are doing, helping to put this man on his feet again.'"

One of the girls at the seminary told me a similar story. Once, during a class with Sarah Schenirer, a fashionably dressed young man, a total stranger, ran into the classroom in severe distress. He came right up to our dear teacher and, tears pouring down his cheeks, begged, "Frau Schenirer, please come and help me. My child is very sick. The doctors have already given up on him. Only God Almighty can help him recover. Please come with me," he implored, crying bitterly, "and pray at the grave of the saintly Rema, which you do so often, and ask that great sage to plead with Heaven to heal my child."

Frau Schenirer did not think twice. "May Hashem give me strength," she prayed, "to help this poor man." She excused herself from the girls. "Sorry, I know you'll understand," she said. "I must go to help this man. Review your lessons and continue on your own with whatever you can. I will see you soon, God willing, but in the meantime, pray with me for the recovery of this child." Thus, as important as her classes were, she set her work aside to help a stranger in trouble.

All through the years, up until she passed away, we always found Chavah, Sarah Schenirer's true disciple, emulating her revered teacher's way of helping people in need and distress, regardless of their identity and origin.

❧ *Chapter 32* ❧

Frau Schenirer loved people, all people, whether they were committed Jews or not. She gave her attention, time, and financial assistance to anyone who asked.

I once had a problem with a girl in my Bnos group — a bright, intelligent youngster who, although from a non-affiliated home, took an interest in her Jewish heritage. She yearned to grow in Jewish knowledge and, in her eagerness to learn, bubbled with questions. She required more attention than the other girls, and I apportioned my time accordingly. It was a pleasure to discuss and answer her intelligent inquiries, and I was pleased to observe her growth in Jewish knowledge and commitment to mitzvos and Jewish law.

This, of course, made the other girls in the group jealous. They wanted me to minimize the attention I gave her. They told me the following: "She can't stay in Bnos forever. There'll come a time when she'll have to get married. *Frum* boys demand a dowry from the girl's parents, and her parents will never agree to that. They'll ask her to meet nonreligious boys who won't demand a dowry. So we'll lose her to *Yiddishkeit* anyway. You're just wasting your time with her," they reasoned.

I consulted Frau Schenirer for her opinion and advice on how to handle the situation. Frau Schenirer listened attentively as I described this girl and the other girls' arguments. I finished my story and waited for an answer. After a moment of silence, she replied with her usual vigor: "Let me tell you a little story about a simple kerosene lamp.

"It's a small lamp with a tall glass chimney, a hurricane lamp. The wick burns and produces soot. The more it burns, the more soot accumulates in the chimney glass. The tube turns black. You look at it and you see no flame in it, just darkness. But if you remove, clean, and polish the chimney, you'll see what a beautiful flame shines through the glass.

"The same is true about a human being. We live in a world that produces an awful lot of soot and dirt. It attacks one's innermost being and blackens one's clear surface. All we can see is darkness, blackness.

"But you should know that a little flame burns inside every human being. We just have to clean the surface lovingly. Once you scrub off the black soot and dirt that accumulated there, you'll see the flame of Godliness shining through.

"It is our responsibility to do this for our children, our youth. We must educate them to be aware of their God-given mantle of glory and splendor. We must pursue our calling with compassion and loving care, so that our girls will stand up proudly and be happy to perform their duties as Jewish daughters.

"Don't spare any effort to do the job properly! Some glass surfaces are darker than others; they require more time, more attention, to clean and polish. Don't worry about the outcome. We don't know how our labors will affect a person. We don't know when they will touch his soul and what consequences they will have for his future. We have to do our share; the rest is up to the Almighty. Only He knows the effects that our efforts will have. But be confident that your labor is not in vain; it will yield results.

"So go, my child, continue doing your duty, and may Hashem bless your efforts."

❧ *Chapter 33* ❧

The Nazis liquidated the Tarnów ghetto on September 3, 1943. Having accomplished this, they employed a different scheme to annihilate the 10,000 ghetto inhabitants who were still living. They loaded them into boxcars on the pretext of transporting them to labor camps. As it later transpired, the cars never left the Tarnów vicinity. Instead, the Nazis placed deadly chemicals inside them and sealed the doors and windows tightly. The fumes killed everyone aboard.

Thus the thriving and beautiful Jewish community of Tarnów — leaders, rabbis, scholars, professionals, the young and the old, and our precious children, everyone who had been interned in Ghetto B — met its demise.

Some two thousand Jews who worked in Madritch's Tarnów factory, myself among them, were left on the square under the supervision of Tich, Madritch's assistant, to make sure that we would be transported back to the Plaszów camp and continue to work in Madritch's factory. After waiting in the square for two days, we, the fortunate few who had been selected for life, were marched five abreast to the railroad station, accompanied by shouting two-legged beasts and barking four-legged dogs.

However, we had a problem. One woman in our column had concealed a little boy under her trenchcoat. Luckily, we successfully passed Amon Göth, the experienced liquidator, who busily pulled women with suspicious rucksacks or bulges out of the ranks and withdrew the poor youngsters to satisfy his lust for

Jewish children's blood. The rest of us safely headed for the waiting boxcars, in which we were tightly packed at about 120 to a car. The cars were locked. Although we nearly suffocated inside, we were pleased to have the chance to save the mother and her child.

Suddenly, the door of our car was opened and there on the steps stood Göth.

"Where's the boy?" he roared. "Mother and child, out!" he screamed, his face red with hatred. "Where's the boy?" he repeated. "If you don't hand him over I'll shoot you all!"

"There's no child here," someone dared to say.

"I saw him entering the car," retorted Göth in a rage. "I'll blow up the car if you don't hand him over at once."

He was capable of it, we all knew. Most of us had already been in the Plaszów camp before, where we had often seen him exact collective punishment.

Trembling with fear, I looked around to observe the others' reactions. My partners in the boxcar were all young, all lucky to be chosen to live. I observed the concerned faces of my friends, my campmates, and I scanned the many unfamiliar faces. They came from all walks of life, and from different kinds of schooling, upbringing, and religious and political orientations.

"Move out with the boy," Göth barked, fuming. "I'll kill you all, you smugglers, you dirty pigs."

He was determined, but so were we. We pressed together into a large knot of bodies, its one tremendous heart pulsating with love. Nobody moved forward, nobody said a word, nobody betrayed the boy. Nobody among 120 people.

We had one great thing in common: we were all Jews. The little flame of Godliness that flickers in each Jewish heart roars to the surface at crucial moments and radiates loving-kindness and mutual responsibility. Now, all the people in that boxcar were ready to sacrifice their lives, which had just been granted to them, to save *one Jewish child.*

In the suffocating blackness of that boxcar, my heart's eye could see a brilliant light, aglow with 120 flames, blazing against the profound benightedness of man's animal side, his unbridled killer instinct, his unquenchable thirst for human blood.

Indeed, the beast did not give up. Desperate to lay hands on mother and child, he ordered his adjutant to climb into the boxcar and seize them. Brutally the SS thug shoved us to one side of the car, made us cross to the other side one by one, and scrutinized us, lest we were concealing the wanted boy. Eventually no more shelterers were left. Triumphantly the SS man seized these great enemies of the Third Reich, a helpless woman and her son, who trembled with fear as he tendered them to his boss, Göth.

Göth stood on the steps, an arrogant smile of victory on his lips. "I told you the Jews are smugglers. I saw them smuggling that kid into the car," the beast of beasts remarked as he kicked the victims down the boxcar steps.

Again the doors were sealed tightly. Again darkness and utter silence reigned inside. Instead of hopes for a miracle, we heard two terrifying gunshots — one for the smuggler-mother and one for the "nefarious" little boy.

Nobody spoke. There were no words of consolation. We all felt the gnawing pain of helplessness. That massive body of humanity was heartbroken and deeply wounded. More than a hundred people, ready to sacrifice their young lives on the altar of love and responsibility, could not save even one Jewish child.

How painful, how sad.

Even then, having seen evil triumph, I was proud to be part of this wretched, tortured, yet great and noble people.

❧ *Chapter 34* ❧

I usually spend the High Holidays in Israel. The atmosphere, even the air, of *Eretz ha-Kodesh*, the Holy Land, elevates a Jew spiritually and makes him feel closer to Hashem. There it is easier to communicate with Him, to talk to Him in one's own language, to pour out one's heart, to beg, to implore, even just to ask. We Holocaust survivors have much to ask for — and much to be thankful for.

It was the night after Yom Kippur 1983 and I was in Israel when I received exciting news from New York: my grandson had just been born. What a great feeling it was to become a grandmother again. Only another grandmother can fully appreciate the feeling of joy and gratitude to the Creator for granting her another miracle of life. Holocaust survivor grandmothers, who had often stared death in the face, who were fed chemicals in their watery soup to destroy their reproductive facilities, can best value the marvelous gift of motherhood — and grandmotherhood — that God has bestowed upon them.

Who would have imagined while laying on a dirt floor in Bergen-Belsen, gripped by typhus, burning with fever, dying of thirst, that one could live through that hell; become a normal human being; marry; and bear children?

But a miracle happened. I and others recovered. God blew a spark of life into our desiccated bodies. We began to breathe, walk, live. We fanned the spark into a flame of hope. We planned for the future and encouraged others to do the same. Wonder of wonders: the dry bones acquired a mantle of flesh

192

and began to look like human beings again. They married. And they bore children. Their lonely world became alive with children, their own children, Jewish children. O, God, Jewish children!

Becoming a mother is the greatest joy in life, especially for people whose lives are devoid of loved ones, family, and relatives. What a joy it is to have a child, somebody of *one's own,* someone to love, to care for, to teach, to rear, to enjoy, and to *shep nachas* from.

We sing Hallel to the Almighty not only on Rosh Chodesh and festivals, but every day of the week. We bless Hashem and exalt Him for enabling us again to fill the *yeshivos* and Bais Yaakov schools with our children. We see them grow into adulthood, treading their parents' path with joy. They become wonderful human beings. They build their own lives, start their own families, and bear children of their own. Thus, joy of joys, we become grandparents.

Baruch Hashem, another grandchild was born that night, after Yom Kippur — another soul to love, hug, enjoy, worry about, and pray for. The excitement for this grandson was the same as with the first.

The *bris* was scheduled for the morning of the first day of *Chol ha-Mo'ed Sukkos.* To be able to attend, I rushed to make arrangements for my flight to New York. Two days before Sukkos, I boarded the Tower Air plane on my way to the happy occasion.

The beginning of the flight was pleasant and relaxing. Then, suddenly, I heard the captain announce over the loudspeaker, "We are sorry, but due to technical difficulties we have to make an emergency landing in Hamburg, Germany. Keep calm, everything will be all right. We will do our best to minimize your discomfort." Some people showed signs of panic, but the crew tried to put us at ease, explaining, "There is a crack in the windshield. The window must be replaced. You will soon be able to reboard the plane and continue to New York."

After landing, we were advised to leave the plane and take

our belongings and a blanket. We were directed to the waiting room of the airport, which was large enough to accommodate everyone aboard our aircraft — more than three hundred passengers. People tried to settle in comfortably for the wait. Before I could relax, however, I wished to understand the situation in greater detail. The woman who had booked me for the flight had been on the plane. I looked for her but could not find her or any other member of the crew. There was nobody to answer questions, to explain matters, to offer assistance.

It being late at night, the cafeteria was closed. We had neither food nor drink. We spent the night unescorted. Finally, in the early hours of the morning, the airline's German representative showed up and apologized for the inconvenience. "The cafeteria will open in a couple of hours, at eight. You'll be able to get coffee and a snack. Whatever you choose."

How generous!

Eight o'clock finally came. The cafeteria opened; the passengers queued for coffee. I overheard anti-Semitic remarks about Jews, about Israelis. I saw sneers on the faces of early-rising German travelers who came to the airport to catch their planes. I was back in Germany. Decades after their defeat, they still treated us as ugly Jews.

O, God! Of all places in Europe, did our emergency landing have to take place in Germany? I had promised myself never to step on German soil again. But since Providence had brought me here, there must have been a reason. Then I understood: Providence wanted me to see the same hatred on the Germans' faces that I once saw, to witness the same Germany, the same Germans, the same anti-Semitism, the same ugly enmity. Providence meant to remind me: "Germany has not changed and never will."

No matter how thirsty and tired I was, I could not make myself queue up on German soil for a cup of coffee. What painful recollections the very idea brought to mind! Only due to my husband's foresight did I not experience serious hunger. He never let me travel without sandwiches and fruit. "You never know what can happen," he insisted. Now I was refreshed by the food he had so lovingly packed in my carry-on before I left. What is more, that food sustained several other passengers who otherwise would have gone hungry, as they too did not want to eat the snacks in the cafeteria.

Several hours later, the airline's German representative came back. The passengers delegated a young man to speak with him. He did not have good news for us. "So far, I got no information from the Tower Air office about replacing the windshield window or the plane. Let's be patient. I'll tell them to inform us of any new developments," he assured us.

I did not like this information, and expected no "developments" that would allow me to reach home before the holiday. Determined to leave Germany quickly and be home in time for Sukkos, I approached every airline in the airport to determine which were flying to New York. After much searching, I found a Pan American flight leaving at two o'clock that afternoon. I described my predicament to the woman at the desk and asked her to save one seat for me. She told me that there were seventy seats available and instructed me to report half an hour before boarding with whoever wished to use her airline to get to New York.

I was overjoyed, and grateful to Hashem for the *hashgachah pratis* that would allow me to reach New York in time for the festival. I went back to my co-travelers in a relaxed frame of mind, knowing that I had a chance to complete my trip in time, albeit at a double fare.

Shortly before one o'clock, the Tower Air representative showed up. "I am sorry to inform you," he said with typical German coldness and indifference that I remembered so well, "that you will not be able to travel today. I made all necessary arrangements for your accommodations in a fine hotel. I also asked the Jewish community of Hamburg to provide you with kosher food for the festival and a *sukkah* for those who will require it. We regret the inconvenience, but under the circumstances this is the best we can do to minimize your discomfort."

Our liaison translated his oration into Hebrew.

There was no reaction from the crowd. Realizing that I could not depend on the young delegate to represent us, I asked for the floor and turned to the German agent. "I know there are seventy vacant seats on a Pan Am flight to New York that is leaving an hour from now. There are forty Sabbath observers among us, who are not satisfied with your arrangement and must be home for the festival. Besides, I am rushing home for the circumcision of my grandchild. I suggest that the forty Sabbath observers, women with small children, and other urgent cases fill the available seats — at your airline's expense." I waited while my request was translated into Hebrew for all the passengers to hear.

The agent countered me. "I am not allowed to do that. I am responsible for all the passengers. I cannot accommodate just seventy people. What about the rest? They will all attack me. Nobody wants to give up his chance for a seat for someone else's convenience. Lady, I am not looking for trouble." He finished with a note of finality.

"Sir," I persevered, "let me talk to the people. Maybe I can convince them to go along with my plan." He laughed, "You should know, in my many years of experience I have never seen that kind of cooperation among so many travelers in a case like this. I wish you luck," he concluded, sneering.

I turned to the crowd: "Dear fellow travelers, as you heard, our plane will not leave today and I doubt that it will leave tomorrow. The Sukkos festival begins tonight. Some of us are Shabbos observers who will not travel tonight or tomorrow, or the next day. We will be stranded and unable to celebrate the festival properly. We need kosher food, a shul, and a *sukkah*. Furthermore, all of these must be within walking distance, because we cannot travel on the festival.

"On top of it all, I have a special problem. I am traveling, thank God, to the *bris* of my grandchild, which I would not miss for any amount of money in the world. Every one of you knows and can understand the joy and gratitude a grandmother feels upon the birth of a grandchild. Especially we Holocaust survivors, who saw our precious children being thrown like rag dolls into black trucks on the way to Auschwitz; we, who after the liberation raced about, nearly insane, combing the camps for children, Jewish children, and unable to find any because all of them, one and a half million Jewish children, had been tortured, killed and gassed. We survived in an empty world, a world without parents, children, and grandchildren.

"Then, miraculously God revived our people and filled our world with children, Jewish children, and then grandchildren. Many of you here are children or grandchildren of survivors. We are all survivors of the great Jewish tragedy. We all feel the joy of rebirth of our nation, the joy of every Jewish child born.

"You heard me presenting my plan to the airline's representative. Now, I am presenting it to you, my People, for consideration." Our liaison translated my appeal into Hebrew, though many of those present understood English. Sensing a friendly reaction, I turned to the audience again. "Please, would anyone who opposes my plan kindly raise his hand?" I waited for a weighty moment. Not one hand was raised. Thrilled, I continued. "Thank you, my fellow Jews, for not letting me down — first, for your understanding and warm consideration of our predicament and your positive reaction. Second, and more important, for justifying my profound belief in the greatness of my People. And third, most important, for demonstrating to others: 'Yes, we are different.'

"It is late. We have to make the two o'clock plane, but I must tell you a little story." The story I told them was that of the boxcar that carried more than one hundred people who were ready to sacrifice their lives to save one Jewish child.

"My dear fellow Jews, know that there is a little flame of Godliness in each of us. Sometimes it lies dormant and invisible for a while. But when Jews are in danger or in dire need, it surfaces and shines brightly for all to see. A Jew, any Jew, every Jew, is willing to sacrifice his convenience and sometimes his life to save or help a fellow Jew. I am proud of you, my dear ones. May God bless you all. We are all *Bnei Yisroel,* the favored children of the Almighty."

*   *   *

We made the Pan Am flight and landed at Kennedy Airport an hour before sundown. It being our "good fortune" to have no luggage to claim, we rushed home and arrived just before the festival.

On Sunday morning, I proudly attended the *bris* of my new grandson, who was named after his great-grandfather, Yechiel Menachem.

May he grow up to become the Menachem, the comforter, of *Klal Yisroel*, the Jewish People at large — and its pride.

Setting the Stage for Bais Yaakov's Prolific Growth

❦ Chapter 35 ❧

At the same time that Zionism was gaining popularity, the ideas of socialism and communism were pouring in from Russia.

The strong current of these ideas flooded the fertile soil of impoverished Poland. Jewish youth, too, were influenced by their slogans. "We want to bring peace to the world," the Communists proclaimed, "to ease the anguish of the needy, to rescue the starving masses. No child should cry for bread; no man should walk in tatters. We want equality and justice for all."

Who were the first to join the Communist organizations? Orthodox youth, of course. Who else had been raised to feel the anguish of the needy? Who else had been shown by their parents to feed the hungry and to open their homes and hearts to the dejected? Those humanitarian slogans could not but appeal to teenagers who had been brought up to practice loving-kindness. Thus, unfortunately, many of our precious children fell victims to these treacherous and Godless ideas.

An agonized Frau Schenirer responded: "If only I could open their eyes and show them the truth! There can be no justice without fear of God. The needy cannot be helped, the hungry fed, the dejected cared for, without belief in Hashem. He is the source of loving-kindness. He cares for all His creatures and meets all their needs. Only by emulating the Creator can we bring true peace and justice to the world."

But the young people, already attracted to the false ideas, were deaf to her cries for truth. To be fair, however, it was not

201

easy for those young Jewish girls to withstand the tremendous external pressure. It was very hard to be a Jewish girl in Kraków at that time.

Jewish girls attended Polish public schools, there being no Jewish day schools for girls in Poland. A post-World War I baby boom was under way; the schools were overcrowded. The Kraków board of education made girls attend school in two shifts — one from eight o'clock in the morning to one in the afternoon, the other from two to seven in the evening.

I was assigned to the afternoon shift. As my classmates and I walked down the wide steps of our school on Sebastiana Street every evening, young people from a broad variety of organizations lined the way on both sides, bombarding us with temptations to join their respective movements — Zionist, Socialist, Communist. Each offered the most exciting ideas, the most interesting programs and activities, and great co-ed entertainment.

We were between twelve and fourteen years of age. It was no simple matter to resist the agitators' crushing pressure, remain true to our own ideals, and adhere to our parents' teachings.

Frau Schenirer could not deliver her timely message to the masses of Jewish youth who had come under the spell of the false idea of Communism.

From the 1920s on, poverty was on the rise in Poland, especially in large industrial cities, to where young people from small towns were streaming in large numbers in search of work. Poland could not cope with its own economic woes, let alone those of its poor. Much of Polish Jewry, too, suffered from hunger and need.

Self-help — *tzedakah* (financial aid) and *gemilus chessed* (acts of kindness), delivered with love and compassion — is a hallmark of the Jews. Individual Jews extended themselves in various ways to care for others. Members of shuls tried to help needy members make ends meet. *Tzedakah* and *gemilus chessed* organizations toiled away. Our Bnos girls had their own *tzedakah* association and worked hard to cook and deliver meals to the hospitalized and the needy.

One of the Bnos girls, Sarah Luftglass (later Bodner), worked hard to support herself. An orphan, she was loathe to accept help from relatives or friends. Just the same, she spent her every spare moment collecting meals and — one struggles to imagine it today — pieces of challah to distribute to the poor for Shabbos. She lugged a heavy bag from door to door, begging for a donation of a piece of challah or a slice of cake.

However, none of it sufficed to elevate the standard of living of the poor or even to make them more comfortable.

Teenagers and young adults composed songs that portrayed the pitiful situation and sang them with passion. Unemployed young men tried to earn a few zlotys by performing those songs in the large tenement courtyards, accompanied by a guitar and, in some cases, a parrot in a cage. Each performer had a young child in tow. As the jobless sang and played with deep emotion, the children collected such coins as good-hearted Jewish women threw from their windows.

The most popular song at the time, portraying the bitter poverty that gripped much of Polish Jewry, follows:

אין א קלײנעם בוידעם שטיבל
פון אלע זײטן בלאזט דער װינט
אינעם װינקל אויפן שטרוי זאק
ליגט דאס בלאסע קראנקע קינד

און דערנעבן שטייט די מאמע
שלינגט א טרער נאך טרער
זאג מיר קינד מיינס ליבעס טײערעס
זאג מיר װאס איז דיין באגער

איך האב געזען װי אנדערע קינדער
אויפן פלאץ פון מאגיסטראט
האבן זיי געגעסען קיכלעך
און אזוי פיל טשאקאלאד

אוי מיין מאמע טײערע מאמע
איך בין פון טרוקן ברויט שוין זאט

גיב מיר מאמע ליבע טייערע
כאטש א שטיקל טשאקאלאד

ווען דער טאטע וועט געלט פארדינען
געלט פארדינען גאר אסך
וועט ער טשאקאלאד דיר קויפן
און דיר בויען א פאלאץ

*　　　*　　　*

אינעם קליינעם בוידעם שטיבל
פון אלע זייטן בלאזט דער ווינט
אינעם ווינקל אויפן שטרוי זאק
רואיק שלאפט דאס קראנקע קינד

א פאלאץ פון טשאקאלאד
דערנעבען פון באמבאנעס א בוים
אויפן פנים מיט א גליקלעך שמייכל
זעט דאס קינד אין לעצטן טרוים

In a little attic hovel
From all sides the wind
Blows wild.
In the corner on a straw bed
Shivering, lies a sick
pale child.

At his bedside stays his mother
Painfully swallows tear after tear.
"Tell me, my son, what does bother,
What does trouble you, my dear?"

"I have seen many little children,
Playing in the Town Hall Square,
Eating chocolate and cookies,
Licking lollipops up there.

"O! My Mother, my dear Mother
Of dry bread I am full, quite.
Give me, Mother, if once only,
Of chocolate a little bite."

"As soon as your father finds work,

And earns money, quite a bit,
He will build you a mansion,
Not from bricks but from chocolate."

*   *   *

In a little attic hovel
From all sides the wind
Blows wild.
In the corner on a straw bed
Peacefully sleeps a little child.

A gorgeous house of chocolate
An imposing roof, topped with cream,
Sees the smiling little youngster
In his final, blissful dream.

*   *   *

Many young intelligent Jews who were raised in Orthodox homes joined the Communist organization in Kraków and elsewhere in Poland — a movement that the government had outlawed. Driven by their sensitivity to the plight of the suffering masses, they became Communist activists, so eager to ease the pain of the impoverished that they even risked arrest.

I often visited the home of a good friend who was also a renowned Bnos leader. Sometimes, mostly on Jewish festivals, I found her oldest sister there — a charming, beautiful, and very intelligent girl who, unfortunately, got involved in the Communist organization and became its leader and its main activist. She traveled all over Poland, preaching in towns and cities about the Communist idea and the great salvation it would bring to the needy. To avoid hurting her parents, whom she loved and highly respected, she never spoke in Kraków. She visited Kraków only to spend Jewish festivals with her family. On those occasions, I enjoyed speaking with her and probing her mind.

"I am doing what I was taught and saw in my parents' home. I am emulating the compassion and loving-kindness that they give the impoverished," she explained, defending her actions. "We are trying to bring the idea of communal life to the masses. Possessions should be apportioned equally among all. There should be no more poor or rich. We wish to free the world of poverty and hunger and to bring joy and happiness to humanity, the whole world, all people."

"Yes, my dear friend," I countered. "You are trying to save the whole world, but you begin by destroying the happiness of your family, causing them pain and distress. Day and night they worry about your safety, knowing the danger that you face, constantly hunted by the police. Think about it."

One wintry Friday night, after the Shabbos meal, I heard a knock at my door. "Open up. Police," an official sounding voice ordered. I opened the door and faced two policemen. "Which apartment does Shymek G. live in? Here, or one floor up?" they asked.

My heart skipped a beat. Intelligent, well-liked Shymek was the only child of the prestigious G. family. What do they need him for? I thought. I mumbled that he didn't live in our apartment. I left the door open to see what would happen. As I heard their heavy bootsteps going up the stairs, I waited and worried. And hoped, for Shymek seemed to be busy of late and was often absent from home.

Now I looked on in terror as the policemen led Shymek down the stairs in handcuffs. A moment later, I heard light footsteps: Shymek's mother, running down the steps with a warm blanket over her arm.

"Please," she begged the policemen, "let him take this." They refused. "Please," she entreated the older policeman, tears in her eyes, "he'll be cold in this freezing weather. Please have pity *on me!*"

The older policeman, observing the motherly love and concern on Mrs. G.'s face, finally relented and took the blanket from her.

I could not take listening to this tragic scene anymore. Not

wishing to face Shymek's mother and thus compound her agony and distress, I closed the door.

Thus the Jewish People lost another youth, the only child of
a prestigious religious family, another victim of the Communist
lie. How devastating, how painful.

❧ Chapter 36 ❧

Unlike the Communist movement, the Socialist movement was legal in Poland. Its organization strove to force the government to establish basic rules that would ease the plight of working people. Exploitation of workers was real and widespread. The eight-hour workday existed on paper only. People were expected to work all week long, with an occasional Sunday off. National health insurance and social insurance did not exist at all.

As time passed, the Socialists secured several entitlements for members of their unions: an eight-hour workday, a six-day week with Sunday off, and the *Kasa Chorych,* a health insurance program of sorts.

None of these benefits, of course, convinced Orthodox Jewish workers to consider joining the Socialist Party. Thus, in 1922, they established their own organization under the auspices of Agudath Israel: Po'alei Agudath Israel, "Workers of Agudath Israel," also known by its initials, PAI. Many serious young members of the Agudah, understanding the plight of the religious worker, joined the new organization and offered it all possible assistance.

Reb Yehudah Leib Orlean was one of the founders of this important movement. What is more, after it was up and running, he became its ideologue. He wrote a tract called *Tzu Zate und Tzu Hungerike* (To the Satiated and the Hungry) that argued the case of Jewish workers' rights in view of halachah. Reb Yehudah Leib wrote in anguish about the plight of the religious Jewish worker, who not only shared the problems of the

208

Reb Yehudah Leib Orlean, one of the founders of Po'alei Agudath Israel and director of the Bais Yaakov Seminary in Kraków.

working class but had a particularly severe quandary of his own: *shemiras Shabbos.*

Major Orthodox leaders, wealthy manufacturers who employed thousands of workers who had formed strong unions, were loathe to accept religious workers who refused to work on Shabbos. They sold their businesses to a gentile for Shabbos with a special — and controversial — *shtar mechirah* ("bill of sale") so they could operate their factories on Shabbos. "Since our workers have to work on Saturday, so should the Jewish workers work also," the Socialist unions argued.

PAI took up their cause, foremost in large cities such as Warsaw and Lodz (the country's largest industrial towns), and in smaller industrial centers as well. Activists in the new movement worked hard to encourage large manufacturers to employ Orthodox workers. "They are eager, capable, and proud young people who'll do any kind of work. Just give them a chance," they pleaded vehemently. The activists themselves, dedicated, idealistic, and energetic, were not ashamed to do manual labor such as housepainting and construction; proudly they carried their tools and ladders in their Chassidic garb. By day, they performed any work that would provide them with a living. In the evening, until late at night, they diligently learned Torah; many of them were great scholars.

One of their leaders was Reb Dovid Tzvi Silberstein, a young man and a dynamic speaker who helped edit the *Bais Yaakov Journal*. He pledged all of his spare time, talents, and energy to PAI, striving in many ways to find jobs for unfortunate unemployed Orthodox young men.

"Unfortunate" hardly expresses the plight of the jobless, whose agonies included hunger. My husband Shymon, one of the energetic PAI activists at the time, remembers:

> At the evening study and activity session, we served the members a meal, knowing that for many it would be the only meal for the day.
>
> It was tough going for the leaders and the capable members of the movement — speaking in shuls, visiting manufacturers and trying to impress upon them the dire need for employing those people. Apart from having to deal with the employers, they had to fight the well-established Polish Socialist Party and even the Jewish Socialist party, the Bund. Their strong unions were reluctant to accept the religious worker who would not work on Shabbos.

Just the same, the PAI members were strong and unbending in their *Yiddishkeit*, and tenacious in their campaign for the sake of *shomer Shabbos* workers. They were active in education, established trade centers, and published a monthly journal — the *Yiddishe Arbeiter Shtime* — to enhance public consciousness about the problem of the unemployed and alert the rich to the existence of poverty and need among Jews.

PAI established "kibbutzim" (training collectives) where boys studied agriculture and other trades in preparation for life and work in Eretz Yisroel. Unfortunately, the Sochnut (the Jewish Agency for Palestine, representing the Zionist establishment) allotted only a small quota of immigration certificates to the Agudah and its kibbutzim. Notwithstanding the members' eagerness and enthusiasm for *aliyah*, they had to wait years for their chance. In the meantime, they also worked hard outside the kibbutz, accepting any sort of work in order to diversify their training and prepare themselves to be breadwinners in *Eretz ha-Kodesh*. They became known as reliable, competent workers, their conduct on the job highly admired. Their exemplary idealism and pride in combining work, Torah study, and *yiras Shamayim* was a real *kiddush Hashem* — sanctification of God's Name.

Inspired by the idealism and sincerity of the PAI core group, many young people joined PAI and embraced its goals: easing the plight of the hungry, impoverished worker and fighting for religious workers' rights in the spirit of Torah. By means of its conduct, PAI spared working youth from victimization at the hands of the false and Godless ideas of Socialism and Communism.

The Movement Flourishes

❧ Chapter 37 ❧

By 1925, forty-nine Bais Yaakov schools had come into being in Poland (unbelievable as it might sound), with 6,585 students attending (see graph on page 99).

As the movement grew, so, thank God, did its young teachers. Now, apart from Frau Schenirer's handwritten lectures, the newly established *Bais Yaakov Journal,* and scarce educational material, they were able to attend the summer in-service training program created by Dr. Schmuel Deutschlander, the Fortbildungs Kurs. The diverse educational contents of the course, coupled with the warmth and depth of those who presented them, expanded the girls' knowledge and broadened their minds.

The love and dedication of these wonderful teachers created an atmosphere of *mesirus nefesh* (self-sacrifice) for the Bais Yaakov cause. The teachers maintained their incredible devotion throughout their entire careers. Also aiding their spiritual growth was the opportunity they had to be in the proximity of Frau Schenirer. Witnessing her way of doing mitzvos, observing her behavior, and listening to her saintly soul speaking strengthened the girls even more.

After they finished the course, the girls returned to their positions as Bais Yaakov teachers enriched with wisdom and experience. They started the new school year with new energy, enthusiasm, and dedication.

Under these young teachers' tutelage, the children developed into intelligent teenagers who embraced their Jewish heritage with knowledge, love, and excitement. Finally, the first classes reached the ages of fourteen and fifteen and were ready to graduate from the Bais Yaakov program.

Frau Schenirer was puzzled and concerned: What will become of those young teenagers who, although imbued with love of Torah life, are about to enter a hostile world? They will be vulnerable to all those faithless "isms," which will bear down on them with tremendous pressure. It is so difficult for youngsters to repel the pressure that activists in the service of those ideas will apply. "These are my children and I must protect them," she wrote. "We must establish a strong Orthodox youth organization, in which the girls will continue the Jewish education and their dedication to the Torah ideal that they acquire at Bais Yaakov."

It was a dream that Frau Schenirer never relinquished. What is more, she assigned the as-yet-nonexistent organization an additional and broader task: to restore the Torah ideal among misled Jewish youth. "What we accomplished with our Bais Yaakov youth is not enough," she reminded us. "We must strive to bring every Jewish girl under the banner of Torah."

To bring her dream to fruition, she turned again to her "Executive Director," that ardent supporter of Bais Yaakov, the capable publisher Reb Gershon Friedenson, who with enormous dedication, energy, and sacrifice had answered her fledgling Bais Yaakov movement's dire need for literature. As noted above, it was he who published the beautiful and interesting *Bais Yaakov Journal* for Bais Yaakov and Bnos girls and *Kindergarten* for younger children. Both publications were crucial in making the Bais Yaakov idea grow and flourish. This most important endeavor was carried out with little funding but with unbelievable determination on the part of Reb Gershon and his staff. Reb Gershon responded to Sarah Schenirer's new project with his usual enthusiasm. He adopted her initiative to establish an Orthodox Jewish youth organization as his own. With characteristic vigor, he immediately began to plan the founding conference.

It convened in 1926. In a small auditorium on Piramovicz Street in Lodz, a group of young Orthodox women gathered: Bais Yaakov teachers under the leadership of Sarah Schenirer, several Agudah leaders, and, of course, the initiator of the conference, Reb Gershon Friedenson.

A name was chosen for the organization: Bnos Agudath Israel, a branch of the Agudah. *Bnos* means "daughters." Frau Schenirer liked that name. Its members would be daughters of the King of kings, doing His will with joy.

The initial program was drafted. Frau Schenirer explained its essence: "The program of this organization was established thousands of years ago, at Mount Sinai. Hashem, the Creator and Leader of this world, revealed Himself to us and gave us His commandments in our eternal Torah. That is our eternal "program," always refreshingly new in all its details. Hashem has chosen the Jewish People as His everlasting organization, the *Am Kadosh* [Holy People], and we will wave its banner. *Na'aseh ve-nishma*; with love and dedication we will follow all the precepts of His program."

Although pleased to see her dream come true, Frau Schenirer found her joy marred by doubts. This was her third attempt to found an Orthodox youth organization. Twice she had failed. Would the new initiative thrive and progress as she had envisioned it?

It did. With no resources save the dedication and unshakable resolve of Reb Gershon and his staff, Bnos quickly became a strong organization with a large and quickly growing membership in both major cities and small towns.

"For a whole year I prayed and hoped for its success," Sarah Schenirer wrote. "After I visited various Bnos chapters, seeing them flourish in our important work, my happiness had no limit. Finally I called out a joyous '*Mazel tov.*'"

It is no wonder Frau Schenirer had a warm spot in her heart for the Bnos organization. Those girls, she knew, would bring the enthusiasm of Torah study and performance of mitzvos into their daily lives by implementing everything they were taught.

At Bnos they would be readied to become wives and mothers. There they would learn to build a true Jewish home, fill it with an atmosphere of sanctity and purity, and imbue it with zest for the study of Torah and the joy of fulfilling the mitzvos.

Frau Schenirer placed much hope in this organization. She pictured it growing into a strong movement. She spoke with excitement about her Bnos.

"Do you know what youth means, my sisters?" she asked rhetorically. "Youth is joy, enthusiasm, a life of optimism, of belief in an ideal. Young people have courage and desire to make the world into a happier, more enjoyable place to live. They are full of energy and take delight in attaining their goals. How much more joy and excitement my Bnos organization should have, knowing that they're striving for the ultimate goal — the true, everlasting ideal of a Torah life. With their behavior and vigorous activism for the welfare of mankind, they will become an example for other youth organizations to follow.

"The Kotzker Rebbe once extrapolated that just as Yitzchak was so excited as he went to the *Akeidah*, even though Hashem neither revealed Himself to him nor commanded him, it follows that Youth will be the one that will continue the limitless love and *mesirus nefesh* to fulfill God's command, as our forefathers did before us. Therefore, the Kotzker befriended the young more emphatically.

"To attain perfection in fulfilling our Torah commitment," Sarah Schenirer concluded, "we must have both the excitement and vigor of the young, and the wisdom and experience of the elders."

*   *   *

The Bnos chapters in large cities had large memberships.[37] Our Kraków chapter had over five hundred members, the Lodz chapter had seven hundred, and the branches in Warsaw,

---

37. In Kraków, there were also a couple hundred Basya girls who attended the Bais Yaakov elementary school in the afternoon and had Basya programs on Shabbos and holidays.

Tarnów, Sanz, Chrzanów, and other major cities had several hundred apiece. Smaller chapters existed in towns, townlets, and every location that had a Bais Yaakov school.

The Kraków Bnos chapter and several others had extensive programs that began at 7:00 P.M. and ended at 10:00 P.M. The schedule of activities was diverse. We learned Torah, *Nevi'im*, *Kesuvim, tefillah, Yahadus*, Jewish history, Hebrew, and secular subjects.

There was also an array of committees. Members of the *tzedakah* committee collected meals from generous women and delivered them to patients in non-Jewish hospitals. Other girls collected pieces of challah and slices of cake — hard to believe now — and distributed them to the needy for Shabbos. Another committee prepared the Rosh Chodesh evening, a very important event on our schedule. Frau Schenirer liked to attend it from time to time; considering Rosh Chodesh a holiday given especially to women, she believed we should honor it with special festivity.

As stated earlier, Frau Schenirer loved her Bnos and strove to attend their events whenever she could. She was proud of her Bnos girls and happy to see them following her teachings. Every Wednesday, time permitting, she taught us halachah and *Yahadus*. We in turn appreciated her sacrifice. Having her with us once a week, listening to her inspiring lessons and observing her personality was a special treat for us.

After Frau Schenirer passed away, Reb Yehudah Leib Orlean wrote an article in the *Bais Yaakov Journal* entitled, "Sarah Schenirer the Program." We at Bnos truly considered her our program. We tried to emulate her ways, follow her example, and, above all, practice what she often repeated to us: learn with joy but remember the lessons in order to implement them in your everyday life, even if it is sometimes difficult.

As soon as World War II began, masses of Jews reached Kraków after unsuccessfully attempting to escape from the Nazis by fleeing into Russia. Unsurprisingly, the Bnos girls were among the first to establish public kitchens to feed them. They also established refugee shelters in schools and *yeshivos* which became vacant after the Nazis prohibited Jewish children from attending school. They delivered meals to masses of captured young men who were being held in an insane asylum that had been forcibly vacated for this purpose. Then, the girls devised a scheme to release them one by one, and implemented it at great sacrifice.

Afterwards, in the ghettos and camps, Bnos girls risked their own lives to save the lives of others — to help, to share a scrap of bread or a sip of water. According to Frau Schenirer's teachings, when a Jew is in danger one must not hesitate to risk one's life to save him. Her Bais Yaakov and Bnos girls risked their lives and, worse, subjected themselves to torture, in order to save the lives of others. Thus they fulfilled that quintessential Jewish ideal expressed in the *Shema*, and which Sarah Schenirer so often repeated: "Love Hashem with all your heart, all your soul, and all your might" — meaning your life. Frau Schenirer further elucidated that we should love His children that way, too.

✳   ✳   ✳

Bnos was not only an educational and *chessed* organization. With its array of small groups, it was also a unique girls' club in which strong bonds of friendship formed. Younger girls were counseled by slightly older girls who had been handpicked for this unique task. The older girls were called leaders, and so they were.

The Bnos leader was a role model to look up to, to love, to admire, to be eager to emulate. She was a friend but also a mentor, a big sister but also a teacher in whom one could confide, discuss personal problems, ask questions and receive answers, and resolve occasional confusion. The girls continually sought her advice and guidance, which she delivered with an attentive ear and a caring, understanding heart. She consistently offered loving, soothing, sensible advice for her girls' personal problems. No wonder they all wanted to pick her up from her home and take her to Bnos meetings in order to have an extra few minutes alone with her.

She always had time for a brief audience with individual girls who needed her guidance. We gave such sessions a Polish name: *dushne,* denoting spirituality, a soul-searching walk.

In that setting of small Bnos groups, we girls worked hard to emulate one of Frau Schenirer's most sterling attributes, as described in her autobiographical writings:

"Late at night, after a difficult day of hard work, I was able to start working on myself. I studied my favorite *seforim* and worked on self-improvement."

Trying to emulate our great teacher, we began our Shabbos mornings at 6:00, investing two hours in a *mussar* (Jewish ethics) workshop. Amidst the tranquil surroundings of the Wavel, the castle grounds of the Polish kings, we studied *mussar.* We concentrated on a particular *middah* (character trait) each month. We practiced it constantly until it became part of our very fiber. Then we went to work on another *middah.* Throughout, we tried to emulate Frau Schenirer's self-improvement methods.

What an enchanting, happy, meaningful, satisfying adolescence we had. Even as young and sometimes rebellious teenagers, we knew this well.

It happened one Thursday night in Kraków, in 1932. We were celebrating Rosh Chodesh with a special evening program, as we did each month. We read and recited from the monthly paper that we published. One girl gave a speech; a few others performed a skit on something related to current events. Everyone in Bnos attended — about five hundred girls in all.

We had a large auditorium but not enough chairs. To solve the problem, the girls had decided to buy inexpensive wooden folding chairs. But they were one and a half zlotys each — too much for the girls to afford. So we agreed that each pair of girls would buy, and use, one chair. We became so accustomed to this arrangement that, to this very day, I sit on only a half a chair. I cannot make myself comfortable on a whole chair, no matter how my children urge me to do so for safety reasons.

Having solved the seating problem, we went on with our program, excited about what we could do on our own, without our teachers' help. Suddenly, the door opened and Frau Schenirer entered. Even today I picture her vividly as she walked to the left-hand corner of the room and sat down on a whole chair that two girls offered her. She was tired. She had just come from the railroad station after a week of traveling from town to town, visiting Bais Yaakov schools, talking to the children, asking them questions, and complimenting them on their achievements. How they loved those visits. Most of all, however, she came to visit the young teachers, bolster their morale, help them with their problems, and give them new teaching materials that she had prepared.

Her shoes were dusty, her clothing wrinkled. She placed her heavy black briefcase on the floor. I see her closing her eyes; she cannot keep them open. She is exhausted, yet she came. Not to give a lecture at the seminary, not even to teach a class at Bnos. She came to her Bnos girls just to join them for a Rosh Chodesh evening — to listen to them and take pride in their accomplishments. She opens her eyes from time to time, not only to listen but to see her dear children.

Now that the speech and the recitations are over, the girls start singing and dancing. Frau Schenirer steps into the circle. Never mind her exhaustion. She is there, full of joy and vigor, joining the girls in dance and song. Now, she sings "*Ve-taher libeinu,*" "Purify our hearts," with the girls. Hands outstretched and face uplifted, she turns to Heaven: "Oh God, purify our hearts so that we can serve You in truth." She dances with us and sings and sings. But it is a prayer, not a song. Now she sings it in Yiddish, again imploring Hashem to keep our hearts pure so we may serve Him in truth.

Years passed after that magical evening — bitter, tragic years, years of pain, torture, and agony. In Auschwitz, there were times when we were so cruelly beaten that we could no longer recite *Tehillim*, recall the lessons we had learned, or even think. But one thing stood out: the sight of Frau Schenirer with her outstretched hands and uplifted face, singing and praying, begging Hashem, *ve-taher libeinu,* purify our hearts. In that valley of death, that dungeon of existence, surrounded only by ugliness and bestiality, we prayed with her: Dear God, help us to keep our hearts pure, lest we become beasts like them. Make us able, even under these circumstances, to love, to care, to help others, to keep ourselves pure as You willed, Hashem, "and to serve You in truth."

❧ *Chapter 38* ❧

As stated, our marvelous Bnos organization in pre-war Kraków had over five hundred members. A leader was appointed for each group of ten to fifteen girls, to lead and educate them. Every cluster of ten or so groups was formed into a larger unit, a *kitah* — *kitos* in the plural. *Kitos* were led by older and more experienced girls, who helped the group leaders carry out their programs, discussed problems they had with the girls, and conducted classes and lectures for the *kitos*.

Thus, we had group leaders, *kitah* leaders, and leaders of various workshops, educational and recreational programs, and community activities such as *tzedakah* and *chessed* projects.

An appointed body composed of a few girls made policy, rendered organizational decisions, and solved major problems. However, there was no official president, vice-president, or treasurer — in a nutshell, no titles.

Looking back at our beautiful life in Bnos, I marvel: How was it possible to maintain an organization of such magnitude, with scores of leaders and heads of different programs, without any power struggles? How, in fact, did members treat each other with uncommon respect, each member always holding the *other* in greater esteem than herself? How could one girl forgo any honor given to her for the benefit of another whom she considered more deserving?

If a girl was offered a prestigious position, she would decline it, saying, "I don't deserve this distinction; please give it to someone who's worthier." The only way to convince the girl to take the job or position was by showing her that it was difficult to accomplish. Then she accepted the responsibility gladly.

When I occasionally mention this remarkable relationship among the Bnos members, people shake their heads in disbelief. I do not blame them. I, who witnessed it, can hardly believe it. Yet it is the absolute truth!

"How can it be," I muse, "that in a competitive world, where striving for domination is the rule of the day, where every organization, every institution, is mired in power struggles that cause internal strife and intrigues, disunity among members, and discord within the leadership? How," I ask again, "could this amazing oasis of friendship and comradeship have existed in such a world?"

Only Frau Schenirer, this remarkable teacher of pure and noble character, unblemished by even the slightest shade of jealousy, could have produced a movement and organization that would thrive under her tremendous influence, proudly following in her footsteps, evolving into one united persona, as it were, unblemished by the destructive trait of jealousy.

*   *   *

Sarah Schenirer did not want her picture to hang in any Bais Yaakov school. She felt so strongly about this that nobody dared go against her wishes. "I don't want you to hang my picture on the wall," she would say. *"Carry it in your heart."* So we did. Just as Yosef ha-Tzaddik, Joseph the Righteous, carried his father's likeness in his heart to help him overcome temptation, so did we carry the image of our revered teacher in our hearts and minds.

In the most tragic times, when we were thrown into pits, interned in ghettos, confined to concentration camps, and — unlike Yosef — brutally beaten, degraded, denied food and water, left to die of hunger and thirst; when our lives were unbearable, when we were ready to give up, Frau Schenirer's image stood before us. Her lively dark eyes penetrated us with her uncommon love and encouragement. Her warm smile urged us,

"*Kinderlach*, don't give up, hold on. 'Proclaim [God's] steadfast love at daybreak, [His] faithfulness each night.'[38] It is night. Keep on hoping; Soon the day will come with its everlasting light and joy."

Yes, her girls were put to the test not only by one deceiver or seducer, as Joseph was, but again and again, every day, every hour. They were subjected to the strongest temptations to surrender their unsullied morals — for a piece of bread, a bowl of soup, an offer of better working conditions, and in some cases even a promise of survival by a gentile, who offered to place them in safe hiding. In those trying times, the picture of Frau Schenirer helped them endure the trials. They would rather starve or be put to death for disobedience than to submit.

Indeed, Frau Schenirer did not allow her picture to hang on the wall. "Carry it in your heart," she said, and her children have obeyed her to this day. In no Bais Yaakov school in the world does her picture hang on the wall. But her children, scattered to every continent, keep her image alive in their hearts and minds, to this very day and to the end of days.

In their lengthy journey in the desert, the Israelites carried two arks. One held the *Luchos*, the Tablets of the Covenant; the other held the remains of Yosef ha-Tzaddik. Passersby found this bewildering. "Why are you carrying two arks?" they would ask. "We understand why you carry one of them. It holds God's commandments. But why are you carrying the second heavy ark, with its contents of dry bones?"

"We are indeed carrying a second ark," the Israelites replied, "but its contents are not the dry bones, *atzamos,* of Yosef ha-Tzaddik, but his *atzmus* — his personality, his unshakable faith, his devotion. It sustains our devotion to the ark that holds the Tablets at all times, under the most trying circumstances. Yosef's teachings, his exemplary behavior, his blessings, and his hopes for the redemption of his beloved people — these are what we proudly bear in the second ark."

---

38. *Tehillim* 92:3.

We, like the Israelites, crossed a vast, dry desert, a wilderness full of haunting beasts, ready to devour us at any time. With neither food, nor manna, nor even bitter water — just with pain, torture, and ugliness all around us — we still carried two arks in our hearts. One contained tablets that bore the message, "I have not swerved from Your Torah";[39] the other contained the *atzmus* of our martyrs, who sacrificed their lives to keep the Ark of the Covenant alive. Even to their deaths they went with *Shema Yisroel* on their lips.

Even when we left the desert, our emaciated bodies with their dry, bony arms carried those two arks into our renewed life. Hashem gave us the privilege of bringing forth a wonderful new generation. Today, we proudly carry those two arks on our shoulders together with our children and grandchildren. May they all know and remember how crucial both these arks are for the existence of our people. Then, with prayer and hope, may we be privileged to carry them into the glorious future of the End of Days and be able, at long last, to sing a *shir chadash,* a new song, *al geulaseinu ve-al pedus nafsheinu,* a new song of our physical deliverance and spiritual redemption.

---

39. Ibid., 119:51.

❧ *Chapter 39* ❧

Any discussion of the Bais Yaakov Teachers' Seminary, already functioning at 10 Stanislawa Street, must make mention of Reb Yehudah Leib Orlean, who became its director in the early 1930s to help Frau Schenirer manage her fast-growing Bais Yaakov movement.

While still a young man in Warsaw, Reb Yehudah Leib was renowned as a great *talmid chacham,* a talented educator, and a gifted orator. He became involved in the Agudah movement after the Kenessiah Gedolah in 1923. A brilliant speaker and thought-provoking lecturer, he devoted all his talents to the shaping and development of Zeirei Agudath Israel, the Agudah youth organization. When the need arose, he and Reb Dovid Tzvi Silberstein, along with other Agudah activists, established Po'alei Agudath Israel (PAI), an Orthodox labor organization that aimed to combat the pressure of the powerful Socialist movement, which refused to offer work to Shabbos-observant workers.

As a leading figure in PAI, along with his passionate activities to help struggling young men to find work and earn an honest living, Reb Yehudah Leib wrote the tract *"Tzu Zate und Tzu Hungerike,"* as mentioned previously. This essay expounded on the socio-religious *halachos* that both Jewish employers and Jewish laborers must observe. In the tract, Reb Yehudah Leib stressed the obligation of Jewish employers to hire Jewish workers and treat them in accordance with a set of rules, and the duty of workers to give their employers an honest day's labor for which they were hired and paid.

Reb Yehudah Leib was a follower of the Gerrer Rebbe (the Imrei Emes), and in the late 1920s the Rebbe advised him to leave his promising career in the Agudah world in Warsaw and become the director of the Bais Yaakov Seminary in Kraków. "You are the ideal person for this position," the Rebbe emphasized, "and the Bais Yaakov Seminary needs you more than the Agudah does."

Thus, in an act blessed by the Rebbe, Reb Yehudah Leib moved to Kraków and took the helm of the Bais Yaakov Seminary. His brilliant mind, educational talents, knowledge of youth, and ability to understand their problems made him the most beloved leader of this crucially important women's institution.

The girls there spent hours discussing and pondering the creative ideas he expressed in each of his thought-provoking lectures. Each of them felt as though he was talking to her personally. Herr Orlean, as he wanted to be called, somehow eased their doubts and answered their questions before they asked. He shaped their minds and forged their characters.

Even though more than sixty years have passed, I remember vividly one of his *Yahadus* lectures before Yom Kippur. He spoke about the *viduy* of *Al Cheit* in the Yom Kippur prayers, in which we enumerate and confess our sins repeatedly and ruefully and beg our merciful Father for forgiveness. Regretfully we count out the forty-four sins and pledge to correct them. Herr Orlean expounded on every one of them in his original way, impressing upon us the duty of thoughtful, sincere repentance and responsibility to fulfill our obligations.

Among his comments, the most memorable was his mind-boggling interpretation of *Al cheit she-chatanu... be-yod'im u-ve-lo yod'im*. Ordinarily, this is translated as, "We regret the sins that we committed before You knowingly and unknowingly. We understand our liability for transgressing a precept knowingly, but why are we responsible for sins we did unknowingly?"

"*Be-lo yod'im*," Herr Orlean explained emphatically, "refers to sins of *not knowing*. We must regret those sins deeply. We are commanded to know. We live in a world where everyone is wrapped up in himself. He knows only how to satisfy his own needs, his own concerns. He is oblivious to everyone else. He does not care to *know* about others' needs or concerns.

"You're in the street. To be able to help, you have to *know* what's going on around you. A woman falls down. A child is lost. Someone cries in distress. An old man is confused. Someone needs help crossing the street; someone else needs help walking. A woman carrying a heavy load needs help, and so on. You are obligated to *know*.

"You live in an apartment house. The neighbor below you is ill and alone. She needs bread and milk. She is hungry and lonely. You pass her door and rush down the stairs. You *did not know* she needs your help. You *should have known*. You should have knocked on her door, asked how she is, and determined what help she needs.

"You have to repent and ask Hashem's forgiveness for the weighty *sin of not knowing*. It is your duty to care and to know where and when your help is needed."

This simple truth touched me so deeply that I remember it to this day. I taught it to my children, and they to theirs, and so on forever.

Herr Orlean's teachings, leadership, interest in and concern for others, and his constant striving to *know* their needs and help meet them, made a lasting impression on his students and is still evident in the educational messages of the Bais Yaakov schools.

*   *   *

When World War II began, Herr Orlean and his family had to leave Kraków and return to Warsaw. Even then, however, he did not forget his beloved Bais Yaakov. With great sacrifice, he smuggled his weekly lectures to us. We gathered on Shabbos in small groups in private homes, to study his precious lessons.

His words of faith, courage, and hope sustained us week after tragic week. The mere experience of waiting for his next letter, for another ray of light, made our bleak, gloomy lives bearable.

Unfortunately, even that small happiness came to an end. His treasured letters stopped coming. Herr Orlean could no longer smuggle them to us at any level of risk. Thus, we lost contact with our dear teacher and mentor, and did not hear from him again until, in pitiful condition, we reached Bergen-Belsen. There we discovered that Reb Yehudah Leib and his family, as Swiss subjects, had been interned in the foreign citizens' compound of the camp. We tried to get in touch with him but failed. His compound was encased in a high brick wall; even the Germans in our part of the camp could not enter it.

After the war, when the doors of all camps were pried open, we made inquiries about Herr Orlean. To our immense pain and sorrow, we received tragic news. He was to have been released as a Swiss citizen, but was brutally murdered a day before the papers arrived, on *Chol ha-Mo'ed Sukkos*. It was one day too late for his students' tireless efforts to provide the necessary documents in order to save Reb Yehudah Leib Orlean, director of the Bais Yaakov Seminary and leader of all Bais Yaakov schools in Poland, one of the greatest personalities of the past century, whose impact lives on in the Bais Yaakov movement to this day.

Hashem yikom damo — may God avenge his blood.

❧ *Chapter 40* ❧

Sarah Schenirer realized that her girls were torn in their daily lives between the agitators' pressure to join various organizations and the truth they were taught in Bais Yaakov. She also knew that many of her charges had to work to supplement their household's income and that some actually supported their families.

From the start, she established trade schools for girls that taught appropriate occupations for Orthodox women, the sort that would allow them to make a living in the privacy of their homes. Students in these schools learned to help their families make ends meet by making dresses, men's shirts, women's felt hats, embroidered objects, etc. Photographs of such classes in Kraków and Warsaw survive.

Bnos also tried to place girls in selected positions in Jewish factories.

Eretz Yisroel was part of Frau Schenirer's initiative. While aware of her students' love of *Eretz ha-Kedushah* and their profound desire to live there, she also realized the difficulties they would face. They would have to work hard to support themselves in their new surroundings. After their physical *aliyah* — the trip and resettlement — they would have to prepare themselves for the more difficult labor of achieving spiritual *aliyah* — a mighty reinforcement of *emunah* (faith in God) and *bitachon* (trust in God) to overcome the odds that they would face there.

In consideration of the problems, the Bnos "Centrale" in

Bais Yaakov Hachsharah trade school, Powanzek (near Warsaw).

Lodz set up the first Bnos *Hachsharah* (training center) in Powanzek, a suburb of Warsaw. This beautiful educational facility equipped girls with various trades, as well as dressmaking, shirtmaking, and simple and fancy embroidery on dresses, tablecloths, and bed linen made for rich brides' dowries. The center operated under the auspices of Agudath Israel, which screened the participants to verify their intentions and devotion to *aliyah*, and obtained their parents' consent.

In edition 115 of the *Bais Yaakov Journal* (April 1933), we read an interesting article about Rabbi Yitzchok Meir Levine, president of Agudath Israel at that time, and Reb Gershon Friedenson, as they visited the *Hachsharah* in Warsaw.

The visitors were greeted by several familiar verses of the Torah on the walls of the auditorium, classrooms, and workshops. Among the various quotations was hung an interesting slogan, reiterated (next to the most important one, *mesirus nefesh*) in bold lettering at every turn: "*Hish'amus* (obedience)," it screamed. "*Hish'amus, ha-madreigah ha-rishonah le-aliyah.*" Obedience, the first step toward settling in Eretz Yisroel. The next sign explained the object of this obedience: "Obedience to Torah and devotion to the *yesodos* [foundations] of our kibbutz" are the first steps to *aliyah*.

"That's right," the camp leader, Devorah Gur-Aryeh, said as she explained the slogans. "Obedience is the main theme in our education of the girls. Discipline yourself, learn to obey. Obey the Torah's commandments; obey the Sages, the Jewish leaders, the kibbutz leaders. Only by achieving the *madreigah* of obedience will you achieve true *hachsharah*, preparation, for *aliyah*.

"With discipline, you will be able to withstand the material and spiritual difficulties that you may encounter in Eretz Yisroel. Only by obedience can you attain true *aliyah* — spiritual ascent. Then you may satisfy your profound quest for moral ascendancy in *Eretz ha-Kodesh*."

The Bnos Centrale in Lodz, of course with the cooperation of Frau Schenirer, established two additional *Hachsharos* — one in Melava (near Warsaw) and one in Lodz — to answer the growing yearnings of Bnos youth to settle in the Holy Land. One need not be surprised about those yearnings. Listening to Frau Schenirer express her love of Zion and her profound wish to be in *Eretz ha-Kedushah*, even if only for a short while, made a great impression on her girls. Their longings only intensified when they read in the *Bais Yaakov Journal* about Frau Schenirer's desire to tread on the holy soil where our prophets and *geonim* had walked, to breathe the air that had been filled with Hashem's *Shechinah,* to hear every tree, every blade of grass retell the erstwhile glory of our Land. The *Tehillim* lessons, taught by her and others, inspired the girls even more by exalting the holiness of the Land that Hashem chose as the abode for His Presence.

Aware that her favorite youngsters in Bnos truly aspired to perform the mitzvah of *yishuv Eretz Yisroel* — settling the Land of Holiness — Frau Schenirer fully cooperated with Reb Gershon Friedenson in establishing those three *Hachsharos.*

Aided by teachers and the leaders of various Bnos chapters, Frau Schenirer personally hand-picked the most capable and responsible candidates. Carefully she scrutinized their *yiras Shamayim*, *middos* (character traits), and devotion to the Bais Yaakov ideal. Only the most devoted and reliable Bais Yaakov teachers and Bnos leaders were placed in charge of the *Hachsharos*.

Devorah Gur-Aryeh was a member of the first group from the *Hachsharah* in Warsaw who "made *aliyah*." (Additional girls came on *aliyah* from the other two *Hachsharos*.) Settling in Tel Aviv, she organized a kibbutz on Kalisher Street in that city.

There were several very important young women in this collective. They included Bais Yaakov teachers and Bnos leaders such as Devorah Siedlecky, Sarah Lehmann, and Leah Kalmanowitz, along with others who became the nucleus of the Tel Aviv Gerrer community. One of them was our Ita Goldknopf, subsequently the daughter-in-law of Rabbi Gershtenkorn, the founder and first mayor of Bnei Brak.

As noted earlier, the *Hachsharos* in Poland were very successful. These wonderful training centers equipped members with trades that they could use to support themselves in Eretz Yisroel and, even more important, prepared them spiritually to fight the odds and accomplish their goal of *yishuv Eretz Yisroel,* settling the Holy Land, according to the teachings they received in Bais Yaakov.

After years of fighting with the Jewish Agency for their right to make *aliyah*, Agudath Israel finally received a small quantity of "certificates," the entrance visas that the British Mandate authorities so sparingly doled out. The "certificates" allowed Jews to legally enter the country that the British called Palestine.

The first Bnos *aliyah* group was scheduled to depart in early March 1934. Frau Schenirer received the great news with tremendous joy and enthusiasm. Before the girls embarked on their great voyage, Frau Schenirer wrote an inspirational parting letter to them that was later published in the *Bais Yaakov Journal*.

Her love and trust of the girls upon their *aliyah* are evident. So, however, is her concern: "Are my girls sufficiently prepared for the struggle in Eretz Yisroel?"

> My dear daughters, remember your great responsibility there in the Holy Land, where every blade of grass reminds you that *mipnei chata'einu galinu me-Artzeinu,* that we were exiled due to our sins. What a great responsibility it will be for you, to be even more vigilant than in the Diaspora not to transgress God's mitzvos.
>
> Remember the great trust our people have invested in you and especially that of Agudath Israel, which gave you this great opportunity to live in the Promised Land. You are about to go to Yerushalayim, the city of unity, of perfection, as her name proclaims. Only in Yerushalayim can you feel Hashem's Presence so closely. It is the center of the universe that God created, the place where His *Shechinah* rests.
>
> Our *shevatim* [tribes] came to the Land, inspired by the giving of the Torah on Mount Sinai, eager to spread God's truth to the world. As it says: *Ki mi-Tziyon* [from Zion] Torah will come forth, and God's word from Jerusalem.[40]
>
> You too, my dear children, are going to the Holy Land with a purpose. Realizing the great *zechus* of *yishuv Eretz Yisroel,* inspired by the *kedushah* [holiness] surrounding you, you should fulfill the mitzvos with more enthusiasm and joy than you do here.
>
> May Hashem bless you with success in your ways and everything you do. May you also influence the estranged Jewish youth in our Land to heed Hashem's word. May the Almighty watch over you and help you in all your holy endeavors.
>
> Sarah Schenirer

---

40. *Yeshayahu* 2:3.

*   *   *

Lodz, Poland's premier industrial city, brimmed with huge factories that worked around the clock and blanketed the town in black smoke. Each of them employed thousands of workers who turned out tons of cotton products and immense bolts of linen. Gigantic mills spewed tremendous quantities of cotton and woolen fabrics each day. Smaller plants manufactured stockings, socks, sweaters, gloves, and other garments. And craftsmen plied their trades with the assistance of a few workers and apprentices.

On a little side street, at Naritovicza 41, another "factory" labored at full speed. This unique facility forged character and turned out women of valor. The sign over the building identified the establishment in simple terms: "Hachsharas Ohel Sarah of Bnos Agudath Israel in Lodz." Ohel Sarah, the "tent" of Sarah, was named for our matriarch Sarah.

In the same issue of the *Bais Yaakov Journal* mentioned above, we find a beautiful description of a visit of Agudah leaders to this unique facility. They had decided to spend a Shabbos in Ohel Sarah.

> There, forty girls are preparing themselves for *aliyah*.
>
> *Hachsharah* means preparation. Other kibbutzim understand the term only in reference to the six days of labor; they engage only in *chol*, in mundane affairs. In contrast, at this *Hachsharah*, the six days [of the week are days] of preparation for Shabbos, for spiritual *aliyah*. You can see it in the girls' faces and feel it in their behavior as they go about everything lovingly to create an atmosphere of sanctity as they greet the Shabbos.
>
> Guests entering the dining room were greeted with a hearty, joyous "Good Shabbos." The girls sitting at the table with their leader rose to receive their esteemed guests with the respect they deserve. Their leader, a Bais Yaakov teacher, was especially chosen for this difficult task by Sarah Schenirer.

The table was prepared magnificently, with love and feeling, in the expectation of the glorious guest, the "Shabbos Queen." This time, however, the girls added a special touch in their delight upon receiving some very prestigious guests — the Agudah delegation.

One of the invitees, Reb Gershon Friedenson, the sponsor of the *Hachsharah*, beheld this idyllic scene and exclaimed enthusiastically, *"Shalom aleichem! Aleichem*

שבת אויף הכשרה, אדער הכשרה אויף שבת

(פֿון אַ באַזוך אין דער לאדזשער בנות־מחנה)

Copy of the article which appeared in the Bais Yaakov Journal.

ha-shalom. Shalom upon you girls, who are striving for 'Shabbos ha-shalom,' a *Shabbos shleimus*, perfection in life.

"God bless you," he addressed the girls, "for enduring the difficulties and, at times, the painful situations you have encountered, with love. You know and understand that through suffering we earn the privilege of Hashem's precious gift, Eretz Yisroel."

The next speaker, Reb Dovid Tzvi Silberstein, expressed his deep passion for Eretz Yisroel, "Our *oleh* [settler in Eretz Yisroel] needs to be *neki kapayim u-var leivov*,[41] of clean hands and pure heart," he exclaimed excitedly. "Clean hands to work and a pure heart to embrace, to love every human being. Only with clean hands and a pure heart," he cried out, "can you light the Shabbos candles and bring light and peace to the Holy Land and to the world."

Kibbutz Ohel Sarah, a Hachsharah in pre-war Lodz. Sitting on the first left over the sign is Sarah Luftglass Bodner.

41. *Tehillim* 24:4.

Reb Nuteh Berliner, a thinker, a renowned writer, and a great teacher [from whom I had the merit to learn *Tehillim* at Chavas Schmuel] recited a saying from *Chazal*: "Anyone who sleeps seven days without dreaming is called evil" [*Berachos* 14a]. Reb Nuteh explained it thus: "One who takes the dry reality of weekdays without a dream of Shabbos is called evil. You have to live every difficult day of the week with a dream of a joyous Shabbos, with a dream of *aliyah* — spiritual ascent — on Shabbos, the ideal time of rest, of silence, of being with yourself," the dreamer intoned passionately. "But now I see the dream of the Bnos *Hachsharah* becoming a reality — a place where dreams are forged in daily struggle and become a reality on Shabbos."

Embodying Our Holy Writings

❧ *Chapter 41* ❧

"Serve Hashem with joy." (Tehillim 100:2)

𝒫*eople often ask me to explain* the secret of Frau Schenirer's success. The answer is the joy and enthusiasm that she instilled in her students for observance of mitzvos and worship of Hashem. One of Sarah Schenirer's five most important mottoes was *Ivdu es Hashem be-simchah,* "Serve Hashem with joy." She embodied this adage. Her every action, her every mitzvah, filled her with such delight that her entire personality radiated enthusiasm and joy. The thought of doing God's will — to help the needy, to care for the sick, to encourage the downtrodden, to give and give without limit, and to do it all with joy — simply made her ecstatic.

She derived her greatest joy, however, from teaching us girls about the holiness of Shabbos, the beauty of the Jewish festivals, and of course all the mitzvos involved in these holy days. Her happiness knew no end when she observed the girls listening with interest to the truth that *"Bashefer,"* as she often called Him, had revealed to us. It delighted us, in turn, to absorb her unusual gift of transmitting thoughts and feelings. We were impressed not only by what she said but by the way she said it. We felt her *neshamah* speaking. Thus, her teachings became part of our selves.

Decades after she delivered those teachings, I recall so many of them because they guided me through life, especially in situations when crucial decisions had to be made.

When she taught about Pesach, she stressed the joy of becoming a free people; Shavuos, the happiness of receiving the
Torah; Sukkos, the virtue of humility as an antidote to the sin
of arrogance. The lesson of Sukkos was especially memorable.
Hashem commanded us to leave our sound, beautiful, comfortable dwellings, fancy furniture and all, and move into a primitive *sukkah*, unlocked and accessible to all, without a
permanent roof, vulnerable to all of nature's vicissitudes. For
seven days we are to feel that nothing is ours, that everything
we possess is a gift of God's loving-kindness to use for mankind's benefit, to His Glory. We should know that we are sheltered from calamity not by material powers but solely by our
Creator's benevolence.

In her personal diary, Frau Schenirer wrote:

> Sukkos — we have to leave our permanent homes and enter
> the *sukkah*.
>
> Thus there comes a time when Hashem urges us to
> leave our beautiful dwellings and all our precious posses-
> sions and enter the *sukkah* — a *sukkah* built of four
> wooden boards, with open cracks, vulnerable to an infesta-
> tion of crawling insects and worms.
>
> Take with you, I beg you, the treasures of which you
> may never be deprived — the 613 mitzvos and your
> *ma'asim tovim*, the acts of loving-kindness that you have
> performed in this physical world.
>
> Do not despair, *kinderlach*. This festival is called
> "*zeman simchaseinu.*" In everything you do or think
> *lichvod Shem Shamayim*, in honor of God's Name, do it
> with joy, and Hashem will surround you with *sukkas sha-
> lom* — a *sukkah* of peace and ultimate joy.

For Simchas Torah, Frau Schenirer emphasized the supreme delight that a Jew experiences by holding the Torah in
his arms and his heart. "Rejoice in the knowledge that God has
given it to us," she taught. "It's ours."

At every happy occasion, she impressed upon us the joy of

experiencing the significance of the event. "It is easy to share others' sorrow, pain, and grief, and even to cry with them," she used to say. "But it is much more difficult to share wholeheartedly, with genuine joy, the happiness of your friends, your family, the people around you." Frau Schenirer mastered this skill. No one could even approach her level of empathy with others.

Once, after I spoke at Frau Schenirer's *yahrtzeit*, emphasizing her *middah* of *simchah*, a girl stood up. "Tell me," she asked, "was Sarah Schenirer a *chassidiste*?"

"No," I answered. The girl was crestfallen; other faces expressed disbelief. "No," I repeated, "she was not a *chassidiste*, but she was a chassid in the full sense of the word. Her whole being personified *Chassidus*. Her entire life was a chain of acts of *chessed*, performed at a level of excitement and joy that one rarely finds even among chassidim."[42]

Indeed, Sarah Schenirer worshiped with joy, spoke with joy, taught with joy, and admired all God's creations with joy. Everything she did was filled with joy. In a nutshell, Frau Schenirer was a powerhouse of joy.

*   *   *

Frau Schenirer's joy peaked in the month of Adar. "When Adar enters," she explained, "we are explicitly commanded to increase joy. We rejoice *ad b'li dai*, boundlessly, as we celebrate the great miracle Hashem performed for our people. Instead of the mass murder of Jews that Haman had decreed, Hashem brought tragedy and death to Haman, his family, and his people — and joy and happiness to the Jews."

Each year before Purim, Frau Schenirer taught us Megillas Esther and the many facets and nuances of this unique scroll. "You see, girls," she would say, "on that day when God transformed our sorrow into joy, our mourning into revelry, we are

---

42. A *chassidiste* is a lower level than a true chassid. In my talk, I emphasized that Sarah Schenirer was a true chassid, greater than many chassidim. In fact, there were Chassidic rebbes who used to stand up for her when she entered a room.

commanded to make a great and joyous feast and be happy without limit, without bounds. As it says: 'They were to observe them as days of feasting and merrymaking....'[43]

"But what is the significance of this lengthy peroration about 'feasting and merrymaking'? What is its purpose? Let's see how the verse continues: '...and as an occasion for sending gifts to one another and presents to the poor.'

"If so, what is the pinnacle, the greatest expression of joy?" Frau Schenirer continued. "What is the zenith of your happiness? Here is the answer." She pointed to the text: "'Sending gifts to one another and presents to the poor.' The greatest joy one can experience is the joy of giving — giving to your children, your family, your friends, the needy.

"And who are the needy?" she asked with a disarming smile. "Each of us lacks something at one time or another. If we are privileged to know about someone else's need, our greatest joy is to be able to satisfy it." These were more than Frau Schenirer's teachings; they were the markers that guided her in life, as we, her students, knew. She was a symbol of giving and giving with joy. She gave herself, her energy, her knowledge, her time, and, at the end, her health and her life, so that others could live happier and more meaningful lives.

I once heard an interesting interpretation of *Bereishis* 15:6, "*Ve-he'emin b'Hashem, va-yachsheveha lo tzedakah*" — because Avraham had faith in the Almighty, God considered it a charity on Avraham's part. What kind of charity was it? To whom did Avraham give the charity? What is charity? The explanation offered was this: whenever one gives a person or a community something that he or it lacks, one engages in charity. In Avraham's time, the world lacked belief in the Almighty. Avraham, with his belief in Hashem, performed an act of charity for mankind by giving it what it lacked: faith in Hashem.

---

43. *Esther* 9:22.

"*Kimu ve-kiblu ha-Yehudim,*"[44] Megillas Esther relates: the Jews made an undertaking and an acceptance. After their deliverance, they stood up and rededicated themselves to the Torah and mitzvos that they had neglected. This time, however, they did it with joy.

Years ago, I was privileged to hear Rabbi Gedaliah Koenig of Jerusalem deliver an elaborate and inspirational speech in New York on precisely this topic. "They rose from their lethargy and rededicated themselves to the Torah and to its great Giver," he said. "But this time they did it with joy."

"Yes!" Rabbi Koenig continued with emphasis. "The first time they received the Torah, they did so with wonder, with great awe, fear, and trembling at the great revelation. But what happened after this lofty experience? They made themselves a golden calf and worshiped it with joy, dancing, and merriment. The joy of *matan Torah,* the giving of the Torah, was missing. Now, after Hashem's great miracle for the Jews on Purim, they disavowed the indifference to their heritage and rededicated themselves to Torah and mitzvos. This time, however, they did it with joy, jubilation, dancing, and merriment. '*Ivdu es Hashem be-simchah.*' They worshiped Hashem with joy. Only by serving Hashem with joy can we assure a lasting commitment to Torah and *Yiddishkeit* for generations to come."

*   *   *

Sarah Schenirer treated *Kimu ve-kiblu* as a guiding ethos. She had grown up during a time of emptiness in Jewish women's lives. The beauty of the Jewish heritage had somehow passed them by. They lacked faith in Ribono shel Olam, the refreshing spring of Torah knowledge. Insofar as they performed mitzvos, they did so because of pressure from parents or to avoid hurting them. Above all, Sarah Schenirer realized with her sixth sense, they strayed from *Yiddishkeit* because they missed the joy of serving Hashem. She set out to make up what

---

44. Ibid., verse 27.

they lacked: faith in Hashem and joy in worshiping Him. The dictum *Ivdu es Hashem be-simchah* was always on her lips.

Frau Schenirer's students first perceived and then internalized her enthusiasm. Eventually they did everything — study, worship, good deeds — joyously. The entire seminary rang with song and laughter. Girls danced down the steps, singing, between and after lessons. Frau Schenirer's enterprise restored not only Jewish girls' faith in Hashem but also their joy in worshiping Him. She gave them their own *Kimu*, spiritual stature, and their own *kiblu*, rededication to Torah and mitzvos. She restored their pride in being daughters of Israel.

Frau Schenirer did for the spiritually starved Jewish women in her time what Avraham Avinu accomplished in his own era: instilling faith in Hashem and joy in serving Him. In so doing, she performed *tzedakah* not only for the women but for all of Jewry, since she saved both her generation and posterity for Torah-true *Yiddishkeit*.

Thus, in this frame of mind, with Frau Schenirer still alive to witness it, the Jewish neighborhood in Kraków erupted in a tremendous outpouring of joy on Purim night. Krakowska Street filled with people in all manner of costumes and uniforms — kings and emperors, dignitaries on foot and on horseback. Scenes of Jewish and world history flashed by as in a kaleidoscope. One could hardly circulate in the streets, so crowded were they with performers and onlookers. We girls had to navigate the congestion on Krakowska Street to reach the Bnos center at Augustianska 30.

At Bnos, too, Purim night was an occasion of continual joy. The girls came in a variety of costumes, each trying to be different from the others. Every year, to maximize the happy and joyous Purim atmosphere, they came up with unique ideas on how to portray distinctive personalities by means of appropriate uniforms. They also performed the *Purim shpiel* (play), an annual ritual whose themes changed from year to year. Frau Schenirer personally wrote the scripts for many of those plays — *Hannah and Her Seven Sons, Yehudis, Esther and Achashveirosh*, etc.

A view of Krakowska Street, the main street in the Jewish neighborhood of pre-war Kraków.

The stately Alte Shul of Kraków.

Often, too, she came to watch her girls perform; this gave her *nachas.*

That Jews celebrated Purim so freely in *galus,* in the streets of Kraków, seems unbelievable today. However, they did so every year until three or four years before World War II, when the climate toward Jews in Poland changed. Once that happened, the Jews' own mood changed and, unfortunately, they stopped celebrating Purim in the streets of Kraków. By that time, too, Frau Schenirer was no longer with us.

*   *   *

Sarah Schenirer's *talmidos* went on to experience dark times — times of bitterness, pain, torment, and hopelessness. Even then, the bleakness was punctuated by moments of joy — the joy of being able to give, to share.

I will never forget Naomi's tall figure bending down to the ill and half-dying Jews on the dirt floor in Bergen-Belsen. "Naomi, Naomi," they called from every direction. How her face glowed and her eyes sparkled with joy as she placed in each feverish, parched mouth a sip of ersatz coffee and a few precious granules of sugar that she had pilfered from the German mess hall where she worked. She smuggled these treasures to the barracks in the hem of her skirt. She risked her life to be able to give, and give with joy.

Some of us were relatively fortunate. As "turnip girls" who worked in a special peeling room that was separated from the main area by barbed wire, we could eat as many turnips as we wanted when no one was looking. The girls in the camp, however, were starving. We contrived innumerable ways to pilfer and smuggle turnips into the camp. For weeks, we were successful; the guard who searched us at the camp gate did not discover the contraband. Then a new guard was posted to the gate. A thorough workman, he found most of the concealed turnips. We paid a very steep price for our perfidy and were reluctant to take further chances. However, we could not endure the sight of our starving friends who came to the gate to wait for us, hoping that we would again be able to slip them some camouflaged turnips.

One day, I said to my fellow turnip girls, "I have an idea: let's make insoles from the turnips and put them into our shoes. The guards will never find them; they check only the exposed parts of the shoes." Said and done. Thus, when our Sturmführer (supervisor) was away, we beat turnips into insoles as one of us stood watch. That evening, we passed through the gate half an inch taller and delivered the insoles to the starving girls in the camp. The joy on their faces as they consumed the delicious shoe inserts, memorable though it was, cannot compare to our turnip girls' boundless joy in the knowledge that once again we were able to give.

*　　*　　*

If I wish to recall the greatest joy in my life, I return to the Männerlager, the men's camp, in Auschwitz, to which I and some other girls had just been transferred from Birkenau. We were separated from the men's quarters by electric fences. There I was reunited with Cylka, a great woman who had been in charge of the Neistube, the sewing room, in the Prokocim camp.[45] A proud and independent young woman back then, she had tried hard to ease the girls' plight amidst the misery of the camp, and was always willing to help. Now, in Auschwitz, I encountered a different Cylka — dispirited, disengaged, and spent of her will to live.

"Cylka," I cried, "don't give up! We must still hope that with God's help we'll survive. Have faith, Cylka, have faith!"

"You know I'm not a believer," she interrupted. "I always envied you for your faith and hope, and I still do. But I cannot believe in your God. He deserted us. He deserted you. Where is He?"

"If you ask where He is, then you believe He exists. He will surely help you, especially for what you did that fateful Shabbos

---

45. See *To Vanquish the Dragon*.

in Prokocim — how you risked your life to spare me from dese-
crating 'my' Shabbos. I explained to you that under threatening
circumstances such as we were under, I would be allowed to
help you sew and, in fact, must do so. You did not let me. I will
never forget your answer: 'As long as I live you will not dese-
crate your Sabbath.' Our God remembers that, watches over
you, and will help you to survive. Cylka, have faith. We must
not lose hope."

Just then I recalled that a neighbor of mine, who had recognized me, had thrown me a piece of bread over the electrified
fence. Miraculously, I still had it. I gave it to Cylka.[46] My joy, my
happiness, knew no limit. I had something to give.

During my stay in Auschwitz-Birkenau, however, there was
a time when I had nothing, literally nothing, to give. After a se-
lection and "shower," I and the other women in my transport
were pushed naked into a chamber where — as we found out
later — all our hair was to be sheared. We were the only transport that had not been shaved. We were the lucky ones.

Entering the chamber, we faced a group of young Jewish
women armed with scissors and razors. With kicks and slaps,
we were lined up, one queue for each "barber." Waiting my
turn, I observed these haircutters as they mercilessly hacked
the hair of their "customers" off their heads and gouged their
flesh, leaving their victims bruised and bleeding. What had the
Nazis done to those teenagers to make them so bitter and so indifferent to human pain? I thought with pity. Then I found out:
as members of the *Sonderkommando* (the "special detail"),
they were given the task of untangling masses of gassed
corpses, carrying them to the crematoria, and extracting hidden
treasures, i.e., gold teeth, from their bodies.

Now it was my turn in line. The girl to whom I was assigned
looked at me with soft, caring brown eyes. She cut my hair and
looked again. Amazingly, she wanted me to look decent. She
was not bitter. She did not seem to remember how mercilessly

---

46. Cylka survived the war and rebuilt her home in Israel.

her own hair had been shaved off.

After observing the other haircutters, I marveled at the miraculous treatment I was receiving. Who is this girl? I wondered. I wanted so badly to show my appreciation to this great person, who risked her position if not her life by treating the inmates humanely in a place where you were not allowed to be humane. I felt an urge to express my admiration by giving her something. But I was naked; I had nothing, really nothing, to give.

But Frau Schenirer used to tell us that one always had something to give. Yes, you were right, my revered teacher: I still had my life and a residual spark of hope. "Bóg zapłać," I whispered to my hair stylist. "May God reward you." It was a popular Polish blessing. I gave her a meaningful smile that carried a gleam of hope. Even in my pitiful state, I felt happy; I still had something to give.[47]

47. Some time later, after inquiries, I found out that my "hairdresser" was a Bais Yaakov girl from Oswiecim, the Polish town the Nazis renamed Auschwitz.

❧ *Chapter 42* ❧

Hevei mekabel es kol ha-adam be-seiver panim yafos — "Greet everyone with a friendly face,"[48] was another of our Sages' sayings that Sarah Schenirer loved to repeat.

I lived around the corner from Frau Schenirer and a short block from the Bais Yaakov Seminary. It was my great privilege to encounter her often, especially on Shabbos. It gave me pleasure to see her, surrounded by her students, passing my house on the way to shul. "Good Shabbos," she would say, her face wreathed in smiles. She always greeted people before they could greet her. No matter how hard we girls tried, we could never beat her to it.

One Shabbos, as I walked home alone, I saw Frau Schenirer from afar, walking briskly toward me in the accompaniment of a group of girls. "My God," I thought, "here's my chance to greet my esteemed teacher first." I quickened my pace. When I came into eyeshot and earshot, I opened my mouth. However, before I could make a sound, I heard Frau Schenirer's happy "Good Shabbos!" Her smiling face and sparkling eyes invited me to have a great Shabbos — a day of rest, a day of peace, a day of basking in Hashem's Glory. Frau Schenirer had beat me to it again! Still, I considered myself the victor, not the vanquished. I had gained an extraordinary experience: I received living evidence of greatness — both of my teacher and of our Sages' saying, "Greet everyone with a smile."

---

48. *Pirkei Avos* 1:17.

*   *   *

It was Friday night when our transport from Plaszów arrived in Auschwitz-Birkenau. We had been transported in cattle cars but treated worse than cattle. Now we disembarked under a rain of clubs and bayonets and were marched to the crematorium side of the camp.

We spent that entire night standing in front of the gas chambers, spent of strength, waiting and waiting. For what? we wondered. Then we prayed that the heavy doors would open up and swallow us for good. We had already said our *viduy*, our confession, and were ready to meet our Creator and rejoin all the loved ones who had preceded us. However, the doors did not open. God had different plans for us. We were marched to a nearby building, identical to the previous one and equipped with the same sign, "Sauna." In this building, however, the shower heads spouted water. "Oh, God," I thought, "you have given us another chance to live and suffer....but we do not know for how long."

Brutally we were shoved from one chamber to another. Finally, we came out dressed — a short girl in a long, cutout gown; a tall girl in a small dress. I had the good fortune of receiving a man's pajama top. We could not recognize each other in those outfits and our choppy hairdos. It must have been the weirdest fashion show on earth. Only by calling our names did we identify each other.

In the morning, after hours of *appel* (roll call), we were grouped into a column for the march to the women's camp in Birkenau. Suddenly, we heard three voices calling our names. Who could they be? Who dared to come from the women's camp to this, the crematorium area?

Then we recognized them: our teacher, Tzila Orlean; her student and our friend, Tyly Yogel Rinder, the White Angel of Auschwitz; and Tony Katz. After hearing that the Kraków transport had arrived, they came, at mortal risk, to see what they could do to help.

"Good Shabbos, girls," Tzila said after recognizing us.

Good Shabbos?! How do those two words sound when uttered in front of the towering crematorium chimney, belching fire and black smoke? How do they sound when one's nostrils smell the stench of burning human flesh?

"Good Shabbos, girls," Tzila repeated, smiling, eyes sparkling with joy. Yes, this was Frau Schenirer's *talmidah* greeting us in her teacher's authentic way, telling us that even in this jungle of existence it is Shabbos. The Shabbos Queen does not respect boundaries. She vaults the barbed wire and the electric fences to visit us. Although we offer her only two paper-thin slices of bread for Kiddush, we receive and greet her with joy — the joy of being alive; the joy of being Jewish; the joy of keeping our hearts pure in this pit of evil, amidst this ugliness of human decay. Thanks to our late teacher, her *talmidah,* and the Shabbos Queen, we will never become such beasts as our oppressors are.

*   *   *

Come Friday night, all shuls resound with the lovely strains of *Lecha Dodi.* How happy, how eager a Jew is to greet his beloved bride, the Shabbos Queen. After every stanza, he lovingly repeats the refrain, "Let's go and meet the bride." The very thought brings to mind a beautiful idea expressed by the Tiferes Shlomo of Radomsk, one of the great Chassidic leaders in Poland. "This song contains many different greetings," he explained. "One of them is the expression *Rav lach sheves be-emek ha-bacha,* 'You have spent long enough sitting in the vale of tears.' Don't read it as it is written, *'sheves'* [sitting], but as 'Shabbos' [as the same Hebrew letters are used in both words]. How great is your Shabbos when you observe it in *emek ha-bacha,* the vale of tears."

It pleases Hashem to see how Jewish men in their shuls greet His Shabbos with joyful prayer and song and how Jewish women at home light their candles in lovely candelabra and set their white-mantled tables with sparkling glasses and shining silverware, all for the glory of their special guest, the Shabbos Queen. How delighted the Almighty is when the angels, after visiting Jewish homes, report to Him: Great are Your children! They greeted Your holy Shabbos with ecstasy, joy, and peace.

But how much greater is His joy when He sees His children, with great sacrifice, honor the Shabbos Queen in the valley of tears, nay, in the valley of death.

Frau Schenirer, too, in her place in Gan Eden, takes pride in seeing her *talmidos* emulating her and greeting everybody with joy, as she impressed upon them. But how much greater must have been her satisfaction upon seeing how her children joyously greeted each other with "Good Shabbos" in the valley of death.

✳   ✳   ✳

In 1994, while visiting Haifa for a family celebration, I spent Shabbos with my sister-in-law there. As I left for shul on Friday night, she suggested that I save strain and time by using a shortcut through a park. I took her advice and enjoyed a walk through the beautiful park, admiring the colorful flowers on both sides of the path and inhaling the pleasant scent of recently cut grass.

From afar, I noticed a group of young girls happily strolling in my direction. As they came closer, I recognized them as Bais Yaakov girls and presumed that they attended the nearby school. I greeted them with a joyous "Shabbat Shalom" and a smile, as I had been taught.

The girls were bewildered. "Who are you, Ma'am?" they asked. "Do you know any of us?"

"I do," I answered. "I am a member of your family. I am a Bais Yaakov girl, too, part of this great, worldwide sisterhood called Bais Yaakov."

They began to study me with interest. I had my chance. "Do you have a few minutes?" I asked. A resounding "yes" told me that they wanted to listen.

"Girls," I began my story, "I had the privilege to be a

talmidah of a great teacher. Her name was Sarah Schenirer. I and her other young students admired her greatly and were always eager to learn from her. We learned from her in the classroom, where she revealed the treasures of Jewish thought. But we learned even more from her by observing her exemplary behavior and her extraordinary love for her people. Her willingness to listen and to try to help everyone in need was amazing. The most exceptional thing, however, was the way she greeted every human being. Her unique warmth and joy, her smiling face, and her sparkling eyes gave everyone the same message: I noticed you; I care. You can imagine what a great and lasting impression it made on us young people. We always tried hard to emulate her ways. We still do.

"Girls, did you ever stop to think what a tremendous impact a greeting makes on people? Tomorrow morning, as you walk to shul through the park, observe the lonely women sitting on the benches. Notice the blank expressions on their faces. As you pass by, say a heartfelt 'Shabbat Shalom' to one of them and ask with concern, 'How do you feel today?' You will see how her face lights up. Her fear that even God has forsaken her slowly vanishes. You will have restored a spark of faith in Hashem's goodness to this woman. Go over to another woman and do the same. Your warm greeting will restore her faith in people, after she felt neglected and unwanted by the world. Yes! she will think, there are still people who care. Then go over to a third woman, one who sits on the bench after having put on her finest clothing. No matter how difficult it is, she wishes to look like a human being and to be treated as one. Your 'Shabbat Shalom' and a compliment — 'you look great in that pretty outfit' — will make her feel good. She will return the smile with a hearty 'Thank you,' happy that she still looks nice and that someone has noticed it. Your greeting will have restored her faith in herself and will give her the courage to try even harder.

"That was Frau Schenirer's way. She greeted people with such charm that the recipient was always strongly affected. She greeted every Jew in the street, whether he was *frum* or non-committed. Instead of screaming '*Shabbes, Shabbes*!' her hearty, joyous 'Good Shabbos' made an impression on those to whom it was addressed. Her greetings for strangers and gentiles, with a smile and a good wish each time, were a *kiddush Hashem*. 'What a nice Jewish woman you are to notice me and give me your blessing,' gentile women would say happily, returning her greeting.

"I am proud of you girls. You have revived the principles of the Bais Yaakov movement and the ideals of the late Sarah Schenirer. Now, let's revive the forgotten art of greeting everybody *be-seiver panim yafos* — with a friendly face. Let's do it with genuine joy, as our great teacher taught us. Thank you for listening. May you have a wonderful Shabbos and succeed in everything you do."

"We're the ones who should thank you, ma'am, for making us aware of the great mitzvah of greeting every human being with joy. May you have a *gut Shabbos*," they replied, using Frau Schenirer's Yiddish pronunciation of the Sabbath greeting. "May God help us do what you've just taught us." As I moved on, each girl gave me a great and joyous parting smile.

*   *   *

One morning on the way to work, as I passed a tollbooth to cross the bridge, the young attendant stretched out her hand indifferently to accept the money and said "Thank you" in the perfunctory way that people do in such situations. "Good morning, how are you this morning?" I replied, giving the lonely girl in the isolated tollbooth a greeting of my own. "Have a pleasant day." Her face lit up. With a big smile, she answered, "Thank you, Ma'am. You already made my day." I often think about this little episode. It confirms to me the great power of a friendly greeting. It can change a person's mood and spirit. It can bring joy and hope to the downtrodden.

❧ Chapter 43 ❧

After she left the seminary in Kraków, Dr. Judith Rosenbaum remained in close contact with Frau Schenirer and many of her students. She was always ready to help the school and the individual Bais Yaakov girl in whatever way was needed.

It is no wonder, then, that Frau Schenirer's happiness knew no limit when she heard that Fraulein Doktor, as we called her, was about to marry Rabbi Dayan Dr. Yishai (Isidore) Grunfeld. To express her great love and admiration for Judith, Frau Schenirer sent her as a wedding gift the *Tiferes Shlomo*, her favorite Chassidic *sefer,* by the Rebbe of Radomsk.

When I visited Dr. Grunfeld at her home in London years ago, she nostalgically showed me a beautiful "treasure chest" in which she kept cherished mementos from her students. With love and emotion, she withdrew faded letters and small gifts that she had received from her favorite pupils — her beloved Hanka Grossfeld, Gittel Teitelbaum, Escia Goldstoff, and a few others.

Then, with visible pride, she showed me the wedding gift she had received from her esteemed and admired mentor, Sarah Schenirer. She called my attention to the inscription Frau Schenirer had written on the front page of the book — a beautiful piece of rhymed verse. Mrs. Yaffa Mandel, one of Dr. Judith Grunfeld's many admirers, graciously copied it for me. I am happy to print it here in its entirety, in free translation:

Inscription from Frau Schenirer and her husband, Rabbi Landau, on the front page of the Tiferes Shlomo, which Dr. Judith Grunfeld received as a wedding gift from them.

Mazel Tov!
Gold, silver, crystals from your good friends
You will receive,
To help you establish your home with material goods
They believe.
I present you this *sefer*
Of a special kind,
In which you will great treasures of thought
And advice find.

It surely will provide you with
Strength to overcome
Some difficult days,
And Hashem will bless your household and help it
To observe the Torah's ways.
Then, the rays of joy into the
Jewish world will spread
To show that true happiness can only be had
In a home by Torah and *kedushah* led.
It is my warmest wish that you
From the well
Of *Chassidus* draw
Even if only
In a small measure;
It will make your
Life aglow
With joy and true pleasure.

I hope that this *sefer* will you lots
Of material give.
To realize my wish;
To see you a little bit
In spirit
Of *Chassidus* live.

> "*Le-zikaron*" [for a memento],
> Sarah Landau (Schenirer)
> Kraków

Frau Schenirer's husband, Rabbi Yitzchok Landau, added a blessing of his own for the newlyweds, wishing them a happy life together:

> May the merit of the Tiferes Shlomo, the great Rebbe of Radomsk, make you *zocheh* [privileged] to witness the rebuilding of Zion and Jerusalem soon.

> Yitzchok Landau,
> his grandson

৩ Chapter 44 ৩

"Hashem created the world in six days," Frau Schenirer taught us, "and He rested on the seventh. The day of peace and rest, the holy Shabbos, marked the pinnacle of God's creation. With this act, His work was completed, ready for man *la'asos*, to continue — to work, to produce, to strive in six days, and to rest on Shabbos."

Hashem gave man the material domain, the entire plant kingdom and all living creatures, to master. He bestowed upon man all manner of skills and tremendous possibilities to search and discover the powers concealed in each of God's creations. Man was given these abilities so that he might develop them to their full potential. "However, man," God warned, "remember to use those great discoveries only for the benefit of mankind!"

Frau Schenirer gave us a seemingly mundane example: water. She noted the tremendous power of water, which, when turned into steam by man, propels additional human creations, ships and locomotives, across oceans and continents.

"Isn't it great," she remarked, "that I can take a train and visit so many more schools in different cities than I could by horse and carriage?" She spoke appreciatively of the incandescent lamp, which made it so much easier for her to write her lectures and answer her letters into the early hours of the morning. She commented on the invention of the telephone with admiration: "You speak here and they can hear you far away," she would say with a smile. Then she extended the significance of that idea to the spiritual: "See, girls, how careful you have to be with every word you say. You speak down here and they hear you up there." She broadened this comparison of physical and spiritual discoveries into additional domains.

Hashem also gave man, Sarah Schenirer taught, the potential to discover himself and develop his spiritual powers to the highest *madreigah* (degree). "Know your talents, your skills, your abilities. Every human being is created with a special faculty that is his alone. Only he can develop it and perform his acts of kindness and his mitzvos in his own unique way. Yes, every person has something special to give. Everyone can achieve, take action, and be productive — and the world is eager to receive the results." To emphasize the point, she frequently added an adage: *"A nar is der vus denkt az er can ales tuen ober noch a greserer nar, is der vus zugt az er ken gurnisht tuen* — A person who thinks he can do everything is a fool, but one who says 'I cannot do anything' is the most foolish of all."

Frau Schenirer despised arrogance. "Never be too sure of yourself," she admonished. By saying this, however, she did not mean to instruct her girls to feel inferior. She bolstered the egos of girls whose confidence flagged: "You can do it, just start, just try, and you will see how you'll succeed. Never say, 'I cannot do anything,'" she cautioned. "Everyone is given specific qualities with which to fulfill his purpose in God's creation. Everyone must make his unique contribution, the share that is his alone, to the absolute purpose of Creation.

"The ultimate goal is attained only by the combined efforts of each and every individual's unique abilities, by the power of the united Jewish People."

*   *   *

Several weeks after I wrote those remarks, I was amazed to encounter the same thought in the writings of one of the greatest Chassidic thinkers and rabbis, the Sefas Emes of blessed memory, the saintly Gerrer Rebbe.

In the weekly Torah portion *Bechukosai*, the Rebbe in his sacred *sefer* quotes the *mishnah* in *Pirkei Avos* (Ethics of the

Fathers), "*Im ein ani li, mi li? U-keshe'ani le-atzmi mah ani?*" "If I am not for myself, who will be for me? And when I am [only] for myself, what am I?" The Rebbe explains, "Every person was created with special abilities to accomplish his specific purpose. Only he can perform it. No one else can do it. *Im ein ani li mi li?* If I do not add my *Ani* to the fulfillment of man's mission in this world, who will? *U-keshe'ani le-atzmi* — if I keep it for myself only and do not share it, as Hashem willed, with *Klal Yisroel*, then who am I? Where is my uniqueness, my *Ani?*"

So this ethic was not Frau Schenirer's personal invention. But her marvelous ability to communicate profound thoughts such as these to young girls with a simplicity that emanated from her soul — this was the special faculty that only her *Ani* could express.

❧ *Chapter 45* ❧

A Bais Yaakov teacher in a small town once invited Sarah Schenirer to attend the girls' final examination. Frau Schenirer never turned down an opportunity to participate in a special event at an out-of-town school. In the case of this important test, she knew how much joy her presence would bring to the children and what tremendous encouragement it would provide the teacher, who, as she knew, had worked so hard to prepare her pupils. The parents, too, would *shep nachas* from their young daughters. Above all, the teacher wanted Frau Schenirer to enjoy the children's intelligent answers, for that would make her proud of her Bais Yaakov girls.

Indeed, it was a real joy to hear the cute little girls answering the questions with such confidence. The children relaxed after their successful performance. Beaming mothers hugged their daughters. The greatest satisfaction and happiness, however, were those visible on the face of Frau Schenirer as she observed the teacher questioning and the children answering properly. Her joy and *nachas* knew no limit.

Then the children began dancing. A moment later, Frau Schenirer and their teacher joined in. All burst into a lively rendition of Frau Schenirer's favorite song, "Ve-taher Libeinu." This completed, Frau Schenirer heartily thanked the children for their successful performance and presented them with her own question:

"Tell me, girls," she asked with a charming smile. "You just sang 'Ve-taher Libeinu.' 'Purify our hearts.' So tell me: what

Typical picture of a Bais Yaakov school in a Polish village.

virtue, what *middah*, will best help you to purify your hearts?"

"*Yiras Shamayim*," came the first answer.

"*Chessed*."

"Be nice to your friends."

"Respect your parents and teachers."

"Love your teachers, friends, and neighbors."

One little girl said nothing. Frau Schenirer turned to her: "What do you think?"

"I don't know," the girl answered, embarrassed.

"You are quite right," Frau Schenirer said, kissing and hugging the child. "You've told us the greatest truth. It's man's noblest virtue to say, 'I don't know.' After learning, acquiring, searching, reading all the worthy *seforim*, listening to great scholars, drawing from the well of exalted minds, absorbing the wisdom of our *geonim*, trying to emulate them, striving to follow their ways…if after all that one can say 'I don't know' as humbly, as innocently as you just did, that's the highest *madreigah* that man can use to attain a pure heart."

*   *   *

Bais Yaakov schools in cities and small towns eagerly awaited those visits from Frau Schenirer. The children who participated in them never forgot them — as the anecdotes presented here prove. Indeed, Frau Schenirer found time to visit almost every Bais Yaakov school in Poland. She used the visits to provision the teachers with three badly needed commodities: educational material, advice, and encouragement. Above all, however, her visits boosted the children's love for and pride in being Bais Yaakov girls.

One can only marvel at the pride those little children took in their school and their teacher. Dr. Schmuel Deutschlander's report on Bais Yaakov schools in Poland in 1928 highlights this by describing an interesting event in Felenice, a small town near Warsaw.

When the community leaders in Felenice closed the local Bais Yaakov school due to a shortage of funds, the heartbroken children decided to fight to reopen it. They refused to part with both the school and their beloved teacher, who taught them such interesting lessons and showered them with so much care. One Shabbos afternoon, as the town's householders enjoyed

One of the many Bais Yaakov schools that Frau Schenirer visited.

their *shalosh se'udos* in shul, an army of a hundred little girls marched into the shul and surrounded the assemblage.

"We are not leaving," they announced, "until you promise to reopen our school. It's as important as any other institution in town."

After the town activists discussed the matter heatedly, the community's tax collector promised the children that the school would reopen. Only then did the young fighters leave, pleased to have resurrected their school and their education. Such was the Bais Yaakov spirit. The Jewish daily newspapers in Warsaw reported the story enthusiastically.

*   *   *

As already mentioned, in Poland it was compulsory for all children, Jewish and gentile alike, to attend state-run elementary schools — up to seventh grade in some cities and to eighth grade in others. No private schools were available, and Bais Yaakov was yet only an after-school program.

There was only one exception: the Agudah somehow managed to establish a few day schools for religious boys, where they learned Jewish subjects in the morning and secular subjects in the afternoon. Fortunately, we had one school of this type in Kraków, known as Yesodei ha-Torah, and one Talmud Torah. They were both recognized educational institutions and were headed by an Agudah representative.

For girls' schools, the process was slower and more difficult. Frau Schenirer's dream was to establish a Bais Yaakov elementary day school where girls could avoid the public schools without forgoing secular education.

High school was not compulsory; one could take it or leave it. There were private high schools, trade schools, and business schools in Poland. In Kraków, one of the Zionist organizations ran a large and very successful high school called the Hebrew Gymnasium. Understandably, however, our Bais Yaakov girls did not attend it.

Our Bais Yaakov Seminary in Kraków was an accredited

high school due to its high educational standards. Apart from the seminary, Bais Yaakov high schools were established in several towns in Poland and Lithuania. The first one, Chavatzeles, was up and running in Warsaw in 1928. Two Yavne high schools were in existence by that time: one in Kovno, Lithuania, and one in Telz, Poland. Another was founded that year in Ponivezh (Poniwierz), in Polish Lithuania. The initiative for the latter school was taken by Rabbi Yosef Kahaneman, the renowned Ponivezher Rav, who also did the hard work that brought the school into being and placed it in a beautiful new building. Below is the original photo of this building. Note the inscriptions of the name of the Jewish philanthropist who financed it.

One of the few Bais Yaakov high schools that were established in Lithuania and Poland. This one, in Ponivezh, Lithuania, was founded and supervised by the Ponivezher Rav, Rabbi Yosef Kahaneman.

*   *   *

Miriam Lubling *née* Albert was born in Konskie (Kinsk), a small Polish city near Lodz, and spent her childhood and youth there.

A daughter of a renowned Chassidic family, she was surrounded by her family's love and understanding, and basked in an atmosphere of Chassidic fervor and dedication to Torah study and girls' education.

She was especially fond of her grandmother. "My Bubbe Chayale's house," she recalled long after the events, "was always busy. Great rabbis, Agudah leaders, and fundraisers for Jewish institutions found a home away from home there.

"The Bais Yaakov teacher boarded there, too. That made it easier for the community to maintain the school, which was quite large.

"I attended that school as a little girl, of course," Miriam related. "We all loved it and admired the teachers," she continued nostalgically. "It was an afternoon school, and we couldn't wait for the afternoons to begin.

"However, the most important and most exciting events in our lives were Frau Schenirer's visits. We awaited them impatiently. I can still see her face light up with joy whenever she heard "her" little girls answering her questions correctly. 'I'm happy, *kinderlach*,' she would say, 'to see how your learning progresses every time I visit you. Keep up your good work,' she added with an encouraging smile. 'May Hashem bless you by allowing you to continue making progress in your studies and *yiras Shamayim*.'

"Then she expressed her joy by dancing with us and singing her favorite songs.

"During those visits, she stayed with her friend, my Bubbe Chayale. My bubbe allowed me to sleep over whenever Frau Schenirer visited. I cannot describe how happy that made me. It was a great *zechus* for me to serve and cater to this great *tzaddeikes*, and especially to prepare *negel vasser* for her.

"I followed her around, watching how she behaved and performed the mitzvos. Listening to her praying and reciting *berachos* left a lasting impression on me. Her heartfelt 'Thank you' and warm blessing whenever I did anything for her were the most precious rewards I ever received.

"I can still hear her lovely voice and see her sparkling eyes and the love and concern that they radiated. To this very day, her saintly image stays with me, warming me and urging me to emulate her ways of loving-kindness and concern for every human being."

When Miriam was still a young girl, she received an enlightening postcard from Frau Schenirer, dated Rosh Chodesh Elul. Below is a free English translation:

> My beloved Miss Albert:
> Probably you have already heard about Miss Steier's illness.[49] I visited her yesterday. The doctor gives her hope for recovery, thank God, but her condition is still serious and he said the recovery would be slow.
>
> First, make sure that the children in school say *Tehillim* every day for the speedy recovery of Feiga bas Chaye Yitta. Second, please arrange to have the older girls teach the younger ones. Make sure the Bnos get together every evening. They should read (and study) *Sha'arei Yitzchak* and also read the current *Bais Yaakov Journal* and other material [on the subject of the Days of Awe].
>
> May we, with Hashem's help, be able from now on to share only *besoros tovos*, good tidings.
>
> Wishing everyone a *kesivah ve-chasimah tovah* [a good inscription and sealing in the Book of Life] from me.
>
> Sarah Schenirer

The message in the postcard suggests that Frau Schenirer saw two traits in this young Bais Yaakov girl: leadership qualities and the potential of becoming an energetic activist for the care of the sick and needy.

Miriam, in turn, took her role model seriously and respected Frau Schenirer's advice and guidance. She considered them an instruction to concentrate her efforts in the direction of *bikkur cholim* (care for the ill). She did this in Israel but carried it to higher levels after she came to the United States. There, Miriam's preoccupation with the well-being of the ill grew tremendously over time. Her determination and self-sacrifice in

---

49. Miss Steier was Miriam's Bais Yaakov teacher.

serving the ill, reflected in her efforts to meet their needs at almost all hours of the day and night, has earned her the respect and admiration of the medical profession.

Doctors know better than to say "No" to Miriam Lubling. Her every request and demand has to be satisfied. In her spirited way, she stops short of no action to obtain treatments that her patients need or the best surgeon to perform an intricate emergency operation to save someone's life. She is universally known as the "Angel of Mercy," whom Hashem sent to this world as a messenger to help heal His sick children.

"Miriam," I sometimes ask her, "I know Hashem gives you special energy and strength to do the job. But tell me your secret: where do you get the time to accomplish it all? Does Hashem give you more than twenty-four hours a day?"

The Bnos in Konskie, the hometown of Miriam Albert (Lubling). She is in the center, behind the banner.

✦ *Chapter 46* ✦

Shivisi Hashem le-negdi tamid — "I am mindful of Hashem always"[50] — was another of Frau Schenirer's maxims. It was posted in every Bais Yaakov school, in the classrooms, in the auditorium, and in all places of assembly. It greeted you wherever you turned, reminding us to "be mindful of Hashem always." This puzzled the girls: "How can we be mindful of Hashem *always* as we go about ordinary daily chores?"

God's first lesson to the Jewish People was this: "Don't be afraid." Thus spoke Moshe[51] in the name of God. "Stand, concentrate, and you will see the salvation that the Almighty will bring upon you today." Moshe delivered this teaching as the Jews stood trembling with fear in front of the turbulent Sea of Reeds, the pursuing hordes of Egyptians behind them.

The Jews obeyed. They *looked* and they *saw* the evildoers drown in the sea, just as they had *seen* the miracles God had performed for them in Egypt. The Hebrew verbs in these verses follow in the corresponding order: *va-yar* — they *saw. Va-yir'u* — they were filled with awe. *Va-ya'aminu* — and they *believed.* At the dawn of Jewish nationhood, we were instructed to *look,* to *see,* and to *believe.* It was a lesson for eternity. *Be-chol derachecha da'eihu* — "In all your ways acknowledge Him."[52] Wherever you turn and whatever you do throughout your life,

---

50. *Tehillim* 16:8.
51. See *Shemos* 14:13.
52. *Mishlei* 3:6.

Embodying Our Holy Writings

look, see, and admire His everlasting Glory.

*   *   *

It was early May, when nature bursts to life after its long winter sleep. The two most beautiful parks in Kraków, Royal and Krakowski, were alive with colorful flowers and the scent of red and yellow roses. Frau Schenirer was teaching us the blessing that one recites upon sighting the first fruit-bearing tree in efflorescence.

"Girls," she instructed us, "go to the park, look, and see how beautifully the trees are blossoming. Stop and admire God's creation and cry out the blessing we have just learned: 'Blessed are You, O Lord, our God, Master of the Universe, Who has withheld nothing from His world and has created beautiful creatures and beautiful trees for people to enjoy.'

"That's right, girls, we are a nation of seers. We are brought up to look and see. Wherever we go, whatever we meet on the way, we should look intently. If we do that, we will be 'mindful of Hashem always.' Is it a bird singing, a colorful butterfly aloft, a flower blooming, golden wheat in the field swaying, trees in the woods rustling, or a refreshing spring breeze whispering? All of them tell you, 'God created us to serve *you*, man.'

"We Jews are commanded to look, to see, and to know: 'In all your ways acknowledge Him.' When you see a beautiful sunrise, a colorful rainbow, a new moon, lightning that splits the sky, or thunder that shakes the earth, you recite a blessing to acknowledge the greatness of our Creator."

*   *   *

Once Frau Schenirer entered our classroom and heard us singing a popular Yiddish song. I remember the stanza well because of the commotion it caused:

עס איז איין ליגענט
עס איז איין ווילדער טרוים
דער מדבר האט קיין קוואל
קיין פעלד און קיין בוים

> It's a lie!
> It's the wildest dream.
> The desert has no field,
> No tree and no stream.

"'It's a lie'?" Frau Schenirer responded angrily. "The *song* is a lie! The desert has a tree to shade the wanderer from the scorching sun, a stream of refreshing water to quench his thirst, dates from a tree to ease his hunger. No matter how tired and thirsty a traveler may be, he need only to look for these things intently and to pray and hope that Hashem will help him *see* them. Then he will be able to praise the Merciful One for His compassion in providing man with an oasis in the hot, dry desert.

"You learned about Hagar as she was crossing the desert with her son, Yishmael, on the way to Egypt. The boy was dying of thirst and cried bitterly. God heard him, pitied him, and *opened Hagar's eyes. She saw the well.* It had been there all along, but she had not looked intently enough. You have to look. But once you do so, you will discover Hashem's Glory even in a wasteland."

*   *   *

In the ultimate wasteland, the concentration camps, we saw neither a blooming tree nor a blossoming flower, neither a butterfly aloft nor a bird in flight. Even the sun was invisible, concealed by billowing black clouds of crematorium smoke. We saw only barbed wire, electric fences, two-legged beasts in green uniforms and shiny black boots who kicked and tortured human beings to death, and dogs that they turned loose against people to tear them apart. Where could we see Hashem's Glory in this jungle of wild beasts, of hate, ugliness, and evil?

Frau Schenirer, you continually reminded us to behold Hashem always, everywhere. But even here?!

Yes. We looked and saw Hashem's Glory in the great human beings who sacrificed their lives to emulate the Almighty, who cared for others and tried to ease their pain, who helped the sick and the starving, who saved others' lives at the risk of their own.

Our Sages have a beautiful saying: *Afilu cherev chadah munachas lo al tzavaro shel adam, al yimna min ha-rachamim* — "Even if a sharp sword is laid on one's neck, one mustn't despair; there is always hope for mercy."[53] Rabbi David Hollander interpreted the saying in an even more profound way than its simple meaning: "Even if a sharp sword is laid on one's neck, one should not despair; *he can still do rachamim, still practice mercy on others.*"

They proved it in Auschwitz. I saw those outstanding girls have mercy on others as they faced threats worse than a sword on their necks. Even when threatened with lethal torture, they courageously continued to practice mercy toward others. Indeed, in their actions and sacrifices they glorified God's Name.

In view of those girls' behavior, I understood why Frau Schenirer had become angry when she heard the girls singing that song. She was right: one can see the greatness of the Creator even in a desert, even in a jungle of two-legged beasts — when one discerns the nobility of human beings.

---

53. *Berachos* 10a.

✣ *Chapter 47* ✣

We were ready for morning prayers. Frau Schenirer asked me for a *siddur*. What a delight and privilege it was to offer Frau Schenirer my own and allow her to grace my *siddur* with her *tefillos*. Frau Schenirer flipped the pages to the *Shacharis* (morning) prayers and then, before she started, glanced at the *Shemoneh Esrei*. Suddenly she turned to me. "Peraleh, please give me another *siddur*."

"Frau Schenirer," I dared to ask, "what's wrong with my *siddur*?"

"I don't pray from a *siddur* in which the special *yehi ratzon* [request for God's grace] at the end of *Shemoneh Esrei* is missing. Let me have another *siddur* and I will show you what I mean."

I obliged. Frau Schenirer turned to the proper place and asked me to read the appropriate prayer aloud. I did. Here is a free English translation:

> May it be Your wish, my God and God of my fathers, that I not be an object of human jealousy and that I should not envy others. May I not become angry [with people or with myself] and not anger You [with my behavior]. Spare me from the evil inclination, which lurks every morning anew. Every day it gets stronger, inciting me to anger and to arrogance. Instead, Hashem, please help me to be humble and to love and respect people, all people. Then, our Lord, our King, may Your Name be known in the world as *Echad*, the One and only One, Creator of the Universe. Then may You

278

build Your holy city, reestablish Your Holy Temple, and return Your Presence there. May You gather us from our dispersion around the globe, liberate us from our exile, and bring eternal joy to our people.

Now Frau Schenirer turned to the class and embarked on a spontaneous lesson. "My dear children, we study the meaning of the *tefillos* and try to understand them when we pray. We find these beautiful prayers of ours express our every wish, need, feeling, and thought. But why should I omit this little '*yehi ratzon*,' which is so precious to me? Children, I want you to remember what you already know: that jealousy is a transgression of one of the Ten Commandments, *Do not covet*. Don't envy others for what they possess. Hashem gave them their share, what they need to perform their obligations. He gave you your own share, to accomplish the purpose of your life. Be *same'ach be-chelko*, happy with your lot. Be happy with *your share* and know that it contains everything you need to attain your goal.

"Unfortunately, the evil impulse does not rest. It infects us with that terrible feeling of envy at every occasion. We covet everything that others have. Girls, jealousy is one of the most dangerous things that exist. It can lead a person, God forbid, to irresponsible actions — cheating, stealing, robbing, even worse. As our Sages say [in *Pirkei Avos*], it can destroy one's life.[54] This is why every morning we must pray and beg Hashem to help us overcome this sinful feeling in our hearts."

Everyone's attention was focused as Frau Schenirer continued.

"There is something else that I cannot omit in my daily prayers: to implore the Almighty to help us overcome anger, the blemish that is the most difficult to fight. We get angry at people, members of our families, and ourselves so easily, for whatever reason and for no reason. Anger ruins our days, our lives. How can we let a day pass without praying for help in overcom-

---

54. Cf. 4:28.

ing this horrible trait?

"How much more should we beg Hashem to help us acquire another difficult attribute: to be unassuming and humble in our actions, behavior, and dealings with people. I know it's not easy. We must constantly pray and beseech Hashem to help us make this noble characteristic part of ourselves. However, people can reach those heights. We should only strive for them earnestly and pray.

"Now, look at the end of this little prayer and you will see how God rewards those who attain those moral heights. The reward is *geulah shleimah,* the Final Redemption of our People, the eternal joy. Now you can understand why I insist on praying from a *siddur* that contains my favorite little *'yehi ratzon,'* the one that's so essential to starting my day, everybody's day."

We understood the concept easily because the great teacher who just taught it to us personally embodied those traits she spoke of. We, her pupils, always found her personality more inspiring than her lessons, remarkable though they were. Observing her, we added our own brief prayer: "Hashem, help give us the merit to emulate our extraordinary teacher and guide, if only in a minute way."

We also understood the secret of Frau Schenirer's command of the traits of humility and modesty. Her genuine interest in helping people fill *their* lives with joy and purpose was driven by her deep faith in and love of the Master of the Universe. As she often said, *"Far Zain liben Numen"* — it's all meant only to glorify Hashem's Name. Needing nothing for herself, she was unassuming.

Thus, I could not understand why Frau Schenirer herself needed so strenuously to ask Hashem for help in fighting the terrible sins mentioned in the special *yehi ratzon.* Was she ever jealous? Did she ever desire anything beyond the bare essentials? No, she insisted, "I have everything I need." It was true. She cared and worried only about others. For years, her students tried to persuade her to accept a Persian fur coat as a gift. She needed a fur coat badly; frequently she traveled from city to town, from town to hamlet, from hamlet to rural locality in the freezing cold and blizzards of the Polish winter. The girls tried various arguments. Nothing helped; she shook them off with a charming smile. "I'm not cold," she explained. "The thought of visiting those faraway Bais Yaakov schools, their children, and their brave, devoted young teachers makes me warm, if not hot!" Indeed, the flame of her enthusiasm could thaw any frozen heart.

One day, however, one of the girls came up with a new suggestion: "Frau Schenirer, you collect money for your *tzedakos.* You have to look presentable. It makes a difference in the amount of charity you receive."

With that, Frau Schenirer accepted the gift. "*Far zain liben Numen,* to glorify God's Name, I will even wear a Persian fur coat if I have to." And she did.

So much for envy.

Any doubts I ever had about the matter were dispelled again and again. Once I asked Dr. Grunfeld, *née* Rosenbaum, about her arrival in Kraków. I wanted to know her impressions of those early days and months.

One of those impressions concerned a situation that often causes professional or personal jealousy to erupt. A young woman of exceptional beauty and charm — Dr. Judith Rosenbaum — came from Frankfurt at that time to help Frau Schenirer train students at the seminary to become Bais Yaakov teachers. The girls were instantly impressed with Judith's personality, intelligence, worldly appearance, and academic title. Immediately they nicknamed her "Fraulein Doktor." Soon she inspired them with her knowledge, her enthusiasm for *Yiddishkeit,* her warm interest in them, and her dedication. They fell in love with this adorable teacher. Dr. Rosenbaum, herself a virtuous woman of the highest order, felt uncomfortable about this situation, fearing that it would distract attention from Frau Schenirer.

At second glance, however, she saw how delighted Frau Schenirer was with "Fraulein Doktor's" success, how her face lit up with joy when she saw the girls admiring their new teacher, whom she herself adored. Dr. Rosenbaum noticed how Frau Schenirer took delight in seeing her pupils becoming teachers and succeeding in their work. She observed Frau Schenirer's joy upon hearing how those teachers were beloved by their pupils and respected by the community.

Dr. Grunfeld said to me, "I then realized what a privilege it was for me to work with this great *tzaddeikes*." This noble woman was totally unmarred by jealousy. "*Frau Schenirer hat doch keyn yetzer hora* — Frau Schenirer was immune to the evil inclination," I thought admiringly.

*   *   *

Was Frau Schenirer ever angry?

I do not recall her ever losing her temper with either pupils, teachers, or staff members. Only at seeing *chilul Hashem* (profanation of God's Name) or hearing a statement against the Truth would she react angrily. In other contexts, however, she condemned anger as man's worst inclination, implored us to overcome it, and alerted us to the difficulty in doing so. "It grabs you and does not let go," she said. "You have to gird yourself every day anew to fight this *yetzer ha-ra*; otherwise it will attack you every day when you are young, and even more viciously when you get older." At the time, I did not understand why she stressed the matter of aging. Today I do: older people are more easily irritated and more prone to erupt in anger.

Why is that so? I wondered. The evil inclination loses a lot of ground in older people, so it tries to succeed by invading areas that it had previously ignored. It seizes every opportunity to incite an older person to anger. The elderly are prone to get upset about the smallest problem, the slightest inconvenience. The unrelenting war on anger, however, is a struggle for people of all ages. "Every day, all your life," said Frau Schenirer, "you have to pray and beg Hashem to help you overcome this terrible trait." How right she was.

*   *   *

Although Frau Schenirer would display anger when she saw or heard *chilul Hashem*, in mundane matters she always yielded with a smile. Whenever she heard a girl in school speak disrespectfully to another girl or call someone names, she reproved the culprit. Even then, however, she spoke affably. "Oh! I didn't expect to hear that from my Bais Yaakov girls," she would say with a pained expression. For the girl, this was punishment enough; she regretfully apologized for her wrongdoing and sincerely promised not to do it again. This brought a glow to Frau Schenirer's face. "I'm sure you'll keep your word," she said. She believed it, too. I was amazed how she believed her young charges, took all people at their word, and never doubted a promise given to her. I sometimes treated those promises skeptically. Frau Schenirer never did, and somehow no one abused her trust.

What is more, she turned her reproach into a moral lesson. At the next appropriate occasion, she would casually mention the episode — avoiding names, of course — and remind us how important it was for Bais Yaakov girls to speak respectfully to each other and to everybody else as well. "Girls," she stressed, "never call your friends names, even in a friendly manner."

This statement sufficed to impress her children with deep respect for each other and an unusual drive to meet Frau Schenirer's every expectation of them. They realized their wrongdoing just by observing the expression of their teacher's face and chose to adjust their behavior to Frau Schenirer's satisfaction.

One of the most influential teachers at the Bais Yaakov school in Kraków, Esther Heitner *née* Rosa, wrote in the *Bais Yaakov Journal* about her experiences with Frau Schenirer when the latter visited her school:

"On many occasions, I watched Frau Schenirer's very special way of responding to occasional misbehavior by young Bais Yaakov girls," Esther Rosa wrote. "She reacted with just a facial expression and silence. Her silence was more powerful than words, stronger than a verbal reproach." Esther Rosa continued in her admiration of Frau Schenirer's sincere way of instilling the right values in her children.

"Her silence was enough of a rebuke," Esther points out, telling a story to prove it. "Once Frau Schenirer visited one of my ill girls to lift her spirits and wish her a speedy recovery. She noticed a pillow on the couch with a beautifully embroidered but inappropriate picture on its cover. She turned the pillow around with the picture facing down and did not say a word.

"Her silence and facial expression, coupled with her soft smile of expectation, did wonders and taught volumes."

*   *   *

Frau Schenirer often quoted *Tehillim* 34:13 – 14: *Mi ha-ish heh-chafeitz chaim...* — "Who is the man who is eager for life, who desires years of good fortune? He who guards his tongue from evil, his lips from deceitful speech." According to Frau Schenirer, it also meant not to talk harshly to our friends, to use only clean language, and to express love and care when speaking to people.

"Girls, be careful not to embarrass your friends or your siblings. Remember, a word can bring joy and happiness to people; it can restore their confidence, their faith in God and man. And a word can kill; it can destroy a human being.

"You can discern a person's character and personality in his voice. *Ha-kol kol Yaakov* — your voices should sound like that of our patriarch Yaakov."

To prove her point, she told a story about Reb Avrohom of Lublin:

"Reb Avrohom had a produce stand in the marketplace. He advertised his fruit and vegetables and loudly touted their fine qualities. 'They're fresh; they're tasty; they're juicy,' he intoned in a melodious voice.

"Once a great rabbi passed by and heard Reb Avrohom lauding his produce. Something about Reb Avrohom's voice made him pause. Astonished, he cried, '*Ha-kol kol Yaakov*, that's a voice of Yaakov, a voice of *kedushah* and *taharah*.'

"Intrigued, the rabbi made further inquiries about this man. He followed him, observed his behavior, and monitored his actions. Eventually he discovered that this man was one of the thirty-six *tzaddikim* whose merit sustains the world.

"*Tayere kinderlach*, dear children," Frau Schenirer continued, "this story teaches us how a person's voice expresses his personality and his character traits. This is why we must be careful with every word we say, lest it hurt or embarrass someone, God forbid. However, it's not enough to watch our words; we must also be careful with our tone of voice. We must pronounce our words softly, lovingly, and respectfully, because the mere tone of our voice can make or break a human being.

"I expect my Bais Yaakov girls to behave this way."

*   *   *

Frau Schenirer softened her approach when necessary. The seminary had a rule about girls' hair: they must not cut it but had to wear it in a bun or a braid. Once a girl from the West explained a problem that this caused: girls in her area of residence wore only short haircuts, and her mother would be aggravated to find her with such long hair. "I'm going home for the Holidays and I don't want my mother to get upset," she lamented. Frau Schenirer calmed her: "You have my permission to cut your hair before you leave. *Kibud eim* [honoring a mother's wishes] is a very important mitzvah; it can break my rule."

In matters of *din*, however, she was unflinching. She neither yielded nor compromised on even an iota of the *Shulchan Aruch*.

✣ *Chapter 48* ✣

Hevei mi-talmidav shel Aharon, Frau Schenirer often urged us, quoting Hillel the Elder in *Pirkei Avos* 1:12. "'Be of the pupils of Aharon.' Follow his teachings: 'love peace, pursue peace, love all fellow creatures, and attract them to Torah.'

"Yes," Frau Schenirer would stress, "the highest form of love of people is expressed in attracting them to the truth, to Torah. To do this successfully, our love must be absolutely genuine and unlimited. When we emulate Aharon and follow his ways of love and peace, we give testimony to the greatness of our teacher."

Frau Schenirer's *talmidos* followed in her ways, striving to emulate her limitless love of all God's children and sparing no effort to bring them closer to Hashem — the greatest act of loving-kindness one can do for a human being. Her pupils, through their behavior, bear witness to the greatness of their teacher.

*　　*　　*

At the commencement ceremony of the two-year seminary program, Frau Schenirer would gaze down at her graduating class with her usual love and joy. The words which followed would send a flame of faith, enthusiasm, encouragement, and inspiration to the future teachers.

"You have chosen the greatest and most rewarding profession in life: to cleave and polish the most precious diamonds — the souls of Jewish children. You are the *kohanim*, the teachers of this generation."

Sometimes she would continue by turning to everyone in attendance: "We, all Jews, are teachers. With everything we do, every step we take, every word we utter, every act of kindness we perform, we teach. Our children, our friends, and everyone around us are influenced by our behavior."

Then she refocused her gaze on the graduates:

"We are all a *mamleches kohanim*, a kingdom of teachers. Hashem dispersed us among the nations to instill in them faith in Him by means of our actions. We are to teach others how to love and care for people. We gave the world the concepts of philanthropy and justice. We continually remind the gentiles of the expected moral behavior of human beings.

"The gentiles hate us because our mere existence among them curbs their animal instincts. They wish to free themselves of our passive but powerful influence."

It is exactly as King David, the sweet singer of Israel, said so beautifully in Psalm 2:

Lamah ragshu goyim… — "Why do the nations rage, why are their masses so furious? Kings of the earth take their stand and regents intrigue together against Hashem and His anointed." They discuss, scheme, and advise each other about the actions they should take against the Israelites. "Let us break the cords of their yoke," they cry out in anger, "and shake off their ropes from us."

Rabbi Samson Raphael Hirsch stresses that the yoke of God's anointed hangs heavily around the necks of the gentile nations. The Jewish People, by being ethical and acting morally, gives them an uneasy conscience by continually reminding them that they are human; as such, they must behave decently and be loving and faithful. "Let us shake off their ropes from us" — the reins that restrain their passions and lusts. Let us be free to follow our evil inclinations, they say. Let us rid ourselves of the Jews, so we can live uninhibitedly.

"[But] He Who is enthroned in Heaven laughs; the Lord mocks them. Then He speaks to them in anger, terrifying them in His rage," the Psalm continues. Ultimately, He will redeem

His beloved People and make all gentile nations their inheritance.

*   *   *

Ve-ha'amidu talmidim harbeh — "Raise many pupils."[55] This is what Sarah Schenirer did best: she raised many *talmidos*. She inspired them with her love and enthusiasm for Jewish faith and knowledge. She taught them how to love people, how to care for them, how to give. And what is the most precious gift one can bestow on others? *U-mekarvan la-Torah*[56] — teach them the truth of the Torah.

"*Hevei mi-talmidav shel Aharon*,"[57] says Hillel the Elder. Do not be like Aharon; just be one of his students. The students give testimony to the greatness of their teachers. Mankind has had great individuals, great minds, great leaders. But where are their students, their followers, their children?

Jewish history has known great ideologues and scholars, men of exceptional minds, like Moses Mendelssohn, who possessed faith and even practiced Torah precepts. However, his creed, which became a slogan among the uncommitted: be a Jew at home and a German [a man] in public life, was his undoing.

Was his faith genuine? Even if it was, nothing remains of it. Where are his followers? Even his own children did not remain Jews.

How different Sarah Schenirer's legacy was! "Be one of the *talmidos* of Sarah Schenirer," went the slogan in the hearts of the girls and women who knew her. Their teacher's followers give testimony to her greatness. By emulating her ways, devoting themselves to her ideals, and perpetuating her goals, they bore witness to our mentor's superior virtues. They acted as she did — with love, caring, and kindness — even to the point of forfeiting their lives.

---

55. *Pirkei Avos* 1:1.
56. Ibid., *mishnah* 12.
57. Ibid.

❧ *Chapter 49* ❧

The last time I met Feiga Zelicka, my dear teacher and friend, was in Lodz at the beginning of the war. I had gone to Lodz under strained circumstances to discover the whereabouts of my friend, Rivka Horowitz, who was visiting with her sister-in-law, the daughter of the Kalisher Rav (the brother of the Gerrer Rebbe). I knew she had run away together with a well-known Gerrer family to escape the Nazi scourge. Unfortunately, they had to come back to Lodz, where I hoped to find her. Feiga Zelicka's address was the only one I had in Lodz, so I went there first when I reached the city. I was eager to meet Feiga again, to see her lovely smile, to listen to her words of encouragement, and to be in her presence, however briefly.[58]

I was pleased to make the acquaintance of Feiga's family, since such a lovely flower can grow only in a beautiful garden. I spent several days with them until I found Rivka and passed some time with her; after all, it was for Rivka that I made the trip. Feiga then took me to the railroad station to see me off. Trains were running infrequently by then; one sometimes had to wait for hours. I had already thanked Feiga, expressed my feelings about our painful parting, and begged her to go home and not wait under those wartime circumstances for my train to arrive. But she refused to leave me there alone, as I should have known.

We discussed the situation in Kraków and Lodz, where con-

---

58. Details of that trip are described in *To Vanquish the Dragon*.

ditions worsened with each passing day.

"You know, we have to be strong," Feiga said to me — and to herself — in a tone of urgency that I can still hear. "We can see that hard and bitter times are coming. We have to be ready. We have to stay on guard in order to help others overcome the ordeals. We've got to encourage and support each other. We'll have to implement everything we learned over the years. We're going to face a great test. May the Almighty help us to endure the ordeals and give us strength to help others do the same." That concluding prayer still resonates clearly in my mind.

I never heard from her again. The terrible conditions in the ghetto and the camps ruled out any form of contact. Only after the war did I meet people who told me about Feiga's remarkable feats in the Lodz ghetto.

"The hunger in the ghetto was unbearable," relates Chaya Erlanger *née* Gutterman. "We had to sell everything we possessed for bread until there was nothing to sell and no money. Fortunately, I had a friend who planted radishes in her backyard and who allowed me to sell them for her.

"I was lucky; I earned a few zlotys to buy bread for my family. One evening after a difficult day of work, when I visited my friend to pay her for the radishes I had sold, she told me, 'Chaya, I'm rushing to a lecture that I organized. There's a group of twelve girls who get together in the evenings to listen to an extraordinary teacher, Feiga Zelicka. Come with me. It's a long walk, but when you come back you'll be glad you went. Each of us pays her twenty *groschen* per lecture, but as you will realize, it's a bargain.' I agreed to join them.

"Her lessons," Chaya continued enthusiastically, "elevated us from this world of bestiality and ugliness into a different sphere, a world of light, truth, goodness, and loving-kindness. Just listening to her uplifted us, gave us courage and hope, and made us forget about our hunger and misery.

"Feiga shared a little room with her father; the rest of the family had already died of hunger in the ghetto. The thirteen of us packed into this tiny space, changing places intermittently because there were only four chairs available. All wooden furniture and implements in the ghetto were gone; they had been used to heat up a little water or to warm someone's room.

"Despite the discomfort, I ran to the lecture every night after work. By that time I was working in a feather plant. I had replaced my mother, who could not take the feather dust any more because it gave her a heavy cough. It was tiring and unhealthy work. Still, after a whole terrible day of it, I ran home to say hello to my mother — my father had already died of starvation — and then, without food and without rest, I rushed to the class in order to be there on time. Freezing from the long walk to the outskirts of the ghetto and back again, I came home to a cast-iron stove that had long since gone cold. I put my legs into the ashes to warm up a little and then went to bed without food, saving my bread for the morning. I had no need for food now. Feiga's elaborate lecture had filled me with spiritual nourishment. I dreamed of a lofty world of fulfillment and satisfaction.

At a summer seminary camp in the thirties. Stretched on the grass to the left is Feiga Zelicka. Standing, from the left, are Tonka Neiman, Basia Leiser, Ruchel Schowzer. Yenta Werdiger stands to the far right. Sitting on the right is Rachel Luria.

"After a while, Feiga decided that she could no longer give us any classes. When we insisted, she agreed to resume, but under one condition — without pay. 'I cannot take the little you have,' she stressed. She then set up a charity fund. Under those conditions! She asked every girl to bring a half-teaspoon of sugar, a teaspoon of flour, etc., from her monthly rations, for distribution to the very ill and the half-dead.

"Feiga felt guilty. With the two zlotys she earned per week, and other earnings that she could acquire, she still could not feed her father properly, even under those circumstances. She always thought that she was not doing enough for her father. Still, no matter under how much stress she was, her face was always calm and relaxed. Her lectures always radiated faith, hope, and wise counsel.

"She not only taught her 'class' but also used to speak to us personally," Chaya recalled. "She knew the girls and how to approach them.

"Once she asked me and my friend, Sarah Urbach [née Zelver], to speak to the group. We spoke about the fact that every person has a special purpose in life, based on their abilities. One is better in this skill, one in another. It is our goal to offer the world the best that our individuality can provide.

"She encouraged us girls to think independently, to learn on our own, and to acquire Torah wisdom by dint of our own efforts. I try to follow her advice to this very day," Chaya told me proudly. "I impart it to my children, my grandchildren, and others."

Chaya's story impressed me deeply. What a true *talmidah* of Frau Schenirer's Feiga was. How effectively she communicated her great teacher's ideas and thoughts. What power Frau Schenirer had, to be able to implant her ideals in the hearts of the teachers, for retransmission to future generations.

This reminds one of Dr. Judith Grunfeld's parable mentioned earlier: "You throw a stone into a pond and observe the impression it leaves: one round wave and then another bigger one, followed by a third larger still; circle after circle, each larger than the one preceding it." What a powerful throw it must have been to set such a process in motion.

*   *   *

Feiga Zelicka did not survive the war. During a *Selektion* in Auschwitz, she ran to join her ill father, and they both perished. However, she left a legacy that continues to grow: the impact that she made on the people whose lives she touched.

❧ *Chapter 50* ❧

"Die Grosse und Kleine Menschenliebe"

Frau Schenirer subscribed to *Der Israelit,* a Jewish weekly published in Frankfurt from 1860 until Kristallnacht (November 10 – 11, 1938) and edited in the early years by Dr. Marcus Lehmann. She encouraged us to read this Orthodox Jewish paper due to its high literary level, and suggested that the Bnos leaders study some interesting articles and discuss them with their groups. One of them carried the title cited above, which means, "The Great and Small Love of Humanity." The meaning and moral of the fascinating story left such a deep impression on the young readers that one of them — this author — and probably many others, remember its crux more than a half century later.

"There was once a great teacher," the story begins, "who successfully educated many talented and capable students. Apart from knowledge, he instilled love of humanity in them. One day, he decided to send three of his most promising pupils to the large cities in the district to show men the great virtue of love of humanity. 'Go out into the world for two days,' he said, 'and see what great acts you can perform for the benefit of humanity. Then come back and tell me what you accomplished. May God bless you with success,' he wished them as they eagerly set out.

"The first student came to a large city, climbed onto a wooden box, attracted a crowd, and began to preach passionately and excitedly about love of humanity. The crowd grew, listening to him with interest and inspired by his sincere oratory. He progressed in this fashion from city to city, successfully communicating the message of love of humanity to enthusiastic audiences of all kinds.

"The second student, in his travels, gathered notables and impressed them with the importance of building large institutions of study for the benefit of the population at large. At one of his stops, he noticed that the town leaders were oblivious to the citizens' health problems and explained the importance of building a hospital for them. So he went, from city to city, doing great deeds for the benefit of humanity.

"The third student, flush with love of humanity, was also eager to do his teacher's bidding and bring love and peace to humankind. Right off, however, he encountered a problem: his elderly mother fell ill and he had to summon a doctor and order medication to help his father care for her. This delayed his departure for several hours. After completing the arrangements, he rushed to the railroad station, anxious to make up the lost time.

"Suddenly the young student noticed a group of young people at the town well, drawing water for their families. He helped some of the girls hoist the heavy pails. Then he noticed an older and homely girl trying to get her turn at the well so that her family, evidently poor, might drink as well. The young men, stronger than she, pushed her away repeatedly. Disgusted by the injustice, the student approached the well, forcibly made room for the girl, and helped her to fill her two heavy pails. Then he chastised the young townspeople for their inhumane behavior.

"'Oh, my goodness,' he thought. 'Again I've lost precious time for my assignment.' He flung his small bag over his shoulder and hurried to his destination, humming a happy tune. Then, however, he heard a man and woman screaming and could not but stop to see what was happening. As he approached, the sounds of a severe quarrel between husband and wife, replete with cursing, reached his ears.

"The traveler felt he must help the troubled young couple — to calm them or even, perhaps, to establish peace between them. He wrote down the name of a neighbor several houses away and, armed with the slip of paper, knocked on the door of the shouting couple.

"'Good evening,' he greeted them affably. 'I'm lost in this neighborhood. Could you please tell me where I might find these people?' He showed them the name. The shouting stopped and the woman invited him inside pleasantly. 'What brings you here at this late hour?' she asked. The student explained his need to reach the capital, where he would do an assignment for his great and widely renowned teacher. He had been delayed, but fortunately he had been given the name of their neighbor, who might put him up for the night.

"'Oh, you don't have to look for him,' the woman interrupted hastily. Turning to her husband, she said, 'Wouldn't it be our pleasure to let this young man stay with us?'

"'Of course!' he nodded. 'And we'll be glad to take you to the railroad station tomorrow morning. The train to the capital leaves very early.'

"The next morning, our young man happily reached the station under the guidance of his now calm hosts. After lengthy and friendly farewells, he rushed to board his train. Once aboard, he made himself comfortable and made plans to carry out his great assignment.

"Soon a young woman entered the compartment carrying a baby who looked severely ill. She began to explain why she was traveling to the great city. She had left her older children with her husband and was taking her ill child, who could not be helped in her hometown, to the city where a good doctor might treat his terrible disease and save his life.

"Finding the young man attentive to her distress, she poured out her heart to him, tears streaming down her cheeks. 'We are poor people,' she confided. 'I can't afford the treatment that I am trying to arrange in the great city. I can only trust and hope that God, in His beneficence, will somehow help me.'

"Without thinking twice, our young man asked the woman to follow him with the baby. 'We'll go from compartment to compartment,' he explained. 'I'll describe your plight to the passengers and ask them to help you. I'm sure they'll respond.' Indeed, he raised enough money to pay for a specialist and even for hospital care, if needed.

"This put the mother at ease for the rest of the trip. As they approached the great city, however, she became nervous again. 'Where should I go? I don't know anyone here.'

"'It's still early in the morning,' thought the young man. 'I've still got the whole day. I'll help this poor woman.' He found her a doctor, who advised her to take the baby to the hospital at once. The student then escorted them to the hospital.

"The hours passed. By the time he reached the downtown area, where he might at last accomplish something for love of humanity, it was late afternoon. Before he could set his great plans in motion, however, night fell. The two days were up. His teacher had instructed him to return by then.

"Patiently and lovingly the teacher waited for his favorite students. Two of them returned promptly, before sundown. The first one told his story: 'Dear mentor, I left for the big city right away, as you told us. I gathered a crowd in front of City Hall and spoke to them about loving-kindness, charity, and helping the needy. They listened to me with interest and enthusiasm,' he said proudly, 'so I went to another city and had the same success. People with tears in their eyes told me about the great impression my speech made on them and how it would help them to live more meaningful lives.'

"'And you?' the teacher turned to the second student. "'What did you accomplish in those two days?'

"'I made people understand the need to act for the community in large ways, like building schools and hospitals. I'm sure these important people took the message seriously and will follow it up,' he finished with confidence.

"The third student arrived long after nightfall. 'Why are

you so late?' the teacher asked. 'What did you accomplish for love of humanity in those two long days?'

"The student lowered his head in shame for having disappointed his mentor. 'Raise your head, my beloved boy,' the teacher said softly, 'and tell us what you did during those two days.'

"'I...I'm sorry,' the young man stammered. 'Please forgive me, my revered teacher. I did not do the very important task you gave us. I was delayed repeatedly and lost so much precious time that I did no great acts for humanity. Forgive me,' he pleaded again.

"'But tell me,' the teacher continued in an encouraging tone, 'what it was that delayed you so much.' Our young man, put slightly at ease, began to retell the events of the past two days — from helping his ill mother to assisting a stranger with a sick baby. He finished his story and humbly awaited his beloved mentor's verdict.

"After a lengthy pause, the teacher turned to two of his three favorite students and declared with conviction, 'Know that what your fellow student did — acts of care and devotion for people in distress — was the most important accomplishment of my assignment. His deeds are the *true* love of humanity!'"

Sarah Schenirer embodied this "true love of humanity" at both levels expressed in the title of the article: the *grosse* (grand) and the *kleine* (minute). With the vast breadth of her love, she spared Jewish girls from assimilation by introducing the novel idea of *chinuch ha-banos,* systematic Orthodox schooling for girls. Her Bais Yaakov movement had an extraordinary impact on Jewish life in her own time and spread its influence to all future generations worldwide.

In her all-encompassing love of humanity, she did not neglect love of and concern for every individual human being everywhere. Her *ahavas chessed,* loving-kindness, was extraordinary. Regarding every individual as an entire universe, she found him or her worthy of her utmost attention. Her eyes and ears were always open to human pain and woe. She "made time" to help in every way necessary, from great deeds for the ill to the smallest acts of bringing joy to a pupil or any human being.

The title of that article — *Die Grosse und Kleine Mensch-enliebe,* the "great" and "small" love of humankind — encapsulates the marvel that was Sarah Schenirer.

Our Teacher's
Final Year

✧ *Chapter 51* ✧

Frau Schenirer spent the summer of 1934 at her usual activities — teaching, visiting newly established schools, sitting with teachers to discuss their problems, planning the coming year's programs with the staff, and above all, maintaining her correspondence.

She wrote letters until 3:00 or 4:00 in the morning. At such hours, girls stepped into her room and begged her to retire. "You've got a hard day ahead. You must rest," they implored, worrying about her health.

"Dear girls," she replied, "I *am* resting. Writing to my children is my rest, my joy. I am with them."

During this, her last summer, Frau Schenirer's *tzedakah* and *chessed* activities kept her unusually busy. She traveled to all manner of vacation spots — spas, summer resorts, and hotels in the mountains — where people fled from the sweltering, muggy weather in the cities. There she could raise more funds for her diverse responsibilities.

That summer, she also took a lengthy trip to Lodz to visit the *Hachsharah*, Ohel Sarah, which she had not seen for a long time. It was a good time to visit; the people there were not on vacation. She brought her girls encouragement and blessings for success in their daunting goal: physical and spiritual *aliyah*, ascent, to *Eretz ha-Kodesh*. Her display of interest and the strenuous effort she had invested in the visit filled the girls there with joy and enthusiasm. In fact, however, the mere fact of her presence would have done the same.

At the end of the summer, in Jordanów, Frau Schenirer answered a letter she received from the first Bnos kibbutz (collective) in Eretz Yisroel. The first *aliyah* group, made up of the most important Bais Yaakov teachers and Bnos leaders under the leadership of Devorah Gur-Aryeh, had arrived in Tel Aviv in Adar (February) 1934. The letter read as follows:

Elul [August] 1934

My dear Bnos daughters,
I have your letter from Eretz Yisroel, from the Bnos kibbutz in Tel Aviv, in front of me. You asked me to write an article for the forthcoming brochure that will be distributed in newly established Bnos chapters.

I am deeply moved by your request that I write a few words of encouragement and advice to the Bnos girls in our Holy Land. The words, "Bnos girls in our Holy Land," awakened a deep love and yearning for Zion in me.

Although I cannot come, you, my daughters, have been *zocheh* to live in *Eretz ha-Kedushah*, where Hashem's Presence resided. Even now, Hashem is *doreish osah*;[59] He continuously watches over Eretz Yisroel and its inhabitants.

You walk the streets of Jerusalem, where our *Nevi'im* and *Nevi'os* [Prophets] gave their prophecies. You breathe the same holy air. Excitedly you walk the narrow cobblestone lanes and touch the tiny pebbles that tell you about the gorgeous past that we have lost.

Mipnei chata'einu galinu me-Artzeinu — "due to our sins we were exiled from our Land." Now that you are *zocheh* to live in our Promised Land, use your strong religious presence there, your abilities, your knowledge, and your enthusiasm, to influence the estranged youth and bring them back to our precious heritage. Show them how the words of Torah bring joy into our lives, how its teachings are a refreshing spring in scorching summer heat, a shelter in wintry weather, a balm for our painful existence.

---

59. See *Devarim* 11:12.

We hope and pray that, against all difficulties and obstacles, you will manage to spread the idea of Bnos and Bais Yaakov in the Holy Land. Just as we in Poland managed, with God's help, to surmount all the objections and make our presence felt in the Jewish community, so will you, God willing.

The month of Elul, in which I am writing to you, will help you to stay strong and unbending in serving Hashem with joy. This month of repentance will also give you the strength and ability to bring your Jewish sisters to *teshuvah*.

Frau Schenirer also used this opportunity to appeal to parents:

Dear sisters and brothers in the Holy Land,
Just as you care about your children's physical needs, do not neglect their spiritual needs, which are even more important. Send your daughters to Bais Yaakov, where they will be brought up in the true, original Jewish spirit.

Let us hope that with Hashem's help we will witness the time when *Bais Yaakov, lechu ve-nelchah be-ohr Hashem* — when Bais Yaakov will pave the way, and others will follow in God's glorious light.

Sarah Schenirer

*   *   *

On *Chol ha-Mo'ed Sukkos*, the teachers returned from summer vacation to their positions in the various cities and towns. This year, one of them demurred and approached Frau Schenirer to discuss her problem:

"I can't go back to teach. I don't feel well," she pleaded.

Instead of convincing the teacher to carry on, as Frau Schenirer usually did, she answered, "I understand you. I never knew what it meant to be ill, but now I can commiserate."

People who overheard this remark became alarmed. Closely observing Frau Schenirer, they realized that she was not well.

She was in pain and had lost her appetite; she forced herself to eat. Although she remained active, illness had made inroads.

As time passed, her family and staff insisted that she stop her activities and take care of herself. Their entreaties were in vain until Frau Schenirer collapsed one Friday evening after lighting the Shabbos candles. Severe pain and weight loss had taken their toll.

Realizing that she could not go to the seminary that night, Frau Schenirer burst into tears. Nobody had ever seen her weeping before, and those who witnessed it that night asked her in concern, "Is the pain getting worse?"

"No, I am not crying about the physical pain," she replied. "I am bothered by a different and stronger kind of pain. I cannot be with my children and recite *Shir ha-Shirim* with them in my usual way on erev Shabbos."

Usual, indeed. Every Friday night she poured out her heart and love to the Ribono shel Olam for His concern for and admiration of His beloved bride, *Am Yisroel.* Her beautiful and passionate recitation of that monumental work, *Shir ha-Shirim*, made such an impression on her students that they recite it with fervor and ardor to this very day.

That erev Shabbos in late 1934, however, Frau Schenirer could not share with her children her emotive message about the exquisite relationship between the Almighty and His People. That was her greatest pain.

Nevertheless, she quickly regained her composure. "It is Shabbos today. We have to greet the Shabbos Queen with joy!" Then, with a lovely smile, she transformed the atmosphere of worry and concern into an aura of faith, trust, and hope in the Ribono shel Olam.

*   *   *

As Frau Schenirer's condition worsened, she entered the local hospital for treatments. Although bedridden, she continued to correspond with her children at the seminary and made sure the letters would reach them in time for each Shabbos.

One of those letters follows, in free translation from the Yiddish:

B"H, Chanukah 1934

Although I am no longer with you physically, I am among you with my soul and heart. May Hashem help us to be *zocheh* together to celebrate *chanukas ha-bayis* [the consecration of the *Beis ha-Mikdash*] in Jerusalem.

Yours,
Sarah Schenirer

Another letter from the hospital:

B"H, November 16, 1934
Friday, erev Shabbos *Vayeitze* 5695

Good Shabbos to each and every one of you, again through the medium of this cold paper. If Hashem so decreed, it is surely for the best.

Sarah Schenirer

Some time later, Frau Schenirer was discharged from the hospital, although she showed no signs of improvement and remained bedridden and immobile. One day, however, she made up her mind to visit her children at the seminary.

Over the entreaties and remonstrations of her family and friends, she dressed and made her way to the seminary by dint of sheer willpower.

When she arrived, she found the girls about to conduct a *siyum* for having completed the study of one book of the Torah. Her happiness knew no limit. "I've come home to my children!" she exclaimed joyfully. "Here I feel that I will recover."

She felt somewhat better after that visit, but not for long. To everyone's distress, her condition worsened and her family and friends decided to take her to Vienna for major surgery, it being known that the best hospital, surgeons, and medical staff for the procedure were there.

Below in free translation are excerpts from Sarah Schenirer's last letter before her departure for Vienna, written from her sickbed to her students on the occasion of their graduation. More than a letter, it expresses a testament, her last will and last wish.

My beloved, cherished children, *amosh*!

What should we say? Of what can we speak? How can we justify ourselves?[60] There are many thoughts in man's heart, but only Hashem's guidance will prevail.[61]

Our thoughts are powerless and uncertain; only God knows and does what's good for us.

May Hashem be blessed for all the acts of loving-kindness that He bestows upon us.

Since this morning, I have not been able to restrain my tears. I, who always complained of an inability to cry while praying, now cannot control the flow of my tears.

Now I realize the strength of the spiritual ties that bind me to you, my dear children. You remember how often I used to repeat the Polish saying, "Blood is thicker than water." Now, I say: "The soul is thicker than the body." Yes, the spiritual ties are much stronger. They last forever.

I feel that just as my tears flow as I write to you, so will your tears flow as you read my words. With our merciful Father's help, may our united tears reach the throne of His Glory and bring us complete redemption and speedy recovery for all sufferers.

Now I turn to you, my beloved children, who are heading into the wide world to educate and guide Jewish daughters.

I trust that you understand your lofty calling. We have a good Father in Heaven, Who helps us all to perform the tasks we undertake.

Throughout my years of difficult endeavor, Hashem always sent me dedicated people who helped me in my work. I

---

60. Based on verses from *Tachanun* and *Viduy*.
61. *Mishlei* 19:21.

hope He will do the same for you.

I just want to make you aware of two grave dangers that will threaten you, my dear children. They are your two greatest enemies; they lurk to attack you. You must fight them, especially when you practice your lofty calling. First, the feeling of pride and arrogance that you will feel when you succeed, and second, the other extreme: the sense of inferiority that causes you to slacken your efforts to succeed at your work (as we discussed earlier).

Remember, then, to recite the verse in *Parashas Eikev* after your prayers: "And now, what does Hashem request of you? Only to fear the Lord your God, to walk in all His ways, to love Him, and to serve the Lord your God with all your heart and soul."[62] Just be sure that you are doing your work with dedication and love for the Almighty. Do it all with the joy of being able to heed and fulfill His commandments.

My dear children, you have all taken your written and oral exams. All of you passed, thank God. But now comes the most important and difficult test — *life*.

Life is often hard and replete with trying circumstances. But remember, you also possess the most powerful weapon to fight the ordeals — *yiras Hashem*, *ahavas Hashem*, and *avodas Hashem* [fear, love, and service of God].

Sometimes, despite myself, I am overcome with a painful thought: do my dear children, those young pioneers, really feel how much I trust them? Do they understand the great responsibilities they will have to shoulder to bring up a new generation? Do they realize the great trials awaiting them on their new path of life's hardships?

A silent prayer wells from within my heart at times like this. Then I pray, "Almighty God, please continue to help my devoted children in their holy work. Do not test them too severely on their thorn-strewn path. May our Sages' promise be fulfilled in them: 'He who comes to purify him-

---

62. *Devarim* 10:12.

self is helped by Heaven.'

"My children surely have the purest of intentions. Thus, please help them, Father in Heaven, to transform those intentions into good and beautiful deeds."

Years ago in Rabka, at the final examination, our revered Herr Orlean spoke to the girls. His words still resonate in my ears: "The tests showed us that you can learn and teach, but throughout the examinations we were troubled by the thought that you may not realize that you are venturing into the wide world to train young Jewish souls.

"We thought of the young *kohanim* who, before entering the Holy of Holies, were asked to treat the holiness of the Sanctuary cautiously. Now that the *Beis ha-Mikdash* has been destroyed, every Jewish home has become a temple. Your responsibility now is to go into the world to build temples.

"Your goal is to implant holiness in the souls of pure children and help them to grow up as true God-fearing Jews and passionate human beings. In your hands lies the future of the Jewish woman and, with it, of the Jewish People."

On the occasion of your celebrating the *siyum* of almost the entire Tanach, I want to remind you of a Chassidic story that I just recalled. A student came to his rebbe with joyous news. "I just finished learning the whole *Shas* [Talmud]!" he said proudly.

"And what did the *Shas* teach you?" the rebbe asked.

That is the crux of the whole matter, my dear children: what all the education you received taught you.

I wish to end my letter with some old *pesukim* of mine (not really mine, but King David's), which should always accompany you in life. They are, as you all know:

Ivdu es Hashem be-simchah
    (Serve Hashem with joy).
Shivisi Hashem le-negdi tamid
    (I always keep Hashem in mind).

Reishis chochmah yiras Hashem
(The origin of wisdom is fear of Hashem).
Limnos yameinu kein hoda
(Teach us to count our days rightly).
Toras Hashem temimah meshivas nafesh
(The teaching of Hashem is perfect, renewing life).[63]

May Hashem protect you as you go and as you come. May He listen to our prayers and send to us the Ultimate Redemption speedily. Amen.

Yours,
Sarah Schenirer
Kraków, January 1935

Before Frau Schenirer left for the train station on her way to Vienna, Hanka Grossfeld visited her at home to see her off. Frau Schenirer sensed her presence near the door and called her into her room.

"I'm going to Vienna for surgery," she explained. "We all know that surgery is a serious matter. We hope, with God's help, that all will go well and that the doctors of Vienna will be God's faithful emissaries.

"Please take this note from me," she continued in an imploring tone. "It is important for you to have it; it lists all of my personal debts."

Hanka took the note. Inspecting it, she found no true personal debts, but records of loans Frau Schenirer had taken to cover important *chessed* activities, plus a list of notes that she had co-signed for people in need.

At the station, Frau Schenirer found herself surrounded by relatives, friends, and members of her seminary staff, all wishing and praying for her speedy recovery. They could hardly restrain their tears, but Frau Schenirer was in good spirits. She spoke loudly, for all to hear:

"From Vienna I brought spiritual recovery for the daugh-

---

63. *Tehillim* 100:2, 16:8, 111:10, 90:12, and 19:8, respectively.

ters of Israel. So, too, I hope to receive my physical recovery there." Then she added, in jest, "I'll surprise everyone, you'll see. I'll yet give a lecture to the Bais Yaakov girls in Vienna."

Providence did not allow that to happen. However, from Vienna, too, despite her grave condition, her letters continued to reach the seminary in time for every Shabbos. They were different from her previous letters in one sense: they reflected the seriousness of her illness. Many letters ended with a plea: "Please pray for my recovery, but don't forget to pray to and serve Hashem with joy."

Below is a translation of one of those letters from Vienna, written after Frau Schenirer's operation:

B"H, Vienna, *Parashas Terumah* 5695

Another week has passed, bringing us one week closer to the Final Redemption. Do you remember what I said in Jordanów? There is a *mikdash* [a temple] in the heart of every Jew, and as you know, every holy place has its Holy of Holies. It was there that Hashem told Aharon ha-Kohen to kindle the flame of *yiras Hashem* and *ahavas Hashem*. Although that was to be a perpetual flame, God told Aharon to add two pieces of wood every day. Yes, my dear children, we should ourselves add two pieces of wood to this fire every day — one of mitzvos and one of *ma'asim tovim* [good deeds] — to keep the fire aglow.

That's enough for today. Good Shabbos to each and every one of you individually.

Please pray for the *refuah shleimah* [full recovery] of Surah bas Roiza [Sarah Schenirer]. Be aware that Hashem is close and listens to all who call Him.

Sarah Schenirer

Frau Schenirer returned from Vienna after the operation but showed no improvement. Instead, to everyone's distress and anguish, her condition worsened. Her *talmidos* and friends intensified their prayers for her recovery...and hoped.

❧ *Chapter 52* ❧

It was two weeks before our dear Frau Schenirer passed away. Her sister took care of the ailing patient and tried to conserve her strength by limiting the number of visitors. Taubka Mushel Jacobi came from her hometown of Chrzanów to see her beloved teacher.

"When I came in," Taubka related, "her sister told me, 'Frau Schenirer is very weak today and cannot see anybody.' I was heartbroken to think of my dear teacher in that condition. I left despondently, praying for her speedy recovery. But before I reached the bottom of the landing, I heard her sister running after me. 'Sorry,' she said. 'Come right back, please. Frau Schenirer wants to see you.'"

In fact, Taubka said, Frau Schenirer scolded her sister for her good intentions. "Taubka came to see me and you didn't let her in? Maybe she needs something. Bring her right back."

"I ran up the steps back to Frau Schenirer's room," Taubka continued. "I could not bear to look at her ill, tired face. I regretted disturbing her. But she wanted to know everything; she was interested in every detail. She knew all my problems in school and asked me how I was managing. In general, she was always aware of everything that went on in each school. Now, seeing my dear teacher in this state, I could hardly restrain my sobbing until after I left."

All other visitors felt the same way. They tried not to show their dear teacher how worried they were about her condition. However, Frau Schenirer noticed their concern as they surrounded her sickbed. Once she responded: "My dear children, don't worry. You see that I'm not worried. We should thank Hashem for everything He does.... *Al ha-tov ve-al*...." She fell asleep in mid-sentence under her sedation.

Once, when Reb Binyamin Süssman and another man came to visit, Frau Schenirer was sleeping, and so the visitors moved from her room to the next room so as not to disturb her. Suddenly she called out. The girl who served as her regular attendant rushed in. Frau Schenirer was awake and had overheard the conversation in the next room. "Please," she asked the girl, "call in Mr. Süssman." Reb Binyamin and the other visitor came in. After giving them her usual friendly greeting, she exclaimed, "I'm so upset about what I overheard you saying. Is it possible that a young man did not daven in a *tallis* today because his old one was burned and he couldn't afford a new one? Please," she continued, turning to Reb Binyamin, "buy him a *tallis* right away, and don't forget an *atarah*. Tomorrow, please God, he should daven *Shacharis* proudly in his new *tallis*."

Only Sarah Schenirer would struggle under sedation to regain enough consciousness to restore a stranger's pride.

Several days before Frau Schenirer's passing, Dr. Heshel Klepfisch traveled to Kraków to pay a *bikkur cholim* visit to the great woman whom he admired.

"It was a rainy, cloudy day when I arrived at her home on Kordeckiego Street," the noted Agudath Israel activist and regular contributor to the *Bais Yaakov Journal* writes. "But when I entered her room, I found it even darker and gloomier.

"Her students surrounded the bed of their beloved teacher with tears in their eyes and bitter pain and sorrow etched into their faces. With love and dedication they gazed at their mentor's dear face, its suffering evident despite heavy sedation. They waited for those precious eyes to open and show them a sign of her usual love and concern."

Dr. Klepfisch sat down together with them and waited.

"Suddenly she stirred, opened her eyes, and tried to raise her head. The girls rushed to prop up her pillows so that she could attain a sitting position. She withdrew a hand from under the cover and whispered, 'Paper, pen, ink.'

"She could hardly speak, but she spoke:

"'I must answer the letter I received from the founders of a Bais Yaakov school in Eretz Yisroel. They asked me for advice and suggestions on how to educate our girls in the Land of Holiness. I must answer.'

"With her last strength, her hand shaking, she grasped the pen and wrote her last letter, concerning the obligations of Jewish girls in the Land of Holiness.

"Even on her deathbed," Dr. Klepfisch explained enthusiastically in his article, "she was a great writer."

She was not appreciated as such, as we have noted, but Dr. Klepfisch urged us to read her *Gesamelte Schriften* (*Collected Writings*), and the many articles that she had contributed to every edition of the *Bais Yaakov Journal* and *Kindergarten*. Read and admire her beautiful writings, he said, and appreciate her style, her meaningful thoughts, and her deep feelings, expressed in prose and poetry.

*   *   *

On that fateful Friday afternoon, Frau Schenirer's last day on earth, one of Frau Schenirer's exceptional students and one of my beloved teachers, Escia Teitelbaum, came to visit her. She set the table for her mentor, covered it with a white tablecloth, and brought out Frau Schenirer's two large candlesticks. Escia was about to leave when Frau Schenirer stopped her: "Escia, before you leave, please bring me the *leichters* [candlesticks] and two candles. Today I want to light my Shabbos candles early." Escia did as told. From her bedside, Frau Schenirer lit the candles with deep emotion and recited the blessing with great enthusiasm and joy. Seeing the two large candles illuminate her home and the whole world like a pair of torches, she peacefully fell asleep.

❧ *Chapter 53* ❧

Va-tamos Sarah — *"And Sarah died" (Bereishis 23:2)*

At this writing, sixty-seven years have passed since that day — dark, terrible years, years of suffering and pain, years of horror and fright, years of losing nearest and dearest in the cruelest manner imaginable. None of it, however, could erase the sad recollections of the day when our beloved mother, the unforgettable Sarah Schenirer of blessed memory, passed away.

It happened on Shabbos eve, 26 Adar Alef 5695, March 1, 1935. After the kindling of the Shabbos lights, I meant to go as usual to my Bnos group, where my friends and I would pray together and joyously greet the Shabbos Queen. As soon as I stepped into the street, however, the terrible news hit me: "Frau Schenirer has passed away."

She is gone. We are alone, orphaned. She had always shown us the way, the path to follow to *ohr Hashem,* Hashem's luminance. That expression came from one of her favorite verses: "House of Jacob [*Bais Yaakov*], let us walk in the light of Hashem."[64] Continually she expounded on that verse, explaining its meaning and teaching us how to achieve its intention.

She is gone. We are still so young, Mother; you left us too early. Who will lead us? A sudden despondency and darkness swept over me, the other girls, and our whole world.

Immediately I turned in the direction of her apartment,

---

64. *Yeshayahu* 2:5.

which was around the corner from mine. With a heavy heart, I ascended the stairs. The door was open. The house was lit. The table was covered with a white tablecloth in honor of Shabbos. However, the holy Shabbos did not reign here as it did elsewhere in the world; the suffocating atmosphere in the house weighed heavily on our tender hearts. We passed the dining room and entered the room where the holy body of our dear mother, the great *tzaddeikes*, lay. The room was dark except for the two candles in the tall candlesticks at her head, which she had lit before she fell into eternal sleep.

I and several girls who had preceded me into the room had come "to mourn for Sarah and to bewail her,"[65] to part with our dear mother. For the last time we surrounded her holy body, reciting *Tehillim* with broken hearts and tearful eyes. I gazed at those burning candles and wondered what would become of the holy flames she had kindled in our hearts and the great torches she had lit in the world. In our despair, we cried bitterly, "Dear Mother, how could you leave us at this difficult time? Who will keep your holy lights from being extinguished?"

Hearing our weeping, Frau Schenirer's husband, Rabbi Yitzchok Landau, stepped in from the dining room and tried to comfort us. "Girls, it is Shabbos. You are not allowed to cry," he said. "It would make Frau Schenirer sad." Like magic, the sobbing stopped immediately. God forbid that we would ever distress our dear mother!

This thought and feeling accompanied us for the rest of our lives. Amidst the most trying ordeals, we asked ourselves, "How would Frau Schenirer want us to act? How should we spare her from pain and make her proud of her Bais Yaakov girls?" Just as her daughters guarded her holy body that entire fateful Shabbos, day and night, so did they guard her saintly legacy — the two torches, love of Hashem and love of fellowman, that she had kindled in their hearts. They protected that legacy to their last breath, at great sacrifice. They kept the torches burning

---

65. *Bereishis* 23:2.

amidst the tragic tumult of the war years. Neither the ovens of Auschwitz, nor the bullets of the murderers, not even the hunger pangs and the rivers of blood could extinguish that fire. During the long, cold, dark nights, harassed by the cruel Nazi beasts, her candles gave us light and warmed our souls.

The funeral took place on Sunday morning. To escort this holy woman to her resting place, people from all over Poland transformed the roads into a mass of black that streamed the Kazimierz section of the Jewish quarter. Young and old, congregational leaders and laypeople, they all came, grieving deeply, to pay their last respects to Sarah Schenirer. Many came to salute this great personality who had revolutionized the Jewish world in her own time and for all future generations by introducing the novel idea of Orthodox Jewish education for girls. Others came to part from this woman who, like a mother, had felt everybody's pain and helped everyone with love.

Her Bais Yaakov daughters cried, the Jewish People cried, even the heavens cried. Torrential rain pelted Kraków — the large and sorrowful tears of the firmament, bemoaning man-

Frau Schenirer's obituary notice.

kind's great and tragic loss.

It was difficult to walk behind the coffin. The way was packed with people — along the streets of Kraków, over the bridge and through Podgorze to the new Jewish cemetery. Although the old cemetery was still being used to inter important and wealthy people, Sarah Schenirer, in her last will, expressed her wish to be buried in the new cemetery, where she could stay with the plain, simple people whom she loved.

During the Holocaust, the Nazis established the Plaszów concentration camp on the grounds of the new cemetery. Bais Yaakov girls were forced to help build the camp and, later on, to uproot the tombstones and with their own hands use them to pave the camp paths. The old cemetery in Kraków, in contrast, remained intact. Thus Frau Schenirer shared her daughters' fate, as she had wished. Just as they had neither graves nor tombstones, so had no trace of Frau Schenirer's resting place survived. [After these lines were written, a tombstone was erected in the presumed site of Frau Schenirer's grave.]

The same was said of Moshe Rabbeinu: *Lo yada ish es kevuraso* — "No one knows his burial place until this very day."[66] Moshe, who suffered with and dedicated his life to his People, died in the desert together with his entire generation. No trace of his burial place is known. Thus was our mother Sarah reunited in fate with her daughters and her People: as their place of burial is not known, so, too, is hers not to be found.

✳   ✳   ✳

It not being the custom in Kraków for Jewish women to attend burials, we girls did not follow the hearse to the cemetery. Instead, we went to the Bais Yaakov building at 30 Augustianska Street and sat there, Sarah Schenirer's daughters, lamenting and mourning the loss of our dear mother. As we wept, one of the Bnos leaders, Ruchka Iliker, came in.

"Girls, what is going on here?" she asked. "Frau Schenirer

---

66. *Devarim* 34:6.

surely would never have wanted you to sit around and just cry like this. Come, let's learn something for her sake. Let's turn the time of mourning into a time of learning, for our mother's merit. It will give her genuine *nachas ruach* [spiritual satisfaction]."

"That's easier said than done," we protested. "How can we concentrate on learning now? It's impossible." Now our sobbing expressed additional despair: that our crying might be hurting her.

"Ruchka, please, let's talk about Frau Schenirer," I suggested, "her actions, her sayings, her lessons. It's like studying a book of *mussar*."

Ruchka accepted this. Thus, we sat until late that night learning Torah by retelling stories and anecdotes about our noble mentor's great acts of piety and loving-kindness. Episode after episode, the girls poured out their love for their great teacher. My contribution was an account of Frau Schenirer's last lesson, which made an impact on me that has lasted to this day. It was one of the *Yahadus* lessons that she gave every Wednesday evening at Bnos when she was in town. Since it was before Purim, we learned Megillas Esther, of course. The theme of the lesson impressed me very deeply. She emphasized Mordechai's personality and relationship with Esther. Although a queen, Esther still considered her uncle Mordechai her teacher and mentor. Even after her coronation, she followed her uncle's advice and instructions as she had when she was his ward. Mordechai asked her not to reveal her origins, and she did not reveal them. Mordechai had raised her to make no personal requests, and she made none. She followed and cherished his every word.

Even after Esther became Queen of Persia, Mordechai always kept an eye on her and concerned himself with her well-being. The moment came when Mordechai had to inform his beloved niece, Queen Esther, of King Achashveirosh's terrible decree against the Jews. He asked her to approach the king and intervene on the Jews' behalf and plead for the lives of her brethren. Esther sent Hasach to bring back her answer: "Don't you know that approaching the king without being summoned can cost a person his life? And I have not been summoned to the king for thirty days."

Mordechai replied, "Do not imagine that you can escape the fate of the Jews. How can you, a Jewish daughter, be indifferent to the tragedy of your People?"

"*Al tedami be-nafsheich*,"[67] Sarah Schenirer repeated, her unique smile lighting up her face. "Do not imagine it." With a twinkle in her lovely black eyes, she continued with a pun: "*Al te-dami* — don't be an *alte dame* [in Yiddish: an old lady, a spoiled madam]. Be young, act with enthusiasm, be ready to sacrifice even your life to save your People. Who knows if you were not created just for that moment, to save your brethren?"

She leaned over us and, flashing a charming smile, asked rhetorically, "Who knows if all your beauty, charm, talents, and abilities were not given to you for that very moment when your people need your help?"

Esther responded to Mordechai's message by telling him, "Go and gather all the Jews." She rose to her task. We discover a different Esther, not the humble, reserved girl who hid her origins and asked for nothing. The Esther who personified the ideal of *Kol kevudah bas Melech penimah*,[68] the King's daughter who reflects His honor in her modesty, turned into a dynamic leader. Her organizational talents rose to the surface. She became a capable diplomat, scheduling and planning her actions in a grandiose scheme to rescue her people.

"You see, girls," Frau Schenirer explained, "a Jewish girl has to have two pockets" — she put her hands in her own. "In one pocket she should carry *Kol kevudah bas Melech penimah*; but in the other pocket she must carry *Eis la'asos l'Hashem*.[69] There are crucial times in Jewish life which demand excep-

---

67. *Esther* 4:13.
68. *Tehillim* 45:14.
69. Ibid., 119:126.

tional actions of the Jewish girl. At those times she must pull out the *Eis la'asos* from the other pocket and go into the world on behalf of Hashem and the Jewish People."

We did not realize then how prophetic her words were. Our revered teacher did not give us a test on this, her last *Yahadus* lesson. But that important lesson guided us for the rest of our lives. When life tested her children in the most daunting ways, subjecting us to starvation, thirst, all manner of lethal threats, and daily torture, we proudly passed the test, our mentor having taught us how to live *and* how to die *al kiddush Hashem*, in sanctification of God's Name.

In the deepest dungeon of human decay, Sarah Schenirer's daughters sparkled like diamonds and proclaimed to the world that *tzelem Elokim*, the spark of Godliness, still exists *ba-adam*, in human beings.

So be proud, our teacher! Your children, in the darkest era in Jewish history, to this very day proudly carry the torch you lit in their hearts: "*Bais Yaakov*, let us walk in the light of Hashem, and they will follow you in His radiance!"

Bais Yaakov Is Orphaned

❧ *Chapter 54* ❧

Ruchka Iliker

𝒲*ho was that young girl who* had the inner fortitude, at that time of extreme distress, to "turn the time of mourning into a time of learning?"

She was one of the older Bnos leaders, beloved and admired by us all. She had lost her father at a very young age; her mother tried to be both mother and father to Ruchka and her siblings. She had a little stand in the Sukienice, a prestigious shopping center in Kraków. Ruchka, the oldest child in the family, immediately placed herself at her mother's side and relieved her of as much responsibility as she could. Although hers were narrow shoulders on a tall frame, she carried her heavy duties with grace and charm.

She spent her days in the business with her mother, from morning until the evening — in the freezing cold of winter and the scorching heat of summer. The open stand had neither heat nor air conditioning. Its three walls hardly protected them from blizzards and rain. We girls tried to avoid the place, not wanting to embarrass her. Inadvertently, I once passed by on a cold winter day and saw her warming her frozen fingers over burning coals on a makeshift potbelly stove. I turned around as fast as I could and rushed home on the other side of the square.

Ruchka's responsibilities did not end when she came home. She helped with the household chores and tried to make her siblings' lives as comfortable as possible. She was also the most responsible Bnos leader we had. Following her revered teacher's path, she emulated Sarah Schenirer's way of showing concern for people, helping the needy, and listening to the troubled.

When her eighteen-year-old brother passed away, we young girls came to comfort our beloved leader at that time of personal tragedy. We wanted to express our deep sorrow and condolences, but somehow failed to find the words.

She responded by comforting *us*. "God gave us a wonderful gift," she said simply, expressing sublime faith in Ribono Shel Olam. "A devoted son for my mother, a great brother for us to enjoy for a while. Now He has taken him back. Probably we no longer deserved him. The Lord gives, the Lord takes away. We have to be grateful to Him for the time He gave us with our dear brother."

Decades later, I still see Ruchka's calm face and hear her consoling words. I will never cease to admire the greatness of a girl of such tender age. Her powerful personality imbued us with her unusual faith and trust in Hashem.

The entire Iliker family perished. However, Ruchka's image is still with us, carrying that powerful message of belief and trust in the Almighty's ways.

*   *   *

After our dear Sarah Schenirer passed away, Dr. Schmuel Deutschlander came to comfort us. He spent several months at the seminary and then, unfortunately, he, too, passed away. Reb Yehudah Leib Orlean took over full responsibility for the seminary and was joined by Sarah Schenirer's most capable, dedicated, and talented students, who became the teachers and pillars of the Bais Yaakov movement. Among the most outstanding were Hanka Grossfeld, Ida Bauminger, Bella Gross, Frau Zlota Waciarz *née* Scharansky, Escia Goldstoff, and Gittel Pass *née* Teitelbaum.

Our great loss evoked an outpouring of sorrow and also, thank God, a great consolation: hope and trust in the powerful dedication of the capable new leadership. Their responsibility and devotion to Sarah Schenirer's ideals and ways put us at ease and gave us reason to hope that the authentic Bais Yaakov ideas would endure.

Herr Orlean invited Betty Rothschild Wreschner, a young widow with four children, to return from Germany to help the staff. Even under her tragic personal circumstances, she was the same cheerful young woman as when she had taught as a girl. "Fraulein Rothschild" brought joy and happiness into the life of the girls and tried to fill the void they felt after Frau Schenirer's death.

Frau Wreschner had much motherly love to give. Apart from being a great teacher, she spared no effort to serve Frau Schenirer's orphaned daughters as a mentor and to replace Frau Schenirer as a source of motherly love. She took full charge of the girls, accompanied them to shul on Friday nights and Shabbos mornings, sang with them, and danced with them. Eagerly she shared her effervescence with her beloved charges. She also assumed responsibility for housekeeping.

Once she noticed that the ground-floor dormitory rooms lacked curtains. How could the girls get dressed and undressed without curtains? she asked, outraged. She solved the problem by appropriating money that had been set aside for fish on Shabbos and using it to buy curtains for all the ground-floor windows. When it came time to serve fish the next Shabbos, there was none. When the girls inquired about the missing course, Frau Wreschner pointed to the curtains and said, "There's your fish. *Tzeniyus* (modesty) is more important than Shabbos fish."

*   *   *

Frau Wreschner took care of her two daughters, Tirtzah and Gusti, by enrolling them in public school in the morning and Bais Yaakov in the afternoon. Such was the typical arrangement for our Jewish girls. Then she registered the boys at the Yesodei ha-Torah *cheder* which, as mentioned previously, was run by Agudath Israel. The children there devoted the en-

tire morning to religious studies, of course, but for a couple of
hours in the afternoon they were taught secular subjects as required by Polish law. Since the administration there knew and
respected her, it was pleased to admit her boys. When she asked
the registrar how much each boy's tuition would cost and was
told, "Fifteen zlotys per month," she replied in her native German, "*Ach, das is doch fül zu venig* — that's much too little to
teach a child for a whole month." The story circulated throughout Kraków and was found to be very humorous, since other
parents always argued about tuition.

The Agudah activists who were involved in running Yesodei
ha-Torah, such as Senator Moshe Deutcher, a member of the
Polish Sejm (parliament), and Reb Uscher Spira, a wealthy
realtor, also worked devotedly on behalf of the Bais Yaakov
Seminary. Later on, the ghetto administration in Kraków
praised Senator Deutcher for donating the beds of the seminary
dormitory to the ghetto hospital.

Indeed, even at that tragic time, when the Jews of Kraków
were surrounded by hate and bestiality, and when many people
thought and dreamed only about how to save their own skin,
the representatives of the Bais Yaakov schools thought about
how to alleviate others' pain, help the sick, and make conditions
more bearable for ev-
eryone. At that time,
Bais Yaakov as a
movement, too, dis-
played its ideal of true
loving-kindness.

*Board of Directors of Bais Yaakov, Kraków,
1936. From left: Dr. L. Deutschlander, Rabbi
Lau, Senator M. Deutcher, Senator I.
Bauminger, Ch. Freylich, Rabbi Dr. L. Jung,
Rabbi Tobias Horowitz, Reb Uscher Spira, S.
Rosenfeld, M.S. Frankel, Reb Moshe Heitner.*

❧ *Chapter 55* ❧

It was one year after Sarah Schenirer's passing. The *Bais Yaakov Journal*, of course, dedicated its monthly issue to the first *yahrtzeit* of the founder of both the movement and the *Journal* itself.

Her children wrote, her teachers wrote, and her admirers wrote. They expressed their love for and admiration of Mother Sarah and their deep bereavement over their great loss.

Reb Binyamin Süssman was also asked to contribute. "What can I write about Sarah Schenirer?" he mused. "I cannot laud her for her great *middos*, her dedication, her love for every human being, and her exceptional caring. She would be angry at me; she would never approve of it. She always stayed in the shadows, never wishing to be in the limelight. Even at her most festive moment, the groundbreaking ceremony for her seminary building, the realization of lengthy years of toil, she stayed in the shadows, hiding among her students.

"How can I write about the multitude of great deeds that she performed, using me as her emissary, sworn to secrecy?

"Then I remembered: five years ago I visited her one afternoon. It was her father's *yahrtzeit*. I found her seated at the table learning *mishnayos* (probably *Pirkei Avos*) for her father's soul.

"When she noticed me, she exclaimed happily, 'It's good that you're here, but before you tell me why you came, please explain to me a *mishnah* that I find difficult to understand.'

"After I explained the thought that had given her difficulty, she asked, with satisfaction and with gratitude, why I had come.

"Truth to tell, after having immersed myself in the difficult passage of the *mishnah*, I had completely forgotten the purpose of my visit that day. At times, I visited her to share personal problems; she sometimes visited me to engage my help with her personal endeavors. Now I just sat there, uneasy about my forgetfulness.

"To dispel the discomfort, she said, 'I know, Hashem sent you to me just in time to help me clarify the *mishnah*.'

"Then she began to talk about her father's *yahrtzeit* and the importance of every *yahrtzeit* generally.

"'You know,' she exclaimed, 'I don't like the great celebrations that people make at any occasion, but I like the celebration of the *yahrtzeit* for departed members of our families or *tzaddikim*. It is important for them, and for us, the living, to commemorate their passing with an elaborate event, even with festivities.

"'Today is my father's *yahrtzeit*,' she added. 'Recalling his pious life, his great deeds, and my wonderful upbringing gives me more strength and courage to carry on with my work than all other memories in my life.' It seems that she wanted her *yahrtzeit* to be celebrated, too."

In fact, Frau Schenirer's students organized a special event in her memory for each of her *yahrtzeiten*. We should indeed tell our children and youth about the great personality of the founder of the Bais Yaakov movement, about her diverse deeds and the way she performed them. Our Sages say that our great people do not need monuments; their sayings are their memorial.

So it was with Sarah Schenirer. She had no monument; her words and teachings were her memorial.

Reb Süssman then emphasized this point by adding a saying of Frau Schenirer's that she had told him on that *yahrtzeit* day. She commented on a verse from *Koheles*: "The greatness of a worthy person can be evaluated and praised after he is gone, according to the living whom he left behind. In other words, his influence on the generation he left behind allows us to evaluate and praise him accurately."

When we observe the Bais Yaakov movement growing and flourishing all over the world, and contemplate the generations of loyal daughters of Israel walking in her ways and building wonderful Jewish homes and families as a result, we can truly evaluate and admire the achievements of Sarah Schenirer, and honor her in the manner that she deserves: with the praise of the great.

❧ Chapter 56 ❧

In June 1937, Bnos held its first official convention at the prestigious Philharmonic Music Hall in Lodz. Some two thousand delegates attended, representing chapters from all over Europe and Eretz Yisroel. Leaders of Bnos *Hachsharos* and principals of trade schools represented their institutions as well.

This impressive assembly of young women had not convened to proclaim women's rights. The delegates had gathered to show the world that a powerful youth organization that awakened Jewish womanhood to the Torah way of life had come into being.

The conference was also attended by Agudah activists, rabbis involved in the Bnos movement, and officials at the Bnos Centrale (central office) in Lodz, directed by Rabbi Gershon Friedenson. The staff and contributing editors of the *Bais Yaakov Journal* were represented as well. Only one person was missing: Sarah Schenirer, the dreamer who had envisioned a strong Orthodox youth organization. Fortunately, she had lived to see it come into being. What joy and *nachas* she would have derived from this tremendous outpouring of dedication to her Bnos idea.

The convention was addressed by three notable leaders in Agudath Israel: Rabbi Fischel Lieberman, Rabbi Y. L. Minzberg (a senator in the Polish Sejm), and Rabbi Yitzchok Meir Levine, president of Agudath Israel and an ardent supporter of Bnos. Additional renowned rabbis and educators made congratulatory remarks as well.

Afterwards, Mrs. Zlota Waciarz, *née* Scharansky, of the Bais Yaakov movement, greeted the assembly on behalf of the Bais Yaakov Seminary in Kraków. With emotion and nostalgia she recalled the beginnings of both movements, Bais Yaakov and Bnos: "We witnessed the birth of Frau Schenirer's Bnos idea. We stood at the cradle and watched the child growing and developing into a strong movement."

Then she cried out in passion, "It is such a privilege for me to experience this great Bnos convention. With its two thousand delegates, it proclaims with its presence that we have come to revive the traditional Jewish woman's commitment to Hashem, His Torah, and His people. You should know that we at the seminary are teaching our students not only how to instruct young children but also how to lead and advise the end product of the Bais Yaakov movement, the Bnos organization."

The next speaker, Escia Goldstoff, a pillar of the Bais Yaakov Seminary, underscored Mrs. Waciarz's point. "Bnos is not only an educational and *chessed* institution; it also forges personalities of knowledge, wisdom, and character. Our work is non-stop. From childhood to youth to adulthood, it helps young women to continue their spiritual growth."

The Bais Yaakov teachers were indeed devoted to Bnos, spending their precious free time teaching, advising, and befriending Bnos leaders and members. However, Bnos strove to be independent. The girls wanted their own teachers and leaders. They fought to establish an instructors' course for Bnos leaders, to enrich their education and teach them leadership skills.

Again it was our energetic Bnos patron, Reb Gershon Friedenson, who with his hard work and uncommon zeal organized the first Bnos instructors' course. He named it Chavas Schmuel, after Dr. Schmuel Deutschlander.

I was privileged to attend this first very successful course, led by Tzila Neugröschl-Orlean (later Soroczkin), which advanced the Bnos leaders' Jewish knowledge and gave them professional advice on how to organize and lead their chapters and groups. One of the most important suggestions at the convention was to make this course permanent, with one month-long course each summer. A resolution to this effect passed unanimously. A year later, the Bnos leadership set up a Chavas Schmuel instructors' course, this time led by our very capable Feiga Zelicka. The course proved to be an essential and promising tool in the training of Bnos leaders. Unfortunately, it was brutally cut off by the tragedy of war.

Then additional delegates from various Bnos chapters and institutions — in Poland, Austria, England, Slovakia, and Eretz Yisroel — took the floor in succession and reported on their local activities. Some of them described problems that their organizations faced; others offered suggestions and proposals. A delegate from Brisk retold a tragic episode as the grief-stricken audience listened. In anguish, she recounted the recent pogroms in her city, when for sixteen hours a Polish mob plundered Jewish homes, shattered store windows, stole property, destroyed synagogues and schools, and battered the helpless Jewish population. She urged her audience to help the victims. A committee was formed immediately to take care of the Brisk community's needs.

A delegate from the Ohel Sarah trade school and kibbutz had a very important suggestion. First she stressed how essential such schools were for our girls in those grim economic times. Small towns were engulfed in such poverty that the girls had to work to help support their families. With jobs scarce in the provinces, they went to large cities in the hope of finding jobs.

Bnos, the delegate continued, is not only an educational and social organization. "We care for more than our members' spiritual needs; we should also look out for their material well-being." Passionately she appealed to Bnos chapters in larger cities to help these girls to find work and to set up these lonely, hardworking out-of-towners with local families. The assembly transformed this cry for help into an applauded resolution and immediately established a committee to work on the project.

The assembly heard additional speeches, suggestions, and proposals that led to plenary discussions. Some were more important, some less. However, the most moving and passionate speech was that delivered by Devorah Gur-Aryeh, who had settled in Eretz Yisroel as the leader of the first Bnos *aliyah* group in March 1934.

Assisted by the local chapters of Agudath Israel and Po'alei Agudath Israel, she had established the Bnos kibbutz (collective) on Kalisher Street in Tel Aviv for all girls who had made *aliyah* from the *Hachsharos* in Poland. It was a beautiful facility; the girls supported it by taking on various jobs during the day. They continued to work into the night, this time for their spiritual ascent. The kibbutz had a special collection of members, such as Rivka Halberman, Devorah Gur-Aryeh's deputy; Ita Goldknopf, (subsequently Gershtenkorn), her co-leader as far back as the Warsaw *Hachsharah*; and Devorah Siedlecky, who from the first moment was one of the most beloved teachers in the Bais Yaakov school that Rabbi Meir Scharansky had established in Tel Aviv. She used to bring her Basya girls to the kibbutz for Shabbatonim and special events. It is no wonder that, with their help, Devorah Gur-Aryeh organized a Bnos movement within a short time.

In due course, the kibbutz became a Bnos center with branches in Haifa, Bnei Brak, Petach Tikvah, and other locations.

The members of Bnos and Basya (the movement that had been set up for younger girls) visited the kibbutz to learn, attend lectures by prominent rabbis, enjoy and share in the happy events of the kibbutz, and bask in its warm, friendly atmosphere.

Devorah Gur-Aryeh's ideal was to establish the nucleus of a strong Orthodox organization which, by means of its activities, behavior, and Jewish ways, would attract youth to the Bnos idea by its very presence.

This daring traditional Jewish movement of the young,

amidst an ocean of faithless Zionist kibbutzim and institutions — not to mention other obstacles — paved the way for a religious presence in the Holy Land. Devorah's brilliance, passionate love of and concern for people, abilities, and, above all, devotion to the Bnos idea, made her an ideal leader of such a movement. Now she addressed the Bnos convention in Poland as the delegate of her kibbutz and the Bnos girls in Eretz Yisroel.

"In the name of Bnos," she began, "I bring you greetings from the Holy Land." She then commended the Bnos *aliyah* pioneers who, at great sacrifice, were investing all their energies in keeping the Holy Land holy. "Thanks to them, a Bnos movement exists and prospers in Eretz Yisroel against all the odds and difficulties."

In Eretz Yisroel, Devorah explained, the Agudah leaders and local rabbis were assisting the kibbutz in various ways. So was a Mr. Mondry, who, after organizing the Bnos *Hachsharah* in Melava and inspiring the girls there to make *aliyah*, made *aliyah* along with his family. Now settled, he helped the kibbutz with all his energy. He found jobs for the girls in a *tallis* factory, a publishing house, and the Lieber chocolate enterprise. He devoted all of his spare time and vigor to easing the girls' adjustment. "You, my sisters in Bnos," Devorah cried out with emotion, "know how difficult it is to find work for girls in Poland. Can you imagine how much harder it is in Eretz Yisroel? There, jobs are handed out by the Histadrut [the Zionist federation of trade unions], and you cannot get work unless you belong to the Histadrut, which of course our girls refuse to do.

"We are so isolated," she continued, raising her voice in agitation. "We get no encouragement or help from the outside world. There's no longer a Sarah Schenirer to write us letters of encouragement and advice. The Orthodox are not interested in this *aliyah*. They call it a hallucination, a dream that will never work out.

"How wrong they are! These girls are filled with love of Zion. They left their homes and families to come to the Promised Land and make it again blossom with holiness. They struggle against physical and spiritual obstacles to reach their goal. Yet they do it all with love and joy.

"Two years ago, we organized a Bnos conference in Tel Aviv. It was much smaller than the one we witness here today. But it was a powerful revelation of Jewish women's desire to lead a Torah way of life in the Holy Land.

"Only one person from abroad attended that impressive conference: Reb Gershon Friedenson. He spent a whole week with us, encouraging, advising, suggesting improvements, helping in whatever way he could in his limited time.

"Unfortunately, after his visit we again felt neglected and forgotten. No word from Bais Yaakov or Bnos in Europe reached us. We have no leader here, no older generation to guide us.

"Please," she entreated the assembly passionately. "We have all of your problems but worse. We have no teaching materials, no books, no periodicals, not enough leaders for the 400 Bnos members in different towns. We reach out to the local youth, but again we have no literature for them in Hebrew."

She ended her speech with an emotional appeal to the Bnos center in Lodz, the Bnos leaders at the chapter level, and the heads of Agudath Israel: "*Im eshkacheich Yerushalayim...*[70] Don't forget Jerusalem. Teach the girls about the Holy Land, about the great mitzvah of *yishuv Eretz Yisroel*. Tell them about the two hundred pioneers from the Polish Bnos *Hachsharos* who, with their deep love of Zion and their ardent desire to establish an Orthodox community there, are the bricks from which the *Beis ha-Mikdash*, God's eternal Sanctuary, will be built in Jerusalem."

The assembly, deeply moved by Devorah's words, dedicated a session to the discussion of the problems facing Bnos in Eretz Yisroel. It formed a committee to maintain contact with the Bnos leaders in *Eretz ha-Kodesh* and to help them with their

---

70. See *Tehillim* 137:5.

needs in every possible way.

After various additional suggestions, proposals, and resolutions, the convention was ready for the concluding speech. The speaker was Reb Yehudah Leib Orlean, the God-blessed educator who directed the Bais Yaakov Seminary in Kraków.

Taking the floor, Reb Yehudah Leib summarized the proposals and resolutions and spoke of their importance. He urged the respective committees to act immediately to help solve the problems addressed at the preliminary sessions. Then, as the audience waited in eager anticipation, he began the speech proper.

"*Bereishis bara Elokim es ha-shamayim ve-es ha-aretz.* In the very beginning, God created heaven and earth, the basic matter of which the universe is formed. In this first sentence, the Torah proclaims the entire truth of Creation. In the very beginning, *Hashem Echad,* the One Omnipotent God, created this world out of nothingness. First He brought *ha-shamayim ve-ha'aretz,* the basic forms of matter, into being. And the earth was *tohu va-vohu* — all elements were entangled in chaotic disorder. The turmoil was enveloped in darkness. The mass was waiting to be separated into individual components.

"With His first utterance, Hashem called light into existence. Then, with each subsequent statement, He created separate elements. In six days, God created the world — light and darkness, water and dry land, the luminaries, the vegetable world, and all living creatures, from the smallest creeping thing to the mightiest beast.

"Hashem provided each creation with sustenance and a place and time for its functioning. He endowed every living creature with the potential and the natural urge to carry out its intended purpose.

"The whole universe, with its existence, performance, and harmonious unity, proclaims the truth loudly: *Hashem Echad.* There is only One Omnipotent Creator and Ruler of this world.

"At the end of the sixth day, God created man. He entrusted the entire universe to man, *le-ovdah,* to work, to continue, to create, and to develop and explore its elements — *u'le-shomrah,* to use its abundance and goodness for the benefit of mankind.

"Hashem worked six days to create and bring order and light to the world, and on the seventh day *va-yishbos,* He rested. He blessed this day and sanctified it as Shabbos, the day of rest, tranquility, and genuine happiness and joy, the day of *menuchas nefesh,* inner serenity and peace, the day of closeness to Hashem and to the truth. Shabbos — Hashem's most precious gift to humanity.

"With the creation of Shabbos on the seventh day, God's act of Creation was completed.

"Hashem gave man absolute control over everything that exists in this world and commanded him to use it all to accomplish the end purpose of creation; to serve the Creator, in contrast to all other creatures, with his own will and love. Man is to proclaim the existence of the Almighty, the Creator, ruler, and director of all human affairs, Who shapes the destiny of man and the future of the world.

"Man has to realize that God created both extremes during those six days — light and darkness, refreshing water and cold, dry land, friendly animals and dangerous beasts, joy and pain, peace and suffering.

"The weekdays in our lives are difficult. They combine happiness and sorrow. Hashem gave man the wisdom to separate them, to put each into perspective, to know that they are all part of God's great design.

"Man must learn to cope with life's challenges, joys and sorrows, by focusing on the seventh day, Shabbos — the day of ultimate joy and peace, the day of closeness to Hashem and to the purpose of life.

"A Jew gets up every morning with the perspective of drawing nearer to Shabbos. Longing for that day, he counts: *yom rishon* to Shabbos, *yom sheini, yom shelishi,* and so on. Everything he does during the week is accompanied with yearning for that special day.

"You must live with the concept of two worlds," Reb Yehudah Leib stated emphatically. "The weekday world of activity, challenges, preparation, and yearning for the world of Shabbos, the world of light, of joy, of truth and genuine peace. This concept of two worlds will continue throughout your lives. *Olam ha-zeh,* the world of the here-and-now: the time of labor, action, creativity, and pursuit...and longing for *olam ha-ba,* the world to come: the world of light, of only happiness and delight; a time of closeness to Hashem and of understanding His ways. A blissful time of knowing and experiencing the truth and basking in everlasting joy and peace in a world *she-kulo* Shabbos, a world that is entirely Shabbos.

"The idea of regarding all challenges in this world as preparation for the world to come makes life's struggles bearable. Longing and hoping for that time opens your eyes to observe and appreciate the goodness and loving-kindness that Hashem showers upon you. They enrich your life with *nachas ruach,* true contentment and peace."

Now Herr Orlean focused his remarks on the Bais Yaakov teachers and Bnos leaders. "You are young. Now is the time for action. Continue to work on yourselves and impress the girls whom you're leading with the two-world concept that we discussed.

"Don't stop here. Don't forget the estranged Jewish youth out there, those disappointed young people who are searching for meaning in life. Their souls yearn to find the truth. They search and search in vain and cannot attain the inner peace they desire. It is our responsibility to reach out to them. We, the Jewish People, are the carriers of the truth. We believe in its power to inspire every Jewish heart that craves and searches for it.

"It is our responsibility to make those youth aware of their heritage. Show them the beauty of Shabbos, the genuine happiness, the tranquility, and the inner peace that it brings.

"Your behavior, your sincere and enthusiastic observance of the precepts of the Torah, its ways of love of Hashem and love of every human being, will surely impress these youngsters and open their hearts so they may listen. It will enable you to accomplish your task of attracting them to the truth.

"This achievement, and all other acts of loving-kindness performed with such devotion and care by Jewish women, will be the greatest merit for the Ultimate Redemption. Then it may be said, as upon the redemption from Egypt, "From the merit of righteous women came the salvation of our people."[71]

---

71. *Sotah* 11b.

The War Ends: Picking Up the Pieces

❧ *Chapter 57* ❧

We're free! we screamed. "We're liberated! The gates of the concentration camps are open." We attempted to reassure each other that it had really happened. "Didn't you see our liberators? Are they Russians, Americans, or British?"

The liberators expressed human feelings. They cried, seeing our pitiful state. They cared. They gave us whatever they could spare.

This evidence of love for another human being, after all those years of world-spanning hatred — interest for someone else's welfare and genuine willingness to help — made us cry with them. Our dream of waking up to a better world had come true, we thought.

How naive we were. The world, we soon discovered, was indifferent to our plight. We lone survivors had nowhere to go. No country opened its doors to us. Even the Land of Liberty, home of the great statue whose base carries a plaque with the message — an excerpt by a Jewish poet, Emma Lazarus — "Give me your tired, your poor, your huddled masses…" did not find us sufficiently tired, poor, or huddled for admission. We were left to fend for ourselves and reestablish our lives with our own inner strength, willpower, and initiative.

As I wrote in my book, *To Vanquish the Dragon*, we Bais Yaakov girls started a Bais Yaakov school in Bergen-Belsen immediately after the liberation. We discovered the sparks that still flickered in the piles of ashes and fanned them into flames. We brought encouragement and hope to those lonely girls and willed them to start over and continue the chain of Jewish family heritage. We revived their faith and trust in Hashem. We tried to rekindle belief in human beings among youngsters who had seen only bestiality in man. We instilled an atmosphere of love and care. Soon the girls started flocking to us.

All over Germany and Austria, former Nazi camps and other locations quickly metamorphosed into DP camps. Bais Yaakov schools sprang up in all of them. There were no special buildings, but girls sat on beds, on floors, wherever they could find room, to learn Torah and how to fulfill its precepts as they remembered from home.

The survivors were now eager to start new lives. Matchmakers proliferated — older and younger women, and men as well. They did their work well. Thus young people married and picked up the loose ends of their families' chains.

There were neither parents nor siblings at the weddings. At first, there were no couples to escort brides and grooms to the *chuppah* (wedding canopy). The first couple in Bergen-Belsen to escort a bride and groom to the *chuppah* were Shulim Dovid and Nadia Horowitz, who were already engaged, having been introduced by Rivka, Shulim's sister. Rivka continued to practice her new trade of matchmaking, invested much effort in it, and had much success.

It was the first erev Yom Kippur in Bergen-Belsen. Our Rivka, always energetic and bursting with ideas, had a plan. She somehow obtained two portable sewing machines and made Eda Laufer (now Rebbetzin Piekarsky) and her friend, Sarah Bodner (later Mintz), sew yarmulkes for the young men. The waiting lines were dauntingly long, Eda remembers: "We had to eat our erev Yom Kippur meals at the machines. But scores of young men went to services that night wearing yarmulkes for the first time since the war."

That was the girls' greatest reward.

Eda worked for the *Bekleidungskammer*, the Apparel Board at Bergen-Belsen, which gave her a beautiful dress as a reward for her work. Although the board intended it for her, she considered it more important to have Rivka wear it. Rivka, she reasoned, represented Bais Yaakov in the camp offices and had to meet foreign dignitaries; she must look presentable. Eda altered the dress for Rivka and presented it to her with love and a little sacrifice.

Several days later, she saw another girl wearing a dress that strongly resembled that precious garment. Checking the alterations, she found that it was true. "It's the dress I gave Rivka," she thought with displeasure.

Marshaling her courage, she asked Rivka, "Why did you give away the dress that I gave you? How could you?!"

She was heartbroken until Rivka replied, "*Shah* [Be quiet]! That girl is about to meet a boy today; she has to look good."

As time passed, Eda saw many girls wearing that dress for the same reason. Rivka made sure to marry off "her" girls before she got married herself. When she and the rest of us moved on to the kibbutz for Jewish survivors in Zeilsheim, she met

Zeilsheim, 1945. Here, survivors are demonstrating for their right to immigrate to Eretz Yisroel. The banner reads: "Thank you, President Truman, for helping us in our struggle for free immigration to Israel."

Reb Leibel Pincusewitz, who had already established a yeshiva there and, through the American occupation forces, obtained a kibbutz from the Germans for us, which we named Kibbutz Chofetz Chaim.

Rivka and Reb Leibel got married and stayed in Zeilsheim, where they worked together for the benefit of boys and girls. They were active in the Kenessiah Gedolah of Agudath Israel in Europe, where Rivka established an organization named Novai — the initials of *Neshei u'Vnos Agudath Israel*.

The young couple, of course, planned to settle in Eretz Yisroel. Rivka had entertained this dream even before the war. However, as we all know, our dreams and plans cannot always be fulfilled; various situations and circumstances force us to change them.

The worldwide Agudath Israel organization applied tremendous pressure on Rivka and Reb Leibel to move to Belgium. The Agudah leaders considered Reb Leibel the right person to head their office in Antwerp, in order to strengthen and rebuild the Orthodox community there. After he relocated, Reb Leibel worked tirelessly as the general secretary of Agudath Israel to help refugees from Eastern Europe settle in Antwerp. His love of people, his willingness to listen to their problems and attempt to solve them, and his warm personal interest in each individual made him the most beloved personality in town. As a dedicated Agudah activist, he was involved in the operations of religious institutions and helped the Antwerp Orthodox community to flourish and regain its pre-war importance.

Rivka, too, did not stay idle. Always the energetic organizer, she established a large Bnos group for girls arriving from Poland, Russia, and other locations in Europe. She also founded a "Neshei" for women and has remained active in it to the present day, giving lectures and speeches to the Jewish women of Antwerp.

She was especially involved with young girls who had been removed from gentile homes and farms in Poland. After years of life and labor as Poles, they were now returning to their roots as Jews. One can imagine their ignorance of Jewish matters. Rivka showed them the beauty of our Jewish heritage and made them proud to be daughters of Israel. She met their needs and tried to solve the financial and spiritual difficulties that they encountered in adjusting to their new lives. Her efforts extended to job placement and matchmaking; even today she continues to practice the latter vocation. Her greatest joy was to see these young women survivors happily building Jewish homes.

As one of Sarah Schenirer's favorite *talmidos*, she lectures on *Tehillim* and, with her dynamic speaking style, imbues women and girls with the authentic Krakowian Bais Yaakov spirit.

Each year she organizes a large celebration on Sarah Schenirer's *yahrtzeit*. The rich program she prepares for the occasion leaves the participants with a profound impression of Sarah Schenirer's personality and teachings.

Below is the original Yiddish and a condensed free English translation of the poem by Rivka Pincusewitz, written and published for Frau Schenirer's *yahrtzeit*:

צו דער מאמע שרה שענירער
צו איר יארצייט

מ'וואלט וועלן
אויסוויינען ס'הארץ
פאר דיר,
דערצ
יילן נסיונות
און קאמפן אן שיעור.

אוועקלייגן דעם מידן קאפ
אויף דעם קאלטן שטיין
און אוועקגיין פון דיר
געלייטערט און ריין.

אזוי ווי אמאל
אויף דיין מצבה קוקן
טראכטן, מאכן דין וחשבון

בשעת די טרערן שטיקן.

אבער אויך דאס האבן די רוצחים
אונדז אוועק גענומען,
מיט ערד גלייך געמאכט דיין קבר
ווען זיי זענען קיין קראקע געקומען.

בית-עולמים געשענדעט,
מצבות צושטערט,
אבער נישט די קראפט פון גייסט
ווייל אייביק איז זיין ווערט.

לעבסט אין אונדז, א מאמע,
אינם הארץ ביסטו שטענדיק דא.
געפילט דיך גאר נאנט שטענדיק
אין שווערער גורל שעה.

ביסט אויך אין לאגערן געווען
צוזאמען מיט דיינע קינדער,
געגעבן זיי מוט, גבורה
צו באווייזן גרויסע וואונדער.

אויך הונדערטער קדושות
נעבן דיר האבן זיך געשטעלט,
נאכן אפהאקן זייער יונג לעבן,
נאכן אומברענגען פון דער וועלט

און דאן פון דיינע גוטע אויגן
געפאלן איז א טרער,
געמיינט אז אין חורבות
ליגט דיין ווערק.
נישט געבליבן קיין שפור מער.

נישט אמת, מאמע,
זע, בית-יעקב לעבט.
פון איין עק צום צווייטן
פון דער גארער וועלט.

זע אין הייליקן לאנד,
וואקסן טעכטער ווי אמאל,
מיט אידיש חן און שטאלץ
לויטן אידעאל פון ישראל.

און אין אמעריקע, זע,

ס'ארא דור צו ערציען, האבן באוויזן
דיינע תלמידות, מאמע,
די פאר גייסטיקע ריזן.

און אויף די חורבות פון איראפע
אויפשטעלן בית יעקב'ס בנות
זיך דיינע תלמידות גענומען,
און אזוי האט ס'אידישע פאלק
זיין פרויען-דור צוריקגעוואונען.

אויף אייביק וועט דיין ווערק
אויף זיינע יסודות שטיין,
וייל מיט אמת האסטו עס געבויט
דיין כוונה געווען ריין.

און אינם טאג פון יארצייט,
קומען מיר אלע דיר טרייסט געבן
מאמע! דיינע קינדער
בית יעקב עקזיסטירט,
מיר לעבן!

To My Mother on Her Yahrtzeit

I desire
To pour out my heart
To you, my mother,
And start

To tell you about
The unending chain
Of bitter tortures,
Struggles and tests
Endured in pain,
Day and night,
Without rest.

I long to embrace
Your monument,
And as before,
To lay my tired face
On the cold stone,

And once more
Moisten it with my tears,
And leave refreshed, atoned.

But even that
The murderers
Took from us away,
No grave to be found,
No monument, no sign.
Of everything, bereft,
Only straight, empty ground
Of nothingness
Is left.

But Mother, stop crying,
Seeing masses of your children
Dying.
Like mother Rachel,
Wipe the tears
From your face,
Because Hashem
In His grace
Spared some of your *talmidos*.
They made deserts bloom
With Bais Yaakov schools,
Where your spirit rules.

Mother, don't worry,
On your great teachings we thrive.
Your life's work flourishes,
We are alive.

The first time I visited Rivka in Belgium, I arrived shortly before Pesach and, of course, helped with the pre-festival cleaning. As she removed precious silver objects from her china cabinet to be cleaned and polished, Rivka picked up a small tin box tenderly and lovingly, and showed it to me. "This is the most cherished item in the case," she explained, her eyes moist with nostalgia. "A tin tea box I got as a wedding gift from a friend in the camp...." Such was the value of wedding gifts in the DP camps: a cotton kerchief priceless, a nicely wrapped safety pin or hairpin greatly appreciated.

Although content with the most basic necessities, the young survivor newlyweds were eager to start normal lives. However, instead of returning to the lands of hatred, many of them wanted to "make *aliyah*," settle in Eretz Yisroel and establish their homes in the Land of Holiness. These lone survivors hoped that the world community, aware of the inhuman tortures they had suffered under the Nazis, would open the doors of the Jewish homeland to them. After all the degradation they had experienced, they thought the world would allow them to embark on meaningful, honorable Jewish lives in the Land of their dreams.

Again the level of the world's humanity proved disappointing. Where compassion should have been shown, the survivors were treated with cold political calculation. Still, young people from the many organized kibbutzim in Germany, who had been preparing for *aliyah*, did not give up. They set out for Eretz Yisroel on the dangerous clandestine route offered them by the Jewish Brigade.

They progressed from place to place, sometimes without lodging and often without food, until they reached a port where a boat bound for Eretz Yisroel was waiting. What a pitiful sight such a boat was! A small vessel, built to navigate small distances with several hundred passengers aboard, was now to accommodate thousands of young men and women. Although aware of the unsafe conditions, the travelers boarded the ship happily and kept one prayer in mind: may it deliver us to the Land of our hopes and dreams.

The voyage was slow and dangerous. The would-be immigrants and their crews encountered difficulties that they tried to solve with their primitive equipment and scanty maritime experience. Miraculously, many of these boats eluded the British guards and reached the shores of the Promised Land. Passengers who could swim the short distance to land did so; the others were transported to the shore in small unnoticed boats.

Other vessels were not graced with this good fortune. One such boat carried my husband Shymon and members of the kibbutz in Landsberg that he had organized and led — three thousand people in all. After weeks of dangerous sailing in the unsafe boat, the passengers rejoiced at the sight of the coast of Eretz Yisroel. Their happiness, however, was short-lived: armed British border guards brutally intercepted their vessel and ordered them to board their large boats for transport to the island of Cyprus.

The emaciated camp survivors refused to disembark. A fight ensued between them and the husky guards, who summoned heavily armed reinforcements. Our people had no weapons except for empty tin cans of food, which they threw vigorously at their opponents. They could not overcome the well-equipped soldiers, of course. However, even under the threat of live ammunition, they refused to leave the ship voluntarily. The British had to carry them forcibly, one by one, all three thousand of them, to the boats that would haul them to Cyprus.

❧ Chapter 58 ❦

Cyprus

The group from our kibbutz, Zeilsheim, experienced all the tribulations described above. After plying gypsy trails, on erev Pesach they finally reached a beautiful little Italian coastal town with a breathtaking view.

They spent several months there. Wasting no time, they carried on with their kibbutz activities until their boat to Eretz Yisroel came in. "The boat was old and dilapidated; it did not look safe for the voyage," Chavah Olstein, my kibbutz comrade, told me later, "but we boarded it happily. Nothing mattered except the chance to reach *Eretz ha-Kodesh*.

"We spent four weeks at sea, stopping and going because the worn-out engine needed frequent repairs. We endured all the hardships as long as we felt we were nearing our goal.

"After a month of dangerous sailing, we put in at Haifa port. We took this as a miracle. My happiness knew no limit as I saw the lights of Haifa, blinking us a warm greeting and a hearty invitation. I knew that one of those lights might be from the home of my brother, who was waiting for me impatiently. Oh God, how wonderful it was! I would finally take a warm bath after four weeks of travel, have a hot mug of coffee served with love; and rest my battered body in a clean and cozy bed. It would all happen in just an hour or two."

Chavah paused, pondered, and resumed talking with a greater passion.

355

"But my great dream of reaching *Eretz ha-Kodesh*, and my little dream of a shower and a hot drink, were brutally shattered. Several large boats manned by British soldiers blockaded our ship, preventing us from reaching our goal. Can you imagine our disappointment?

"They ordered us to abandon our shabby boat and board a large English vessel that was waiting for us. We refused. Right off, the Brits summoned reinforcements from a large army unit that had been trained to put down such 'rebellions.'

"I couldn't believe my eyes," Chavah continued, her anguish showing through. "Each of us had a personal escort, a soldier, who forcibly led him or her to the vessel. A whole British army unit, a large one, came to disarm a boatload of survivors of hell and transport them to another hell.

"I couldn't walk; I had to be carried off by two soldiers. I noticed tears on the face of one of them. I knew it could only have been a Jewish boy who had enlisted in the British army.

"After a short voyage at sea, our group disembarked at Cyprus. From the dock we were mercilessly loaded onto military trucks and driven across rocky soil until we reached a camp encased in barbed wire. There we encountered thousands of Holocaust survivors who, like us, had been forcibly interned in that concentration camp, with its Nazi similarities. The inmates were from kibbutzim in Germany, Poland, and Austria. They were of all sorts of political orientations and levels of religious observance.

"But they had one thing in common: they had all experienced the same hardships and dangerous travel, and they all entertained the same hope to establish a new life in the Land of their dreams, where they could finally have a place of their own in which to raise a new generation in peace."

How tragically matters unfolded. After all their hardships, the survivors finally reached their destination and, to their unspeakable disappointment, were placed in a camp surrounded by barbed wire, a great prison with insufficient food and primitive sanitation. They lived in cloth tents that exposed them to the scorching summer sun and torrential winter rains that filled the tents with deep pools of water. After one night like that, Shymon woke up the next morning in his tent — which had moved to a different location! Other tents also floated off in different directions.

Yet even in this desperate situation, the survivors did not despair. They were young and, although still emaciated, full of uncommon willpower and determination. They continued their cultural activities, each group in its own way. There were Hebrew and English lessons, drama classes that produced plays of interest to entertain the internees, and a weekly "wall newspaper," which was literally pasted to the walls of those office tents that were made of aluminum. The Orthodox established a shul and yeshiva, and arranged lectures on Tanach and various religious topics. An ORT[72] school trained young people in occupations that they could use in Eretz Yisroel.

Professional art teachers provided instruction in their fields. Shymon attended the classes for professional guidance in his hobbies of painting and sculpture. Once, the teacher instructed the students to paint a picture depicting the past, the present, and the future. It was quite a challenge, but the students tackled it diligently. Shymon's picture showed a young man in a striped concentration-camp uniform and a cap that obviously had been acquired after the liberation. The man sat on a chair and played a violin, his face projecting hope and joy. The picture won the instructor's special praise. To Shymon's great regret, however, it got lost in travel.

Our Bais Yaakov girls kept together, helped and encouraged each other, and waited and hoped for the Final Redemption.

Delegations from relief organizations often visited the camp to attempt to augment the meager rations with larger quantities of solid food. The resiliency and steadfastness of the survivors amazed them all. During the High Holidays in the autumn of 1946, the *dayan* Rabbi Dr. Yishai Grunfeld and his wife, Dr.

---

72. Organization for Rehabilitation through Training.

Judith Grunfeld, visited on behalf of the Jewish religious community of London in order to try to alleviate the inhuman conditions and ease the internees' plight.

The survivors greeted their enthusiasm with hostility. The troubles the British had caused them, and British Foreign Secretary Ernest Bevin's intransigent opposition to Jewish immigration to Palestine, had made "Britain" a dirty word among survivors. They considered anyone from Britain, including British Jews (!), an enemy. Thus, the internees gave the London delegation a chilly reception, and even the Bais Yaakov girls cooled to Dr. Grunfeld when they discovered that she had come from Britain.

"But I broke the ice," Dr. Grunfeld recalled with a smile, "simply by telling them that I had worked with Frau Schenirer and had known their teachers. Hearing that, the girls became excited and the atmosphere immediately changed into one of a friendly, enthusiastic Bais Yaakov gathering.

"You know whom I met there?" she continued in amazement. "A Zukerbrodt girl by the name of Henia.

"I told her that her oldest sister Fruma had been my student. She recognized my name but not me, since she had been very young when her sister went away to the seminary.

"What a pleasant encounter it was!"

"Yes, Henia was in our kibbutz in Zeilsheim," I interrupted. "And it was her older sister, Ruchka Reinhold, who gave me her own precious labor-detail number, which enabled me to go to Plaszów as the Kraków ghetto was being liquidated. Her gesture spared me from deportation to the death camps. She had young children; she had no choice but to go into hiding.

"I will never forget her unusual and life-saving generosity," I added. "I spent the rest of the war moving from camp to camp as Ruchka Reinhold. My gratitude to her can never be measured. May Hashem reward and bless her very name."

The camp on Cyprus became a fixture. Weeks turned into months, months into years. The struggling inmates spent that time hoping and waiting for a favorable outcome. The population in the camp grew, swelling into the thousands as the British delivered new transports of survivors who had had the *chutzpah* to try to enter their homeland "illegally."

On November 29, 1947, with the grace of Hashem, "in Whose hands lay the hearts of kings and rulers," the United Nations resolved in favor of a plan for Eretz Yisroel that would open the gates of our country to Jews. The UN, representing all nations, gave the Jews permission to settle and occupy the Land of Israel. The Cyprus barbed-wire camp would be liquidated. The Ribono shel Olam, in His loving-kindness, made a home available to the survivors of all manner of camps — concentration, death, and even Cyprus — a home where they could start over and build a future for their children and all *Bnei Yisroel*.

No other nation wanted to admit the distressed and ragged victims of Nazism. Even the Land of Liberty, who urges the world to "give me your tired, your poor, your huddled masses," kept its doors firmly shut to the survivors at that time.

Now, thank God, masses of Jews from Cyprus and elsewhere had where to go. Again transports left one after the other, this time sailing from Cyprus to Israel, until the camp was dismantled for good in February 1949.

My brother-in-law, Pinchas Reichman, was the chairman of the camp committee and an activist in cultural enterprises, especially education for the internees' young children. As such, he was the last internee to leave the camp. When asked to specify the most moving moment in his life, he replied without hesitation, "February 10, 1949, at 2:30 P.M." It was then that Pinchas, together with a British captain, locked the gates of the Cyprus detention camp.

A photograph of this historic event is reproduced on the next page. The gates of the detention camp, encased in barbed wire, are clearly visible. It has been evacuated and the last two men are locking its gates. Pinchas, the proud detainees' representative, embodies will and determination. The other man is a captain in the powerful army of a *compassionate* country. He is smiling.

I will never understand the reason for that smile. However, the vision of how humane, cultured, democratic Great Britain treated the homeless Jewish victims of the Holocaust will forever remain acute in my mind.

Pinchas Reichman, the last internee to leave Cyprus, locks the gate of the detention camp with a British captain. February 10, 1949.

Pinchas leaving the camp with his small valise containing all of his belongings.

A Tribute to
Frau Schenirer's Students

❧ *Chapter 59* ❧

"I will give them an everlasting name which shall not perish"
(Yeshayahu 56:5)

Most of Frau Schenirer's talmidos perished during the war. However, the lone survivors who struggled to reestablish their lives also fought to establish institutions for religious survival. Wherever they were fortunate enough to find homes, they made a tremendous impact on the community. With their meager means, they turned wastelands bereft of *Yiddishkeit* into blooming Jewish centers.

To some of them who have not been mentioned elsewhere in this account, a deserving tribute follows in the next several chapters.

Rachel Kaimovitz Greenbaum

Rachel Kaimovitz Greenbaum was born in Lomza, Poland, to an Orthodox family. An exceptionally gifted girl, she was fortunate to have intelligent, understanding parents who, realizing their daughter's potential, enrolled her in the Bais Yaakov Seminary in Kraków. They wanted her to become a teacher and to spread the ideas of Sarah Schenirer, whom they admired, among Jewish girls.

Rachel reached the seminary in 1931 and was assigned to the advanced classes. Eager to make the most of the two-year seminary program, she imbibed the lectures with her natural vigor and enthusiasm. After she completed the program, she fulfilled her dream of becoming a Bais Yaakov teacher. Excited, she started her first job in Szeratz; then she moved to Zdunska Wola. Her last position was in Zgiersz, where her work at the fine large Bais Yaakov school left a long-lasting impression on her young charges.

I reencountered Rachel in 1998 in Brooklyn at the home of her daughter, Mrs. Pearl Altschuler, the principal of the Bais Yaakov High School of Gur. I recognized her right away — the same pretty face, the same lively eyes, the same lovely smile. She was exactly as I remembered her, a young girl who passed my house on her way to and from the seminary. I was excited about this reunion, after so many years apart, and was eager to hear her life story.

She began by describing what happened when she visited her relatives in Lodz after the 1936/37 school year. They were about to introduce her to a second cousin, Shmuel Greenbaum, a handsome young man, a student at Yeshivas Chachmei Lublin, and well-versed in secular knowledge. The encounter culminated in a God-blessed marriage in 1938.

The war and its concomitant, the Nazi persecution of the Jews, broke out a year later. Soon Lodz became the most dreadful ghetto, infamous as the Nazis' target for bloody mass deportations to death camps. Those left behind in the ghetto were not much better off. Illness, starvation, and death were their daily companions. People died on their feet, while standing, and as they talked. The Devil of Death — one hesitates to call him an angel — frolicked gleefully among the ill and the starving. My father-in-law, Reb Chaim Pinchas Benisch of blessed and sainted memory, sat at the Pesach table conducting the Seder service. In the middle of Hallel, he stopped. He had crossed the barrier. He completed the rest of Hallel accompanied by a choir of angels, in the sublime world of peace and plenitude.

Observing one's loved ones in hunger pangs or terminal illness was even worse than experiencing it oneself.

I previously mentioned Feiga Zelicka, one of Sarah Schenirer's favorite students and a talented teacher, who faithfully answered her calling under those tragic circumstances. Feiga continued teaching the starving girls, giving them faith and encouragement and helping them face another gruesome day. Through her, they vaulted from the darkness of the present to the glory of the future.

Our Rachel was Feiga's associate in her charitable endeavors. They collected meager teaspoonsful of food to help the ill and the dying. She became a source of moral support, guidance, and outreach for Bnos girls. They helped each other keep Shabbos under the inhuman working conditions.

At our reunion in Brooklyn, Rachel told me about Tzipora Levi, a friend with whom I had attended Chavas Schmuel, the first Bnos instructors' course before the war. I found it a pleasure to study with this intelligent, witty girl and to discuss the material we had learned.

After the war began, Tzipora was transported from her hometown to the Lodz ghetto. She arrived in a pitiful state; as an utterly dispossessed newcomer, she was even worse off than others. However, as a Bais Yaakov *talmidah* she had not been stripped of her pride and did not wish to burden anybody. She tried to hide herself and her desperate condition from acquaintances.

I next met Tzipora in Bergen-Belsen, where she shared a bunk with Ryska Yoskowicz. "How are you, Tzipora?" I asked her.

"I feel fine," she replied feverishly, her face skin and bones, prostrate with typhus. "Look, I'm sitting at a beautifully set table," she hallucinated. "There's a whole loaf of bread on it. It's fresh and crisp; it's waiting for me to start eating it. There's a beautiful platter of fruit on the table, and a young healthy girl is serving a meal. Her cheeks are as fresh as peaches, like the ones on the table."

"I'll be pretty, too," she continued in her delirium. I stared at her, half-laughing, half-crying. She turned to Ryska. "When I die," she pleaded, "and you survive, please find my brother and tell him that I died with dignity." Illness had not sapped her pride.

However, Ryska did not give up on Tzipora. She continued to provide encouragement, support, assistance, and care. Tzipora survived due to her friend's love and self-sacrifice. I met her decades after the war in Tel Aviv. She had raised a beautiful family and continued to help and encourage others. Although she was ill and hardly able to walk by that time, she dragged her ailing legs to visit friends in the hospital or in nursing homes. The sight of her continued loving-kindness for others made one forget one's own problems.

This is how Bais Yaakov girls went through the ghettos, the camps, the ordeals, and then the times of rebirth — always encouraging, helping, sharing.

Rachel Greenbaum and her family were placed aboard one of the last transports to Auschwitz. There she parted with her loved ones and embarked alone on the tortuous life of a camp prisoner. After surviving this inferno, she found herself in

Bais Yaakov seminary in the Salzburg, Austria, DP camp. On the bench, fourth from left, is its founder, Rachel Kaimovitz Greenbaum.

Salzburg, Austria, at the end of the war. Like other *talmidos* of Sarah Schenirer, however, she did not rest there.

In cooperation with Agudath Israel and PAI, Rachel began to work with young girls who had survived. She organized the young girls in a Bais Yaakov setting and the older girls into a seminary, where she trained them to teach and lead other survivors. In response to the motherly love she gave them, they treated her as they would a mother, especially since she was a married woman.

Soon she was informed that her husband had also survived. Delighted, and armed with her usual vigor, she set out to look for him. She visited men's camps in succession but failed to find him. Exhausted, she returned to Salzburg to rest up before starting her search again.

Her friends urged her to stay put. "Your husband probably found out about you, too, and is trying to locate you. You'll keep on missing each other. Stay where you are," they advised her. "You'll have a better chance of finding each other." But she was not so sure.

The next day, as she went to the railroad station to see a friend off, she suddenly noticed a tall young man boarding the train. "Shmuel!" she called excitedly. "Shmuel, Shmuel!" she screamed in a crescendo. Shmuel turned around and rushed to her. Thus the husband and wife, having survived such bitter ordeals, were happily reunited. After greeting each other with cries of "Thank God," the grateful couple started a new life together.

Amidst their happiness, the Greenbaums were concerned about the young Jews in the Salzburg DP camp. Enthusiastically they stirred the ashes in search of lonely Jewish sparks, fanned what they found into flames, and encouraged the reclaimed souls to start their lives over again. Shmuel led the young men to the yeshiva that he had helped to establish, and Rachel enrolled the girls in the school she headed.

Soon they began arranging *shidduchim* among the young people. A year later, photographs show young mothers carrying

אינדהאלט פון לער־פראנראם:

יהדות: פון ה' ארלעאן ז"ל.

9 לעקציעם פאר די יונגערע גרופען און 9 לעקציעם
פאר די עלטערע גרופען.

חומש: נח, לך לך, דאם ראנגלען זיך פון דעם סלאך
מיט יעקבן, די ברכות פון יעקבן פאר זיגע זיהן,
פ' ויחי, פ' שמות, או ישיר און פ' קדושים.

פעדאגאגיק: פארלעזונגען און אנווייזונגען איבער קינדער־
ערציהונג.

תהלים: קאפ. א, ב, ג, ח, ט, י, ס"ד, צ, צ"א שיר המעלות.

געשיכטע: די תקופה פון די שופטים, די שפאנישע
תקופה, געשיכטע פון הזידיזם און מתנגדים.

פירוש התפלה: שמונה עשרה, ברכת המזון, ברכות השחר,
קריאת שמע.

קיצור שולחן ערוך: הלכות פון ליכם צינדן, פלייש זאל־
צען, חלה נעמן און נאך איינינע אקטועלע שיעורים.

עברית, אנגלית

ארעאלאנני

פאלעסטינאראפיע

The curriculum taught at the Bais Yaakov seminary in the Salzburg, Austria, DP camp.

babies — the very first Jewish children born after the war, a new generation to continue forging the chain of Jewish eternity.

The seminary, under Rachel Greenbaum's leadership, grew in numbers and stature, as she had set up a new, professional educational system. The school identity card indicates as much and attests to the propitious involvement of Agudath Israel and PAI.

In retrospect, it gives us pride to note the seminary's outstanding, devoted staff, made up of Bais Yaakov *talmidos*. They included Devorah Kostman, a talented Bais Yaakov student from Kraków, and Itka Asch, who had completed one year at the Bais Yaakov Seminary in Kraków before the war terminated her studies.

The administrative board consisted of Agudath Israel and PAI leaders: Yaakov Elbaum, Nesanel Radziner, and the aforementioned Ryska Yoskowicz.

One who studies the curriculum we reproduce here can only marvel at the work done in the DP camps immediately after the liberation, by survivors who could hardly stand on their own feet.

Rachel Greenbaum, too, became the happy mother of a sweet little boy. She and her husband were eager to settle in Eretz Yisroel. At the time, however, our homeland was accessible only by means of the clandestine and hazardous "Aliyah

*Shmuel and Rachel Greenbaum, together
with their little boy, leaving for Australia.*

Beit."[73] The Jewish Brigade, which organized those perilous voyages, was loathe to assume responsibility for mothers with infants.

Under these circumstances, the Greenbaums made their home in Sydney, Australia, where they were sponsored by relatives. There, as in Salzburg, Rachel worked with the women while her husband, Shmuel, spent his spare time helping to es-

---

73. Literally, "Immigration B," denoting clandestine immigration to Eretz Yisroel, under the hostile noses of the British authorities there. To immigrate to Eretz Yisroel in an ordinary way, one needed an entrance visa ("certificate") from the British, who strictly limited the number of these documents.

tablish and lead a shul for the survivors and a boys' *cheder* that they called "the Yeshiva." She created girls' groups that she called Bnos Sarah, in which students learned to teach and lead other groups in the footsteps of the organization's namesake, Sarah Schenirer. Bnos Sarah spread the ideals of Bais Yaakov to young girls and, under Rachel's leadership, organized diverse evening lectures for youth and events for women. Again we witness a *talmidah* of Sarah Schenirer's emulating her, standing up proudly before the ignorant Jewish girls of Australia, and inspiring them with the joy and beauty of their Jewish heritage — imbuing them with pride in being a Jewish daughter, a princess, a daughter of the King.

Before leaving Salzburg, Rachel stayed on a few months to transfer her work and responsibilities to her successor, Itka Asch.

Rachel Greenbaum, surrounded by her students, receives a letter of recognition and appreciation for her work with young people in the camp from the chairman of the D.P. community in Salzburg.

✣ *Chapter 60* ✥

Itka Asch

Itka Asch came from Nowogródek, Poland. When her
parents applied to the seminary to have her admitted as a student, Reb Yehudah Leib Orlean came to town to test her and
other applicants. He was impressed with Itka and accepted her
application.

Itka's happiness knew no limit. Imagine: spending two
years at the Bais Yaakov Seminary and quenching her thirst for
learning at the very fount of knowledge. She prepared to bask
in the spiritual atmosphere of the seminary and looked ahead to
the next phase: realizing her dream to teach, to share her
knowledge with others.

Her dream was brutally shattered. She attended the seminary for only one year; the tragedy of war kept her from returning to Kraków to finish her studies. She was ghettoized in
Nowogródek, like all the Jews in that town. There, the Germans promptly cut off the water supply to kill the Jews by
thirst. Aware of their intent, Itka's brother arranged to have
the family escape from the ghetto. One night, they slipped out,
crossed a little wooden bridge, and hid in the woods.

There, they encountered the three sons of the Bielski family, owners of a mill and a farm in Nowogródek. When the Nazis
came to town, the occupiers immediately established a ghetto,
forced the Jews to enter it, and sealed it tightly. Then they
rounded up four thousand of the seven thousand Jews of

Nowogródek — men, women, and children — and slaughtered them brutally.

Some of the Bielskis were among the victims. The oldest sons, Tuvia, Zus, and Asael, were assigned to a labor detail. Realizing the tragic situation and benefiting from a measure of good luck, they escaped, went into hiding in the dense forests in the Belorussian countryside, and formed a small group of fighters. After moving from hideout to hideout in the woods, they finally found a place that they considered safe. There they established a partisan community that they called the "Base."

It was a very unusual partisan group: each family had to dig its own dwelling deeply into the ground, cover it with grass, and ventilate it with special holes. This was done on a forested "island," where the members of the group hid during the day and performed underground operations at night. The Base was surrounded by dangerous marshes. When the Germans entered the area, they did not dare to venture into the deep marshes even though they suspected that partisans were there. They could not even force their dogs to enter. Only the partisans knew how to cross the swamps safely.

The three Bielski brothers — robust, aggressive individuals — dominated the group of fighters, both Jewish and non-Jewish. Tuvia, the oldest, assumed the overall leadership. A self-confident and tough commander, he demanded complete and unquestioning compliance with his orders. All partisans were to carry weapons to protect themselves, acquire food, and carry out their duties. One of Tuvia's orders, given to rescuers whom he sent to the ghetto, was, "Save whomever you can. No matter who they are, children, the elderly, or the ill, deliver them all safely to the Base."

He had a motto that encapsulated his priorities: better to save one ailing Jew than to kill ten Germans.

The nearby German forces cordoned off the area and shot at the Base from afar, cutting off the fighters' supplies of food and water. After ten days, however, they were forced to leave without engaging the determined partisans in battle. After the Nazis left, the Base did something unmatched by any other partisan undertaking: it organized itself into a community. Its members established a shul, an infirmary, a public bath, and a bakery. Then it renamed itself Shtetl Bielsk, population 1,500.

Tuvia Bielski was the commander-in-chief, Asael commanded the armed forces, and Zus was chief of reconnaissance. The community members who observed them astride their white horses felt that they had an army behind them. An accurate depiction, as that "army" rescued 1,500 Jews, by Jews, in the midst of the Nazi reign of terror.

Young, beautiful, blonde Itka was one of those rescued by the Bielski partisans. She became a resident of Shtetl Bielsk, together with her family. Apart from her duties in the community, she struggled to keep Shabbos and eat only kosher food. The Polish partisans, aware of her commitment, often dropped *treif* meat into anything she cooked. Whenever she discovered this, she threw out the cooked food, kashered the only tin pot she had, and cooked another meal for her family.

Even the non-Jewish partisans, however, respected her for her unusual sense of direction. At night she guided groups of fighters to an assigned place. She had no compass; navigating only by the moon and stars, she found her destination time and again. Still, it was an arduous, difficult, and dangerous life. Young Itka had to employ strength and determination to fight the enemy within — her personal ordeals — as well as the enemy without. Furthermore, she had to struggle every week anew to keep Shabbos and fend off Shabbos-desecrating duties given her by her superior.

Then Providence stepped in. The doctor of the Base, the renowned surgeon Dr. Mesnik, contracted typhus. Who but Itka would risk her own health to treat a man with a contagious disease? She took the risk and nursed him back to health. From then on, she was the nurse of the Base. Both commanders and the rank-and-file admired her sacrifice and selfless dedication. They nicknamed her the *Swieta Partizanka*, the saintly woman partisan.

The adjective fits. Among the hard, ruthless, cold-blooded underground fighters, she was a walking sanctification of God's Name. Throughout those difficult, trying times, she remained the pure, untouched Itka — a true *talmidah* of Sarah Schenirer.

*　　*　　*

After the liberation, Itka and her family reached Bad Gastein, Austria. Itka busied herself organizing older girls into Bnos groups and younger ones into Basya. Bustling with energy, she circulated among the DP camps, creating study groups and kibbutzim to prepare youth for *aliyah* and encourage the young people to start life anew.

Agudath Israel was already active in Bad Gastein, and she worked with its leaders to match boys with girls and marry them off. She was a talented, God-sent teacher whose ability to impart Jewish concepts inspired girls with the beauty of their Jewish heritage. Apart from teaching, she loved, cared for, and helped her troubled pupils. The Polish and Hungarian girls clung to her, excited by her interesting lessons and attentive to her sensible advice.

One day, a delegation of British, American, and French officials visited Bad Gastein to find out how and where the survivors wished to start their new lives. So they said, at any rate. The meeting took place in the Kursaal, a large auditorium in this renowned spa city. Leaders of every organization in the DP camp were invited. Itka represented the girls' educational groups and kibbutzim.

After three speakers addressed the delegation, Itka was asked to take the floor. She delivered a dynamic speech that held the visitors spellbound. She expressed the Jewish survivors' feelings and, especially, their profound desire to obtain a country of their own at long last — a peaceful place where they could establish a new home for their families.

"We survivors," she cried with pathos, "will strive and fight for the right of entry to the Holy Land, the land of our ancestors, where we will raise our children.

"We will not return to the countries of our youth; we do not wish to live among people who even today continue to hate us, among nations that never acknowledged our tremendous role in their growth and development.

"Now, after what has happened, their hatred of Jews has become even more evident. They express their anti-Semitic feelings openly and shamelessly. They greeted with malice the few Jews who returned to see their homes and visit the tombs of their great rabbis and the mass graves of their brethren. Even worse, they greeted them with pogroms in which they killed fellow citizens.

"As they shed the surviving Jews' blood, they asked malevolent questions such as, 'What are you doing here, in our land? Didn't Hitler finish you all off as he had promised?'"

The visiting officials found Itka's passion, enthusiasm, and staunch commitment inspiring. They were touched by the sincere words of this young girl who expressed the survivors' pain and disappointment. In admiration, they promised to support the survivors' claim. "We'll do whatever we can," they assured them.

However, help arrived slowly and painfully at best. In desperation, young people set out on dangerous and illegal routes to their homeland. Within sight of their destination, they were forcibly turned away and transported to yet another camp encased in barbed wire, this time in Cyprus, where inhumane conditions awaited them.

Despite mistreatment and degradation, however, they did not despair. Courageously they improved their lot by means of cultural endeavors and religious education and observance. Apart from making their lives as productive and enjoyable as possible, they prepared themselves for life in the Land of Holiness by studying professions, agriculture, and diverse trades.

After two years of organizational activities in Bad Gastein (see photos of her two Bnos groups on pages 376 and 377), Itka Asch was summoned to Salzburg by Jewish activists in that DP

One of Itka's Bnos groups in Bad Gastein, Austria.

camp to become headmistress of the Bais Yaakov seminary and school that they had established there. Rachel Greenbaum was about to depart; she and her husband were waiting for a immigration "certificate" for Eretz Yisroel. As mentioned above, unable to enter the Holy Land legally, the Greenbaums eventually accepted visas for Australia, which were arranged by relatives of Rachel's there, and made their home in Sydney out of necessity.

Rachel used her extra time in Salzburg to acquaint Itka with her duties and responsibilities. The two idealistic Bais Yaakov girls also became close friends. Before Rachel left for Australia, Itka gave her a farewell present: a book of poems by the Ibn Ezra, with a beautiful inscription:

> My dear sister:
> Take this small gift
> On the day of our parting.
>
> Itka
> Salzburg, Austria
> 25 August 1948

Rachel kept the gift lovingly.

Itka also yearned to go to Eretz Yisroel, but having an ill father whom she had to take care of, she decided to follow him to America. *Kibud av* (honoring one's father) was her highest priority. It was there, in the United States, that I had the privilege to meet her, learn about her past, and appreciate what she did later on.

Itka's continual selfless acts of limitless giving and helping for the benefit of mankind were exemplary. A believer in a healthy soul in a healthy body, she promoted health food at every turn — among

Salzburg, Austria. Itka is seated, third from left. Notice a few of the redeemed children sitting in front. They were all in kibbutzim such as this one before the kinderheimen were established.

pupils, friends, and neighbors. She also gave public lectures on health problems, recommending various health foods and supplements. Doctors respected her unselfish interest in the ill and needy and lowered their fees at her suggestion, whenever necessary.

She was a great advocate of natural cures and vitamins. When my son's first baby was born, he was unable to have his *bris* at the appointed time due to jaundice. I mentioned the matter to Itka.

"Tell your daughter-in-law," she advised firmly, "to give

him vitamin E." Observing my hesitation, she added, "It's easy. If she applies the vitamin to the nipple, he will drink it with the milk he sucks."

I let my skepticism show. "I don't think I can do it," I said. "I don't feel comfortable enough to suggest it to my daughter-in-law."

"If you can't do it," she answered quietly but decisively, "I'll call her." And she did.

My daughter-in-law followed her advice. In two or three days, my grandson was ready for his *bris*.

Her activities to heal the body were as important to her as her efforts to heal and improve the human soul, to help minds to grow, to understand, to love, and to care.

As for Itka Asch's remarkable teaching abilities, it is best to let her students describe their beloved teacher. A copy of one student's letter of January 1981 to the late Rebbetzin Vichna Kaplan, principal of the Bais Yaakov where Itka taught, and a poem submitted to *The Jewish Press* by another of her students after Itka's death, expresses the tremendous impression her teachings made on her pupils.

Friday, Sept. 26, 1980 • JEWISH PRESS • Page 57

A Remembrance
Of Rebbitzen
Itka Lerner
(Zecher Tzadakes L'vracha)
(How Did The Heros Fall?
(Samuels 2, 1,)
And the Heroine,
How did she fall?
Heroic was her heart,
A heart that could embrace the whole world,
Yet, you thought at the moment
She hugs you alone;
As sound waves,
A beat of her heart moved thousands of others,
and gave them a pulse!
Many hearts were calmer,
Thanks to her over active one...
The couragous Partisaner,
Who fought the enemy within and without;
Who raced evil all her life, to overcome it in herself...
Who thought her mission in life,
Is to live for the other,
How did the Heroine fall?
Heroic were those eyes,
Rays that were pulled to earth,
To hint to us, how the angels be,

A glimpse of those eyes,
And our neshoma was drawn to something higher...
Great were her lips,
That shrank from lies and slander,
That only opened to truth and faith,
And always called in the name of Hashem
How did the Heroine fall!
Our hearts tremble,
For we have lost a heart of calm faith,
A heart that beat for others,
Our eyes are darkened by tears,
for we miss the light
Of her neshoma's eyes,
Our lips are too small,
To form all the words of praise,
For we knew a fraction of her,
We can only murmer,
The echo of her existence ...
She fell, to be remembered as a giant,
We fell with her,
For we are all the more dwarfed,
We no longer have the merit,
To come to the giant,
To lift us up...
How did the Heroine fall!
By A Friend

A tribute to Itka Asch Lerner

IN LOVING MEMORY OF REBBETZIN ITKA LERNER, A"H
From the Private Correspondence of Rebbetzin Kaplan, A"H

January '81

Dear Rebbetzin Kaplan עמו"ש,

I want to express my feelings and thoughts about a most remarkable teacher who made an everlasting impression on me.

In '50 - '51, I was a freshman in Bais Yaakov. An out-of-towner from Elizabeth, New Jersey, I had a day-school education. Raised by *Torah* - true parents who fortunately had arrived here just before World War II, they did their utmost to raise their three children religiously, but the atmosphere certainly wasn't Williamsburg.

One of my teachers that semester was Miss Itka Ash (later Lerner) a young girl fresh from the nightmare of *Churban Europa*. What a warm, wonderful person she was! She kept us enthralled with reminiscences about her friends, the Bais Yaakov girls, who in the face of the worst *tzaros*, were always full of *Bitachon*. She would say, "Girls, you don't know how priceless a Bais Yaakov education is. It will accompany you from here to the *Olam HaEmes!*"

Her mannerisms, her love for *Torah*, filled us with awe. The forty-five minute classes flew by too quickly for us. Once when I received a 98% on a test she praised me and made me feel that I was the smartest student ever. I tried so hard to please her, and truly enjoyed her classes. The longest lasting lesson I learned was when she said: "Kinderlach, what is the most valuable treasure in your home, and where is it kept?" We didn't understand, until she explained, with shining eyes. "The *seforim*, the *Torah*, why are they not placed in the most *chashuv* room for all to gaze at? This lesson never left me. From the first day that I made my home, my husband's *seforim* were placed in the dining room, our most important room. Now, 23 years later, they are still there, more than a little more used, a lot more torn (I have seven sons קן יעה), the *seforim* occupy the place of honor in my home.

As I sit and write this letter, I am filled with sadness at this wonderful womans' passing, but I am deeply grateful that I had the opportunity to know her. I am proud to have been her student and I feel sure that I learned her lessons well, and transmitted them to my children faithfully. They will, בע"ה, always know what the jewels of our nation are, and the value of their own lives in the tapestry of the *Am HaNivchar*.

With much love for Bais Yaakov,

Respectfully,
Penina (Edith) Neuman Tesser

Another tribute to Itka Asch Lerner

❧ *Chapter 61* ☙

Leah Galler

$\mathcal{B}$*efore the war, Leah Galler* of Rzeszów had been a beloved Bais Yaakov teacher in Uszczyki Dolne, a fine Polish town with a large Jewish population led by the renowned Bluziver Rebbe, Rav Yisrael Shapira, *zt"l*.

After her tragic war experiences, *hashgachah* delivered Leah to a DP camp in Föhrenwald, Germany. There she re-met Rivka Horowitz, who came to visit survivors who had formed a Jewish community in the camp. Happy to see Leah, Rivka suggested that she relocate to Landsberg, a larger town in the vicinity.

"A rather nice group of Bais Yaakov girls from Polish towns and villages is living together on the same block," she explained. "They need to be organized into a Bnos kibbutz."

Leah, eager to help the forlorn survivor girls stand up courageously and reconstruct their lives, gladly acted on Rivka's suggestion and resolved to do whatever she could.

Shymon, my future husband, was glad to meet Leah, the talented Bais Yaakov teacher who had come to Landsberg to work with the girls. Promptly he arranged comfortable accommodations for the girls' kibbutz and acquainted Leah with the agencies that funded and maintained survivors' kibbutzim, such as HIAS (Hebrew Immigrant Aid Society) and Va'ad Hatzalah.

Applying her usual vigor and enthusiasm, Leah established

a home for unaccompanied girl survivors and called it Ohel Sarah, Sarah's Tent, after her great teacher and mentor, Sarah Schenirer. The new kibbutz attracted so many girls, and did it so quickly, that soon it became the most important girls' kibbutz in Germany.

* * *

By that time, several Po'alei Agudath Israel activists — Shymon Benisch, Dovid Adler, Chaim Banker, and a few others — had already established a PAI organization in Landsberg.

From the first moment of liberation, Shymon combed the area for tiny Jewish sparks that glowed in the still-smoking ashes. He fanned those sparks — lonely, desperate boys who had already given up — until they began to blaze again on their own. He literally dragged several survivors from the gutter. He picked up others from the dirty roads on which they lay, waiting for their lonely, tragic lives to end. He gathered them together and established a home for them. As a PAI official, he requisitioned a large military compound where German soldiers had been housed and turned it into a kibbutz — a warm family home where his wards felt loved and wanted. As word of this large "family" quickly spread, additional young people joined to bask in the atmosphere of affection and friendship. That loving relationship persists among the members of the kibbutz to this very day.

Almost eighty boys lived together. Shymon and several other young *talmidei chachamim* among the kibbutz members gave classes in Talmud and Tanach. They also studied Jewish history and Hebrew avidly. Having a large garden across the street, they were able not only to study agriculture but also to practice it, an important prerequisite for *aliyah*.

The boys also undertook a very dangerous mission: traveling in small groups to Poland, where, following leads from Jewish organizations, they searched for Jewish children. "You'll find them in gentile homes or Christian convents," they were told, "where desperate mothers placed them to keep them alive until they could reclaim them after the war, as agreed."

Chaim Banker, one of the influential members of the kibbutz, retold one of their escapades:

"We went into a Polish city," he began, "equipped with names and addresses of places where we might find Jewish children. We stayed there for quite a few days, spying on the children as they moved about and looking for opportunities to abduct them.

"One of our group received a tip about a Jewish child who was staying in town with a Polish family. He did some reconnaissance and discovered that the maid took the boy to the park to play at the same time every day.

"By offering the boy a piece of candy, he lured him out of the park and loaded him into a waiting car that delivered him to our hiding place. A few minutes later, another colleague of ours brought in a little boy in rags whom he had snatched from a pasture, where the poor child was grazing cattle.

"Another member of the group kidnapped a girl from a lengthy column of children that was coming out of an orphanage. The teacher suspected nothing and continued walking as the child was driven away.

"Some of the children knew they were Jews; they were the easiest to handle. Others cried, 'We don't want to be Jewish! We want to go back to our parents!' They had to be taken by force.

"We led the children across the Tatra Mountains and spirited them over the border into Austria. There, trucks were waiting to take them to *kinderheimen* in Germany, where they awaited their turn for Youth Aliyah to arrange their immigration to Eretz Yisroel.

"In those Polish cities and towns, we also encountered Bais Yaakov girls who had been given the same dangerous assignments," he noted in conclusion.

*   *   *

On one of my visits to Landsberg, I was surprised to find the camp in an exceptionally festive mood, the inhabitants dressed in holiday attire and excitement permeating the air. Soon I came upon the reason: a makeshift, primitive *chuppah* composed of a tallis supported by four tree branches.

I got caught up in the tumult and joined the crowd surrounding the *chuppah* in anticipation of the great event — the first wedding in which these reborn war survivors were to participate.

The first wedding in the Landsberg, Germany, DP camp.

In a departure from tradition, the groom and bride were escorted to the *chuppah* by their unmarried friends. Married couples ordinarily discharged this privilege, but, tragically, none had survived. The nuptial blessings, serious and meaningful, were recited under the *chuppah* with exceptional love and passion. After the groom broke a glass, in symbolic remembrance of the destruction of Jerusalem and our bitter past, the wedding ceremony was over. The newlyweds were surrounded by a crowd of hugging, kissing, and singing well-wishers. It was everybody's *simchah*, a courageous first act of reconstruction. The resounding *"Mazel tov"* was addressed not only to the new couple but to every person in attendance, as a warm, sincere expression of wishes for a happy future for all.

Those in attendance burst into joyous song and hundreds of *heftlinge* (camp internees) clasped hands and danced. Soon the entire community joined in with singing, dancing, and merrymaking.

A short time later, however, painful memories marred the happiness and sighs and tears infiltrated the songs. A sudden silence took over as we felt the profound presence of the invisible but most important invitees: the departed. Their souls descended to earth to participate in the *simchah* of their children and friends, and to wish them *Mazel tov*. As they mingled with the living, they conveyed blessings straight from Heaven for the happy beginning of a new wonderful generation. Indeed, Hashem has blessed us survivors with three very special generations: children, grandchildren, and great-grandchildren.

Then a thunderous recitation of *Kel Malei Rachamim* shattered the silence, pierced the earth and the heavens, and rent our broken hearts, too.

*   *   *

Leah Galler directed Ohel Sarah with a strong hand and a loving heart. She taught her girls Tanach, *Pirkei Avos*, Jewish history, Hebrew, and other subjects. What they needed more, however, was a warm home, a loving family life, and the courage to start anew. Ohel Sarah provided them with all of these.

Next came the most important task — matchmaking. Many young people among the survivors had been married before the war, and were eager to perform this most difficult task.

The coupling operation went very well in Landsberg, due to the presence of both a boys' and a girls' kibbutz in the town and the love and dedication of the matchmakers. Shymon once described a matchmaking episode that occurred between the two kibbutzim:

One of his charges in the kibbutz was a fine young man and a *talmid chacham*, of whom he was very proud. He wished to set him up with a nice Bais Yaakov girl from Ohel Sarah whom he knew and thought suitable. Both prospective spouses were short in stature. Shymon tried to convince the girl to meet the young man, but to no avail. "Since both of us are short, our children won't reach the height of a table," she reasoned. "Nothing doing!"

Shymon did not give up; he envisioned them as an ideal couple. One day, before an engagement party at the kibbutz, he had an idea. He asked Leah to bake a cake for the bride and to send it to the kibbutz with the girl he had in mind. Shymon then summoned the young man and kept him at his side until the girl came by to deliver the cake. Shymon introduced the two of them. They immediately found each other interesting and decided to follow up. A short time later, they married and eventually settled in Eretz Yisroel.

I met them in 1967 in Israel. A most wonderful couple, they maintained a warm, friendly home where friends and the needy always found an open door. They started out as very special parents who raised their offspring in an atmosphere of joy and peace, and they went on to become very special grandparents. What is more, all of their sons and grandsons grew up *tall* and handsome, and all the girls turned out beautiful and regal in bearing. But they attained their greatest height in the love and respect they showed their parents.

*   *   *

I reencountered Leah in the United States several years later. Again, she had come at the right time to become involved in the pioneering work again. We needed a kindergarten for our girls and a *cheder* for our little boys.

The Celer Rav, Rabbi Yisrael Olewski, *zt"l*, preceded us to America. Realizing the need, he plunged into the difficult undertaking of starting a yeshiva and a Bais Yaakov for the survivors' children. He embarked on his venture with enthusiasm, great dedication, and vision. His goal for the boys was to establish a great yeshiva along the traditional pre-war lines. He gave it a name: Darchei Noam, "Ways of Pleasantness,"[74] reminiscent of the ways of Torah and symbolic of the act of rebirth and renewal that the survivors' generation would perform.

For the girls, however, he needed help, and so he approached Leah Galler to provide it on the basis of her Bais Yaakov upbringing. She agreed at once, eager as always to serve the cause of girls' education.

Within three years of their modest beginning, the girls' school, Ohel Sarah, and the yeshiva, Darchei Noam, attained a combined enrollment of 275 chidlren. Rabbi Olewski worked hard to maintain a high standard of education and a dedicated staff of teachers. By that time, with Leah's help, he had managed to establish three classes apart from the preschool. (A picture of this courageous beginning appears below.)

The school looked very promising as an educational facility

Third grade at the Ohel Sarah school in New York.

---

74. See *Mishlei* 3:17.

but lacked the funding to endure. Rabbi Olewski received little financial support — no contributions from fundraisers, no outside help, and scanty tuition revenue. It was too much for one man to carry alone, and regretfully, he had to give it up. However, Rabbi Olewski's venture paved the way for the great yeshiva, Yagdil Torah, which thousands of boys attend today. Furthermore, the Gerrer chassidim started a Bais Yaakov elementary and high school for girls, an educational institution of importance in the United States.

Although Leah Galler's first educational endeavor in America did not succeed, she continued to pledge herself to educating Jewish girls in the Bais Yaakov spirit that had been so lovingly bestowed upon her.

Soon her educational capabilities were utilized. Rebbetzin Vichna Kaplan drafted her for the staff of the Bais Yaakov Teachers' Seminary in Brooklyn. There, to this very day, she continues to teach and inspire girls with the authentic spirit of Sarah Schenirer's seminary in Kraków.

✤ *Chapter 62* ✤

Shifra's story

The post-war story of Rebbetzin Shifra Yudasin, *née* Singer, begins in Skarzysko, one of the worst camps in Poland — a so-called labor camp where inmates were worked to death by being forced to handle dangerous chemicals without protection. The message on the large sign over the gate at Camp C of the Skarzysko facility — "Welcome to the Gates of Death" — was only partly sarcastic.

The chemical at issue, called Vitrina, was made of two different substances — one that turned the workers' skin red and one that turned it yellow. The inmates, sometimes unable even to recognize each other, called themselves Reds and Yellows.

Shifra Singer landed in Skarzysko after having spent time at the Plaszów camp, whence she had been transported from the ghetto in Tarnów, her hometown. In the Tarnów ghetto, she had organized lectures for girls and helped the needy and ill in any way she could. In Skarzysko, she was a powerhouse of moral support and advice for lonely girls whose dangerous work had driven them to exhaustion.

From Skarzysko, she was sent to Leipzig, Germany, along with 500 girls — including a group of eleven from Bais Yaakov who had miraculously survived their travails in Skarzysko. In Leipzig, they were interned in a forced-labor camp located on the premises of a munitions factory. Although conditions there were much better than in Skarzysko, the inmates were subjected to the same mistreatments and, sometimes, tortures as in other camps.

There, in a storeroom where scrap metal was kept, our Shifra found a hideout and revealed it to the Bais Yaakov girls, whom she could trust. "I've found a place where we can hide. On Sunday, when we have a couple of free hours before we go to sleep, we can have a short *Yahadus* lecture. It'll be good for our spirits." Indeed, she gave the lecture the next Sunday, and continued to do so throughout her stay in the camp. She also kept a Jewish calendar so that the girls would not overlook the festivals.

During the night shift on Yom Kippur, the SS woman on the camp staff distributed the inmates' most important meal, soup. The girls in Shifra's group refused to eat it; other Bais Yaakov girls, Renia Finkelstein among them, behaved the same way. They asked the SS woman to keep it for later. Furious, she dumped their kettle on the floor. Next she offered soup to other girls who, she thought, would not be fasting. However, all the inmates disregarded their intense hunger and refused the soup, in solidarity with their observant comrades.

The SS woman, her face red with rage, poured the contents of all the remaining kettles on the ground. Although afraid of the beast's retribution, the Jewish inmates, adolescent girls, walked away. Famished but proud to have asserted their Jewishness and humanity in this jungle of predators, they fasted until the next morning instead of the normal twenty-five hours. And when relief came, it was ersatz coffee and no more.

"We were liberated on May 7, 1945," Shifra recalled years later, "and I decided to return to my hometown. My group of eleven Bais Yaakov girls, including my closest friend and associate, Ida Fass, accompanied me.

"The trip back was very difficult and dangerous. The Soviets had liberated us. This created another cause of great distress for the girls — the danger of harassment by Russian soldiers. 'I liberated you; be cooperative,' they kept saying.

The girls hid in village barns, under the hay, to avoid the

soldiers' advances. "One of the youngest girls," Ida related, "was approached by a Russian soldier in the house of a German woman where we were staying. Miraculously, she came away unscathed. A Mrs. Rosenberg, who was with them, knew Russian. She dissuaded the soldier by asking him, 'What do you want with such a dried-out skeleton of a girl? Find someone who's young and healthy!' Although our girl was saved that time, the danger persisted and mounted. The Bais Yaakov group had to leave the Russian occupation zone at once."

Having been liberated by English troops, I avoided the perils of the Russian soldiers. But my friends who had been freed by Russian forces went through Gehenna trying to reach Poland or the American occupation zone. While I was in the DP camp in Zeilsheim, Germany, near Hannover, I received distressing and tragic news about several of my dear friends from Bais Yaakov in Kraków. They had been trying to cross from Russian-occupied territory into the American Zone and were brutally shot while fending off Russians' advances. May their memory and that of other girls who met the same fate be blessed.

Travel in general was difficult in those post-war conditions; every step, every ride, was hazardous. Apart from the personal danger, girls who boarded trains to head from Germany back to Poland had to ride on open platforms or near locomotives on risky, perilous iron plates. Worst of all, however, was the menace of the Russians who traveled on those trains. The trains inched along — it took hours to reach Tarnów from Kraków, a short distance of about forty-five miles, which before the war took only an hour and a half by train. The girls were again subjected to the Russians' harassment.

Twice Shifra and her eleven charges leaped from slow-moving trains to save themselves from the Russians. Now, as they walked along the platform, afraid to take another train, they noticed a decorated Russian general who seemed to be waiting like them. He looked trustworthy, so Shifra marshaled her courage, approached him, and told him the story of the group.

Eager to reach their destination, they related, they had boarded trains twice but had had to jump off on both occasions due to soldiers' harassment.

"Where are you girls heading?" he asked, interested.

"To Tarnów, our hometown," they answered.

"Don't worry," he said soothingly. "I am also going to Tarnów, and I will watch over you."

Trusting the gentleman, they boarded the next train. He was as good as his word; they safely reached their destination. They thanked their protector, the important-looking Russian officer. As he took leave of them, he added, "I work at the headquarters of the military base in this town. If you need my help, don't hesitate to call." He gave them his name and waved a friendly good-bye.

The dangerous journey behind them, the girls headed for the young men's kibbutz in Tarnów. This collective, a far cry from the farming villages in Eretz Yisroel that went by that name, had been organized by several dedicated young men: Reb Nuteh (Natan) Parness, originally from Kraków, Rabbi Meir Lamed, who came to Tarnów from Sambor shortly after Pesach 1945, and Rabbi Chaim Kupperman.

Upon his arrival, Rabbi Lamed asked the *kehillah* (Jewish community administration) in Tarnów, which had already been reestablished, to help him acquire a building where he and others might establish a center to meet the community's religious needs. In response, the *kehillah* procured a beautiful three-story building, formerly a large hotel, near its own center on 5 Goldhammer Street.

The young men went straight to work with vigor and enthusiasm to adapt the building to their special needs. They turned most of the first floor into a shul and yeshiva, which they handed over to Rabbi Kupperman. A part of the spacious floor was made into a kitchen, where starving Jews who had returned from the camps might take meals while they hunted for relatives and acquaintances who, they hoped, had returned from the Soviet Union after having fled from Poland to that country when the war began.[75]

One of the DPs liberated in Germany was a young Bais Yaakov girl named Esther Safran; in May 1945 she arrived in Tarnów, also searching for family. Several additional Jewish girls came after her. Having nowhere to stay, they turned to Rabbi Lamed, who immediately offered the second floor of the building as lodging and took care of their board.

This initiative and other projects required more than the founders' hard work and sacrifice; they entailed funding for maintenance. To acquire it, the three founders contacted the Warsaw *kehillah*, chaired by Dr. Kahane, for financial assistance. Various Jewish organizations abroad provided the Warsaw *kehillah,* which was already well-established, with substantial funding that it could distribute for purposes such as these. Rabbi Eliezer Silver of Cincinnati also had large amounts of money for disposition. The *kehillah* and Rabbi Silver had subventioned many undertakings in Tarnów. They would now do the same for Shifra Singer and her eleven forlorn Bais Yaakov alumnae.

*   *   *

When Shifra and her group reached Tarnów, they asked Rabbi Lamed to help them establish a Bais Yaakov kibbutz of their own. Aware of Shifra's capabilities as a Bais Yaakov teacher, Rabbi Lamed offered her the second-floor facilities. As she got to work, the kibbutz filled with young girls who had survived Nazi death camps in Germany and Poland. Their numbers quickly climbed to forty. Soon, additional girls and young women with children came from Russia and joined. They had to be fed, clothed, and provisioned. It was a tough job for a young woman like Shifra. However, she and her even younger assistant, Ida Fass, discharged this great responsibility seriously, enthusiastically, and devotedly, welcoming newcomers with

---

75. After the war, the USSR and Poland concluded a repatriation agreement that allowed Polish citizens who did not wish to become Soviet citizens to return to Poland.

love. Young children who had been redeemed from the homes of gentiles who had protected them during the war needed especially dedicated care.

Now Shifra extended her activities. The Polish government, in a humanitarian gesture, allowed survivors to travel at no charge to look for families and relatives. Shifra, along with Ida, used this dispensation to visit towns and cities, recruit lonely, despairing girls, and organize them into Bnos groups. She also marshaled financial assistance for the more permanent tenants of the kibbutz. In this effort, she was helped mainly by Va'ad Hatzalah, through Rabbi Silver, and the great benefactor, Reb Nuteh Parness, who was always ready to assist every facet of kibbutz life with funds, advice, and encouragement.

Now it became the daunting responsibility of this kibbutz, other kibbutzim, individual members, and unaffiliated people to redeem and reclaim Jewish children from gentile homes.

An example of a person unaffiliated with political Jewish organizations was Rabbi Shalom Pinchas Wohlgelernter, an American Army captain who, as a representative of the Va'ad Hatzalah, visited survivors in the American Zone to bring them supplies. The most important provisions he delivered were encouragement and warm understanding. After touring the DP camps in Germany, Rabbi Wohlgelernter went on to Eastern Europe to rescue Jewish children from gentiles. He spent most of his time in Poland, where many stories about his exploits circulated. According to one of them, he visited a Polish convent and asked the sisters if there were any Jewish children in their childcare center. Although the nuns received him with respect as an American Army captain, they answered his question with a firm "No." He asked to see the children — a request the nuns could not refuse, since he was a uniformed American officer — and to have them lined up. Observing several distinctive Jewish faces among them, he cried out lovingly and passionately, *"Shema Yisrael! Hashem Elokeinu, Hashem Echad."* Many of the children burst into tears and ran to him. "Our parents used to tell us that at home!" they exclaimed.

Having confirmed these children's Jewishness, Rabbi Wohlgelernter was able to remove them from the convent and deliver them to the survivors' kibbutzim. There, the children were placed in various *kinderheimen* organized by Agudah and Po'alei Agudah activists and led by our Bais Yaakov girls and teachers.

Wherever the gentile caregivers refused to turn over the children voluntarily — as often happened — the rescue activity became very difficult and dangerous. Some rescuers succeeded by giving caregivers large bribes, using funds provided by Va'ad Hatzalah. Other children were removed from gentiles' homes either surreptitiously or overtly; in these operations, the rescue workers risked a kidnapping charge. The young survivors who went about this work were undaunted, sometimes sacrificing even their own lives to save Jewish children from Christian homes. The noteworthy activists in this field include Moshe Zamość, Shimon Zucker, and, of course, our girls from the kibbutzim in Kraków and Tarnów. God privileged each of them with the opportunity to save several young children and to give them the loving, patient, and understanding care that they needed so badly to adjust to a new life. Once rescued, the children were transferred to kibbutzim in Western Europe and thence to Eretz Yisroel.

Shimon Zucker of the PAI office in Lodz was responsible for moving Jews to Eretz Yisroel through "Aliyah Beit." With great self-sacrifice and determination, he sent Jews from all over Poland across the border to Czechoslovakia. From there, they continued by train to various seaports and boarded unsafe vessels that took them on the dangerous voyage toward the land of their dreams.

In the first leg of their trek, Zucker directed young men and women to the kibbutz in Tarnów to rest up. From there, at night, they were transported over the border, where trains awaited them. This foisted yet another task on Shifra's shoulders: to house and feed these hungry, tired refugees. Having accomplished that, she procured transportation to take them over the border. Zucker communicated with her in code: "Shifra, I'm sending you thirty herrings," a typical message read. "Pack them and send them to the kibbutzim." Herrings were people; kibbutzim were trains.

One day she received an urgent telegram: "I'm sending you sixty herrings. Pack them and send them away at 3:00 tomorrow morning." Shifra was beside herself. "How can I get a truck large enough for sixty people at all, let alone tonight?!" she asked Ida in dismay.

They pondered the matter in desperation until Shifra recovered her good cheer. "I have an idea! Let's go to the Communist Party office at the army base and ask that nice general, the man who protected us, for help."

Ida was aghast. "Shifra, you're asking for big trouble. This is a clandestine affair. Nobody should ever find out what we are doing. And you're going to tell a Soviet general about it? Shifra! We're in severe danger; it is a crazy idea." She was shouting by now. "You're going into a lion's den. I'm not going with you."

"If so, I'll go alone," Shifra replied firmly. "Let's pray for success and leave the rest to the Ribono shel Olam."

Despite her fears, Ida was too good-hearted to let Shifra attend the dangerous meeting alone. "I'll go with you and share your fate," she said, and they set out together.

Hearts pounding, they entered army headquarters and asked for the general. He received them amiably and with no further ado asked how he could help them.

Shifra decided to explain matters as tersely as possible, although she knew that even without wasting words her request could condemn her and her associate. "Sir," she said, "I need a large truck to move some people at 3:00 tomorrow morning. I know it's short notice, but we'll be very grateful if you can help us."

"I'll be there at 3:00," he replied quietly.

"We fed the people and let them lie down," Shifra told me long after the fact, "but we were too unsure of what might happen to allow ourselves any rest. When the time came, the people got ready and took up their small bundles. We came down to the lobby in anxious anticipation, trembling with fear.

"It was 3:00! We heard the truck racing down the road. It stopped at 3 Goldhammer Street, the hotel entrance. My heart also stopped for a moment. Then I saw who was driving the truck: the general himself!

"He left the motor running, jumped out of the truck, and came right over to meet me. Noticing our anxiety, he quietly whispered in my ear, 'Don't worry. I am a Jew and I know exactly what you are doing. But be careful not to let anyone else know,' he cautioned. 'And may God bless you.'

"'Hurry, hurry,' he urged the escapees to board the truck. We found out later that morning that the ride had been safe and successful."

❧ *Chapter 63* ❧

Renia's story

As soon as the war ended in May 1945, Renia Finkelstein of Kraków ventured out of the camp in Leipzig, Germany, to return to her hometown and see if anyone else in her family had survived. Although she navigated the dangerous route safely, she found no relatives in Kraków. Neither had any of her friends or neighbors returned. However, she did encounter a group of girls from the Po'alei Agudath Israel kibbutz in Lodz, already making their way to Eretz Yisroel via "Aliyah Beit."

The Soviets had liberated Lodz back in January 1945. By now, two kibbutzim had come into being, one for boys and one for girls. The collectives had been set in motion by the Po'alei Agudath Israel activists Yechiel Granatstein, Shimon Zucker, and a few others, supported by Va'ad Hatzalah through Reb Nuteh Parness.

"After days of tiresome travel, I reached Lodz, joined the kibbutz, and offered my help," Renia explained long afterward. After a brief stay, kibbutz representatives sent her to the kibbutz in Tarnów to replace Shifra Singer, who was away for two months attending a conference of Agudath Israel in Marienbad, Czechoslovakia. There, as a representative of the survivors, she would address the Neshei organization and explain the survivors' conditions and needs.

Renia fell in love with the girls and gave them everything she had — an open ear to listen, a heart to feel, and a devoted, warm intellect that understood their pain — with dedication, concern, affection, and interest. She felt that the most important things they needed now, apart from the *Pirkei Avos* lessons that she delivered, were "love, encouragement, and the will to live and carry on, with faith and hope." Many years after the events, her voice still exuded compassion as she enumerated those values. To put them into practice, she was always ready with sensible advice, a realistic approach, and assistance.

After Shifra returned from the Agudah conference, Renia decided to go back to Kraków. "The sight of our young people roaming the streets there, lonesome, forlorn, desperate, and ready to give up, overwhelmed me with pity," Renia recalled. "It filled me with the desire to raise their spirits, give them hope, and encourage them to start a new life."

Renia gathered a group of girls in Kraków and started a kibbutz on Sheroka Street. Soon afterwards, she met Reizel Wohlhandler, *née* Dym, who came with her husband. Rebbetzin Rachel Cizner also came with her husband and daughter from Russia. Rachelka Dym (a cousin of Reizel's) and Bronia Wiesenfeld also joined. They formed a committee to start an even larger kibbutz.

Reb Nuteh Parness was there to help, as always. Aided by Agudah activists, he provided them with a fine three-room apartment at 29 Dietlowska Street and subsidized their activities with funds from Va'ad Hatzalah. Soon these facilities filled up with girls who had come from labor camps or who had joined the Polish repatriates from the Soviet Union. The Red Auditorium of the Kraków Bais Yaakov Seminary was pressed into service as supplemental housing. The girls' parents — insofar as they had survived — lived outside the kibbutz under very poor conditions, in shelters provided by the *kehillah*.

At its peak, the kibbutz had sixty teenage girls and twenty-five young children. Some of the latter had come from the USSR with their parents under the repatriation agreement. They spent a full day in the kibbutz — from 8:00 A.M. to 9:00 P.M. — and slept with their parents outside the facility. Others

*The Kraków kibbutz on the first yahrtzeit of
Sarah Schenirer after the war. Top row, sixth
from right, is Renia Finkelstein, director of the
kibbutz.*

were children who were redeemed from gentiles and brought to
the kibbutz to be taken care of.

Renia directed the kibbutz with love and devotion; her
co-worker, Reizel Wohlhandler, assisted her. She received
money from Reb Nuteh Parness and kept a strict accounting of
it. She distributed it to Rachelka Dym and Bronia Wiesenfeld,
the administrators of the kibbutz, in order to meet the girls'
needs for food, clothing, and everything else.

In the meantime, Reizel taught the young children the Hebrew alphabet and basic prayers. Rachelka planned and coordi-
nated the activities of the kibbutz. Rachel Cizner and Guta
Silberberg gave classes to the older girls.

It was the most dedicated staff imaginable, as evidenced in
the affection that they lavished on the girls and the self-sacrifice that typified their own behavior. They provided their "clients" with what they needed most: warmth and *harzikeit* (good
cheer), as the girls lovingly acknowledged. The children who
had been redeemed from gentile homes required especially close
personal attention, which they received.

The kibbutz organized for Pesach on an even larger scale.
Aware that the parents of the children who had come from Rus-

sia lacked the facilities to prepare for the holiday, the kibbutz invited them for the entire festival, including both *Sedarim*. Reb Nuteh Parness led the *Sedarim*, retelling with ardor and understanding the account of the Jews' enslavement in Egypt and their miraculous redemption. By this time, his concern for the young survivors' physical and spiritual needs had made him a father-figure among them. Appropriately, the eulogizers at his funeral in Israel interpreted his name as *natan*, a "giver," and *parnas*, a "provider of livelihood and well-being," for so had he been to those lonely children and everyone else in need.

The effort to remove children from gentile homes continued in Kraków and was, in fact, the main purpose of the kibbutzim until *aliyah* became possible. The main activist in this difficult, dangerous endeavor in Kraków was Moshe Zamość of Po'alei Agudath Israel, who abducted children or facilitated their rescue by placing large sums of money in the appropriate pockets. He was assisted by one of the Bais Yaakov alumnae, Balka Grossfeld Drori.[76] Once Moshe removed the children, he delivered them to the kibbutz. They were dirty, neglected, and in some cases literally nameless.

"Once he brought us a nine-year-old girl," Renia once recalled. "She could not sleep that night. Her head itched terribly; her hair was full of lice. I spent hours cleaning her head to relieve her from that terrible malady. Only then did she fall asleep. In the morning, after a few hours' sleep, the poor child woke up relaxed. She kissed and hugged me, saying gratefully, 'You are so good to me. I wish you were my mother.'

"A month later," Renia continued, "a young woman brought me a lovely six-year-old girl named Cesia, and told me to keep her in the kibbutz and watch her carefully.

"'I'm from Krosno,' the young lady explained. 'The mother of this child told me, as well as some other friends and neighbors, that she had given her eighteen-month-old baby to a Pol-

---

76. Balka also taught the girls dressmaking, an important trade for use in Eretz Yisroel.

The Kraków kibbutz.

ish woman whom we all know, and asked her to take care of the infant until the Nazis were gone. Of course, she paid the women a substantial sum in cash and jewelry for her services. She also gave her a family photograph for safekeeping, so that the girl would know who she was even if her parents would perish in the war.

"'A couple of neighbors who survived and returned to Krosno after the war felt obliged to fulfill the mother's last wish. They undertook to redeem the child from the gentile woman and bring her back into the Jewish fold. After strenuous efforts and toil, and aided by a hefty bribe of 40,000 zlotys, provided by Va'ad Hatzalah, they finally managed to redeem the girl and the photo from the Polish woman.

"'I happily took Cesia home with me, thanking Hashem for helping us accomplish this difficult task. Then I spoke to the sweet little girl, now six and a half years old, telling her about her lovely family, whom I knew, and urging her not to worry. I assured her that we would take good care of her and make her comfortable and happy.

""'I'm not worried,'" Cesia answered innocently. "My mother [the gentile woman] promised to take me back soon. I'm sure she will."

"'When I heard that,' the woman concluded, 'I brought her here to save her from that gentile. Please watch her carefully.' With that, we parted. Afterwards, I did as told. I also fell in love with that sweet little Cesia, and we immediately formed a deep, lasting, personal relationship.

"After a while, we were advised to send groups of children to well-organized *kinderheimen* in Germany, where they would be cared for until they could receive legal immigration visas for Eretz Yisroel under the Youth Aliyah program."

For lack of space, the kibbutzim in Germany where the children were first received could not accommodate these large groups of children. Thus, *kinderheimen* had to be organized hurriedly to receive the youngsters who reached the German kibbutzim, mostly from Poland.

It took hard work, lots of determination, and successful mediation with local authorities to acquire those *kinderheimen*. Thanks to the intervention of Po'alei Agudath Israel, Rabbi Moshe Munk visited the DP camps in Germany as a Jewish Agency representative to organize *kinderheimen* and prepare the children for participation in the Youth Aliyah enterprise, a legal mechanism for *aliyah* by the young.

Rabbi Moshe Munk

As a Jewish Agency official, Rabbi Munk was able to help the DP activists establish and, through the UNRRA (United Nations Relief and Rehabilitation Administration), maintain the *kinderheimen*. His unflagging efforts and determination to help the survivors — both children and adults — reach their goal of settling in Eretz Yisroel, the land of their dreams and hopes, were exemplary. Always on the go, he toiled to arrange the survivors' legal *aliyah* without respite. Where this failed, he organized groups of young people for "Aliyah Beit."

One of the most famous *kinderheimen* was the one in Ulm. It started with some fifty children whom Reb Naftali Epstein brought in from Kibbutz Landsberg, where they had been gathered after the liberation. Rabbi Leibush Borenstein of Garmish (who had been contacted beforehand), acting with responsibility and determination, pulled important strings to obtain two beautiful buildings in the picturesque city of Lautersee, on the shores of the lake of the same name, to accommodate the arriving youngsters. After a couple more transfers to different places, they finally arrived in Ulm.

The first group of redeemed children coming from different kibbutzim in Poland to the newly established kinderheim in Lautersee, Germany.

The *kinderheimen* were organized not only to house the children and meet their needs but also to provide a warm, family-like home for these displaced and disoriented youngsters. There they would receive special, skilled attention with love and understanding. The staff had to be sensitive to the problems its clients faced in adjusting to their new lives.

Girls in the Ulm, Germany, kinderheim.

Significantly, the children still felt Christian, and prayed as they had been taught. It took much patience and love to induce them, step by step, to accept their Jewishness. Some of them, bright and intelligent, wished to know the merit and meaning of being a Jew. Others were rebellious and wished to return to their "parents," even though some of those caregivers had treated them harshly. In some cases, peasant caregivers had forced "their" children to do manual labor. Others had turned their wards, six or seven years old, into shepherds and tenders of cattle. Other children had been forced to steal to keep themselves fed. Just the same, many of them wished to go back, if only at first.

There were children aged three or four who had to be circumcised because their mothers, entrusting them to gentiles when they were still infants, had refrained from performing this mitzvah so that the little ones would not be recognized as Jews. These were only a few of problems that the staff had to solve.

Fortunately, in their search for a candidate to direct this difficult, complicated enterprise, the organizers found Ruchka Schanzer. Ruchka had all the credentials — excellent leadership skills, experience, and all other requirements — to educate and guide these troubled children. Always ready to help her beloved people, especially children, she happily accepted the challenge.

She had acquired her experience as a *kinderheim* director under unfortunate circumstances, in the Kraków ghetto. After various deportations, children, including infants, were found in the ghetto streets after having survived for inexplicable reasons. They were gathered and brought to a *kinderheim* that the Germans had established so that they could easily include these innocents in their next *Aktion*. Torn from their parents, lonesome and anguished, they bitterly missed the love and embraces of their mothers. Some had seen their parents shot; others had seen them carted away to the unknown.

There, under the most tragic circumstances, Ruchka had been assigned to work with this collection of wretched, doomed orphans.

Ruchka and her associate, Sarah Blaugrund, invested love, understanding, and uncommon dedication in their efforts on behalf of these children. Attempting to make their existence bearable and to give them some pleasure with a kiss or a hug, they played with them and did everything possible to make them feel like children. But they failed.

Brokenhearted and sobbing, Ruchka explained why: "Working with those children was the most tragic thing I've ever done. No matter how hard we tried, I never saw them smile; I never heard them sing. And most painful of all, I never heard them cry."

How agonizing, I thought.

"They weren't children," Ruchka continued. "They were little Jews, small Jews, baby Jews."

Now, however, she happily accepted her new post-war job. Here in Ulm, she would care for children who, although lonely, had survived. She would help them to embark on a better future, the joyous life of a Jewish child.

She devoted all her experience, brilliance, and dedication…
to see these children smile,
to see them jump,
to hear them laugh,
to hear them *cry*.

*   *   *

Ruchka's staff was also exceptional. At first she was joined by Hilda Hollander, a Bnos and Basya leader before the war, who pledged all her experience, understanding, and passion to the children. By so doing, she immediately became their big sister and confidante.

Girls at the kinderheim being taken care of by their leader, Hilda Hollander.

The next to come aboard, a short time later, was Zlota Borenstein Schnur, a teacher *par excellence* who had been renowned as a top educator back in the pre-war world of Bais Yaakov. She invested all her professional credentials and love in teaching those forlorn children how to appreciate having been born Jewish. With her intelligence and her understanding of the youngsters' psyches, she was able to inspire them with the beauty of Jewish life, each at his or her own level.[77]

The third to join was Renia Finkelstein, who came with her own group of children but stayed on as a mentor and role model for the rest of the youngsters at the Ulm *kinderheim*. She showed the girls how to behave in a ladylike fashion and how to love and respect each other.

After bouncing from one place to another, the youngsters were finally settled in Ulm, where the UNRRA provided a new home that they could fully enjoy: several handsome and comfortable buildings in pleasant surroundings. As time passed, kibbutzim in Poland and elsewhere delivered additional youngsters to the facility until its population surpassed two hundred.

The boys were housed in different buildings, entrusted to the care of male staff members. The boys' *kinderheim* (children's home) was headed by David Hollander, an exceptionally dedicated educator, who was assisted by Mordechai Orzel and several capable boys from PAI kibbutzim.

The older boys already had a rabbi, Ezra Reiman, who instructed them in the behaviors and special responsibilities of Jewish boys, taught them how to learn Torah, and showed them the joys of Jewish festivals and the observance of the mitzvos and rituals related to those great, happy occasions.

The entire staff, with its *mesirus nefesh*, love, and hard work, tackled the goal of inspiring the children to love and grow in the ways of Torah.

After two years of such care, the children were ready for *aliyah*.

---

77. Zlota Borenstein had been married before the war to Alter Schnur, the renowned writer and poet. He contributed meaningful articles and beautiful poems to the *Bais Yaakov Journal*. He also wrote the most touching and emotional poems during the war, passionately portraying the tragic Jewish life in Ghetto Lodz.

After the war, Zlota married Oizer Gebhard and settled with her new husband in Kiryat Ata, Israel, where she founded a Bais Yaakov school and became both its principal and her pupils' caring mentor. Under her leadership, the school grew in numbers and academic quality, Zlota spreading the original teachings of her mentor, Sarah Schenirer.

❧ *Chapter 64* ☙

Several Bais Yaakov teachers and friends of mine, such as Tzila Orlean, Chavah Tauber, Rivka Englard, Ruchka Schanzer, Sarah Blaugrund, and Renia Finkelstein, stayed on in Germany to head kibbutzim, Bais Yaakov groups, and *kinderheimen* for as long as their services were needed. Tzila Orlean and Chavah Tauber went to Bergen-Belsen, where after we left they continued to promote Jewish education and discharged the crucial function of matchmaking. After several months in Ulm, Renia received her last posting in Europe: Kibbutz Eschwege, where she would help the staff by sharing her

Yaakov Aharon Rosen, Renia Finkelstein's husband, appears second from right. Rabbi Binyamin Mintz, the great Agudah activist who organized youth and children in the DP camps, is at the head of the table.

previous kibbutz experience. In Eschwege, she met and married Yaakov Aharon Rosen, a staff member of the boys' kibbutz there. The newlyweds also came to Bergen-Belsen to receive their certificates to Eretz Yisroel.

Eventually, all the Bais Yaakov teachers and Bnos leaders mentioned above received "certificates" (legal immigration visas to Eretz Yisroel). This was arranged by Po'alei Agudath Israel, which at the time was the most active religious organization in facilitating *aliyah*. Due to PAI's tireless efforts, these Bais Yaakov alumnae did not need to risk life and limb to reach the Land of Holiness in the manner previously described.

Upon arrival, of course, they turned to PAI at once, ready to help in any capacity settling youth and children into their new lives in Eretz Yisroel. Ruchka Schanzer went right to work at the PAI office, assisting Reb Yaakov Katz, the legendary rescue worker and untiring immigrant-absorption activist, in his work. His integrity and willingness to sacrifice for every newcomer in all aspects of getting settled, under the difficult circumstances at the time, made him one of the most beloved and admired people in the country. Ruchka was delighted to be his assistant.

In 1947 and early 1948, groups of children from the children's homes in Ulm, Germany, which Ruchka headed, and from other facilities of this type, had been reaching Eretz Yisroel steadily.

It was necessary to set up homes for these children. One of the most prominent ones was Beis Avrohom, organized by PAI in Petach Tikvah under the leadership of Sarah Blaugrund, now married to Yissachar Pfeffer. Sarah was a capable Bais Yaakov teacher whose first experience in preschool education was back in the Kraków ghetto, where she directed a *kinderheim* together with Ruchka Schanzer. She personally fed, clothed, and shopped for over seventy neglected children, aged six through twelve. At considerable personal sacrifice, she served as their mother: she listened to them, comforted them, sent them to school, and received them with warmth and love when they returned. Fortunately, they were aided financially by Youth Aliyah.[78] This difficult job gave her much *nachas*, as she watched the children grow up to be wonderful adults who established staunch Jewish homes and raised great successor generations.

Rivka Englard was assigned almost from the moment of her arrival to set up and direct Beit ha-Chalutzot in Ramat Gan, a short distance from Tel Aviv. Beit ha-Chalutzot was a home for girls who reached Eretz Yisroel alone as orphaned survivors of the Holocaust. Rivka saw to their schooling, placed them in jobs so they might support themselves, and later took care of their *shidduchim* and their establishment of Jewish homes. She was always willing to offer them motherly advice or, for more mature girls, an older sister's friendship.

When it came time to close Beit ha-Chalutzot, Rabbi Joseph Kahaneman drafted her into service in Bnei Brak. He had set up an institution that housed more than seventy girls. Some of them came from underprivileged or faraway localities, others were new immigrants, and still others had fled difficult home conditions. The institution was called Beit Avot. Ordinarily the Hebrew term for an old-age home, here it took on the literal meaning of the term, "parents' home," because it served its residents as a surrogate family home — a home permeated with motherly love, devotion, wisdom, and understanding.

The Ponivezher Rav, as Rabbi Kahaneman was lovingly called, was a man who harbored a great dream: the sweeping vision of creating an immense yeshiva campus on the highest hill in Bnei Brak, overlooking the rest of the city. He also possessed unmatched willpower, unusual drive, and the dedication to carry his monumental dream to fruition. His integrity, knowledge of people, and charm inspired others to help him financially and spiritually in his endeavors. To this day, the Ponivezh Yeshiva, with its beautiful building, towers over the city of Bnei Brak like a crown.

---

78. An organization established for the immigration and absorption of youth into Eretz Yisroel from Nazi-occupied and post-war Europe.

A group of affluent men from Los Angeles once visited the yeshiva. Inspired by what they saw and in admiration of Rabbi Kahaneman, they sat down with him to ask how they could be of assistance. After the Ponivezher Rav delivered an eloquent, moving presentation of his dream of building a citadel of proper Jewish education for youth in the Holy Land, the visitors, touched, offered to finance the construction of one additional building that the facility needed. They had but one condition: the young people who would attend the yeshiva must have neither *peyos* (sidelocks) nor beards. The revered Rabbi Kahaneman promised. They trusted him and financed the construction of a beautiful, comfortable building with a fine dining room and pleasant dormitories.

The facility housed students who had neither *peyos* nor beards. It was occupied by Beit Avot, a vital institution that educated girls in the spirit of Bais Yaakov.

The Ponivezher Rav took a special interest in Beit Avot. He knew Rivka Englard and had heard about her work at Kibbutz Chofetz Chaim in Zeilsheim, her dedication in working with the girls at Beit ha-Chalutzot, and her having been a mother to multitudes of homeless refugee girls. Knowing people as he did, he knew he had found the right candidate for the functions of spiritual leader and, above all, housemother of an institution that needed, more than anything else, someone who could teach, consult, and advise the girls with motherly love and care.

Once he hired Rivka, Rabbi Kahaneman was in constant contact with her — suggesting, advising, and devising strategies on how to educate the girls to perform mitzvos with joy and master proper behavior. Thus Rivka, now Rebbetzin Hoffman, again became a mother to more than seventy girls. Rivka met both their physical and their educational needs. She taught them to learn and to take pride in their achievements, to love knowledge and being educated, to obtain accurate knowledge of the Torah, and to experience joy in performing mitzvos. She placed them in Bais Yaakov schools commensurate with their level — high school or seminary. She maintained contact with their teachers, constantly monitoring their achievements and progress. After they graduated from the seminary, she helped place them in jobs.

Finally, like a mother, she arranged their *shidduchim* and married them off. That was a labor of many years; every time I visited Israel, I found her soliciting donations for this purpose. No wonder; after all, she was a mother to scores of children and was always there for every one of them whenever needed — by day, at mealtimes, late at night, at the Shabbos table; always.

Eventually she began to neglect her own family under the weight of her mounting responsibilities. Her husband, Rabbi Hoffman, himself a great scholar and devoted educator, regretfully had to ask Rabbi Kahaneman to accept his wife's resignation.

"Her job," he explained, "is claiming so much of her time that she has very little left for her own family. She loves her work and cares for the girls dearly. But she must be a mother to her own children."

Rabbi Kahaneman was too distressed to accept Rivka's resignation. "Do you know what it means to turn a child into an orphan?" he cried. "Can you imagine turning more than seventy children into orphans all at once?!"

Rabbi Hoffman could not endure to see the anguish of this great father of thousands of Jewish children and youth. He surrendered, and he and his wife sacrificed much of their own family life for the hundreds of young women to whom Rivka served as a most devoted mother throughout the decades. She stayed on at Beit Avot for many years. Before failing health forced her to retire, she trained her most capable and dedicated *talmidah* to succeed her in this very important, demanding, and gratifying position.

Thus Rebbetzin Rivka Hoffman followed Sarah Schenirer's example in the manner of a true *talmidah* — emulating Frau Schenirer's love of and devotion to people, and deriving joy and pleasure from teaching and spreading the truth of Torah among Jewish youth.

❧ *Chapter 65* ❧

After she settled in Eretz Yisroel, Ruchka Schanzer Teller had two activities in her life: receiving and acculturating new *olim* (immigrants to Eretz Yisroel) and serving as a beacon of strength for anyone who needed it. Her love of people made her everyone's confidante. People approached her with problems and received warm consideration and wise advice. She felt with them; their every pain was hers, as was their happiness. I cannot forget the moment at a personal *simchah* of hers when, as I wished her a hearty *Mazel tov,* I noticed a concerned expression that marred her joyous look.

"Is everything all right?" I asked, worried. "Your happiness does not seem complete."

"How can it be complete?" she replied passionately. "How can I be happy if everyone around me is not? If I'm surrounded with so much sorrow, can my happiness be complete? I can be happy only when I see joy around me."

*　　　*　　　*

Simcha Holzberg, a young man from our kibbutz in Zeilsheim, eventually settled in Tel Aviv and visited Ruchka frequently to consult on personal problems and decisions. He called her "Mamme Rochel," after our matriarch Rachel. "I can cry on her shoulders as I would at the tomb of our mamme Rachel," he once told me. "I can freely tell her about my plans, my successes, and my failures, too — even my flaws. She understands, as 'Mother Rachel' would. I gratefully accept her advice,

413

her encouragement, and even her reproach."

Simcha Holzberg was a unique personality in his own right. Known in Israel as the father of the war-disabled, he displayed remarkable love for wounded servicemen and their families, filling their troubled lives with comfort and joy.

I was visiting Israel when he married off his son. It was an unusual wedding in every sense. It took place at Ganei Ha'ir in Tel Aviv on a beautiful spring afternoon and was attended by thousands of people, including many Israeli dignitaries. Police cordoned off the area to assure order and safety.

"Come stand next to me," Simcha offered. I am glad I did, because this gave me the opportunity to witness a unique procession of well-wishers: young men on crutches or in wheelchairs, with amputated hands or legs. The seemingly endless parade of pain, injury, and disfigurement was the most painful sight I have ever seen. However, their faces glowed as they approached Simcha to congratulate and lovingly to shake the hand of their father, benefactor, and devoted friend. There was nothing perfunctory about their hugs and kisses.

After lengthy preliminaries, the wedding ceremony was announced. Menachem Begin, prime minister at the time and a great friend of Simcha's, delivered a speech of friendship, appreciation, and blessing, with a deep passion that left no one untouched. His remarks were followed by speeches of praise and gratitude to the man who had sacrificed his personal life to benefit and aid the war-injured.

After the orations, the guests burst into thunderous song. The band joined in and the crowd formed a massive *hora* of concentric circles. Young people on crutches and in wheelchairs danced and sang, sharing the *simchah* of Simcha, their benefactor and friend.

Amidst this remarkable scene came one even more remarkable. A man made his way to the center of the *hora* circles and danced with Simcha. His face was burned beyond recognition, his eyes wide open but sightless. Simcha kissed and hugged him. As they danced, I heard Simcha talk to him: "I promised you, and *be-ezras Hashem,* with God's help, I'll keep my word. By Chanukah, you will see with your own eyes. You'll see me and you'll see the world. Just hope and pray to Hashem."

The man's scarred face lit up with hope and joy.

Chanukah came. I was eager to know what happened. I knew that Simcha was working to arrange a corneal transplant that might restore the man's vision.

I called Ruchka to find out. "The operation was successful," she told me happily. "The man can see and Simcha's joy is indescribable."

I visited Israel again for the next High Holidays. On Yom Kippur afternoon, I walked to the Kosel to spend the rest of the day there. Well into the day of praying and fasting, people were tired and thirsty. And there was no restaurant to greet the tremendous crowd in the evening. However, several trucks had been parked nearby before the festival, loaded with electric kettles and tons of sponge cake to break the fast. At nightfall, an army of volunteers emerged to serve the fasting worshipers. Whose idea and work was it? It was Simcha's.

Simcha has gone to a world that knows neither war nor pain. When he went, he took truckloads of his wonderful deeds and tons of his mitzvos of loving-kindness, which he proudly showed to his "Mamme Rochel" when she joined him in Heaven several years later.

❧ *Chapter 66* ❧

"He who saves one Jewish soul…" (Sanhedrin 37a)

The children from various kibbutzim were already waiting in Bergen-Belsen for permission to enter Eretz Yisroel legally. There was also another Youth Aliyah group, made up of children from the *kinderheim* in Ulm, from a *kinderheim* in Aix-les-Bains, France, from Russia, and directly from Poland. Our blond Cesia, mentioned previously, was also part of this group.

Upon arrival in Eretz Yisroel, Cesia and the rest of the children were sent to Beis Avrohom, the children's home in Petach Tikvah that PAI had set up, and that was led by the capable Bais Yaakov teacher Sarah Blaugrund.

Renia and Yaakov Aharon Rosen, now living in Tel Aviv, decided to visit Beis Avrohom to see how they could help Sarah in her dedicated work with the children. There, to her astonishment, Renia found little Cesia, her favorite "kibbutznik" from Kraków. Eager to already have a child to love, to hug, to take care of, and to worry about, Renia "adopted" little Cesia without further ado, even before she had a child of her own.

The Rosens had Cesia come to them during her free time, plus Sabbaths and festivals, in order to fret over her, to satisfy her physical and emotional needs, and to treat her as their own precious little daughter. They were also happy to invite some of the other girls to join them on Shabbos and holidays, to provide them with the atmosphere, warmth and love of a family home.

A few of the invitees were Cesia's friends, especially her best friend Miriam, who most of the time joined Cesia in enjoying the Rosens' friendly hospitality. She too soon became their protégée.

When the Rosens moved to Jerusalem, *hashgachah* had the older girls moved from Petach Tikvah to Ohel Chavah, a Beit ha-Chalutzot in Jerusalem.

That year, on erev Rosh Hashanah, Cesia joined the Rosens without Miriam in tow. Soon it was half an hour before sunset. Everyone in the household was dressed for the festival and ready to go to shul — but Miriam had not yet come.

"Pesia," Yaakov Aharon turned to his young daughter, "let's rush over to Ohel Chavah to bring Miriam home for Rosh Hashanah. I won't be able to sit down at the holiday table without her."

Pesia described the outcome years later. "I went with my father to fetch Miriam. It was quite a walk from our house. My *tatte* rushed along, regal in his holiday attire, until he found and confronted his quarry.

"'I was very depressed before the New Year,' Miriam explained in tears, 'and I did not want to disturb your holiday.'

"Lovingly but firmly, my father did not accept her excuse. He practically forced Miriam to spend the holiday with us.

"Unlike Cesia, Miriam did not know who her parents were or who she was. She didn't even know her real name. Until an Agudah activist in Lodz redeemed her, she did not even know she was Jewish. She kept on searching for her identity unsuccessfully. In that condition, constantly troubled by her lack of identity, she could neither face the world nor make peace with herself."

Miriam was ten years old. How painful and tragic it was, I thought when I first heard the story and whenever I recalled it.

The Rosens tried to help. At their suggestion, a Mrs. Halberstam brought Miriam into her home to make her feel part of the family. Miriam balked at this but eventually agreed to it, at the Rosens' insistence.

Several days later, Mrs. Halberstam visited the Rosens in

tears. "Miriam refuses to speak," she reported, her voice choking. "She doesn't respond to questions; she doesn't say a word."

The Rosens brought her to their home again. Even there, although her distress eased, she was continually haunted by the unknown.

The Rosens tried again. Reb Nuteh Parness and his lovely wife Mania took care of hundreds of children, as they did not yet have any of their own. At the Rosens' suggestion, the Parnesses accepted the challenge and were eager to adopt Miriam. They resolved to treat her as their own *bas yechidah* and meet all her needs with love and joy.

Miriam refused in tears. "I know they are such wonderful people. They want to have me as somebody to love and enjoy. They want to shower me with their goodness.

"But I cannot return their love," she blurted between sobs. "I am too badly hurt, too bitter. I don't want to make their lives miserable. They don't deserve it." Her words stopped; her grievous weeping continued. Renia cried with her.

Miriam was now eleven years old. Her thinking had become permanent; so had her pain. She stayed at Ohel Chavah. A short time later, she had to apply for an I.D. card. As she filled out the forms, Miriam made up the names of "parents" to put on her card.

Bureaucrats at the Ministry of the Interior, who knew from the records of her institution that her parents' names were unknown, noticed the inaccuracy. "Why did you give us false names for your father and mother?" they asked angrily.

"I wanted to have a father and mother like everybody else," Miriam said in courageous self-defense.

In accordance with Israeli bureaucratic thinking at the time, the clerks punished Miriam for her transgression by withholding her I.D. card.

When Yaakov Rosen found out about this, he complained vehemently to the head of the Interior Ministry office. "How heartless your staff is," he charged loudly, "to make this poor child more miserable than she already is!" The official did not budge, but Reb Yaakov appealed to higher echelons at the Interior Ministry and eventually equipped Miriam with an I.D. card. Still upset about what had happened, he took his grievance to Youth Aliyah.

"How could the Interior Ministry do that to a girl who's so unfortunate that she does not even know who she is?"

"You are right," a Youth Aliyah official replied. "They should have been more understanding. Their insensitivity added heartbreak to heartbreak. But you should know," he continued, "that this is not one child's tragedy; unfortunately, it's a national disaster. To our great regret, Youth Aliyah has *two thousand* children without identity. It is as painful, regrettable, and tragic a situation as there can be."

Time passed. Miriam and the other girls in Ohel Chavah grew up. They continued to spend Shabbos and festivals with the Rosens. Then it came time for them to think about the future and learn an occupation that would provide them with a livelihood.

Miriam chose to become an office worker. For that, she had to learn stenography and touch-typing, among other skills. Again, Yaakov Rosen made it his responsibility to help Miriam, this time with her studies. Every day after work, he brought his office typewriter home and hauled it up two flights of stairs so that Miriam could practice on it.

Miriam applied herself diligently. After she passed her course, Yaakov got her an office job at the Ministry of Health, where he held a prestigious position.

At a time when Israeli officials tended to insulate themselves from the public, Yaakov Rosen was known as a unique executive who went so far as to have his office door removed so that citizens could enter without knocking. Anyone with a problem — the ill, the needy, nurses, interns, or even seasoned doctors — could step through Reb Yaakov's unobstructed doorway to request and receive advice, encouragement, intervention, and appropriate help. Above all, they found a compassionate ear and a human heart that knew how to respond swiftly and effectively to help people solve their problems.

Cesia reached adulthood as a beautiful young woman who had a new goal: to become a nurse. Eager to help the sick and to ease their pain and their families' suffering, she pursued this task with passion, hard work, and patience. Throughout that time, she continued to spend her free moments and festivals with the Rosens. She considered Yaakov Rosen her father and Renia her mother.

Their relationship has remained constant to this very day. Cesia, now of Haifa, stays in regular touch with her mother, whom she loves and adores (her father passed away). Often she visits her at her current home in Bnei Brak. Her children and grandchildren never pass up an opportunity to see their dear grandmother Renia. And she never passes up an opportunity to express her overwhelming gratitude to the Rosens — her parents, to whom she owes everything she has, everything she is.

When I met her last, visiting Renia with her lovely family, it moved me deeply to observe Renia beaming with joy and *nachas* as she contemplated the wonderful family that her little Cesia had raised.[79]

*   *   *

The stories of the quiet heroism that these Bais Yaakov alumnae have practiced since the war, in their various communities, are innumerable but no less meaningful for that.

On one of my trips to Israel, I went to visit an ill friend in a nursing home. As I asked for her at the desk, a nurse approached me and spoke admiringly of the patient's friends.

"In my many years of practice, I have never encountered such a group of friends. Every day, in every kind of weather, they come here from great distances to visit their ailing friend and cheer her up. They are elderly women; some of them can

---

79. Miriam married but continued to search for her identity. Her children, aware of the pain this matter caused their mother, continued the search. Unfortunately, their efforts were fruitless. However, now she is comforted by having her own lovely family.

hardly walk! But they come with love and devotion to give their friend a happy and meaningful day.

"That's a very special group of friends," she concluded with enthusiasm. "Where could we find them in our world today?"

"I am not surprised," I answered. "But you are right; this is a very special group of friends. They are products of Bais Yaakov." With that, I took leave of her and rushed to see my friend.

On the way out, I looked up this nurse. "I have to tell you something," I said to her with feeling. "I came to cheer up my ill friend, to comfort her, and to give her courage and strength to fight her condition. Instead, I left comforted, imbued with more courage and strength than I ever could have given her." We both parted in amazement.

❧ Chapter 67 ❧

It was 1996 and I was in Israel for Pesach, that lovely festival at which we remember and retell the miraculous account of our liberation from Egyptian slavery to freedom as the Jewish nation.

I spent an inspirational seder with the family in Bnei Brak; the children asking the "four questions" and the adults answering them by reciting and explaining the Haggadah. We told and retold *yetziyas Mitzrayim* (the Exodus) until early the next morning.

Every year we recite the wondrous tale of our redemption, and the words reveal new meaning each time. That particular Pesach, the expression *Ve-aht eirom ve-eryah* — "You were still naked and bare"[80] — leaped at me from the Haggadah, its seeming redundancy demanding an explanation. "It has a symbolic meaning," Rashi explains: "You [the Jews] were naked of mitzvos in Mitzrayim; you did not perform them." For this reason, Hashem gave them two commandments, both related to blood — that of *bris milah* and that of the Pesach sacrifice — before He took them out of Mitzrayim.

But we were brutally transported to Auschwitz. Upon arrival there, we were stripped of our clothing and mercilessly deprived of our hair — body hair torn along with the flesh, leaving the victim sometimes drenched in blood. After this special treatment, we were *literally* bare...but even in this bloody na-

---

80. *Yechezkel* 16:7.

kedness, we were not bare of mitzvos.

Ve-aht eirom ve-eryah — Yes, you are naked, stripped of everything you own, but you are wealthy, rich in mitzvos. In your bloody nakedness, standing in front of the gas chambers, staring at the towering chimney as it puffed fire, smelling the stench of burning human flesh, you Bais Yaakov girls, Sarah Schenirer's *talmidos*, received the Shabbos Queen by returning Tzila's joyous although hazardous greeting: "Good Shabbos, girls."

"Good Shabbos," Sarah Schenirer's *talmidos* answered, remembering their teacher's hearty and meaningful "Good Shabbos."

It was not only a greeting. It was a blessing.

And Hashem said:[81] *Va-e'evor alayich, va-er'ech misboseses be-damayich, va-omar lach be-damayich chayi* — "*I* looked you over, and *I* saw you drenched in blood, but *be-damayich chayi*: In your blood will you live." You are alive in your bloody nakedness, doing mitzvos. You perform your mitzvah of the blood of *bris milah* — the blood of the covenant of the Almighty. Yes, we are tortured and bleeding because of the covenant You concluded with us. It is because we are Jews, Your People.

Lacking a lamb to offer for the Pesach sacrifice, we gave our own bodies, our flesh and blood, as a sacrifice for performing Your commandments.

And Hashem looked, saw, and promised:

Be-damayich chayi: From this blood you will be reborn, starting a new life for the future of the People of Israel. Hashem kept His promise. Miraculously, new generations were born — of children, grandchildren, and great-grandchildren.

U'vnei Yisrael paru va-yishretzu va-yirbu...me'od — "And the Children of Israel were fruitful and prolific...very greatly."[82] Thus, with God's blessing, Jewish children multiplied amazingly and grew to become a very special generation, a

---

81. Ibid., verse 6.
82. *Shemos* 1:7.

source of pride to Hashem's Glory.

There is no limit to our gratitude to the Almighty for the miracles He has performed for us. We survivors do not wait for Rosh Chodesh to recite Hallel. We sing it to Hashem every morning and exalt His Name.

*   *   *

Back in Mitzrayim, Moshe complained to Hashem: "Since I came to Pharaoh to speak in Your name, he has made things worse with this people, and still You have not redeemed them."[83] "Just wait," Hashem answered. *Atah tir'eh...* — "Now you will see what I have in mind for Pharaoh."[84] So it was in Bergen-Belsen. In the last weeks of the war, we were not only naked but had been stripped of even food and water, lying on the dirt floor among the ill and the dead.

Then You mercifully freed us from torture and death, but You did not redeem us. We remained in the sea of hatred, our people's blood continually spilled. Oh, God, answer us as You answered Moshe Rabbeinu, and say again, *"Atah tir'eh"*: *Now* you will see what I will do to your oppressors. With My strong hand I will avenge the innocent spilt blood and drown them in their own sea of hatred. Finally, I will fulfill my second promise: *Be-damayich chayi,* in your blood will you live. Jewish blood, spilled through the ages, will produce life, *geulah shleimah*, the Ultimate Redemption — a life of everlasting joy and peace.

---

83. Ibid., 5:23.
84. Ibid., 6:1.

✣ *Chapter 68* ✣

Farewell to Tzila

It was early August 1998. Before leaving Eretz Yisroel, I went to Jerusalem to say my parting prayer at the Kosel: to pour out my desire to return soon to my beloved country and to find my holy city, Yerushalayim, as her name proclaims: an awe-inspiring city that spreads eternal *shalom*, true peace.

I also wanted to say a farewell *Shalom* to my dear teacher, mentor, and friend, Tzila, Rebbetzin Soroczkin. I intended to spend an hour there and rush back to Bnei Brak to prepare for my flight to the States. However, the visit stretched to almost four hours, and I left late in the evening.

As we reminisced about the war years, we returned as usual to her experiences in Auschwitz. Whenever I saw her, I encouraged her to write her personal account of those ordeals. Normally, she demurred. This time, she assured me, "I am writing. I've already done quite a bit and I hope to continue."

I was happy to hear that. Again she poured out her stories. I already knew some of them and had written about them; others were new to me. Then she asked about my own writing, considering this a way to motivate me to progress.

"I'm doing well enough, but I won't write about what you just told me. You should tell your own experiences."

"No!" Tzila reacted strongly. "I want *you* to write about them." But she cautioned me, "Don't mention the names of the people involved."

Then we parted. Never again would I see her lovely face, hear her soothing voice, and imbibe her wise advice and guidance. Never again would I hear her remarkable stories about acts of courage and sacrifice, told with matter-of-fact simplicity.

Thus, the stories that follow are presented in the fulfillment of Tzila's last request to me.

*   *   *

Tzila was probably the only woman in Auschwitz who dared to light Shabbos candles under the noses of Mengele and Königel. Every Friday, she withdrew a sheet of white paper from the infirmary office and placed it under a piece of glass that she had somehow acquired. She did this to make her little table look festive. On this glass tray, she melted two tiny candles that the girls of the Kanadakommando sometimes brought her with great sacrifice. Jews en route to Auschwitz had carried these candles in their clothing for use on their final journey, and the members of the Kanadakommando found the candles while sorting the victims' clothing.

"One Friday eve, as I lit my Shabbos candles as usual, I gazed at the tiny flames as they spread a warm glow around the block," Tzila recalled. "The faces of the desiccated inmates around me lit up as well. Their expression changed from bleak hopelessness to warmth and light as they remembered their homes aglow with the Shabbos atmosphere. It was a moment of light, hope, and peace.

"Suddenly a girl stormed in, trembling with fear. An SS doctor was visiting the next block and would come here any minute. The girls in my block, overcome with fright, urged me to blow out the candles. But they were my Shabbos candles. I had lit them, they were mine, and I would not let anyone extinguish them. The girls rushed out to the "Ambulance" (emergency station) where they worked. I was left behind, alone, with my Shabbos lights. I watched them and resolved to shield them with my body.

"I will not leave you," she continued, speaking to her candles now. "I will hide you under my shoulders. Maybe the SS man will not see you. If that happens, he will not blow you out. Maybe he will punish me. Maybe with God's help he will not destroy me, and I will be able to continue to light you. But I'm sure he will never extinguish your flame. The light of Shabbos will shine forever.

"I hear his heavy footsteps nearing my barracks. He opens the door. It turns on its hinges and stands to 'attention,' and so do I. He sees me and sees my candles, their tiny flames burning. He looks at me; he looks at the candles. Again he turns to me and to the candles. Soundlessly. Then he turns around, says *'Weiter machen,'* and leaves the barracks."

Weiter machen: carry on, at ease.

Thus too, to her last breath, Tzila kindled Shabbos candles to spread light, radiance, love, and peace in this world of darkness and hate.

*   *   *

Tzila retold the story of a mutual friend who had married very young and, a short time later, came to Auschwitz pregnant. In the latter part of her pregnancy, Tzila sheltered her to spare her from Selektions. When it came time for her to give birth, Tzila took her to the infirmary, watched her labor, and helped her in delivery. The baby was stillborn. At great personal risk, Tzila buried it on the camp premises. Then she rushed back to the infirmary to take care of the mother. She tightened a rag around the woman's neck to make her look ill.

Soon a woman doctor from the SS came by for the daily checkup. She noticed the new patient and ordered her to climb out of bed for an examination. She wished to determine whether the newcomer was really sick enough to stay in the infirmary.

As frightened as she was, Tzila did not show it. She kept her calm and her senses.

"Frau Doktor," she said, "this girl is seriously ill with diphtheria. The infirmary doctor diagnosed it. I'm trying to place her in quarantine." This frightened the SS doctor; diphtheria was quite contagious under those conditions.

"Let her stay," she said. "I trust Doktor Anna." With that, she rushed out of the barracks.

"Pearl," Tzila concluded. "Haven't I told you that Hashem performed many miracles for me in Auschwitz? That was one of them."

Yes, she had told me. After describing many of her risky feats in Auschwitz and their positive outcome, she always credited them to Hashem and His miracles.

*   *   *

"Something similar happened later on," Tzila related. "One day, a young woman ran into the infirmary well along in labor. She bit her lips to avoid screaming, but I knew her predicament and took her straight to the block.

"I was quite experienced by then; I went to work and quickly delivered a little baby, alive and kicking. He began to cry. The block erupted in panic. The SS might hear the boy crying. They might come and kill the mother, the staff, and the patients.

"'Tzila,' they screamed, 'kill the baby! Don't endanger our lives!'

"'I cannot kill a Jewish child,' I answered. 'The Nazis kill our children. I can't. It reminds me of how the Jewish midwives in Egypt risked their lives to save Jewish children. *Va-techayena es ha-yeladim*[85]; they even helped to keep them alive. No, I cannot do this.'

"Over the protests of the blockmates, I tried to save the newborn. I hid the mother and the baby, made sure the baby would not cry, and fed him a little warm water with milk. This went on for one day, two days, three days. Hashem sent the soul of this tiny infant down to the ugliness of Auschwitz for three days. Then He retrieved that pure soul and sent it to the special

---

85. *Shemos* 1:17.

place in Heaven where Holocaust victims go.

"The mother survived. The block inmates, out of danger, relaxed. Nobody was hurt. Only I, to this very day, have suffered from uncertainty: did I do the right thing? Should I have endangered many lives to save an infant in Auschwitz? Should I have instead let them kill the newborn? Kill a Jewish child?"

"Tzila," I reminded my friend, "you always told me that Hashem guided your actions. You can see that He was with you even that time. The proof is that nobody was hurt. Forget it, Tzila. Don't torture yourself."

My entreaties failed to put her at ease. "We did not learn enough *dinim* to show me how to act," she complained. "One day I presented my *she'elah* to one of the most renowned and respected *poskim* in Israel. 'What does the halachah say I should have done?' I asked him. 'How should I have acted?'

"The story moved the rabbi to tears. 'My child,' he answered, 'I cannot judge; *I was not there*. You acted with love and compassion. You were willing to sacrifice your life to save the lives of others. This time, you did it for the life of a Jewish child.

"'You did what your mind and your heart dictated. Relax, my child, and may Hashem bless you with peace.'"

*   *   *

"I am not Paltiel ben Layish," were Tzila's parting words. She explained:

"King Shaul gave his daughter Michal, who was already betrothed to King David, to Paltiel ben Layish. After the war between the House of Shaul and the House of David, King David sent his trusted servants to Paltiel to reclaim his wife and bring her back to him. Paltiel ben Layish returned Michal to her rightful husband. As he walked her out, he cried.[86]

"Why did he cry? Rashi explains: it was because he regretted being unable to keep continually passing the test and ordeal of living with her — and returning her to King David in purity.

---

86. See *II Shmuel* 3:15 – 16.

"I am not Paltiel ben Layish," she repeated as she walked me to the door. "I do not regret the end of the ordeals and hardships I experienced in Auschwitz. I am grateful to Hashem for relieving me of them. I pray that I and my People may never again be subjected to such trials. Instead, may Hashem give us a taste of the final days, when we will experience everlasting true joy and peace."

Rebirth and Revival: Chinuch ha-Banos in America

❧ *Chapter 69* ❧

It was Chol ha-Mo'ed Pesach 1948 when my first husband, Hirsh Reichman, *z"l*, my baby girl, and I reached the shores of the United States. I would not have chosen America as my family's home; circumstances beyond my control had forced it on me.

My cousin, Ben Mandelker, picked us up at the dock and became a devoted brother who met all our needs and always made himself available with help and advice. He delivered us to my father-in-law, who had preceded us to America. We were also fortunate to meet the American members of the Reichman family, who received us with warmth and affection. Thus my husband was reunited with his father and his two brothers, and all were able to enjoy the rest of the festival together.

After Pesach, I ventured to Williamsburg to learn about the Jewish community of which I heard so much. I hoped not to encounter any familiar faces; I was expecting my second child and my "refugee" dress picked up too much in the front, making it embarrassingly short. To my horror and excitement, I ran into Rebbetzin Vichna Kaplan *née* Eisen, a favorite *talmidah* of Sarah Schenirer's at the seminary in Kraków. She recognized me despite my pitiful appearance. We hugged and kissed, laughed and cried. Tears of sadness mixed with tears of joy flowed freely from one face onto another. I thanked God for having delivered her to America before the war, unscathed by its horrors.

As we began to converse, Vichna's voice, ordinarily subtle and quiet, became agitated as she interrogated me about the war period and about which of our friends had survived. It was then my turn to ask her about her life in the United States. Reverting to her usual soothing tone of voice, Vichna described the Bais Yaakov Seminary that she had established shortly before the war in Williamsburg, and retold her struggles and achievements.

Listening silently, I choked on tears. I recalled those bitter, tragic nights, nights of lengthy nightmares full of pain and sorrow, and dreams of awakening to a gorgeous day, a day of light and freedom. I will again hear Jewish children playing and singing, Jewish boys learning in yeshiva, Jewish girls in Bais Yaakov schools. Oh, God! Jewish children, alive, happy, carefree. Jewish children!

"Petchka!" Vichna roused me from my reverie. "Come with me to the seminary," she urged, quietly but firmly. "Right now."

"I cannot, Vichna. I'm not dressed appropriately."

"You must come with me; you must talk to my girls," she insisted authoritatively. "I'll cover the lectern with a tablecloth. They'll see nothing but your face," she promised.

Unable to resist, I went with her to South Eighth Street and observed the wide steps of the seminary building alive with young girls rushing to their studies. They greeted their principal and mentor with palpable love, and welcomed the strange-looking young woman who accompanied her. We went up to the office and Rebbetzin Kaplan instructed one of the teachers to assemble the girls in the auditorium. The room gave me a sense of *déjà vu*; it reminded me of the large room in my Bais Yaakov at 30 Augustianska Street — bare except for some two hundred chairs, which were now occupied by the girls.

Rebbetzin Kaplan was true to her word. The raised lectern had been covered to the floor with a white cloth. The girls would see only my face and my fine kerchief, a parting gift from my friends in Europe.

I looked down at the hurriedly assembled audience. Bais Yaakov girls! my heart sang out. Bais Yaakov girls here, alive, happy, eager to learn and to listen. Was it really true? my skeptical self asked repeatedly.

The girls waited in silent suspense to hear an unusual story. I waited, too. We were equally overwhelmed and speechless. Suddenly, a thunderous cry shattered the silence. A tearful but powerful voice proclaimed, *"Baruch...she-hecheyanu, ve-kiye-manu, ve-higiyanu la-zeman ha-zeh."*

It was not only my voice, but also the tremendous outcry of all lone survivors, pouring their hearts out in thanksgiving to the Ribono shel Olam, Who has granted us life and given us the opportunity to experience these great moments of resurrection and rebirth.

With that, I found my own voice again and continued: "Girls, you have made our dream come true. You are soldering together the brutally broken chain of the great Bais Yaakov movement."

I described the tortures and atrocities that I and others had experienced. However, I also retold proudly the unimaginable *mesirus nefesh*, tremendous self-sacrifice, that our Bais Yaakov girls had displayed in helping to save human lives. I spoke of the *tzelem Elokim* those girls had exhibited amidst the horrors of the death camps. I showed how the loving-kindness of humanity defeated the bestiality of man.

They responded by thanking me for enlightening them, but I thanked them even more, for the *nachas* they gave me by just being there.

✳   ✳   ✳

Landing in America with a one-year-old daughter, I was a worried mother. How, I wondered, could I raise my children in the Torah-true way, training them to strive for inner beauty and riches in this land of spiritual poverty, a land of golden opportunity where the goal of attaining prosperity and material wealth reigns supreme?

That Sunday at the Bais Yaakov auditorium allayed my fears. My daughters would have a place where they could learn, obtain knowledge, and derive inspiration in how to grow and climb to lofty heights.

❧ *Chapter 70* ❧

The late 1920s and early 1930s found America a desert in terms of *Yiddishkeit*. "Even the stones in America are *treif*," people used to say.

Orthodox Jews who had come from Europe at the turn of the century quickly discovered that the streets of the *goldene medina* were paved not with gold but with the sweat that flowed from the workplaces available to them. Deservingly known as sweatshops, these enterprises operated six days a week, including Saturdays. Employees who refused to work on Shabbos became ex-employees on Monday. Many Orthodox Jews fell victim to this imperative for lack of any other way to support their families.

How painful it is to recall how religious people awakened early on Shabbos morning to pray, and then rushed to work. At lunchtime, they had a hurried *se'udah* and raced through the *bentching* in order to return to their labors on time. As tragic and distressing as these disastrous circumstances were for them, they suffered even more watching their children go astray under these conditions. Other young people did not wait for adverse conditions; they "unburdened" themselves of *Yiddishkeit* from the moment they stepped ashore and had their first taste of American freedom.

Only a handful of observant families withstood the tremendous pressure and avoided working on Shabbos. With great strength, devotion, and self-sacrifice, they strove to bring up their children to follow their ways. They did not give up, but it was very, very difficult.

A vigorous activist, a teacher *par excellence*, and an exceptional educator and organizer named Reb Shraga Feivel Mendelowitz appeared on the American scene before World War I. In 1923 he joined the staff of Yeshivas Torah Vodaath in Williamsburg and shortly afterward became its principal. In this capacity, Reb Shraga Feivel attracted Jewish youth to the study of Torah and observance of the mitzvos. He knew his *talmidim* and worked with each *al pi darko*, commensurate with his personal abilities and needs. He invested his time, abilities, heart, and soul into the establishment of this history-making institution.

Notwithstanding the demanding responsibilities that he had assumed in running the yeshiva, Reb Shraga Feivel did not overlook the importance of *chinuch ha-banos,* Orthodox education for girls. He knew that Jewish girls attended co-ed public schools and participated with their gentile classmates in compulsory social activities that clashed with Orthodox proprieties. Proms with mixed dancing were only one example. Reb Shraga Feivel was concerned about the nefarious effects of immodest and un-Jewish behavior on these girls, whose mothers were equally worried. He also knew that without Orthodox education for girls, Jewish family life in America would have no future.

Reb Shraga Feivel was informed about the 1923 Kenessiah Gedolah of Agudath Israel, where great rabbis such as the Chofetz Chaim, the Belzer Rebbe, and the Gerrer Rebbe had enthusiastically endorsed the Bais Yaakov schools. He was also personally impressed with the Bais Yaakov movement. Although of Hungarian origin — the Hungarian rabbis opposed the Agudah at that time — he felt so strongly about *chinuch ha-banos* that he was prepared to assist any initiative to start a girls' high school and seminary.

His brilliant writings and speeches reflected his pain and commitment: "All nations understand the importance of girls' education; only we Jews consider a traditional education for our own daughters unnecessary. We have neglected our girls, and now we must correct the injustice done to them." He meant it; he spared no effort to encourage any attempt to equip girls with religious knowledge, appreciation of the beauty of the Jewish heritage, and the strength to withstand foreign influences.

One of the most significant efforts in this direction was made in 1934 by Fruma Leah Mandel, a woman of great commitment to Jewish values. Feeling intensely responsible for the future of *Klal Yisroel*, she felt compelled to do something to extricate Jewish girls from their plight. An energetic activist, she established the Beis Ruchel elementary school for girls, subsequently Bais Yaakov of Williamsburg, under the direction of Rabbi Avrohom Newhouse. She was also eager to work on behalf of Jewish teenagers who were already succumbing to the domination of secular American culture. Her idea in this regard was to set up evening groups for girls who attended public high schools during the day.

She turned to Reb Shraga Feivel for advice. Reflecting his own great interest in traditional education for girls, he gave her initiative his warmest blessing and enthusiastically urged her to carry it out. Thus, with sacrifice and hard work, Mrs. Mandel organized evening and Shabbos study groups in many Jewish neighborhoods of New York. She also aimed to establish a teachers' seminary, but notwithstanding her efforts and ardor, she was unable to establish a permanent and lasting educational facility of that kind. Just the same, her sincere efforts were not in vain. They had prepared the ground for *chinuch ha-banos* in America.

✦ *Chapter 71* ✦

It was 1932 when Rabbi Yitzchok Matisyahu Weinberg of New York first found out about the Bais Yaakov Seminary in Kraków and its legendary head, Sarah Schenirer. Knowing of no school in America that could provide his only daughter, Chavah, with a Jewish education, he decided to send her away to Kraków. This was unprecedented; boys were sent to Lithuanian and Polish yeshivos for study, but never girls. Understandably, the girl's mother opposed the move because of the great distance involved, but her father won the argument, especially since his intelligent, adventurous young daughter took his side. She had only one request: assurance of a return ticket, just in case.

Before he sent Chavah to Kraków, Rabbi Weinberg wrote to Sarah Schenirer[87]:

"Please be aware that this girl will need *pi shtayim*, a double dose, of Jewish education, because she has to come back to America heavily armed to combat the American [Jews'] indifference and apathy."

Chavah Weinberg took her risky and unusual voyage in late 1933. After an exhausting trek by ship and train, she reached the Kraków seminary and found herself in an environment of love and warmth. Once she had survived the difficulties that

---

87. This letter was brought to my attention by Rabbi Noach Weinberg, Rabbi Yitzchok Matisyahu Weinberg's son and the founder and dean of Yeshivas Aish Hatorah in Jerusalem.

any beginner faces in a strange land and in strange circumstances, she was pleased with her decision. She definitely got *pi shtayim* from Frau Schenirer, her great teacher and mentor, from Dr. Judith Rosenbaum, and from all the wonderful teachers on the seminary's staff.

Chavah's acquaintance with Sarah Schenirer, who by this time had become a living legend, made a deep and lasting impression on her. "It was a great *zechus*, one that has sustained me through life, to have spent two summer months in Sarah Schenirer's proximity. I was able to observe her ways of acting, of doing mitzvos. The inspiration I got from her simplicity and greatness was a special bonus," she related.

Chavah Weinberg also received *pi shtayim* by traveling all over Poland during the holiday recess with her exceptional teacher Fraulein Hamburger, who like her did not go home for the festivals. This gave her an unusual opportunity to meet several great Chassidic rabbis and their remarkable wives. In Gur, for example, she observed the Rebbetzin preparing the festival table for the women. She used beautiful tablecloths and elegant dishes as a gracious hostess would. However, as Chavah noticed with interest, the Rebbetzin did not put out individual settings. "Is there a special reason for that?" she asked.

"I cannot set the table for a specific amount of people," the Rebbetzin explained. "Maybe I'll have more guests than I expected, and there will be no setting for them. This way, they'll sit down and make their own setting from the prepared dishes. Nobody will be hurt by not finding a personal setting." What sensitivity to others' feelings, Chavah thought admiringly.

"I also had the great privilege on those trips to meet renowned scholars and the important *rashei yeshivos* of Lithuania," Chavah recalls. "We also visited Baranowitz, home of Rav Elchonon Wasserman's great yeshiva, where Rav Yaakov Lubchansky was the *mashgiach*. In Brisk, we were joined by Vichna Eisen, whom Frau Schenirer had sent to that Lithuanian city to attract the women to the idea of Bais Yaakov."

Vichna then drafted Chavah to address a large audience of

teenage girls whom she had assembled for that purpose. After Vichna's own inspiring speech, Chavah took the floor. Her enthusiasm, her dedication to the Bais Yaakov ideal, her charm, and her personality made a potent impression on the assembled youngsters. They could not get over this likable, fashionable "*Amerikanke*" who had left the *goldene medina* to attend the Bais Yaakov school in Kraków. "It must be a very important school," they exclaimed. "It must be worth attending."

This, coupled with Vichna's warm appeal to the women, made such an impact on those present that a Bais Yaakov school was founded right away. It became one of the most successful Bais Yaakov institutions in Lithuania. An additional benefit for Chavah was the opportunity to develop a special friendship with her classmate, Vichna Eisen.

Vichna was one of the most admired students at the seminary. Her keen intelligence, combined with her unblemished character and simplicity, won the hearts of all who met her, from Sarah Schenirer to all her classmates. It is no wonder that Vichna and Chavah, the two finest students at the seminary at this time, formed a special relationship that lasted for years. After leaving the seminary, they shared the ideas of Bais Yaakov and remained dedicated to the movement, albeit on different continents.

After Frau Schenirer's death in 1935, Chavah Weinberg returned to the United States with precious baggage: stronger *yiras Shamayim*, increased Jewish knowledge, and a passion for the Bais Yaakov ideal. She was eager to teach and spread *Yiddishkeit* among Jewish girls in America. Upon her return, she found the Torah way of life being taught to girls in one elementary school, Beis Ruchel, and Fruma Leah Mandel's scattered evening and Shabbos groups only. There was no Bais Yaakov teachers' seminary that could turn out heads of Bais Yaakov schools across America.

Chavah first tried to teach in a Jewish high school but soon found that the Bais Yaakov spirit was missing there. In Kraków she had attended a school that abounded with *yiras Shamayim*, enthusiasm for Torah learning, and joy and pride in being the daughter of the King of kings — an institution where the very air carried Sarah Schenirer's profound inspiration — spread by her saintly personality, her unique character, her *avodas Hashem,* and her boundless love of people.

Chavah also tried to help Mrs. Mandel with her evening groups and Shabbos gatherings, but this did not satisfy her either. It was not what she had come back for. Thus, with a few of her friends, she organized a large youth gathering — this time in America. As in Poland and Lithuania, her charm, eloquence, and enthusiasm infected her young audience with the great idea of the Bais Yaakov movement. As she enlightened her listeners about the great benefits of genuine Orthodox education for girls, their indifference gave way to excitement. It was Vichna Kaplan *née* Eisen who went on to establish a Bais Yaakov seminary in America, but it was Chavah Weinberg's initiative that paved the way.

Chavah Weinberg later married the esteemed Rabbi Chaim Avrohom Pincus and, after many years of accomplishment in Jewish education in the United States, they moved to Eretz Yisroel. There, too, they continued their work in Jewish education. As a supervisor of Bais Yaakov schools, Rebbetzin Pincus helped with curriculum advice and suggestions. She infused the Bais Yaakov schools with the spirit of Sarah Schenirer. She inspired teachers with the original teachings she acquired at the Kraków seminary.[88]

*   *   *

Vichna Eisen had amassed prodigious accomplishments of her own. At the Kraków seminary, she made herself into one of Sarah Schenirer's most capable and talented *talmidos* by practicing the arts of observation and emulation. Thus she absorbed Frau Schenirer's exceptional standards of mitzvos and *middos.*

---

88. Rabbi (*zt"l*) and Rebbetzin (*a"h*) Pincus' son, Rabbi Shimshon Pincus, *zt"l,* was a world-famous *gadol* from Ofakim, Israel, whose life was tragically cut short in an automobile accident in 2001.

In time, she became the embodiment of a Bais Yaakov student. However, Frau Schenirer, recognizing her superb intelligence, phenomenal memory, and unblemished character, saw additional potential in her. "From the first letter you wrote to the school," she said,[89] "I knew you would be able to help the Bais Yaakov movement." A classmate who overheard this remembers her continuing, "You will succeed me, but you will be greater." Rebbetzin Kaplan, of course, never repeated the latter part of Frau Schenirer's remark.

Rebbetzin Devorah Kitowitz, in her article in *The Jewish Observer* under the title, "An Appreciation of Rebbetzin Kaplan *a"h*," brings an interesting episode reflecting Rebbetzin Kaplan's unusual qualities while still a student.

Dr. Judith Rosenbaum, the famed "Fraulein Doktor" from Frankfurt, taught the girls *Shir ha-Shirim* (the Song of Songs) on Friday nights. They could not take notes, of course. "After Shabbos," one of her classmates recalled, "we asked Vichna to repeat the lesson so we could take notes. 'You know it best,' we told her.

"'No, I don't,' Vichna answered, 'but I'll tell you anyway.' Then she repeated the lesson verbatim. Her humility was such that the girls admired and loved her deeply for her continual willingness to help. They were never jealous of Frau Schenirer's special relationship with her."

After Vichna Eisen graduated from the seminary, the Bais Yaakov Central Office, in Kraków, posted her as a teacher to the school in Brisk, which she had organized in her seminary days. There, she earned her students' love and admiration and their parents' respect for her wise and knowledgeable advice. Indeed, the whole community held her in very high esteem. In fact, a Warsaw businesswoman named Leah Schwartz went so far as to write a letter to one of the most influential rabbis in Europe concerning Vichna.

Mrs. Schwartz met Vichna on one of her many visits to

---

89. As related to me by her children.

Brisk. She admired the spirit and enthusiasm that Vichna displayed in teaching the girls the beauty of authentic Judaism. She was so taken by Vichna's personality that she marshaled the responsibility and courage to write to the esteemed, renowned *mashgiach* of the Mirrer Yeshiva, Rabbi Yeruchem Levovitz, *zt"l*, concerning this special girl. Specifically, she asked him to find a student at his yeshiva who would be a suitable match for her.

She described Vichna Eisen as an unusual young lady: "I have no words to describe her exceptional virtues. She is a rare diamond, cut and polished in the house of Rav Yaakov Lubchansky, her uncle, who raised her after she was orphaned.

"She is an outstanding young woman, honest and good-hearted," Leah Schwartz continued. "All her aspirations are *le-shem Shamayim* [for the sake of Heaven]. She constantly works on self-improvement with strong will and inner beauty. I have seen her at different times and in diverse situations and marveled at her dignified reactions. The most impressive thing about her is the intensity of her efforts to achieve the lofty heights she has set for herself. *She was made for greatness*! The young man must be a *ba'al madreigah*, a person who has the stature to be the husband of such a personality." Then, hoping for his help, she signed her name.

*   *   *

Vichna Eisen was introduced to American-born Rabbi Boruch Kaplan, the most promising student at the Mirrer Yeshiva. They met a few times. Before they made any fateful decisions, however, Rabbi Kaplan had to leave for America. They continued to make each other's acquaintance by mail and got engaged the same way. Now Vichna had to follow her *chasan*, though reluctantly, to the United States.

Before she left Poland, however, she asked Reb Yehudah Leib Orlean, Sarah Schenirer's successor, for permission to open a Bais Yaakov seminary in America. As a rule, every new school that opened in Poland had to be under the auspices and regulations of the Bais Yaakov Central Office in Kraków. However, Reb Yehudah Leib gave his dispensation with a blessing.

It was under these circumstances, in 1937, that Vichna Eisen arrived in the United States to become Rebbetzin Kaplan. She knew what Orthodox Jews said about America: "Even the stones there are *treif*." But she had a goal: to turn those stones into pebbles and asphalt, with which to pave a path of Torah in the streets of Jewish neighborhoods. Her paving equipment would be the ideology and passion of Bais Yaakov.

❧ Chapter 72 ❧

Without delay, Rebbetzin Kaplan set out to realize her dream of establishing a Bais Yaakov seminary in America in the true spirit of Kraków — an enterprise that would supply teachers for Bais Yaakov schools across the length and breadth of America. Mrs. Leah Schwartz, in her letter to Rabbi Yeruchem Levovitz, had described Vichna Eisen as destined for greatness. Prophetic words, indeed.

Rebbetzin Kaplan turned to Reb Shraga Feivel Mendelowitz for advice, guidance, and help in this great undertaking. Her vision overwhelmed him at first. Assessing in her the visionary, however, he found her well-equipped for the task in terms of education, experience, enthusiasm, and devotion to the Bais Yaakov idea. He was thrilled. Thus, with his typical vigor, he encouraged her to realize her wonderful plan and offered her his assistance, his warm blessings, and, above all, his two daughters, Chani and Rivky, as her first students. They brought five friends: the two Pilchik sisters, Sylvia and Feigi; Leah Wilhelm; Esther Weissman; and Tzivia Mandel. Thus Rebbetzin Kaplan launched her venture with seven girls in her dining room — just as Sarah Schenirer had in her work room!

Chavah Weinberg, who had returned to the States, became the right-hand woman of Rebbetzin Kaplan, her close friend from seminary days. Together, they planned the curriculum and the teaching methods. The school grew rapidly. Rebbetzin Kaplan's magnetic personality attracted girls at their first meeting; her quiet dignity, intelligence, and vast knowledge impressed teenagers at once. Her compassion and personal interest kindled their love for her. Her kindness and empathy convinced them that she would forgive them for occasional transgressions. Her demands, expressed gently, were always taken seriously and readily fulfilled.

It took an iron fist to direct the rapidly growing school. In this respect, Rebbetzin Kaplan proved to be a true *talmidah* of Sarah Schenirer. "My maiden name is Eisen," she would say. "That means 'iron' in Yiddish." However, she never allowed this characteristic to slide into anger. At times of pressure and difficult circumstances, she drew on her inner strength to maintain her composure. She always kept the trait of anger, which her mentor Sarah Schenirer had termed man's greatest enemy, under control. "I use that iron to fight the most trying situations without getting angry."

A staff took shape, reinforced by many of the most capable students from the Kraków seminary. Rebbetzin Chana Rotenberg reached the United States and joined the faculty shortly before the war. Her scholarly husband, Rabbi Shlomo Rotenberg, also joined the staff. Rabbi Rotenberg was renowned for his prestigious knowledge of the Talmud, as well as for his classic volumes on Jewish history based on Talmudic sources, *Toldos Am Olam*. Rabbi Rotenberg taught every seminary class Jewish history in the most interesting and inspiring way. He left an indelible impression on the hearts of all of his students, both at Bais Yaakov and at Mesifta Torah Vodaath, where he also taught for many years.

Rebbetzin Basya Bender, Rebbetzin Chavah Wachtfogel, Rebbetzin Rivka Springer, and Bat Sheva Ziv reached American shores during the war, miraculously, and also helped Rebbetzin Kaplan in her great undertaking.

The founder's husband, Rabbi Boruch Kaplan, resigned his position at Yeshivas Torah Vodaath to help the Bais Yaakov Seminary grow into a central institution that would provide Bais Yaakov schools all over the country with teachers. To help the Bais Yaakov Seminary to become an institution of the dimensions that it eventually attained, he relinquished the opportunity to become a great Torah personality. Understanding the call of the hour and the dire importance of *chinuch ha-banos,* he made this sacrifice for the future of *Klal Yisroel.* It pained Rebbetzin Kaplan to be credited for Bais Yaakov's tremendous growth without mention of her husband's self-sacrifice.

As time passed, many girls' schools were established by Chassidic groups, *yeshivishe* communities, and Modern Orthodox sponsors. All depended on the seminary in Brooklyn for teachers who would implant the Bais Yaakov spirit in their institutions. Although they carry various names, all these schools realize, appreciate, and are thankful to Sarah Schenirer, who so skillfully dug the well from which they draw knowledge and inspiration. They showed their gratitude in 1985 by attending Sarah Schenirer's fiftieth *yahrtzeit,* organized by Rebbetzin Kaplan, in Madison Square Garden. This display of unity in appreciation of the Bais Yaakov ideal was a memorable event. It was repeated on the occasion of the sixtieth *yahrtzeit,* when seven thousand girls from many different schools packed the Brooklyn Armory to pay tribute to the founder of the *chinuch ha-banos* idea.

*   *   *

Not long ago, while attending an affair in Telz Stone, near Jerusalem, I encountered a middle-aged woman named Mrs. Kaplan. Discovering that I was from Kraków, she described her days as a student at the Bais Yaakov Seminary on South Eighth Street in Williamsburg, Brooklyn, in the school's pioneering phase.

"The conditions were difficult. The dormitory was cold in the winter and sweltering in the summer. Enrollment grew so swiftly that the dormitory rooms were turned into classrooms and we had to move into private homes.

"After the first term, I went back to Baltimore to spend the holiday with my family. By that time, everybody knew about

Bais Yaakov and its technical troubles. My mother's friends suggested that under the circumstances she should send her daughter to a better equipped high school that had more comfortable dormitories.

"My mother asked them," Mrs. Kaplan recalled, "whether that school had Rebbetzin Kaplan. 'No,' she was told, 'but they have a wonderful teaching faculty and a great principal.'

"'If they have no Rebbetzin Kaplan,' my mother replied, 'then I'm sending my daughter back to Bais Yaakov. Her personality and her staff of Sarah Schenirer's original Bais Yaakov teachers cannot be duplicated.'

"And I went back," continued Mrs. Kaplan proudly, "for daily hardships and a glorious spiritual life."

✳   ✳   ✳

The financial burden of maintaining the school fell on Rabbi Boruch Kaplan's shoulders. Despite the pressure, he took a loan to organize a summer learning camp for the girls at a farm in Connecticut owned by a Mr. Engel. This initiative was descendant of the summer instructors' course in Europe. Rebbetzin Kaplan knew how important that course had been. It equipped the girls with spiritual assets that they could transfer to their schools in small towns and large cities. In addition, it kept the girls busy at study and away from summertime city distractions. Rebbetzin Kaplan personally taught all subjects at the camp in Connecticut, sometimes with a baby on her lap when she could not get a babysitter.

Years later, Rebbetzin Kaplan's daughter Miriam described the inner conflict her mother had faced when she had to leave her own children with a babysitter and teach other mothers' children. "For years," Rebbetzin Kaplan once said, "I wished the prophet Eliyahu would come to me and tell me what to do. Then I'd find peace of mind." She continued to build the Bais Yaakov empire. Who knows? Maybe she got a clue from Above. However, the anguish of doing injustice to her own family never left her. She always tried to spend every free moment with her children. On Fridays, when she was at home, she prepared each child's favorite dish. On one Ta'anis Esther, when Rebbetzin Kaplan was off from school, the aroma of fresh hamantaschen from her neighbor's kitchen prompted her to rue the very possibility of depriving her children of that treat. Haunted by the possibility that they would blame it on Bais Yaakov, she hurriedly baked hamantaschen of her own.

Miriam often mentions something her mother used to say: "'We don't realize how great our petty actions are in God's eyes.' I thought of little things that my mother did while walking home — stopping to visit a housebound elderly woman or an ill neighbor to see what she might need — despite her busy schedule." How accurately Rebbetzin Kaplan emulated her beloved mentor, whose personality combined *"Die Grosse und Kleine Menschenliebe"* — altruism in matters great and small. "Small" altruism is reflected in loving-kindness in daily life; "large" altruism resonates on a grand scale of historical dimensions. Rebbetzin Kaplan embraced both as few people could. She was concerned about everybody's needs and wishes. She was always there to listen to every child, to consult, to advise, to help, to satisfy needs.

"How can it be?" I asked her daughter. "A woman with such responsibilities, with such all-encompassing interest in and love for all people, ready to listen to everyone and help whenever needed — was she allotted more than twenty-four hours a day to do it?"

Her daughter smiled. "Our neighbor used to say, 'Rebbetzin Kaplan raised a large family, God bless them, but never raised her voice' — neither at the children nor at anyone else. No matter how busy she was," Miriam continued, "she would never order her child to do a chore. She would ask him or her: 'Please do it if you can, but if you can't, you are not transgressing the mitzvah of *kibud eim*.'"

Now I understood. Rebbetzin Kaplan — the mother — gave her child a wealth of *chinuch* in one brief moment. She must have given them all a multitude of such moments. In a moving remark, Miriam confirmed it: "Before my wedding day, I felt sad about having to leave this home, where one could feel the presence of the *Shechinah* at all times — when my mother was there or when she went to her lofty calling at Bais Yaakov.

"May she derive much *nachas ruach*," she added, "from all her children, seeing their great endeavors in *chinuch* and their sacrifice in following in their great parents' footsteps."

May their memory be for a blessing.

❧ *Chapter 73* ❧

As a resident of Williamsburg for quite a few years, I was able to appreciate and follow the progress of the Bais Yaakov Seminary on South Eighth Street — and to admire its great founder and principal at work.

Sarah Schenirer's *yahrtzeit* fell several months after I reached Williamsburg in 1949, on 26 Adar Alef. I yearned to experience again, after the *churban*, the great gathering that we had held in Europe on this annual occasion — memorial speeches by Frau Schenirer's students, reminiscences about her inspiring lessons, and retelling of her stories, so laden with meaning that they guided us for life.

Shortly before the date, I approached Rebbetzin Kaplan and asked her, "Has a special event for Frau Schenirer's *yahrtzeit* been organized here?"

"Yes, of course," she assured me. "Every year for the *yahrtzeit*, we have an assembly where we tell the girls about the great founder and leader of the Bais Yaakov movement."

"Rebbetzin Kaplan," I continued, introducing my idea, "many surviving students from the pre-war Bais Yaakov schools in Europe are living in the New York area. I am sure they, just as I, need to attend and re-experience the great event of Frau Schenirer's *yahrtzeit*. I know they would be thrilled and excited to have the opportunity."

Rebbetzin Kaplan listened attentively to my words. "I'd be glad to let you use our auditorium for this purpose," she offered at once. "But how will you locate all these people in the vastness of greater New York?"

I discussed that problem with several former students of Frau Schenirer's and we decided to contact *Der Yiddisher Philosoph*, our favorite broadcaster on the Jewish radio station. Toward the end of his interesting half-hour program on Friday afternoons, he announced events scheduled for the coming week.

I wrote him a letter explaining the Bais Yaakov movement. I wrote about Sarah Schenirer, founder of Bais Yaakov and spearhead of the revolutionary idea of *chinuch ha-banos*. Bais Yaakov educated Jewish girls in the traditional Torah way, taught them the beauty of the Jewish heritage, and revealed the treasure of Jewish thought and wisdom. I described the greatness of the Bais Yaakov girls, who had sacrificed their lives to help others and had maintained their humanness amidst the ugliness of Auschwitz, Bergen-Belsen, and other camps. I explained the necessity of an event dedicated to the memory of the legendary educator whose influence continued to reverberate and would do so forever. I presented all the details of the Sunday event and asked him to bring them to the attention of his loyal listeners.

As I cooked my Shabbos meals, I listened intently to the most popular radio station in our community at the time. I strained my ears. Now *Der Yiddisher Philosoph* was speaking. Would he announce our evening? Would he get the address and time right?

He would. Moreover, instead of his weekly program, he read my letter in its entirety. Then came his comments and, finally, a warm appeal to all Bais Yaakov students to attend. I was stunned.

Sunday passed in great anticipation and concern: "Did anyone hear him? Will they come?"

Finally the door of the auditorium opened. Girls and women thronged into the hall, eager to participate, to listen, and again to experience the *yahrtzeit* of their great mentor — and to meet friends, classmates, and maybe even a relative given up for lost.

"What a great event!" they remarked in anticipation of this unusual reunion of the sparse remnants of the Bais Yaakov sisterhood. They filled the seats, then the aisles. They spilled through the entrance back into the hallway. Thus Sarah Schenirer's surviving children expressed their love and gratitude.

They embraced, kissed, and cried. Tears flowed freely — tears of anguish, of recollections of all the wonderful Bais Yaakov girls, students and teachers, who had gone to join their mentor. Then came tears of joy as old friends recognized each other. Each unexpected encounter elicited new outcries and exclamations. The auditorium heaved with emotion. Finally, even after their bitter personal experiences, the participants were overwhelmed by the loss, still fresh in their minds and hearts, of their dear mother and teacher, Sarah Schenirer.

The program began. The atmosphere filled with cherished memories of our devoted mentor. Children reminisced about the dear mother who had accompanied them wherever they went, who invested them with the courage to withstand the most trying of ordeals. They remembered how, when matters descended to nadirs of despair and hopelessness, their mentor suddenly appeared — her face radiating hope, her powerful presence filling them with the strength to endure, to persevere in their struggle, and to live to see the light. The very walls seemed to cry in commiseration with our bereavement.

Then Rebbetzin Kaplan spoke. Her calm, composed voice returned us to the present, a better time than the recent past. She spoke about her resolve to regenerate the genuine spirit of the Kraków seminary in America.

Her very appearance and the glimpse it afforded of her remarkable personality gave the audience a sense of tranquility and confidence in the timelessness of the Bais Yaakov movement. Her appearance and her calm though powerful address reminded us so very much of our great teacher. At the end of that successful *yahrtzeit* evening, we knew we had witnessed the embodiment of a true *talmidah* of Sarah Schenirer's.

The next day, I called Rebbetzin Kaplan and thanked her

for the helpful, inspiring, and encouraging speech she had delivered to our pre-war Bais Yaakov *talmidos*. However, I was upset. After the radio announcement, I knew the event might attract a large crowd. Therefore, I had asked Rebbetzin Kaplan to station a few girls at the entrance to collect donations for the school. "The women are not yet well-off," I told her, "but each of them will surely donate a dollar or two, or maybe even five, at this very important occasion."

Rebbetzin Kaplan had not followed through. There had been no collection at the door. Later on, when I remarked to the teachers about this, they sent girls with plates to solicit among the audience. "What did they get?" I now asked Rebbetzin Kaplan rhetorically. "Quarters!" An excellent fundraising opportunity had been squandered, I felt.

Rebbetzin Kaplan did not share my dismay. "Listen," she said in her quiet, dignified way, "it was not *beshert* [fated from Above] for the school to get money from this special evening."

"Rebbetzin Kaplan," I countered, "aren't we supposed to do our share? I'm upset that we failed to do what we could."

"Don't be upset," she said soothingly. "That was *beshert,* too."

Thus Rebbetzin Kaplan expressed her deep faith and unconditional acceptance of Hashem as the only Leader in our affairs. At first this realization overwhelmed me; afterwards, however, I realized that she had taught me a very important lesson. I will never forget it.

✤ *Chapter 74* ✤

"...How you followed Me in the wilderness, in a land not sown"
(Yirmeyahu 2:2)

After the war, Rebbetzin Kaplan reinforced her wonderful staff by taking on three additional pillars of the student body at the Kraków seminary: Rebbetzins Rachel Cizner, Leah Galler Goldstein, and Shifra Yudasin. They taught excellently and piqued the students' interest and enthusiasm. Most of all, however, they inspired admiration and emulation. No wonder the school grew and flourished.

Rebbetzin Kaplan headed the Bais Yaakov movement in America for almost fifty years by supplying teachers for all Orthodox girls' schools in the United States and beyond. With the assistance of her wonderful colleagues, she tackled and solved all the school's most important problems as well as tended to the minutest details of every aspect of teaching and administration, including paying special attention to students at the individual level.

One could almost see Rebbetzin Kaplan walking in the footsteps of her renowned mentor, Sarah Schenirer. She continually monitored her own behavior, asking herself in every situation, "What would Sarah Schenirer say? Would she approve of what I've done?" Since this was Rebbetzin Kaplan's greatest concern, it is no wonder that she stood shoulder-to-shoulder with her teacher as a pioneer, fighting for and building a school system that would provide girls with Orthodox education on the indifferent American soil. As her teacher had revolutionized Polish Jewry, so Rebbetzin Kaplan revolutionized American Jewry with the novel idea of teaching girls the beauty of the Jewish heritage and influencing them in affirmative Torah conduct.

Rebbetzin Vichna Kaplan passed away suddenly in the summer of 1986, still fully vigorous as the founder and leader of the Bais Yaakov movement in America. Since then, her devoted and capable staff has sustained her great educational enterprise and its purpose — the perpetuation of Sarah Schenirer's heritage. The Bais Yaakov Seminary in Brooklyn turns out teachers for Orthodox girls' schools all over the world. All recently established schools of this type, under whatever name, were launched and are directed by Bais Yaakov alumnae.

At the *shloshim*, her daughter, Miriam, delivered an exceptionally moving and beautiful eulogy: "She was a mother to thousands," she exclaimed, "and concurrently a most devoted and caring mother to each of us personally." What an unheard-of combination in one personality, the listeners thought — although those who had known Frau Schenirer had encountered it before. "You might think that she lost touch with reality by immersing herself in imparting such lofty ideas to her students. Far from it."

Miriam continued by quoting a verse from *Parashas Vayeitze*: "...*Ve-hinei sulam mutzav artzah ve-rosho magi'a ha-shamaimah* — 'Behold, a ladder was fixed to the ground with its top reaching up to the heavens.'[90] Even though her heart and mind reached the heavens, her feet stood firmly on the ground, trying to satisfy and please every student, every child."

*   *   *

The bulletin written for the fiftieth reunion of the Rebbetzin Kaplan Seminary alumnae, held one year after the

---

90. *Bereishis* 28:12.

Rebbetzin's death, was understandably dedicated to her blessed memory. Colleagues, teachers, students, and admirers from all over the world submitted greetings to the bulletin. Below I quote several excerpts from her famed teacher, an associate of Sarah Schenirer's; and from her two most dedicated colleagues, alumnae of Frau Schenirer's seminary.

Dr. Judith Grunfeld writes:

> I wholeheartedly join the gathering of friends and *talmidos* of our beloved Rebbetzin Kaplan. Her humble yet devoted determination to kindle and maintain the flame of Torah in America resulted in an ever-spreading light in thousands of Jewish souls. She is a figure of historical importance because she did her educational rescue work at a time when the powers of Hell had brought the Torah of light, kindled by our great mentor, Sarah Schenirer, to the brink of extinction.
>
> Her penchant for teaching *Shir ha-Shirim* every year in every class gives a clue to her personality. She taught it with a depth of presentation in her soft, heart-warming voice, as she herself personified the ideals she had developed in teaching this beautiful, holy scroll.[91]

Rebbetzin Chavah Pincus, *née* Weinberg, writes:

> We thank Hashem for the heavenly help that made Bais Yaakov a tremendous power in shaping Torah *Yiddishkeit* in this country and the world over.
>
> We can see what one person with dedication and *mesirus nefesh* can achieve, as evidenced by Sarah Schenirer in Poland and her disciple, Rebbetzin Kaplan, in our country. Each of us who was touched by those great lights and pillars of inspiration has a destiny to fulfill: to spread knowledge and love of Torah and mitzvos. We must resolve not only to bring the Bais Yaakov *hashkafah* [outlook] into our homes but also to reach out to others and

---

91. Dr. Judith Rosenbaum Grunfeld was Rebbetzin Kaplan's beloved teacher of *Shir ha-Shirim* at the Kraków seminary.

apprise them of the beauty and holiness of Torah *Yiddishkeit.*

What a *kiddush Hashem* that would create! What a healing for our poor, assimilated, and estranged generation!

Rebbetzin Rivka Springer quoted *Eichah* 4:1:

"Tishtapechnah avnei kodesh be-rosh kol chutzos — The holy stones are spilled at every streetcorner." Our rabbis explain that when the Holy Temple was destroyed, heavenly angels came down, took the stones from the Holy Temple, and scattered them all over the world, so that new sanctuaries could be built from them in those places.

When Polish Jewry existed, the Chazon Ish, *zt"l*, likened the institutions of Torah in Poland to those in Eretz Yisroel. When they were destroyed, he said, the heavenly angels came, took some of their stones, and built new Torah sanctuaries in different places in their stead.

"Who were the angels?" the Sages ask. Their answer: *"Talmidei chachamim* are likened to angels." They took the strewn holy stones that they found, delivered them to their places of exile, and used them to build *yeshivos, batei midrashim,* and holy institutions.

Even before the Bais Yaakov edifice in Poland was destroyed, Rebbetzin Vichna Kaplan lifted up the stones of the Kraków seminary, which were already ablaze, and built of them a new and vibrant Bais Yaakov movement, a sanctuary of Torah, in America.

❧ *Chapter 75* ❧

Sixty years on

𝓘*n the early spring of 1995,* the capable and devoted staff of Rebbetzin Kaplan's Bais Yaakov Seminary, led by her daughter, Rebbetzin Frumie Kirzner, organized a very impressive event to memorialize the *yahrtzeit* of Sarah Schenirer.

Winter still reigned on 26 Adar — February 26 — of that year. Apart from the freezing cold, snow still covered the streets. But that did not stop the flow of buses, one after another, and the throngs of young passengers whom they discharged.

I stood on the streetcorner, reminiscing. Sixty years! Yes, sixty years had passed since that tragic Friday night when we, Frau Schenirer's young students, surrounded the saintly body of our beloved mother. Her children gazed back then at the two candles that she had lit before her passing. They continued to observe those shining lights for the ensuing sixty years, lest the raging gales of life extinguish them.

Now I stood next to the huge Brooklyn Armory in Williamsburg, watching large buses arriving from all boroughs of New York, the suburbs, and small towns farther a field. They disgorged young girls, high-schoolers, and seminary students. All were from Bais Yaakov! Their schools carried various names. Some were sponsored by Chassidic courts and bore the names of their rebbes or rebbetzins. Others belonged to Orthodox communities of various orientations.

They kept on coming by the hundreds, the thousands, to pay tribute to Sarah Schenirer, the towering champion of *chinuch ha-banos* and founder of the Bais Yaakov movement. They came to express their gratitude to the great teacher who so skillfully dug a deep well of knowledge and *yiras Shamayim* for Jewish girls. As they drank from that well, they acknowledged its eternally refreshing properties. Now they came to thank its engineer.

The immense armory filled to capacity. Late arrivals poured into garages that adjoined the building. In all, their numbers came to seven thousand. The facilities were not heated but the excitement and enthusiasm, the joy of being part of this great movement, kept the participants warm.

The program began on time. The chairwoman, Rebbetzin Kirzner, greeted the multitude in a tone of warmth and quiet dignity that reminded those who had known Sarah Schenirer of her special way of addressing her pupils.

The huge audience fell silent. One could hear a pin drop, had anyone dropped one. As the crowd listened intently, the distinguished Rabbis Avrohom ha-Kohen Pam, *zt"l*, Gavriel Ginsburg, and Shmuel Dishon expressed their admiration of and respect for the illustrious person that was Sarah Schenirer. They spoke with gratitude about the woman who had promoted the novel idea of *chinuch ha-banos* and, with responsibility and utter devotion, had turned her great vision into the reality of the flourishing Bais Yaakov movement. Then they praised the movement itself, which had not only returned countless Jewish girls to traditional *Yiddishkeit* but had also left a monumental imprint on Jewish life at large. A few in the crowd who were versed in Bais Yaakov history may have recalled the earliest days of Sarah Schenirer's venture, when such praise was not taken for granted.

The rabbis concluded with an inspirational message for the audience: Continue to follow in the footsteps of your great teacher. Learn the *Heilige* Torah with enthusiasm. Practice its precepts with joy. Acquire and emulate Sarah Schenirer's saintly character traits. And may God bless you with success in attaining the perfection of a Bais Yaakov girl.

It then came the turn of the women, including myself, to speak. I stood up, overwhelmed by the sight of those seven thousand Bais Yaakov girls, may they only multiply. For a long moment, I was speechless, overtaken by distant memories. I saw the large Bnos auditorium in Kraków, filled to capacity at Sarah Schenirer's last *yahrtzeit* before the war. Then I saw the war years — our precious Bais Yaakov girls and teachers decimated by the Nazis again and again, transported under inhuman conditions to the valley of death, to extermination.

Then I saw a post-liberation scene — Bais Yaakov alumnae running half-insane from block to block, looking for a child, a Jewish child, a Bais Yaakov girl, to no avail. We found only a world of emptiness, devoid of Jewish children. Hit by the tragic truth, we faced a world of nothingness.

Then, just a few years later, shortly after I had debarked in America, I was privileged to witness the most gorgeous miracle. Addressing the Bais Yaakov Seminary on South Eighth Street in Brooklyn, at the invitation of Rebbetzin Kaplan, I observed the rebirth of Bais Yaakov. I was spellbound. My eyes had dimmed with tears of joy as I contemplated more than one hundred Bais Yaakov girls — alive, happy, and attending an authentic Bais Yaakov school. I wiped my eyes to assure myself that it was no dream but a great new reality.

Now, almost fifty years after my first speech at the Williamsburg Bais Yaakov, I was again given the *zechus* to address an audience of Bais Yaakov girls, but this time a true multitude. How overwhelming it was to behold the miraculous growth of the Bais Yaakov movement over those last fifty years. Choking on tears of joy and gratitude, I was unable to speak.

Then, without warning, I reenacted the experience I had had when I first met Bais Yaakov girls at Rebbetzin Kaplan's school. An uncontrollable, heart-rending cry erupted from my throat, a powerful blessing to God; "*She-hecheyanu ve-kiyemanu ve-higiyanu la-zeman ha-zeh.*" It was the voice of all the Bais Yaakov survivors, expressing our boundless gratitude to the Almighty for having sustained us to experience this marvelous rebirth of our People. Through my words, they thanked Hashem for the blossoming of our youth, for the privilege of raising such a special generation, one that replenished our nation in great strides after its loss.

Then I found my own voice. I told my enormous Bais Yaakov audience about the late Sarah Schenirer as I had known her, about her great teachings that gave us the strength to surmount the ordeals and trials that daily life had hurled at us during those sixty years.

I retold Dr. Grunfeld's parable of the stone and its ripples with a slight adjustment. It was not a stone that Frau Schenirer had hurled into a pond but a massive, pure diamond into the sea of Jewish life. What a powerful throw it must have been, for to this day it continues to generate waves that not only radiate outward but gain height each time; and it will continue to do so forever.

I shared the feelings I experienced sitting on the dirt floor in Bergen-Belsen, cold and still, unable to stretch for lack of space.

"Who under such circumstances would dream of experiencing today's miraculous event? The dream of resurrecting Bais Yaakov was so far-fetched, so unbelievable, that no one thought it attainable at any future time. But Hashem, in His loving-kindness, realized this dream in our own days.

"Girls," I cried out, "you should know that the dream of *biyas ha-Moshiach,* the coming of the Redeemer, is not as far-fetched today as our dream was back then. Let us hope that the Almighty, in His great kindness and love for His People, will fulfill this dream shortly and send us the Redeemer yet in our days. Then we will be privileged to go *en masse* to greet *Moshiach Tzidkeinu,* our Righteous Redeemer who will vindicate us, carrying the banner of Bais Yaakov: *Bais Yaakov, lechu ve-nelchah be-ohr Hashem* — Bais Yaakov, lead, and others will follow you, in Hashem's glorious light."

Epilogue

I dreamed a blissful dream. I saw a beautiful garden. I gaped in awe and admiration at the gigantic branching trees; at the seedlings that extended their young budding limbs, aspiring to mature; and at the verdant bushes, stubby but shaped to perfection.

I observed the gorgeous, colorful flowers. I saw the precious little buds opening up, spreading a heavenly aroma. So innocent, so promising... .

This was my garden — the garden in which I was raised. My ancestors had planted it with love and devotion.

They arranged the seedlings with tenderness and lovingkindness. They placed them with proper measures (*middos*); they planted them apart to give them room to breathe and grow to their individual potential. And to the precious little buds, looking to the sun for warmth and light, they added their own sunlight and warmth by talking to the sprouts, hoping and trusting that they would develop and send forth exquisite flowers. Then they watered those seedlings with the flow of the ever-refreshing stream of Torah.

I awaken to a frightening reality of emptiness: no garden, no trees, no flowers, no precious little buds... just a vast wasteland of nothingness.

Suddenly the picture of Frau Schenirer emerges from the nothingness. "Don't despair, my child," her lovely face counsels me, offering an encouraging smile. "Look ahead: there is a large stretch of fertile land in front of you. Stand up, gather your strength and energy, and start planting a new beautiful garden. You will succeed," her smile assures me.

Then, with her encouragement, we started to plant. With all of our remaining strength, will, and resolve, we plowed the soil and planted the seeds. And God, in His loving-kindness, blessed our efforts. Miracle of miracles, we grew a beautiful garden with tall branching trees, young seedlings slowly growing to independence, exquisite flowers, and precious little buds that envelop our lives and surroundings with a wonderful, heavenly aroma.

Now, who can match our happiness when we attend a joyous life-cycle occasion, and contemplate our beautiful new garden — our wonderful children, our gorgeous grandchildren, and those precious little buds, our great-grandchildren? Our lips sing Hallel incessantly and our hearts never cease to whisper gratitude to the Almighty for all the miracles He performed for us.

Hashem granted us the *zechus* to raise a special generation and, with His Divine assistance, to plant this gorgeous garden, which fills the entire world with the heavenly aroma of *nachas ruach*.

*   *   *

As we struggled to plant our garden throughout those trying years, we never forgot another dream: to replace another precious treasure that had been brutally destroyed — our *sifrei Torah*.

Now, after having been privileged to raise such a wonderful generation, we began to work for the fulfillment of that second dream: to write a *sefer Torah* that would replace one of the scores of precious *sifrei Torah* that Nazi beasts had burned before our eyes in a towering, agonized pyre.

As the sacred letters billowed aloft, they begged us to remember. Do not forget, the letters implored, to gather us up when the time comes and return us to life in new scrolls. *Kisvu lachem es ha-shirah ha-zos* — "Scribe for yourself this holy (beautiful) song of the Torah."[92]

How well I recalled this entreaty on that beautiful day in June 1999, when we had the great *zechus* to witness the fulfillment of our two wonderful dreams in unison.

*   *   *

My husband and I with the sefer Torah.

It began at 10:00 on a pleasant Sunday morning. Our home, decorated to create a garden atmosphere, was ready to receive the royal bride. The scribe, Reb Yoel, walked in carrying the scroll, which he had draped in a *tallis*. With deep emotion, he hugged and kissed the Torah as he tenderly laid it on the table.

It was his "baby"; he had spent a whole year toiling with devotion to create this treasure of sanctity and love.

He carefully removed the *tallis* and opened the holy scroll. A gorgeous sight unfolded in front of our eyes. Beautiful letters, seemingly in three dimensions, danced as if alive with joy. "We've returned," they pronounced, forming words, sentences,

---

92. *Devarim* 31:19.

parashiyos, and the conclusion of the *Chamishah Chumshei Torah*.

Today it would be our privilege to complete the writing of the *sefer Torah* that we had dedicated to the memory of our dear families who had perished in the Nazi death camps.

At 10:00, as scheduled, the women started to walk in. Apart from our families, we had invited several women who had devoted their lives to the dissemination of Torah and *chessed* in our community.

The scribe had intentionally left a few *yerios* (sheets of parchment) unsewn to give the ladies the sacred opportunity to do the stitching and render the scroll one. By so doing, he allowed the women to take an active part in the great mitzvah of completing a *sefer Torah*. Under the scribe's skilled guidance, we were to perform this holy task now.

It was my *zechus* to make the first stitch. I trembled as my hand touched the special thread, made of sinews, that the halachah prescribes for this purpose. Overwhelmed with awe and elation, I cried out the *She-hecheyanu* blessing, my heart bursting with gratitude to the Almighty for allowing me to live to experience this great moment.

Other women followed me, each having the merit of threading a stitch through the sacred *yerios*. Soon the room was filled with awe mingled with delight. We identified ourselves with the Jewish women in the Sinai desert, who, apart from preceding the men in offering their precious jewelry for the construction of the *Mishkan* (Tabernacle), applied their manual and intellectual skills to bring it to completion. They spun yarns of wool (directly from live sheep), linen, and various types of dyed wool fiber, and wove them into beautiful tapestry for the curtains and coverings of the inner and outer Sanctuary.

So too, we women stitched the scroll together to create a complete *sefer Torah*.

*　　*　　*

Now the men approached the scroll to fill in some letters of which the scribe had purposely only made the outlines, in order to give them the opportunity to fulfill the commandment, expressed in the verse cited above, of writing a *sefer Torah*. After the men performed this mitzvah and the scribe corrected their work and completed the writing, the Torah was dressed in a magnificent, jewel-studded mantel. Two city blocks were lined with "wedding guests," in anticipation of the great event to come. Young children, accompanied by their mothers, carried balloons and flags and enjoyed the *pekalach*, small packages of sweets that were distributed in honor of the occasion as they waited.

The procession began at 4:00 P.M. The "groom," my husband Shymon, representing *Klal Yisroel*, was already standing under the *chuppah*, dressed in his festival attire and embracing his precious "bride," the *sefer Torah*. Older boys clutching torches led the procession, accompanied by music and song. People emerged from side streets to join the jubilant multitude. The streets, closed to traffic, were alive with people dancing and singing — in *horas*, ranks, files, and in every other configuration, all the way.

Be-gilah u've-re'udah, in a joy of holy awe, the procession advanced, its passionate dancing and singing mingling with memories, resulting in an atmosphere of meaning and enthusiasm.

At 6:00 the procession reached its destination, the Gerrer shul. There, the groom, Reb Shymon, holding his treasure, the holy *sefer Torah*, entered the shul. Then he recited with emotion the supremely evocative Psalm 24 (*"Le-David mizmor"*) and, with regret, parted with his beloved bride by depositing our precious Torah scroll in the Holy Ark for safekeeping. In so doing, however, he did not abandon it. He took along the Torah's innermost treasure: its spirit, meaning, teachings, and precepts.

Hashem, you chose *Am Yisroel*, the Jewish People, among all the nations. You loved Your bride and consecrated her *be-taba'as zo*, with "this ring" — a scroll of mitzvos. You lent her Your name: *Am Kadosh,* the holy nation. She accepted the ring with love and promised to obey Your precepts even before You revealed them: *"na'aseh ve-nishma."* I will carry that ring on my finger, on my arm, and in my heart forever, she said.

And she kept her word.

In the most trying times, the Jewish People safeguarded this ring with sacrifice, repeatedly risking their lives for it.

The Jew puts this ring on his finger every morning. It is symbolized by his *tefillin,* which he binds to his arm and wraps around his fingers. After he does this, he proclaims Hashem's commitment to His bride, saying, *Eirastich li le-olam,* "I betroth you to Me forever"[93].... I am bound to you by *taba'as zo,* by the ring of the Torah's spirit of charity and justice, loving-kindness and mercy. *Eirastich li be-emunah,* "I betroth you to Me by your faith."[94]

The Jew puts on this ring every day. It gives him hope and belief in Hashem's everlasting irrevocable covenant, union, with *Klal Yisroel.* The bride waits patiently for her Beloved to return to her with the same loving expression that He showed her at the engagement.

*   *   *

Leaving the shul, we went to a hall for a *se'udas mitzvah* in which we would celebrate two happy occasions: the *hachnasas sefer Torah* (welcoming of a new Torah scroll) and the *sheva berachos* (post-nuptial banquet) of our grandson Hershi. Just three days earlier, he had recited the same words under the *chuppah* to his bride: *Harei aht mekudeshes li be-taba'as zo,* "You are hereby sanctified to me as a wife with this ring." He referred, in fact, to two rings: the band of gold that he placed on his bride's finger and the precious ring of that Torah scroll, which we will carry together in our arms and in our hearts, so that we may know its precepts and act in accordance with them,

---

93. *Hoshea* 2:21.
94. Ibid., verse 22.

at all times and under all circumstances.

This day marked the culmination of my two greatest life's desires — to create another precious *sefer Torah* to replace one of the thousands that the accursed Nazis had burned (I had personally witnessed dozens burned), and to have the merit to see my family tree grow so beautifully, replacing the brutally destroyed garden that my ancestors had planted.

"*Sabeinu mi-tuvecha*," we recite in our Shabbos prayers. Satiate us with Your bountiful goodness, Hashem...but "*ve-samcheinu bi-shu'asecha*," we immediately continue. Impatiently but willingly we still wait, in hope, to witness the joy of Your Ultimate Deliverance."

Afterword

With deep emotion and gratitude to Hashem, we constantly hear that joyous tune, happily sung — *"Kol chasan ve-kol kallah"* — in all Jewish communities. Every day, sometimes several times a day, we experience a miracle in our post-Holocaust life as we see couple after couple, our children, our grandchildren, standing under the *chuppah*.

We hear the groom as he states in awe, *"Harei aht mekudeshes li,"* You are sanctified to me, so that together we may build a true Jewish home, a *mikdash* (sanctuary) in miniature, where peace and joy will reign and God's spirit will dwell.

Now we strain our ears, our aching hearts, longing, pining, waiting, praying, and hoping for the ultimate fulfillment: *"Od yishama be-arei Yehudah u've-chutzos Yerushalayim"* — to hear soon, already, in the cities of Judea and the streets of Jerusalem, that melody of sublime joy, *"kol Chasan ve-kol kallah"*: the Holy Groom, coming out to meet His betrothed, the Jewish People, and proclaiming to her with love that the time has come to rebuild the *Beis ha-Mikdash*, His everlasting home, where He, the Almighty, will dwell with His bride in peace, delight, and ultimate happiness forever.